ROUTLEDGE LIBRARY EDITIONS:
BUSINESS AND ECONOMICS IN ASIA

Volume 32

I0130971

# TOURISM IN SOUTH-EAST ASIA

# TOURISM IN SOUTH-EAST ASIA

Edited by
MICHAEL HITCHCOCK, VICTOR T. KING AND
MICHAEL J. G. PARNWELL

Routledge
Taylor & Francis Group

LONDON AND NEW YORK

First published in 1993 by Routledge

This edition first published in 2019
by Routledge
2 Park Square, Milton Park, Abingdon, Oxon OX14 4RN

and by Routledge
52 Vanderbilt Avenue, New York, NY 10017

*Routledge is an imprint of the Taylor & Francis Group, an informa business*

© 1993 Michael Hitchcock, Victor T. King and Michael J. G. Parnwell

*British Library Cataloguing in Publication Data*
A catalogue record for this book is available from the British Library

ISBN: 978-1-138-48274-6 (Set)
ISBN: 978-0-429-42825-8 (Set) (ebk)
ISBN: 978-1-138-36394-6 (Volume 32) (hbk)
ISBN: 978-1-138-36442-4 (Volume 32) (pbk)
ISBN: 978-0-429-43139-5 (Volume 32) (ebk)

**Publisher's Note**
The publisher has gone to great lengths to ensure the quality of this reprint but points out that some imperfections in the original copies may be apparent.

**Disclaimer**
The publisher has made every effort to trace copyright holders and would welcome correspondence from those they have been unable to trace.

# Tourism in South-East Asia

Edited by
Michael Hitchcock, Victor T. King
and Michael J. G. Parnwell

London and New York

First published 1993
by Routledge
11 New Fetter Lane, London EC4P 4EE

Simultaneously published in the USA and Canada
by Routledge
a division of Routledge, Chapman and Hall, Inc.
29 West 35th Street, New York, NY 10001

Typeset in Times by Witwell Limited, Southport
Printed and bound in Great Britain by
Biddles Ltd, Guildford and King's Lynn

*British Library Cataloguing in Publication Data*
A catalogue record for this title is available from the British Library.

*Library of Congress Cataloging in Publication Data*
Tourism in South-East Asia/edited by Michael Hitchcock, Victor T.
King, and Michael J. G. Parnwell.
    p.   cm.
  Includes bibliographical references (p. ) and index.
  ISBN 0-415-07929-2
  1. Tourist trade—Asia, Southeastern. I. Hitchcock, Michael.
II. King, Victor T. III. Parnwell, Mike.
G155.A743T68   1993
338.4′7915904′53—dc20                              92-18931
                                                     CIP

# Contents

# List of figures

# List of tables

# Acknowledgements

This book grew out of the conference that accompanied the Annual General Meeting of the Association of South-East Asian Studies in the United Kingdom (ASEASUK). The editors gratefully acknowledge ASEASUK and Humberside Polytechnic for hosting the conference (25–28 March 1991). The editors would also like to thank the British Academy's Committee for South-East Asian Studies for funding the Hull programme of research on tourism and development in South-East Asia, and for contributing to the cost of the ASEASUK conference.

Thanks are also due to the Nuffield Foundation and the Foreign and Commonwealth Office for their support, and to the Malaysian Tourism Development Board, the Singapore Tourism Promotion Board and the Royal Thai Embassy, London, for their help. The editors are also grateful to Pauline Kh'ng for her work as a Research Assistant on the Hull tourism research programme. Acknowledgements for assistance given to the individual contributors to this volume are contained in their respective chapters.

# Author biographies for the 2019 edition

**Michael Hitchcock** is Professor in Cultural Policy and Tourism at Goldsmiths, University of London. He has written and edited 14 books and has published over 50 refereed journal papers, as well as many other outputs. He took his doctorate at the Pitt Rivers Museum at the University of Oxford in 1983 based on his field research in eastern Indonesia. He worked at Liverpool Museum (National Museums and Galleries on Merseyside) and then the Horniman Museum, London where he was Assistant Keeper. He then joined Hull University to take part in the world's first multi-disciplinary research programme on tourism in Asia. He was appointed Professor of Tourism at London Metropolitan University in 1995, later becoming a Deputy Dean at the University of Chichester and then Dean at IMI, Switzerland. He then moved to the Macau University of Science and Technology as Dean of the Faculty of Hospitality and Tourism Management and a Member of the Senior Executive.

**Victor T. King** is Professor of Borneo Studies, UBD-Institute of Asian Studies. He is a sociologist-anthropologist and is also Emeritus Professor in the School of Languages, Cultures and Societies, University of Leeds; Professorial Research Associate in the Centre of South East Asian Studies, School of Oriental and African Studies, University of London; and Senior Editorial Advisor in the Regional Center for Social Science and Sustainable Development, Faculty of Social Sciences, Chiang Mai University, Thailand. Since 2012 he has edited/co-edited seven books on topics ranging across tourism in Asia, UNESCO World Heritage Sites in Southeast Asia, ethno-development, Southeast Asian Studies, Borneo Studies, and human insecurities in Southeast Asia. Among these he has recently co-edited two books on tourism for Routledge: *Tourism in East and Southeast Asia* (with David Harrison and J.S. Eades), 2018, a 4-volume reader in the Routledge Critical Concepts in Asian Studies series; and *Tourism and Ethnodevelopment: Inclusion, Empowerment and Self-determination* (with Ismar Borges de Lima), 2018, in the Routledge Advances in Tourism and Anthropology series.

**Michael Parnwell** is Emeritus Professor at the University of Leeds, having held the position of Professor of South East Asian Development until his retirement in 2014. He was then appointed Distinguished Guest Professor in the Faculty of Hospitality and Tourism Management at the Macau University of Science and Technology. His research focuses on various aspects of the development process in several South East Asian countries and mainland China, including tourism, sustainability, localism, Buddhism and development, and intangible cultural heritage. He is presently working on publishing some of the half-million or so photographs taken during his 30-year academic career.

# Preface to the 2019 edition

The purpose of this preface is to review briefly the long-term impacts of what were initially the proceedings of a conference held at Humberside Polytechnic in 1991 under the auspices of the Association of South-East Asian Studies in the UK (ASEASUK). Most of these were then revised as chapters for the Routledge volume that was subsequently published in 1993. On the face of it and, judged by the standards of the twenty-first century, the outputs of a gathering of scholars in a remote northern polytechnic that no longer exists may not seem worthy of further examination, but the picture changes when you consider how unusual this collection of essays was at the time and how it has endured in terms of relevance through to the present. Despite its somewhat drab title, *Tourism in South-East Asia* (looking back, we might have been more imaginative), the volume represents a milestone in research both in its inter-disciplinary and comparative approach and its take on Area Studies, and the result – albeit imperfect in its coverage – was to have long-term impacts that could not have been anticipated at the time, though there were indications that something special was being put together.

This relatively minor conference was part of a wider programme of research undertaken by the Centre for South-East Asian Studies at the University of Hull which had been generously funded by a series of grants from the British Academy's Committee for South-East Asian Studies, and with support from the University of Hull. This research was, in many ways, accidental, fortuitous and opportunistic. Its initial focus was a comparative study of tourism development in Thailand, Malaysia and Indonesia, bringing together colleagues from the Hull Centre from a range of disciplines: geography, sociology, anthropology, history and economics. It was generated by casual conservations that participants in the programme had conducted in Penang in 1990 and the developing interest which one of our co-editors, Michael Hitchcock, had in tourism research.

There were slightly more papers presented at the conference than appeared in the book, and it is perhaps not surprising – given the funding base – that the majority of contributors were British. That said, it is worth noting that the other contributors came from as diverse origins as Israel, France, the USA, Malaysia and Cyprus (albeit a British national). The disciplines covered by the contributors range from anthropology, sociology, history, economics, geography and politics, and the countries discussed in the volume include Malaysia, Indonesia, Thailand and South-East Asia generally, as well as a slightly broader take on the Asia Pacific region in general and how South-East Asia might be perceived in Europe. The subject matter is also not strictly academic – at least by the standards of the time – as it considers publications aimed at tourists, both historical and contemporary, with one contributor drawn from the private sector.

Why did this apparently obscure collection of ruminations of a group of largely British academics in a somewhat out-of-the-way setting go on to be so influential and to be game- changing in ways that can only be hinted at in conventional ways of measuring impact, such as citation indexes? The answer is not an easy one to chart as there is no conventional metric that could address this question, but the impact that this book has had is undoubtedly significant, not least because its publication coincided with a huge expansion of inbound tourism into South-East Asia and then a later outbound growth of tourism from the Asia-Pacific region in general, with the lead in terms of sheer numbers being dominated by China. The book covers the countries of South-East Asia, but its reach is much further as it touches on Asia generally and consequently has always had a much bigger readership than its title suggests. Several of the chapters in the volume have enjoyed considerable attention and some of them have been widely cited; we venture to suggest then that some elements of the book have taken on a 'classic quality' in the development of our thinking and research on tourism in South-East Asia and have therefore played a formative role in research agendas on tourism in Asia and more widely (chapters, among others, by Tom Selwyn, Michel Picard, Linda Richter, Robert Wood, Erik Cohen, David Wilson, Michael Parnwell, Janet Cochrane, Michael Hitchcock, John Walton, Anthony Stockwell, and Graham Saunders).

That the publication of the book coincided with a globally significant intensification of human mobility and behavioural impact, namely the expansion of tourism both to and from Asia, does not in itself explain why it was so influential, as there is a more prosaic reason. The boom in Asian tourism - inbound, outbound, international and domestic – was accompanied by a massive expansion in demand for tourism education at the further and higher levels, not least as companies sought to recruit trained personnel to service this huge upsurge. This growth occurred particularly in Asia, as numerous colleges and universities sought to add the study of tourism and related subjects such as hospitality (and later the creative arts and other subjects) to their curricula. This upsurge in educational provision was not limited to Asia as Western countries ranging from Australia, the USA, New Zealand, Switzerland to the UK also took on board the need to provide Asia-focused courses for students wanting to study tourism. At the time, in the late 1990s and the early twenty-first century, there were remarkably few educational and research resources available in terms of reading materials, and this book ended up serving as a kind of blueprint for what a course on tourism in Asia might look like. The close-up accounts provided by the individual chapters of how these forces were taking shape were used to add empirical detail to the theoretical ideas that were advanced in the volume concerning sustainable development, political economy, cultural interfacing, the spatiality of tourism development, tourism management, and so on.

At the time the book was published, the University of Hull was engaged in a partnership, focused on curriculum development and staff training with what was then called the Agricultural University of Malaysia (Universiti Pertanian Malaysia, now Universiti Putra Malaysia, one of the five leading Malaysian research universities), under the auspices of the British Council. The three editors of this book were involved in this relationship, which, as part of the collaboration, included the development of curricula suitable for students studying tourism. This book was not the only resource that the Malaysian and British partners were relying on, but it was undoubtedly the most significant one to hand. As the Malaysian partner created its tourism curriculum it very rapidly expanded recruitment beyond its immediate hinterland and began to attract students from further afield, notably Indonesia and Bangladesh. The university also recognised that becoming international meant becoming Anglophone and the fact that this book was written in English undoubtedly enhanced its appeal. As the prestige of this university's tourism programmes grew it began to validate the courses taught in other institutes of further and higher education, notably in the private sector. The ripple effect due to such processes was unprecedented as they were not limited to Malaysia and spread out across Asia.

It was not only Asian universities that woke up to the need to have courses with an Asian tourism content, and among the first to realise these possibilities were the renowned Swiss hotel schools. It was in fact a former member of the Centre for South-East Asian Studies, Dr Stephen Kirby, who recommended to a Swiss Hotel School, IMI Switzerland, that they should introduce a course on tourism in Asia in his capacity as a senior member of Manchester Metropolitan University, which was validating IMI's courses at the time. IMI itself went on to validate programmes in other countries, thereby creating a snowballing effect. It was through such processes that this book became influential, and whether or not students were aware of its existence is immaterial as the book's two premises - that tourism is an interdisciplinary and comparative study and that tourism in an Asian context is hugely important - became widely recognised. It is thus not unreasonable to suggest that hundreds of thousands of students, if not millions, have been directly or indirectly affected by this publication.

While this book can be said to have had an undisputed impact in terms of pedagogy, what might be remarked on in terms of its influence on research? If one considers the direct links to the editors and contributors associated with the original volume, then the impacts can be clearly seen. First, the three editors went on to release two additional collections of books dealing with tourism in South-East Asia in 2009 and 2010, and one of the editors, Victor King, released a third edited collection in 2016 and has recently co-compiled a four-volume Routledge reader on *Tourism in East and Southeast Asia* (2018). Two of the contributors to the original *Tourism in South-East Asia* volume, Janet Cochrane and Tom Selwyn, were themselves to release edited books that can be traced in some way or another to the original book. Hitchcock's two co-authored books on Bali can also be said to be descendants of this original volume and all three of the editors also contributed to research in terms of a large number (c. 150) of refereed journal outputs, and those that appeared in tourism journals undoubtedly bear the stamp of *Tourism in South-East Asia*. All three editors not only served in a variety of influential academic roles ranging from the British Academy to the AHRC Peer Review College, which helped to shape the research agenda in the UK, but they were also influential on editorial boards in journals abroad, notably in Thailand, Indonesia, Singapore and Malaysia. Michael Hitchcock and Victor King, for example, also pushed the agenda forward in the early 2000s in organising conference panels on tourism and heritage in Southeast Asia at a conference organised by the School of Oriental and African Studies in 2001 under the auspices of the European Association of Southeast Asian Studies. Several of the papers were published in a special issue of the journal *Indonesia and the Malay World*, 2003, vol. 31, no. 89, which became one of the most widely quoted special issues of the journal. Again, it contained papers that have influenced thinking on tourism development in the South-East Asian region.

The policy impacts of the three editors are a little harder to detect as many policy innovations occurred indirectly as a result of students being influenced by teachings derived in part from the original volume, but sometimes they can be clearly identified such as with the case of Michael Hitchcock's role on the PATA Macau Chapter and his consultancy under the auspices of the UNWTO in Shandong Province in China in 2016. And the impact is far from over, as one of the editors continues to teach a course entitled *Tourism in Asia* at Goldsmiths, University of London.

When the book was first published in 1993 the three editors felt that it would have a wide appeal, particularly among students, and discussed the possibility with Routledge of issuing it in a paperback edition. For various reasons a paperback version did not materialise. We are delighted that after 25 years the value of the original collection has been fully recognised, and Routledge has decided to reissue the book. It has been worth waiting for.

Michael Hitchcock, Victor T. King and Michael Parnwell
June 2018

# 1 Tourism in South-East Asia: introduction

*Michael Hitchcock, Victor T. King and Michael J. G. Parnwell*

Tourism has become one of South-East Asia's foremost industries. Although the region receives less than 11 per cent of the world's international tourist trade, the members of the Association of South-East Asian Nations (ASEAN) are experiencing a boom in both foreign and domestic tourism. The number of foreign visitors has doubled, receipts from tourism have tripled during the last decade, and tourism has become the leading source of foreign exchange in countries like Thailand. Tourism is the second largest industry in the Philippines and the third largest earner of foreign currency in Singapore. In Indonesia tourism has moved into fourth place, outstripping rubber and coffee as an earner of foreign exchange in 1990.[1] Even the non-ASEAN nations such as Cambodia, Laos, Vietnam and Myanmar (Burma), where the income derived from tourism is low, are attempting to expand their own tourism industries. Vietnam has enjoyed an exponential growth in tourism over the last few years, rising from a meagre 20,000 visitors in 1 86 to 187,000 in 1990, and projected to increase further to half a million by 1995. A knock-on effect of the tourism boom in South-East Asia has been the development of tourism in neighbouring regions, particularly in Yunnan, southern China, which has much in common culturally with South-East Asia. Only oil-rich Brunei, an exception among the ASEAN states, seems content to live with only a little tourism. Tourist arrivals in the Asia Pacific region are projected to increase at 7 per cent annually until the end of the century, a much higher rate than the global average of around 4.5 per cent per annum.

The phenomenal growth in tourism in South-East Asia, as elsewhere in the developing world, has been associated with a number of factors and processes. One of the more important of these has been an increase in people's ability to afford to travel to the region. This may be attributed to two parallel factors: first, rising levels of affluence in the main source areas, and second, the steadily falling cost, in real terms, of travel to the region. Before the late-1960s, only relatively small numbers of people travelled to South-East Asia, principally from the wealthy industrialised countries of Western Europe, the United States and Australasia, and consisting of those social groups which could afford the not inconsiderable cost of sea-, and later airborne travel to the Far East. The advent of cheap charter flights and package holidays revolutionised international tourism, initially creating opportunities for mass travel, respectively, to the periphery of Europe (e.g. Spain, Portugal, Greece), Central America and the Caribbean, and the South Pacific, and later including more distant destinations in Asia and elsewhere.

During the 1970s and 1980s the cost of travel to the region remained more or less constant in real terms, and this, combined with rising levels of disposable incomes in the main sending countries, led to a phenomenal increase in international tourism world-wide. During the late 1980s several countries in the Asia Pacific region, most notably Japan and the Asian NICs (Hong Kong, Taiwan and South Korea), became important source areas for South-East Asian tourism (accounting for 23 per cent of tourist arrivals in 1989 – approximately the same proportion as from Europe, the United States and Australasia combined), reflecting not only their own growing wealth but also an increasing amount of time for leisure and a greater inclination to spend this time abroad. At the same time, larger numbers of people within the South-East Asian region, most notably those from the rapidly developing countries of ASEAN, have taken to travelling within the region. In 1989, almost 37 per cent of international tourism occurred within the ASEAN region. Once again rising levels of affluence within the region, coupled with better and cheaper facilities for travel and tourism, help to explain this growth in intra-regional tourism. Also, as tourism infrastructure has developed to accommodate existing tourist demand, so the facilities available have attracted new waves of visitors.

For 'Western' tourists in particular, other factors have also contributed to South-East Asia becoming an important destination area. The gradual shift in the 'centre of gravity' of mass tourism away from the longer-established destinations (in Europe, the Costa del Sol, the Algarve, the Cote d'Azur and the Aegean Islands) towards the Far East and elsewhere is partly a reaction to the over-development of these major tourism centres. The movement in international tourism towards alternative destinations, such as South-East Asia, also reflects changing consumer preferences: the search for something 'different', with new natural and cultural environments placed high on tourists' lists of priorities – provided they can also find the requisite sun, sea and sand. As some of the chapters in this volume highlight, South-East Asia has also established itself as an important destination for 'special interest' forms of tourism, particularly wildlife tourism.

Ironically, although large numbers of tourists may be attracted to the region by its perceived 'differentness', lured by the images of culture and landscape which are vividly portrayed in the promotional literature, few are able or willing to tolerate a great deal of real novelty. Many will remain closetted in hotel complexes or resorts, will follow package tours, may obtain a glimpse of carefully orchestrated cultural performances, and may not be especially interested in what lies beyond the perimeter walls of the hotel.[2] The commonplace view that tourism is a form of escapism may appear absurd at first glance, especially when the destinations (built-up, congested, commercialised, frenetic) are not appreciably different from the ones the tourists left behind. However, 'escapism' depends not so much on a marked change in environment – though it may enhance the tourist's experience – but on a change of behaviour, albeit highly conventionalised. The very fact that the visitor is separated from everyday social realities may be enough to engender much of the sense of 'otherness'.

Another important factor in the recent boom in international tourism in South-East Asia has been the very active promotion of tourism by the various member states of ASEAN and, increasingly, some of the socialist states. To a varying degree, the countries of South-East Asia have banded together to encourage the growth of tourism within the region. They set out to achieve this through a coordinated advertising campaign which strove to promote South-East Asia's attractions world-wide. Up until the early 1980s the members of ASEAN were largely dependent on agriculture and the export of primary products such as minerals, petroleum and timber. In order to reduce their dependence on farming and extractive industries the ASEAN countries tried to develop areas of their economies which had hitherto received comparatively little government attention. It was hoped that the introduction of tourism on a major scale would help diversify the region's economic base and provide a boost for a host of related industries ranging from transport to arts and crafts. It was envisaged that the infrastructure introduced alongside tourism would benefit local communities and assist the process of industrialisation. Environmental interests, especially with regard to the development of national parks, were also catered for.

Following the success of Visit Thailand Year in 1987, the various ASEAN government tourist boards agreed to promote their tourist industries in succession, culminating in a joint venture in 1992, known as Visit ASEAN Year. As was anticipated, the number of visitors from the wealthy countries of the Pacific Rim (Japan, Australia, Canada and the USA) and the European Community rose steadily, a vindication of ASEAN's strategy. In Malaysia, for example, the Ministry of Culture and Tourism, which was established in 1987, received $100 million from the government for its initial promotional expenditure (Bird, 1989, 1). The US and Japanese markets were targeted, and in 1988 a total of $22 million was earmarked for marketing in the USA alone (ibid.). Tourist arrivals in Malaysia were predicted to reach 4.3 million by 1990 and receipts of $3 billion were expected (Bird, 1989, 2). But following the very successful Visit Malaysia Year 1990 the number of foreign visitors reached 7.079 million (*Bangkok Bank Monthly Review*, May 1991, 182).

Tourism, however, is an extremely sensitive industry and ASEAN's strategy was devastated in the first half of 1991 when international air travel declined because of the uncertainties of the Gulf War. Prior to that the Philippines suffered a set-back following the overthrow of President Ferdinand Marcos. The downturn occasioned by the Gulf War hit Indonesia particularly badly and what was supposed to be Visit Indonesia 1991 was quickly dubbed in Jakarta as Visit Indonesia *Nanti Nanti* (Later Later). Tourism did, however, recover later in the year and the Indonesian authorities were able to record an increase on the previous year (see Chapter 4).[3] The problems and successes of the ASEAN campaign will undoubtedly be of great interest to nations in other developing regions.

## THE STUDY OF TOURISM IN SOUTH-EAST ASIA

Along with the growth of the tourism industry in South-East Asia, there has been an increasing awareness of the need to understand its dynamics, the development processes engendered and their consequences for the region and its peoples. Nevertheless, studies of tourism available to date do not provide us with anything approaching a comprehensive view of the social, economic, cultural, environmental and political issues, processes and problems involved in the rapid expansion of both international and domestic tourism in South-East Asia. The only partial exception to this is the substantial, though still far from complete, knowledge of tourism in Bali.

To be sure, there have been some excellent studies of aspects of tourism in the region, some undertaken by various of the authors who have contributed to this present book: Picard's work on Bali, Cohen's on Thailand, Richter's on the Philippines, Kadir Din's on Malaysia, and Wood's papers on South-East Asia generally. However, these are often isolated contributions, which are not part of any multidisciplinary programme of research on a particular region or population, nor has there been much attempt to relate these studies comparatively.

The present volume is an attempt to begin this programme of work by presenting a collection of contributions from different disciplinary perspectives and on a range of different countries and peoples within South-East Asia. The region's great cultural, economic and environmental diversity, coupled with the very rapid changes which have been associated with the tourism boom, make it a particularly appropriate location for an examination of the characteristics and effects of tourism development. At this stage we can do no more than indicate what already has been achieved, and what more needs to be done. What is clear is that the research on tourism as presented in this volume raises certain central conceptual and practical issues in the disciplines of anthropology, sociology, geography, economics and history; it also involves examination of the developmental processes at work within South-East Asian countries and how we might understand these and attempt to plan for them satisfactorily; it has required as well a reconceptualisation of such key concepts in anthropology and sociology as 'culture' and 'ethnicity'.

Much of the debate on tourism in developing countries, including those in South-East Asia, has focused on whether its effects are beneficial or negative, and whether they are developmental or anti-developmental. We can see the main issues in this debate in the present collection. It is still particularly significant in the disciplines of economics and geography in which a predominant concern is the contribution, actual or potential, of tourism to development; it is also a question of importance in anthropology and sociology but, in this case, the discussion has become rather more complex and has to do with the various ways of conceptualising culture and society.

After all, there are some effects which are quantifiable, and, as we see later in the case of the economics contributions, it is at least theoretically possible to draw up a statistical balance sheet of various benefits and disadvantages: foreign exchange earnings, employment generation, infrastructural development and economic diversification set against such items as the leakages resulting from the repatriation of profits, dividends and imports. Economics can compare different economic sectors in these terms and there has been an increasing statistical sophistication in assessing developmental effects, particularly with regard to Singapore. But statistics will always be imperfect and, even in terms of certain economic criteria, analysts will often evaluate these in different terms: for example, whether it is better to encourage the specialisation of economic activity or to diversify; or whether spatial concentration in support of economic efficiency is to be preferred over economic dispersal in the interests of regional development.

Other effects are, however, very problematical to evaluate. We shall consider later various environmental issues appertaining to tourism, which are extremely difficult to cost. For the moment we turn to social and cultural matters. Changes such as cultural denigration, corruption, loss of traditional pride and ethnic identity, and so on are extremely difficult to measure accurately and to interpret objectively. There also been a very marked shift in conceptualising cultural change resulting from tourism, and there is an emerging consensus that it is too simplistic to argue that the effects are either 'good' or 'bad'.

The factors to take into account in examining and attempting to evaluate the socio-cultural effects of tourism are numerous, but we merely outline the main ones below, since they are each developed in some detail in various of the subsequent chapters.

1 The time/period when the research was undertaken. Re-studies suggest that effects change through time: what was considered deleterious at one time may be considered beneficial at another, and vice versa. Snap-shot views of the effects of tourism may equally be misleading, suggesting the need for more longitudinal studies of the effects of tourism. In this connection, Picard's studies of tourism in Bali clearly have contributed to a historically grounded understanding of the transformations of local cultural forms in relation to tourism development (Picard, 1990; Picard, forthcoming). Wilson argues in his chapter for much more attention to the time dimension in anthropological studies of tourism.

2 The particular case study, social class, ethnic group, region or community which has been selected. The effects of tourism are variable; much depends upon the nature of the interactions between hosts and guests, and the circumstances which surround these interactions. It is very difficult to generalise from a specific case, and we need many more studies in a region or country, located in a directly comparative framework, before we can pass judgement on the desirability or otherwise of tourism. At the extreme, two neighbouring communities could be experiencing very different effects from tourism. We already know that people from different

social classes are very likely to react to and take advantage of, or suffer from, transformations and innovations in very different ways.

3 The kinds of tourism promoted in a given region/country. This is not to say that environmental or historical tourism will not have social or cultural consequences. But it is important to establish what governments are promoting and what tourists do and see. A particular country may concentrate on a very specific or a wide range of tourism activities, and different tourism development strategies may very well have different socio-cultural consequences.

4 The scale of tourist activity: in other words the volume of tourist arrivals, how long they stay in particular locations, and how much they spend. Some parts of South-East Asia are still not significantly affected by tourism, while others have been inundated. The intensity of tourism activity is likely to have different kinds or degrees of influence on local societies and cultures.

5 The origins and ethnic backgrounds of tourists: there has been very little research on domestic tourism, and yet it is a very important element in South-East Asia. The popular conception of the deleterious effects of Western-derived tourism on Oriental cultures is a partly mistaken one in South-East Asia. Western tourists, because of their physical appearance and different cultural behaviour, are more likely to be regarded as tourists *per se* than other visitors in some ASEAN countries. In Indonesia, for example, the term *turis* (tourist) designates any person with White European features, whereas Asian tourists are referred to by their respective nationalities. Thus, a German or an Australian will be called an *orang turis* (tourist), whereas a Japanese will be known as an *orang jepang* (Japanese), a Chinese as an *orang cina* (Chinese), and so on. Indeed, in some South-East Asian societies Westerners historically had low social status, as was especially the case in Bali (Vickers, 1989, fig. 9). On the neighbouring island of Lombok the Balinese set themselves and other Indonesians against the Chinese and Japanese, who are viewed as essentially similar on account of their writing. The Lombok Balinese, however, distinguish all East Asian groups from White Europeans who are referred to as *turis* (tourist) or *belanda* (Dutch) (Duff-Cooper, 1986, 214). Further east in Bima, Sumbawa, the word *turis* does not have pejorative associations, though the term 'hippy' may be applied to any White European deemed to have a disreputable appearance.

Not only is local tourism a substantial element in such places as Malaysia and Java, but regional tourism is also vital. For example, about three-quarters of foreign visitors to Malaysia come from the

ASEAN region, and a significant proportion of others from East and South Asia. We must beware then of assuming that local cultures are being transformed in undesirable ways by the secularism of modern Western values. In some respects local cultural forms, as in Java, are responding to local needs and interests, and contributing to either strengthened regional identities or to national consciousness. Tourists are not a homogeneous class or category; they differ in nationality, social background, values, perceptions and motivations.

6 It is often problematic to differentiate the effects of tourism from other processes and effects of change – from industrialisation, urbanisation, enhanced physical mobility, the improvements in communication, and the influence of the mass media.

7 The studies which have tried to argue that tourism has had either positive or negative effects on local cultures have a particular conception of culture, which is now considered to be less than satisfactory. The earlier approaches to the examination of culture tended to view it as something bounded, homogeneous, self-reproducing and passed on as a 'thing' from generation to generation. More recently, as Wood indicates, culture has been conceived of not as a concrete entity acted upon by forces from outside, but rather as sets of symbols; or as webs of significance and meaning; it is variable, relative, contingent, ever-changing. Culture is not a thing, but a process.

Various of the chapters in this volume explore the implications of these current perceptions of culture, and it is useful here to present the outline of some of these analyses.

## TOURISM AND CULTURE

Social scientists with an interest in culture have often treated research on tourism as 'spin-off research' – something of a second order activity – and therefore the various relationships between tourism and culture have tended to be overlooked. Researchers with little more than a passing interest in the subject often conceive of tourism in terms of commonplace assumptions about the positive and negative effects of tourism on traditional culture. Robert Wood has characterised this as the 'billiard ball model', in which a static sphere (culture) is hit by a mobile one (tourism) (Wood, 1980, 565). In some studies, tourism is credited with preserving heritage, while in others it is accused of commercialisation, a process known as the 'commoditisation of culture'.

What these studies usually overlook is the fact that tourism cannot invariably be isolated from many other aspects of culture, and this is particularly true of places such as Bali which have a long history of tourism. By treating tourism as an exogenous force, analysts risk ignoring how tourism may become part of the local reality: in certain cases tourism and traditional culture are inseparable. When culture is conceived of as a static entity, lacking the dynamics of change, the actions, motivations and values of local participants are ignored. By using more actor-oriented approaches, however, one can see how host communities both adapt to and modify tourism in such a way that tourism cannot easily be divorced from the cultural mainstream. This has given rise to what Michel Picard calls 'touristic culture'.

Picard's concept of 'touristic culture' goes beyond the ideas expounded by Eric Hobsbawm and Terence Ranger in their seminal publication entitled *The Invention of Tradition* (1983). Writing in this volume, Prys Morgan showed how many aspects of what might be regarded today as traditional Welsh culture can be traced back to the late eighteenth century. Tourism had opened up passable roads through North Wales and travellers recorded their impressions of the Welsh peasantry. The visitors were struck, for example, by the cloaks and high crowned hats worn by Welsh women, and it is clear that what had been fashionable in lowland England in the 1620s had survived among the poor in Wales. The Welsh woman's attire was not in any sense a national costume, but by the 1830s it had been turned deliberately into a caricature of Wales. The costume became part of the illusion of Welshness and was reproduced on Victorian postcards and dolls (Morgan, 1983, 59–85). Some of these 'invented traditions', such as the Welsh woman's costume, were only thinly rooted in local culture, though today they may be taken for the 'real thing'. Hobsbawm and Ranger reconstructed their social history from material evidence and documentation, and their diachronic perspective provides an invaluable aid for the study of tourism. But they did not have access to the kind of field data, now emerging in South-East Asia, which reveal how the actors themselves perceive and participate in the processes. The notion of 'invented tradition' is perhaps too close to the 'billiard ball model' and represents a stark, albeit historically enlightening, way of describing the divers processes by which tourism has become a part of everyday life in certain South-East Asian regions. Styles of dress, festivals and even local food habits can be understood as indigenous attempts to accommodate to – and in some cases profit from – the cultural and economic experience of tourism. A modified version of Hobsbawm and Ranger's approach, which does take into account the actions of actors, is applicable within the context of South-East Asian tourism, and it is illustrated in some of the chapters in this volume, and in other work on tourism in the region.

An illustration of the interface between tourism and traditional culture in South-East Asia is provided by the work of Annette Sanger in Singapadu, Bali (Sanger, 1988). In her study, Sanger shows how *barong* dance dramas, which are important rites that protect the community from malevolent forces, have been adapted to suit the needs of tourists. Presentations of these dance dramas began in the 1930s, and since then the number of foreign visitors has increased markedly. Although Singapadu is off the beaten track, tourists visit the village around three to four times per week. They usually stay around 70 minutes, enough time to watch the performance and buy some souvenirs. The early groups used to watch full-length performances lasting some three hours, but the villagers realised that this did not appeal to tourists. One of the best village dancers therefore devised a new dance programme, including some slapstick sequences to transcend linguistic boundaries. The performances were reduced in length and female dancers were brought in to play female roles, which had hitherto been played by men. Tourists also found the trance dances with *kris* unpleasant and did not enjoy watching some dancers coming out of trances by eating live chickens. These sections were later modified.

But, as Sanger argues, the villagers do not necessarily see these changes in terms of cultural denigration and justify the commercial use of the dance dramas in the following ways. First, the *barong* is still treated with great respect in performances and the correct prayers and offerings are used. Second, the oldest and holiest *barong* costume is not used for commercial purposes, and is not, therefore, desecrated in any way. Third, the villagers need the tourist revenue and, since most of the remuneration is communal, they are not individually guilty of avarice. Fourth, the villagers argue that the *barong* likes to dance, whatever the situation. Fifth, performances reinforce the solidarity of the community, and during the quiet part of the tourist season the villagers say that they miss the opportunity to come together. Sixth, the performers never compromise on quality, since technical and aesthetic standards are maintained; furthermore, they welcome the opportunity to practise (ibid., 89–96). From Sanger's work it would appear that local traditions have not been supplanted by modified or invented ones, but have been adapted in subtle ways. All these traditions co-exist in the same ordinary time-space, and touristic culture is very much a part of reality.

When considering the interplay between tourism and culture, it is helpful to ask why some traditions are more readily adapted to the needs of tourism than others? To a certain extent this is fortuitous and it does not necessarily mean that all the changes that take place within the context of tourism can invariably be attributed to tourism alone. There are many other factors at play. In Chapter 7, for example, Felicia Hughes-Freeland argues that although the dinner-dances of the Javanese court of Yogyakarta are well suited to the needs of tourism, they came into being long before the advent of the modern industry. Court performances usually accompanied a reception of some kind, and food would be served at such events. This custom persists, and has been transformed into a reception where the guests are tourists who pay to attend. Palace performers were members of the court, not professional performers as such. Court performances were first taken up by national academies to represent national culture, and were gradually made available for tourists on a regular basis. The regularity of performances and their accessibility, staged as they are in urban centres, has been an important contributing factor to court rather than village performance being packaged for tourists.

As is the case with the performing arts, it is not always possible to divide South-East Asian material culture into that which is 'traditional' and that which is 'touristic', though some studies suggest that this is the case. Robert Cooper has argued, for example, that the Hmong of Doi Phui (Thailand) fabricate crude copies of Hmong material culture for tourists (Cooper, 1984). Cooper noted that the 'Meo crossbows' made for tourists are of questionable quality since they will never be fired; productivity, therefore, is high. The input in the tourist business is modest and the output high; but because so many shops sell the same products, the individual's profit is reduced (ibid., 119). In contrast, Lewis Hill has shown how objects that are made specially for tourists in one period, such as the 1930s, may be appreciated by the host community at a later date.[4] There are cases of Balinese *kris* from the early days of tourism being acquired by the Balinese and being used as genuine examples of traditional craftsmanship. Attitudes to objects may change over time, and it is wrong to assume that goods made for tourists are invariably shoddy. Although the majority of goods manufactured for tourists are made using simple processes, which differ greatly from traditional standards of craftsmanship, they cannot always be separated from local practices. Many of the people involved in producing goods for tourists, as is especially the case around the palace in Yogyakarta, are themselves traditional artisans who have simply adapted their products to suit an additional tourist market. Likewise in northern and western Thailand various Karen groups, encouraged by Christian missionaries, weave their traditional striped *ikat* fabrics in subtle colours and longer lengths. This material is popular with Westerners for cushions, bedspreads and casual garments (Fraser-Lu, 1988, 122: citing Thai Tribal Crafts). Tourists themselves can also be discerning buyers, as is evidenced by the growing popularity of books on South-East Asian handicrafts.

It is a commonplace assumption that there are crafts which may be regarded as traditional and that these are denigrated following the introduction of tourism, as if tourism was the only active agent. But changes within material culture can occur for a variety of reasons which cannot invariably be associated with tourism. A good example of this is the Javanese batik industry, particularly on the north coast of the island. Batik makers have a long tradition of designing fabrics to appeal to a variety of ethnic groups, such as the Dutch-Indonesians, the Chinese and the indigenous Javanese. Many fabrics were made with not only a highly fashion-conscious domestic market in mind, but also an important export market in the colonial period. Changes in Javanese batik design can be detected long before the advent of tourism, and it is often impossible to distinguish what might be called a 'touristic' from a 'traditional' artefact. Nelson Graburn's contention that tourist goods may be regarded as those which are 'outwardly directed', as opposed to traditional goods which are 'inwardly directed', cannot be applied with any certainty in the context of South-East Asia (Graburn, 1976, 4–5). Tourist goods are also not necessarily identified as such by the local people, especially when they date from an earlier period. Furthermore, a wide range of goods is made for the important domestic tourist market, and these tourists presumably share similar cultural backgrounds to the makers themselves.

## IMAGES OF SOUTH-EAST ASIA

Some of the chapters in this volume dwell on the images of peoples and cultures promoted in the tourist literature, in brochures, posters and magazines. As Saunders demonstrates, many of these are rooted in the colonial past, and are part of the European stereotyping of the dependent populations. Above all, emphasis was placed on the exotic: on striking body adornments, on such institutions as headhunting, on dramatic funeral rituals and other customs. Much of this European concern was also closely linked to theories of biological and social evolution, to the assumed superiority of Western civilisation, and the belief that non-Western cultures represented earlier stages of human development. Frequently, 'other' people were seen as objects to describe, analyse, classify and 'capture' in word and picture. Despite political independence, many of the exotic features of South-East Asia expressed in colonial literature are retained to promote the region's tourist destinations as different, exciting and, in the words of the Visit Malaysia Year 1990 campaign, 'fascinating' (see King, Chapter 5, and Selwyn, Chapter 6 in this volume). Nowhere are these images so powerfully projected as in photographs.

Photography has long been associated with travel and tourism in South-East Asia, and the images produced with the aid of this medium have influenced the ways in which outsiders perceive the peoples and cultures of this region. Although many of these images are ephemeral, and therefore difficult to evaluate and quantify, sufficient numbers have survived in both private and public collections for us to gain some appreciation of how attitudes to South-East Asia have changed over time. Popular images have a long shelf-life, particularly postcards, and can therefore shape the outlook and expectations of visitors over several decades. Some of the most commercially attuned images from the early days of tourism have been copied and recycled many times; in recent years they have been adapted to the needs of modern advertising. Touristic image-making is by no means unique to South-East Asia, though distinctive trends can be identified, and parallels can be drawn with other parts of the world, notably Africa and the Caribbean.

In the early days of still photography, this medium was used primarily as a means of collecting data and was harnessed to the needs of science. Jurrian Munnich, for example, was commissioned by the Governor-General of the Netherlands East Indies in 1841, not long after the invention of photography. Using the daguerreotype process, Munnich made a record of plants, scenes and other natural phenomena in central Java, albeit with mixed results (*Toekang Potret*, 1989, 16). Three years later, Adolph Schaefer began photographing Hindu-Javanese sculptures belonging to the Batavian Society of Arts and shortly afterwards he moved on to photograph the reliefs of the temple of Borobudur. Explorers and travellers began to appreciate the advantages of the medium, and in 1877 Daniel Veth used photographs to brighten up his travelogue of the Padang Highlands with 'striking scenes and notable types of people' (ibid., 23). Probably some of the most arresting images of Borneo warriors and headhunters were taken by Demmeni during the great Dutch expeditions to Central Borneo in the 1890s (Nieuwenhuis, 1904–7). Commercial photographers became established throughout the region and, though they principally were concerned with portrait photographs of the upper echelons of society, some began to prepare images that were designed to appeal to tourists.

Although commercial photographers prepared large numbers of somewhat conventional images of natural beauty spots and historic monuments, some quickly recognised that there was a demand for exotic pictures of indigenous peoples. These images played on European stereotypes by depicting South-East Asians as members of unchanging and picturesque Oriental societies. Photographers achieved these ends by selecting images that reinforced the prejudices of foreign visitors and Western residents; pictures of naked women, warriors and dancers were especially popular. Studio photographers made use of elaborately painted backdrops and were not averse to equipping their subjects with suitably barbaric props which had little basis in ethnographic reality. The postures adopted by warriors were sometimes so exaggerated that the images were more amusing than threatening, and in any case these fierce-looking 'savages' with their spears and clubs no longer represented a threat to Europeans with their advanced military technology. Also popular were photographs of traditional craftsmen surrounded by strange-looking tools, as well as dancers wearing elaborate costumes and jewellery. Local mores were placed in the service of commerce and by the 1930s Bali had become the 'island of bare breasts' (Vickers, 1989, fig. 14). This colonial- and touristic-inspired exoticism continued to influence the popular image of the Orient until well into the twentieth century (*Toekang Potret*, 1989, 87).

Not all the photographs, however, conveyed such distorted and pejorative views of the indigenous cultures of South-East Asia. Some turn-of-the-century photographs, including those made specifically for the tourist market, were of high quality. They were not only aesthetically pleasing, but provided a sympathetic viewpoint of the lives of South-East Asian peoples. Nevertheless, the tendency to portray local peoples as 'types' (e.g. child, old man, artisan, etc.), rather than individuals persisted well into the tourist mini-booms of the twenties and thirties. Postcards depicting South-East Asia in terms of a traditional world of man, nature and ritual were very common in the inter-war years.

Although the demand for overtly exotic portrayals of native peoples peaked during the early twentieth century, they did not disappear completely. The naked 'native girl' and 'the savage' have fallen victim to both legislation on pornography and changes in outlook on the part of both hosts and guests; but 'the dancer' and 'the craftsman' have endured, albeit in a modified form. While belittling images of South-East Asian culture are inappropriate to the needs of a tourist industry run by independent states, it is significant that two of the images that have featured strongly in the various ASEAN advertising campaigns can be traced back to the colonial period. Although the modern subjects are no longer stiffly posed against studio backdrops, they are recognisably part of the same genre: the dancers are just as richly adorned as their forebears and the craftsmen are still surrounded by a baffling array of tools, some of which are clearly museum pieces. These images continue to be used presumably because they are thought to have a strong touristic appeal – we might even call it 'brand loyalty', if we were to borrow the jargon of the advertising industry. The photographs not only help to sell the region to potential tourists, but they accord well with how South-East Asian peoples – at least in an official sense – want to be perceived. It was, after all, the tourist boards of the respective South-East Asian states which commissioned these promotional images, and we can assume that they had some influence over what eventually was released for wider public consumption. Perhaps they were only recognising commercial realities since it is clear that both 'the dancer' and 'the craftsman' are easily interpreted as symbols of cultural value. Cultural tourism is, after all, the kind of tourism that the members of ASEAN are trying to encourage. Visit Indonesia Year, for example, was preceded by major arts festivals in Europe and North America; '*gamelan* diplomacy' appears to have become a vital element in the promotion of trade and tourism for at least one South-East Asian nation. In Thailand, the concept of *wattanathammachart* (culture and nature) provides the cornerstone for the country's tourism promotion strategy for the 1990s (see Parnwell, Chapter 12 in this volume).

Some commentators on South-East Asia have, however, argued that the images put forward by the tour operators and national tourist boards provide only a partial view of the overall perception of the host culture, as is especially the case in Thailand. Besides the official image there exists, according to Cohen, a subterranean image of considerable attraction to young tourists – the image of a drugs haven (Cohen, 1983b, 309). For some visitors, the presence of opium producers and smokers enhances photogenic qualities of so-called tribal villages set against stunning mountain scenery (Cooper, 1984, 120).[5] National image-makers still face an up-hill struggle in trying to discourage this kind of semi-romantic tourism, given the *frisson* attached to the slight hint of illegitimacy and immorality. Nevertheless, the images used by tour operators are among the most pervasive of all images and undoubtedly help shape expectations, as well as sell the product. As is shown by Selwyn in this volume, brochures have their own conventions, significances and meanings and reveal much about the aspirations and motivations of the majority of modern tourists.

## TOURISM AND DEVELOPMENT

'Tourism is like fire. It can cook your food or burn your house down.'
(Fox, 1976, 44: cited in Richter, 1984b, ATCM18/20)

The growth of the tourism industry has been most opportune for several South-East Asian countries in view of several more general economic and political changes which have taken place in the region over the last two decades. Thailand's early development as an international tourism destination coincided with the waning US military presence after the Vietnam War, and helped to fill a considerable vacuum in terms of foreign exchange earnings and employment. It is also widely suggested that the tourism industry provided a convenient alternative source of livelihood for the several tens of thousands of prostitutes who previously had been associated with the 'rest and recuperation' of American GIs. More recently, tourism has helped to offset Thailand's falling foreign exchange earnings following a steady decline in contract labour migration to the Middle East over the last decade, and particularly following the hasty return of several tens of thousands of Thai migrant workers in the lead-up to the Gulf War. Tourism has also expanded at a time when Malaysia's traditional primary industries, particularly tin and rubber, have been in decline and as international earnings from trade in these commodities have been depressed. Similarly in Indonesia, tourism has helped to boost foreign exchange earnings at a time, during the 1980s, when revenues from the country's main export commodity, petroleum, have fallen.

Just as tourism has earned these countries time and hard currency as they have sought to diversify and rejuvenate their domestic economies, so too may it be expected to play an important role in the development of other countries in the region, most notably Vietnam, Laos and Cambodia, as they too seek to promote economic growth against a backdrop of severe constraints on investment and capital formation, and in the face of woefully inadequate infrastructural provision, technical and managerial expertise, and moribund economic structures.

For many countries in the region tourism represents an attractive and relatively 'soft' means of promoting development. Although competition from other Third World destinations can be expected to increase over the next decade or so, as more countries attempt to jump on the international tourism bandwagon, tourism in general faces fewer constraints in the form of market protectionism than is the case with manufacturing, for instance. Furthermore, the technological and human resource requirements of tourism are in general much lower, and more easily accessible, than for manufacturing and extractive industry. Tourism also faces fewer of the environmental and infrastructural constraints which have restricted the pace of agricultural development in the region.

In addition to the macro-economic significance of tourism in South-East Asia, the industry has also played an important role at the sub-national level. In several countries tourism has helped to spread economic activity into areas which hitherto have been economically marginal and spatially peripheral. Many areas which are attractive to tourists – coasts, islands and uplands – have not in the main been central to the transformations which have recently taken place in the economic structures of several South-East Asian countries, most notably in agriculture, manufacturing industry and the service sector. Thus in Thailand, tourism has breathed new economic life into underdeveloped areas in the north and south of the country. Chiang Mai has become a very important centre for 'hill tribe' tourism in northern Thailand, whilst Phuket, Ko Samui and other islands off the Thai isthmus have derived considerable economic benefits from the recent tourism boom. Tourism is also being used as a means of spreading economic activity to economically depressed areas in eastern Peninsular Malaysia, especially the coastal regions of Terengganu and Kelantan, and islands such as Langkawi off the coast of Kedah.

A classic example of the power of tourism to engender development in economically backward areas is provided by Bali. Although well established as a tourist destination during the colonial period, the island was singled out for very active promotion as an international tourism centre during the 1970s. The policy shared the dual objectives of boosting the country's economy by rapidly developing potential tourism resources, whilst at the same time underpinning the development and diversification of the Balinese economy. The development of tourism on Bali not only provided a model for the development of tourism elsewhere in the archipelago but it also helped to improve Bali's economic standing relative to other parts of the country. In

1980, for example, Bali's Gross Regional Product (198,000 Rupiah) was more or less on par with West Java (208,000 Rp.), one of the country's more developed regions, and indeed enjoyed a faster rate of growth between 1976 and 1980 (13 per cent, compared with 9 per cent). The number of foreign visitors to Bali increased more than twenty-fold to 700,000 between 1969 and 1989.

The myriad economic and spatial benefits which may accrue from tourism help, of course, to explain why South-East Asian governments have been so keen to promote tourism. However, in almost all cases these benefits should be weighed against various economic and non-economic costs. The chapters in this volume by Sinclair and Vokes, and by Walton, analyse the relative balance of the economic costs and benefits of tourism, and suggest that the 'balance sheet' is much less favourable than one might suspect given the current level of tourism promotion in the region. If we add to the economic costs the wide range of less tangible, less easily quantifiable and less immediately apparent effects of tourism, the rather general assumption of the role of tourism as developmental must be questioned. We shall briefly examine below some of the 'hidden' costs of tourism in South-East Asia.

### Economic costs

One of the most important of these costs is the leakage of foreign exchange associated with many forms of tourism in South-East Asia. Leakages are associated with such phenomena as the import of foodstuffs, construction materials, capital goods and other items in support of tourism, and also the repatriation of profits where there is significant involvement of multinational firms in a country's tourism industry. Although such leakages may be less significant than for other forms of economic activity,[6] they nonetheless should moderate the optimism which accompanies the role of tourism in this regard. The net financial benefit from tourism is much lower than the lay public is frequently led to believe. Nonetheless, levels of leakage and foreign involvement in tourism vary quite considerably between countries in South-East Asia (foreign exchange leakages range from 14 per cent in the Philippines to around 59 per cent in Singapore), and also within these countries. In Bali, for example, the tourism industry in Sanur is predominantly owned by foreign or mixed local-foreign groups, whereas neighbouring Kuta is in largely Kutanese hands (Mabbett, 1987, 24). A high level of foreign ownership may also limit the transfer

of skills and technology to local communities, especially where the top
management positions are filled by expatriates.

Other economic costs associated with tourism include the inflationary effects of tourist expenditure on prices for local goods, and of the
demand for land on property and land prices. Tourism may also
displace labour from other forms of economic activity, such as
agriculture, where expected wage rates and job security are higher. It is
also suggested that investment in tourism development may draw
resources away from other projects, enterprises and social welfare
institutions. Linkages between tourism and other economic sectors are
often quite weak in most South-East Asian countries, suggesting that
tourism planning has emphasised most strongly the rapid expansion of
the industry without paying due consideration to the role of tourism in
an integrated programme of development which draws in other
economic sectors. Such a high prioritisation of tourism development
also runs the risk of creating, both nationally and sub-nationally, an
unhealthy dependence on what can be a very fickle and potentially
volatile industry.

Another trade-off associated with tourism is found in the
handicrafts sector. Whilst offering a potentially valuable source of
livelihood in peripheral and economically-backward regions, and
helping to ease problems of regional and economic imbalance and
staving off some rural–urban migration (see Parnwell, Chapter 12 in
this volume), the development of tourist crafts may often necessitate
changes in production methods which draw the industry away from
the traditional craft processes which underpin their attraction for
tourists (Vickers, 1989, 200). Furthermore, not all societies can adapt
easily to handicraft production, especially where local traditions are
not well developed (e.g. Komodo). Hence, brokers belonging to other
ethnic groups than the hosts may be the main beneficiaries of tourist
development, particularly when the brokers come from a society
which has a long experience of tourism (see Hitchcock, Chapter 16 in
this volume).

## Distributional costs

Following on from the above point, tourism tends to be characterised
by, and to further engender, social inequalities. Not everyone can be
expected to participate in and derive benefits from tourism on an
equal basis: this applies whether we examine tourism at the international, regional, national or sub-national level. The capital requirements for entry into the tourism industry may be prohibitive to local

people, leaving the way clear for 'outsiders' – be they in the form of non-local entrepreneurs or international enterprises. The role of local people is thus very often relegated to the more marginal and menial, less well paid occupations. The lion's share of the profits accrue elsewhere, and these are often expatriated. The socially unequal character of much of the tourism industry is one of the principal factors which militates against the whole-hearted acceptance of tourism as a prime instrument of development in South-East Asia (in its broadest sense, not simply in terms of economic growth). Clearly the understanding of the merits of tourism in relation to development is in its infancy, though chapters in this volume indicate areas of potential interest.

## Socio-cultural costs

We have already seen some of the complications involved in assessing the social and cultural consequences of tourism. However, there has been direct condemnation of tourism development as a source of moral corruption, particularly by 'Third World' pressure groups. Much of the blame for this 'cultural pollution' has been attributed to European, North American and Antipodean tourists. Westerners of predominantly White European extraction are much more likely to be associated with the corrupting influences of massage parlours and discotheques than their Asian counterparts. There is, however, no evidence to suggest that Westerners are any more responsible for the kinds of pursuits deemed 'morally degrading' than domestic and other Asian tourists. So-called 'sex tourism', for example, has been condemned by South-East Asian journalists, politicians and anti-tourism campaigners alike, and much of the criticism has been directed towards Western tourists. While there is undoubtedly a market for Western-oriented sex tourism, especially in Thailand and the Philippines, it represents a comparatively small, albeit lucrative, share of the overall market. There are strong indications that the 'sex industries' of many ASEAN countries are heavily dependent on the home market (e.g. Indonesia) or tourists from neighbouring ASEAN states (e.g. South Thailand: see, also, Cohen's examination of 'open-ended prostitution' in Chapter 8 in this volume). There is clearly a discrepancy between what is reported and what is actually happening, and this may have arisen because of the comparatively high visibility of Western tourists in an Asian context: a degree of scapegoating and mild ethnocentrism cannot be ruled out. Nevertheless, there are obviously moral and cultural costs in tourism development which need much more research.

**Environmental costs**

Tourism almost inevitably has an impact, occasionally quite pro-found, on the aesthetic landscape and the natural environment (see Parnwell, Chapter 15 in this volume). As with the effects of tourism on culture, the industry is affecting one of the principal resources upon which it has been built. Tourists require facilities and infrastructure, and where there are few, or only weakly-enforced, regulations to govern their style and forms, the construction of these facilities may quite radically transform the visual quality of natural landscapes. In Thailand, the east coast resort of Pattaya has been transformed into a sprawling, haphazard and congested centre of tourism, just 90 kilome-tres from the capital city Bangkok from where many of Pattaya's domestic and international tourists may travel. High- and low-rise hotels have mushroomed in all the main tourism centres, transforming sky-lines, modifying local micro-climates and radically changing the character of these resorts. Widespread concern has been expressed about the height – often well above the tree line – of new hotels in many resorts. Some commentators, however, have argued against the imposition of regulations on local communities by town planners. Hugh Mabbett, for example, writes about the need to conserve the spontaneity of Kuta and suggests giving responsibility to the village associations, *banjar*, to ensure that the new buildings suit local needs (Mabbett, 1987, 158). And yet in spite of the continuing tourism boom, occupancy rates in most countries are very low because of very weak regulation of hotel construction.

The lack of planning which has allowed the aesthetic quality of many tourism centres to be despoiled has also underpinned a variety of other negative effects of tourism on the environment. In most cases, tourism centres have expanded at a much faster rate than the public and private sector have been capable of providing refuse and sewerage disposal systems, water and energy supply, proper trails through forest reserves, and so on. As a result, the region's main tourism 'hot spots' have increasingly experienced problems of pollution, erosion and other forms of environmental degradation. Souvenir-hunting tourists are responsible, either through their direct action or indirectly through the demand that they generate, for causing damage to fragile ecosystems such as coral reefs,[7] or threatening species diversity by purchasing momentos which incorporate rare birds, butterflies, insects and other of the region's fauna. Of course, tourism is not solely responsible for such forms of environmental and ecological damage but, as we shall see below, many of the effects of tourism in this regard could quite easily be ameliorated by adequate anticipatory planning and the more stringent implementation of the laws and regulations that are presently embodied in the region's various environmental protection acts. One problem is that it often takes a long while before the full environmental impact of uncontrolled tourism becomes apparent, by which time it is often too late to introduce effective reactive measures of the kind which preoccupy most planning systems in the region today. A further barrier is the fact that environmental protection measures cost money, and may therefore either necessitate diverting public sector resources from other forms of development (tourism-related or otherwise), or may eat into profit margins in the private sector. Either way, it is easy to see why there is considerable reluctance to slow the rate of tourism development on environmental grounds alone, and why the full environmental cost of tourism is seldom built in to proposals for new developments.

## TOURISM AND SUSTAINABILITY

Given many of the socio-cultural and environmental effects of tourism outlined above, questions are increasingly being asked as to whether or not the current exponential rate of growth of tourism in South-East Asia can be sustained. In simple terms, the issue of the sustainability of tourism must be focused on the extent to which 'tourism may be destroying tourism': in other words, the effect that tourism is having upon the principal features which attract tourists to the region, notably the region's natural and human landscapes, and its material and aesthetic culture. Although several of the chapters in this volume point to the remarkable adaptability and resilience of some South-East Asian societies, not all peoples are in a strong position to accommodate this industry. Clearly, more culturally sensitive studies need to be built into the planning process. Without adequate safeguards in the form of land management schemes and infrastructural investment, the natural environment is much less resilient, and is particularly susceptible to the effects of over-exploitation and uncontrolled tourism development. There are already signs throughout the region of the more discerning tourists 'voting with their feet', and deserting some of the more developed and commercialised tourism centres in favour of new locations which are nearer the vanguard of tourism development. There are no indications as yet that tourists regard South-East Asia as significantly overexploited in either 'cultural' or 'natural' terms and that overall visitor numbers are about to decline. There are many as yet untapped potential tourism resources, as indeed there are several hitherto unexploited sources of tourists, including a massive latent market for domestic tourism, as well as large numbers of tourists in countries outside the region who hitherto have been prevented from travelling to South-East Asia because the cost is prohibitive.

A narrow assessment of sustainable tourism such as this, which views the industry's future predominantly from the demand perspective, is grossly unfair to the peoples of South-East Asia who must live with both the phenomenon and the effects of mass tourism. This includes very large numbers of people who, because of the nature of an industry which is dominated by international capital and large-scale domestic concerns, have shared very little in the benefits generated by tourism development whilst at the same time enduring disproportionately many of its negative effects. The sustainability of tourism thus should not be centred around concern to maintain the level of tourist arrivals, but should instead emphasise the amelioration of the industry's social, cultural and environmental effects:

> Sustainable tourism development can be thought of as meeting the needs of present tourists and host regions while protecting and enhancing opportunity for the future. Sustainable tourism development is envisaged as leading to management of all resources in such a way that we can fulfil economic, social and aesthetic needs while maintaining cultural integrity, essential ecological processes, biological diversity and life support systems.
>
> (Anita Pleumarom, 1990, 12)

If this can be achieved whilst at the same time maintaining the current scale of the industry, all well and good. If not, it should be the quality of the environment and not the numbers game which determines the future pattern of tourism development.

Such a view of 'sustainable tourism' clearly challenges the established order as far as the growth of South-East Asian tourism has been concerned hitherto. It is also very controversial, in that it largely ignores many of the broader social, economic and political forces which underpin the intense pressure which exists in many South-East Asian countries to exploit resources with tourism potential to the full, such as widespread poverty, unemployment, international debt, shortages of foreign exchange and national prestige. The notion of 'sustainable development', of which sustainable tourism may be considered a variant, has largely been promulgated by the industrialised nations of the North in the context of global environmental processes and concerns, and is in grave danger of being 'imposed' on the poorer nations of the South, regardless of their individual circumstances, needs and development priorities. Thus, whilst mindful of the probable long-term consequences of a *laissez-faire* approach towards tourism development, governments must be free to tailor their tourism policies to suit their particular situation. However, just as it may be naive to assume that South-East Asian governments will, in effect, kill (or restrict) what they perceive to be 'the goose which lays the golden egg', so too is it debatable whether tourism in its present form has been successful in alleviating such problems as poverty, inequality and unemployment.

Also underlying the notion of sustainable tourism is the question of who should be the main beneficiaries from tourism development and, indeed, who should determine its pattern and pace? Hitherto, tourism has functioned primarily for the benefit of the tourist, and its form and dynamics have principally been driven by the industry itself. National governments have taken it upon themselves to act on behalf of the people in respect of facilitating or moderating the development of tourism within their respective territories. In the main, facilitation rather than moderation has ruled the day. Meanwhile, local communities have found themselves largely excluded from the decision-making process, and from full and active participation in the growth of tourism in their localities. However, most commentators now argue that a greater level of local involvement in the planning and development of tourism is an essential prerequisite of sustainable tourism. Notwithstanding people's basic right to participate in decisions which may profoundly affect their lives, the substitution of 'bottom-up' decision-making for centralised directives which pass from the 'top-down' may also lead to a greater appropriateness of planning decisions and a greater motivation on the part of local people to prevent many of the negative effects of tourism.

Whilst laudable in principle, it is very difficult to envisage how sustainable tourism can be engendered in practice. Greater local participation, for instance, requires a much higher level of local democracy than is evident in most South-East Asian countries today. The underlying economic and welfare conditions which lead to pressure to exploit tourism potential would also appear to be intractable. Furthermore, there is an inherent contradiction in the notion of 'sustainable tourism' itself: Edward Niles suggests that it is a myth, in that it is impossible to create culturally and environmentally benign forms of tourism – particularly against the back-drop of mass, commercial tourism which characterises the industry today – when tourism is essentially structured upon the exploitation of these very resources (Niles, 1991, 3–4).

There is mounting evidence, however, that attitudes towards tourism are beginning to change as people, governments, tourists and the tourist industry itself become more aware of the harmful effects of uncontrolled and poorly managed tourism. A host of pressure groups (including Tourism Concern in the United Kingdom and the Ecumenical Coalition on Third World Tourism (ECTWT), based in Thailand), has been established, and through a profusion of publications and fora have advocated the promotion and pursuit of 'alternative', more 'appropriate' forms of tourism, especially in the world's poorer countries.

> Alternative tourism is a process which promotes a just form of travel between members of different communities. It seeks to achieve mutual understanding, solidarity and equality among participants
>
> (Anita Pleumarom, 1990, 12)

A growing number of small tour operators now offer supposedly 'softer', more 'responsible' forms of tourism (Johnston, 1990, 3). These have been given a bewildering range of titles, such as 'ecotourism', 'adventure tourism', 'heritage tourism', 'educational tourism', 'special interest tourism', 'soft-path tourism', 'solidarity tourism', and so on. Each purports, in its own way, to offer an alternative to mass, commercialised tourism.

'Alternative tourism' in its purest form is underpinned by a number of principles. First, tourism should be built upon a dialogue with local people, who must be made fully aware of the likely effects of a tourism project, who must be centrally involved in the decision-making processes, development and management of the project, and whose voice must carry genuine political weight (see also Kadir Din, Chapter 18 in this volume). Local people must be able to ascertain the aesthetic and commercial value of proposed sites for tourism development, and they ultimately should decide whether or not the benefits of tourism in their localities will outweigh the perceived costs.

Second, alternative tourism should constitute a means of giving the poor a reasonable and more equal share in the profits which accrue from tourism. This further presupposes that their involvement in the development of the tourism industry is considerable. Third, tourism must be built upon sound environmental principles, should be sensitive to local cultural and religious traditions, and not exacerbate existing inequalities within the host community (O'Grady, 1990, 10). Fourth, the scale of tourism should be tailored to match the capacity of the local area to cope with it. This assumes that the potential carrying capacity of the locality can be ascertained, and that the volume of tourism can be controlled within the bounds of this capacity. Carrying capacity is defined as 'the maximum level of visitor use an area can accommodate with high levels of satisfaction for visitors and few negative impacts on resources (and the local population)' (Yong, 1991, 1). Carrying capacity is thus measured in aesthetic as well as ecological terms. Finally, alternative tourism might be used to strengthen linkages between the tourism industry and other forms of local economic activity. Tourism should be based upon a demand for locally-produced foodstuffs, building materials, handicrafts and so on, rather than relying on the import of such commodities, as is more often the case in South-East Asia. Indirectly, this may also help to stem the leakage abroad of foreign exchange.

Whilst alternative tourism thus seeks to shift the balance of benefits and participation more squarely in the direction of the host community, the guest is not neglected. Indeed, a parallel objective is that the visitor should also be fulfilled by his or her trip, both educationally and recreationally, through enjoying an enhanced experience of being in a different cultural environment or by making a constructive contribution to the host society. Mark Timm cites the example of Japanese tourists whose 'holiday' in Thailand centres around working on rural development projects in isolated and underdeveloped areas (Timm, 1990, 24).

To what extent do 'alternative' forms of tourism help in the pursuit of sustainable tourism in South-East Asia? By its very nature, alternative tourism can never be expected radically to transform the tourism industry *per se* because of its small scale and specialised nature. Alternative tourism cannot offer the economies of scale which underpin mass tourism. Meanwhile, it is unrealistic to expect the tourism multinationals to press the self-destruct button because of the protests of a nascent alternative tourism movement. Nonetheless, the promotion of the concept of alternative tourism has been successful in encouraging people, both inside and outside the tourism industry, to look more critically and questioningly at how tourism is affecting the principal destination areas in South-East Asia and elsewhere. On the other hand, critics suggest that the popularity of the concept of alternative tourism has created a new market niche which several large tour operators have been very quick to exploit. Thus, in a similar vein to the current trend towards 'green consumerism', many supposed forms of 'alternative tourism' are in reality repackaged forms of 'mainstream tourism' – what Pleumarom refers to as 'pseudo-alternatives' (Pleumarom, 1990, 15). This may ultimately prove counterproductive in the quest for sustainable tourism, as clients are lulled into 'conscience-free' forms of tourism wherein the traveller remains oblivious to the negative effects of his or her presence in the host community. It may also proliferate the movement of tourists.

There are, however, several instances where certain forms of 'alternative' or 'special interest' tourism have had a benign or even positive impact in the host country. 'Ecotourism' is a case in point. 'Ecotourism' may be defined as 'tourism to protected areas of outstanding natural beauty, extraordinary ecological interest, and pristine wilderness with the specific objective of studying, admiring and enjoying the scenery and its wild plants and animals found in these areas' (Yong, 1991, 1). In several instances such forms of nature tourism have provided the economic justification for the protection of areas, such as forests, which otherwise might not have been afforded such protection.[8] The income generated from nature tourism may finance the management of national parks and wildlife sanctuaries, in the process helping to conserve the very resources and environments that nature tourists are willing to pay to experience. Kinabalu National Park in Sabah provides an example of the successful marriage of tourism and conservation in South-East Asia. It is assumed that the people who are interested in ecotourism are also inherently conservation-minded and are very knowledgeable about the vulnerability of natural ecosystems. Tourism may also stimulate the environmental awareness of local people and government officials, encouraging a greater interest in environmental conservation than may otherwise be the case (see Cochrane, Chapter 17 in this volume). Furthermore, the exploitation of ecosystems such as forests for tourism may also help to assuage pressures for other, potentially much more destructive, uses such as commercial forestry, mining, reservoir construction and land clearance for cultivation.

The needs of local people should be taken into account so that they are not marginalised or criminalised by conservation measures. Today's hunter-gatherer or swidden farmer can all too easily become tomorrow's poacher in the eyes of the law. Adequate provision should be made, perhaps through appropriate training programmes, so that indigenous peoples are placed in a position to take advantage of the new opportunities offered by tourism, whether in the public (e.g. rangers, guides) or private (e.g. hoteliers, craftspeople) sectors.

However, there is a fundamental contradiction between the designation of nature reserves for the protection of wildlife and the exploitation of the resources they offer for tourism. This is mirrored by a conflict pitching the 'preservationists' against the 'utilitarians', with the latter increasingly winning the day as more pressure is exerted by central governments in Thailand, Indonesia and Malaysia for areas with tourism potential to be fully mobilised (cf. Cochrane). Only where tourism is very carefully managed and regulated will its impact on these resources be kept within acceptable bounds. Unfortunately, this has not always been the case in South-East Asia. The Taman Negara National Park, containing one of the world's oldest forests and Peninsular Malaysia's last broad expanse of lowland, hill and montane rainforest, provides a good illustration of some of the pressures which are being exerted on natural ecosystems by tourism. In 1989 more than 14,000 tourists visited the Park (Yong, 1991, 4). Because of restrictions on the parts of the Park into which tourists could venture, the impact of this relatively small number of visitors was substantially intensified. The tramping feet of trekkers are responsible for soil erosion and compaction, the exposure of tree roots and the destruction of vegetation. Wildlife, including the rare Indochinese tiger and seladang wild ox, are being displaced or dispersed because of disturbance by tourists, returning only during the season when the Park is closed (ibid.). The disappearance of predators upsets the ecological balance allowing the populations of their usual prey to proliferate. Piles of garbage, and the hand-feeding of wildlife by visitors, encourage parasitism and dependence of wild animals on humans.

Thus, even the alternatives to mass, commercialised tourism have an impact on the human and physical environment of destination areas. This is hardly surprising, because a large segment of the tourism industry by its very nature depends upon the development, enjoyment and utilisation of such environmental resources. This is so whether the guests are international tourists from Europe, East Asia or elsewhere in South-East Asia, or domestic tourists from only a few miles away.

As the Malaysian example clearly illustrates, an important step towards sustainable tourism may lie in the better planning and management of tourism development. One possible step forward may revolve around the development of 'sacrificial resorts' – like Pattaya on Thailand's east coast, or Nusa Dua in Bali – into which tourists who do not seek an experience of 'deep quality' are poured, in the process helping to protect other areas (*In Focus*, 1991, 2). Environmental Impact Assessments are also an important planning tool before and during the implementation of a tourism project although, as Kadir Din's chapter in this volume shows, the system is still open to abuse (cf. also the current controversy concerning the Penang Hill project). Furthermore, tourism should not be treated in isolation from other forms of economic activity – tourism planning should form part of an integrated system of development planning.

A second prerequisite is the better training and education of the agents of tourism, be they the tour operators, the tourists, their local guides or the communities at the receiving end of tourism. Third, as is strongly advocated in the philosophy of 'alternative tourism', a greater level of local participation in the planning, development and management of tourism should be encouraged and facilitated. Finally, the full environmental and social costs of tourism should be incorporated into the evaluation of the costs and benefits of tourism. The 'balance sheet' may change quite radically when this is done (Niles, 1991, 3–4).

## FUTURE RESEARCH

There is a range of themes and substantive topics which requires further research in the study of tourism in South-East Asia. Some of the themes have commanded at least some attention in this volume, but much more needs to be done. Other issues have hardly been considered and we have very little detailed information on them.

One concern which surfaces in a number of the contributions but which is only really coherently treated by Tom Selwyn is that of the images and symbolic representations of peoples, cultures and environments constructed specifically for tourist promotional purposes. However, we do not know very much about the ways in which these images have been developed and changed over time (cf. Saunders, Chapter 14 in this volume), and the similarities and differences between the different media in which South-East Asia has been depicted – in postcards, posters, brochures, tourist guides, film and travel books.

What have been very much neglected are the local perspectives on tourism and leisure, as against the representations of those who promote and sell the tourist product. Furthermore, we do not know whether, and in what ways, images held by tourists prior to the guest–host encounter are translated into particular behavioural patterns and forms of social interaction between tourists and local residents, nor do we know whether these encounters subsequently act to change tourist images, views and prejudices. In this regard, crucial elements in tourism are the tour agents, guides and leaders who act as social and cultural brokers between tourists and hosts. Yet again, we do not know much about how these intermediaries convey information, organise and conduct encounters, and portray local cultures and scenes. This kind of research requires local-level anthropological field-work. At the national level, however, Linda Richter and Robert Wood demonstrate how important it is for us also to have more data on the relations between national identity, political image-building and tour-ism. As Richter and Wood also indicate, these national arenas of representation are also the focus for conflicts over identity and the contesting by various social groups of particular constructions of 'national culture'.

These issues of conflict at the national level should also be examined at the local level. We know that there are many protest groups which lobby on behalf of 'the people' for more caring, sympathetic kinds of tourism. What we do not know much about are local forms of protest and resistance to tourism, examining their organisation and expression. However, we do have a much better idea of how local communities have adapted to tourism. In addition, in these studies of local effects and reactions we commonly do not have material on the ways in which gender differences influence local response.

Aside from social and cultural issues, we also require more detailed evaluations, using a set of related case studies in South-East Asia, of the different processes involved in, and consequences of, different kinds of tourism, and attempts to evaluate these from different perspectives – economic, sociological, anthropological, environmental and political. Furthermore, eve ı though economists have done some research on the developmental impact of tourism on South-East Asian economies, there are still large gaps in our statistical knowledge about the presumed economic benefits and costs of tourism development, especially at the sub-national level.

Finally, and again as Richter has argued, and as Kadir Din has indicated for Malaysia, the whole field of policy-making with regard to tourism is a virtual *terra incognita*. For an industry which has already had, and will continue to have, an enormous influence on South-East Asian countries, the governments of the region, with the partial exception of Singapore, have done little to plan for these developments and effects. We need to know whether there are relevant policies and legal regulations and procedures in place already, cover-ing such matters as environmental conservation, spatial planning, employment regulations and infrastructural development; how policies have been and are being formed, and what else needs to be done.

The present volume, by bringing together a number of writers on tourism, tackling issues hitherto neglected or not treated comprehensively, and raising a whole series of questions and issues, will, it is hoped, serve to draw attention to the vital need for more research on tourism, as a field which provides potentially exciting and necessary studies in both theory and practice.

## NOTES

1 The Economist Intelligence Unit, 1991, *International Tourism Reports*, No. 3, 25.
2 Referred to as 'enclave tourism' by Lea (1988, 14). It is important to note, however, that what is referred to here is the packaged form of mass tourism. A number of the more specialised tour companies go to considerable lengths to provide adequate information on local culture, and arrange itineraries and excursions which employ specialist local guides. This is particularly the case with 'special interest' forms of tourism, such as wildlife tourism, cultural tourism, heritage tourism, and so on.
3 A recent report by the Secretariat of the South-East Asia Trade Advisory Group (SEATAG) suggests that, because of the Gulf War, arrivals in 1991 were expected to be slightly down on 1990, dashing earlier hopes of a 37 per cent rise in tourist arrivals in 1991. Garuda, the national carrier, halved its European schedules, and Bali remained virtually empty in the early months of the year.
4 Lewis Hill, personal communication.
5 Cohen notes the tendency of tour operators to stereotype any minority in Thailand as a hill tribe regardless of whether or not they are highlanders (Cohen, 1983c, 32).
6 Walton (Chapter 11 in this volume) claims that, in general, foreign exchange leakages associated with tourism (27 per cent) compare quite favourably with those which are associated with manufacturing exports (59 per cent) and total exports (72 per cent).
7 The indiscriminate removal of coral (a source of lime) for use in building programmes may also result in the destruction of reefs, and may indirectly lead to severe erosion of beaches due to the removal of protection from seasonal storms.
8 Once again, however, this needs careful consideration, especially when it comes to a choice between a small number of high-paying visitors, some of whom are popularly regarded somewhat negatively (e.g. big game hunters), and large numbers of low budget tourists and the attendant environmental hazards.

# 2 Time and tides in the anthropology of tourism[1]

*David Wilson*

## INTRODUCTION

This chapter examines a problem which I suspect presents a serious research handicap to all those, regardless of discipline, who are interested in the impact of tourism, wherever it has taken place. This problem concerns the provision of an adequate time dimension to tourism research, without which, I would suggest, much current research and analysis must remain highly provisional and contingent in status. Contingent, that is, upon a more adequate contextualisation of data at both the theoretical and substantive levels. There are three distinct but related issues here, all connected through this notion of time, to which I will give some rather pretentious titles, no doubt to be criticised later!

## 'CONCEPTUAL TIME-CAPSULES' IN THE ANTHROPOLOGY OF TOURISM

The first problem relates to changing perspectives over time as to what actually constitutes the 'anthropology of tourism' and the unnecessary intellectual confusion this can produce. Until very recently I would tell my students that one of the difficulties with the anthropology of tourism was that it was still very much in a pre-conceptual or pre-paradigmatic stage, and lacked any firmly grounded theoretical perspective. However, in preparing this chapter, I have changed my mind about this claim. Each academic discipline, or sub-discipline, has its own 'intellectual history'. In the anthropology of tourism, a surprisingly recent branch of the discipline (for reasons considered by Boissevain, 1978, 38–39 and Nash, 1981, 461), definitions, concepts and research priorities have changed rapidly as the following quotations will, I hope, illustrate. But first, a note of caution. A brief survey such as this can be little more than a somewhat arbitrary and personal selection, with many important references omitted for the sake of brevity. However, even if other themes and transformations are discernible this will not alter the conclusions I wish to draw from the exercise.

Nunez, in one of the first major edited contributions to the subject, tells us that 'the study of tourism by anthropologists has been characterised largely by serendipity'(Nunez, 1978, 207). In other words, many anthropologists, wherever they went to do their research, accidentally or fortuitously discovered tourists, and started to write about them. Boissevain calls this 'spin-off' research. They used existing anthropological 'models' such as acculturation as guides to their work. Because touristic interaction between two cultures often tends to be one-sided, the hosts borrowing more from the guests than vice versa, Nunez argues that this led many anthropologists to view tourism as culturally destructive: another reason why they avoided the topic for so long. He suggests that what was needed were studies of the entrepreneurs who acted as 'culture brokers' between the old traditions and the new innovations precipitated by tourism development (in the UK this had already been done by some of F. G. Bailey's students), and a deeper understanding of host–guest interaction and stereotyping. Finally, Nunez warns against the temptation to condemn tourism as intrusive, exploitative and destructive of culture. As anthropologists we should remain ethically neutral and not succumb to the temptation to keep our subjects 'as pristine pets on anthropological reservations' (ibid., 215).

Nash provides another early attempt to speculate on the form that an anthropology of tourism should take. The subject was 'still in its infancy (and) only after we have developed a satisfactory definition of tourism can we begin to think of ways that will help us account for it, its variants, and its consequences' (Nash, 1981, 461). Much of his article is devoted to searching for an adequate definition of the subject matter and associated problems. Many other writers around this time attempted to provide definitions and taxonomies, led by the prolific Erik Cohen – what types of tourism were there, how could tourists be classified, was tourism a manifestation of a universal need and, if so, what was it?

So, at the end of the 1970s anthropologists were still struggling to define and legitimate tourism as an academic field of study with its own distinctive research strategy. Not that Nash was without his critics at the time. Buck (1982), amongst others, argued that he underplayed the value of ethnography, perhaps anthropology's strongest potential contribution to the emergent field. During this period, as indeed throughout the 1980s, the main contribution by anthropologists tended to be of the 'articles and papers' variety, either in edited volumes such as those by Smith (1978) and de Kadt (1979), or in the *Annals of Tourism Research*.

One growth area in the 1980s was a focus on tourism as pilgrimage, ritual or play (e.g. Graburn (1983), acknowledging Turner, MacCanell and Boorstin as his guides). Nash, in his critique of Graburn, specifically points to a shift away from a concern with the study of the social, economic and cultural impact of tourism, towards a growing emphasis on the tourists themselves and the 'ritual' of tourism, especially in the modern Western world. Nash, anticipating the thrust of my own argument, states that 'we should be wary about being trapped into any one conceptual scheme . . . it is important, therefore, to keep our options open and to maintain a healthy empirical orientation in our appreciation of conceptual schemes' (Nash, 1984, 504). Nevertheless, he is sceptical of approaches focusing on tourism as pilgrimage, ritual or play as this involves a 'cognitive reductionism which turns tourism into mental representations' (ibid., 506).

As if such accusations weren't bad enough, enter next the post-modernist anthropologist intent on textual analysis, reflexivity and the 'ethnographic confessional'. Crick, for example, notes the similarities between what anthropologists do and what tourists do, and finds this a 'painful experience' (Crick, 1985, 76). The 'negative emotional forces' aroused by tourism have caused anthropologists to distance themselves from tourists even though, as he goes to some length to point out, a lot of what anthropologists do during their field-work is indistinguishable from the activities of the tourists themselves. Both 'share displacement into non-ordinary space and time' (ibid., 82), both are to a large extent engaged in activities which can be described as 'ludic', both are products of the same social system, and neither can reach an objective understanding of the other.

The story doesn't end here, however, for Errington and Gerwertz have recently attempted to counter the post-modernist critique 'that we have, as anthropologists, lost our authority because, like tourists, we do not reach an objective understanding of the other . . .(that) what we do is for ourselves and in our own terms' (Errington and Gerwertz, 1989, 38). The gist of their argument is that although the practice of fieldwork does involve 'playing the game', these games are essentially political rather than ludic in character.

Errington and Gerwertz go on to contrast 'young travellers' with 'professionally successful tourists' and also with anthropologists in Papua New Guinea. They conclude that the travellers sought out the 'primitive' as part of their own search for individuality and the meaning of life. The tourists, however, compared themselves to the primitive to demonstrate their own success in life. The travellers' desire was for the primitive to remain as it was and they saw change as destructive, whereas the tourists were more positive advocates of the benefits of economic and social development. But what united both these views was an attitude of self-reference where 'the significance of the other is largely in what it does for oneself' (ibid., 46). Anthropologists, however, see things differently. Their aim is 'to convey what the world looks like to the natives and how our world affects them'. They continue: 'Thus, if we cannot easily differentiate our personal motivation from that of tourists, we can differentiate their politics from ours . . . we can and must be political in terms not self-referential and individualistic, but comparative and systemic' (ibid.).

Thus, in little over two decades, the anthropological study of tourism has undergone a series of conceptual shifts, which can be summarised as follows: (a) up until the 1970s, anthropology largely ignores tourism; then, (b) growing awareness of tourism as a legitimate research topic; (c) definitional exercises; (d) studies of the social, economic and cultural impact of tourism on host countries (empirical orientation); (e) tourism as pilgrimage, ritual or play (shift from studying hosts to studying guests, representational model building); (f) reflexive excursions into the nature of anthropological enquiry (anthropology is a subjective and ludic experience similar to tourism itself); and finally, (g) emergent critique of post-modernism as self-indulgent, and a desire to return to more practical and applied issues (to the study of them as well as us, the political implications of tourism development, etc.).

And the point of this little exercise? We must be wary of allowing ourselves to become entrapped by any one conceptual framework. We must remember that they are intellectual products of a given historical moment and, as such, reflect prevailing sets of academic predispositions (currently fashionable research strategies would be another way of putting it). Such awareness of 'moment' allows us to treat the research of others as relative, contingent and diachronically located, rather than in absolute terms as right/wrong, good/bad, old/new, etc. Buck's comments are probably more applicable today than when they were written a decade ago:

Over time, 'schools of thought' may develop, but they are often the result of competitive market and philosophic (political?)

forces rather than deliberate disinterested cooperation. Whose work is cited and how frequently provide useful indicators of the character of a research speciality at any one point in time, but influential figures come and go, 'breakthroughs' are made, and work once shunted aside is rediscovered.

(Buck, 1982, 326).

## 'ETHNOGRAPHIC TIME-TRAPS' IN THE ANTHROPOLOGY OF TOURISM

The difficulty here concerns the lack of an adequate longitudinal time dimension to many ethnographic studies which, when placed in a broader historical context, fundamentally alters the conclusions which can be drawn from them. Many studies, including some which have gained seminal status in the literature, are 'one-offs'. By this I mean that they provide snapshot pictures of a particular moment in time. Interpretations offered and conclusions drawn exhibit a tendency towards polar viewpoints which become fixed in the literature, neither confirmed nor moderated by further research. There is a danger of excessive importance being attached to such studies when they utilise provocative new concepts. Such enthusiasm is understandable in so far as their authors have introduced challenging new ideas into the intellectual arena. As examples of what I have in mind, I wish to reconsider two influential papers: Greenwood's (1977) account of the Alarde festival of Fuenterrabia in Spain and the way it became 'commoditised' by tourism and fell into terminal decline; and Buck's (1978) study of 'boundary maintenance' among the Amish in Pennsylvania and how the total separation of Amish from tourists achieved the opposite effect of reinforcing and revitalising a traditional culture.

Greenwood's deeply pessimistic argument is that tourism turns culture into a commodity which is then packaged and sold to tourists. Local culture is, as a result, inevitably altered and often completely destroyed, and thereby 'made meaningless to the people who once believed in it' (Greenwood, 1977, 131). He takes as his example the Alarde, an annual celebration of Fuenterrabia's victory over the French in 1638, which had also become a potent symbol of local community solidarity. The local municipal government attempted to make the Alarde more accessible to tourists by declaring that it should be performed twice in the same day to allow everyone to see it. Although this apparently was never put into practice, the effect was, according to Greenwood, devastating. 'What was a vital and exciting ritual became an obligation to be avoided' (ibid., 135). He dramatically concludes by saying that 'making their culture a public performance took the municipal government a few minutes; with that act, a 350-year-old ritual died' (ibid., 137).

Now Greenwood's paper has become one of the most powerful indictments of the corrosive effects of tourism in the literature, and one of the most often quoted (see, for example, the use Cohen (1988a) makes of his material). However, I always felt that there were many unanswered questions in his account: the fact that it seemed to be the decision of the municipal government rather than the presence of tourists that was the problem (yet nowhere are we told who the members of this council were); that there were a number of statements suggesting that Fuenterrabia was a deeply divided community, again indicating that local politics could be at the centre of the problem; and if there really was no attempt to keep the festival going this surely implies that it was never a particularly potent symbol in the first place, and so on.

At my suggestion, therefore, Stephanie Young, an undergraduate from the department in which I teach, visited Fuenterrabia in 1988 to see what had become of the poor Alarde. What did she find? A thriving festival! She describes 'a vibrant and exciting ritual which took place in a town alive with expectation and emotion . . . the people, far from feeling that the Alarde was an obligation to be avoided, were enthusiastic in the preparations and enactment of the week long festival' (Young, 1989, 12). And the municipal government? Young's enquiries revealed that 'during Greenwood's fieldwork the municipal government was seen as an undemocratic, corrupt bureaucracy run by Spaniards who had little sympathy for the Basque region' (ibid., 14). She concludes (*pace* Greenwood) that tourism had nothing whatsoever to do with the demise of the Alarde. In fact, what lay at the heart of the festival's continuing success was that it had become a powerful symbol of Basque nationalism and the desire for regional separatism: 'the men no longer march to celebrate a Spanish victory over the French, but rather to state their Basqueness . . . the Alarde has become openly politicised since Greenwood's time' (ibid., 14). She concludes: 'I consider Greenwood's fundamental premise that the development of tourism has led to the commoditisation of the Alarde to be invalid' (ibid., 37).

Another example of an ethnographic time-trap is Buck's oft-quoted study of the Amish (1978), which Cohen describes as one of the 'more important studies' based on MacCannell's work on authenticity (Cohen, 1988b, 35). The question that Buck sets himself is, in a sense, almost the exact opposite of Greenwood's, namely, how have the Amish been able to maintain their way of life in spite of the invasion of tourists into their midst? The key concept he uses is that of boundary maintenance, paradoxically promoted by the tourist industry itself whose brochures and guidebooks continually portray the Amish as different, strange and remote, as people to be left alone. Authentic contact with the Amish is replaced by 'staged' attractions for the tourist to visit such as 'Amish' museums, schoolhouses, weddings, barn raisings, etc. The Amish provide an authentic background to all this, but are left alone, and an almost impermeable boundary is maintained between the Amish and the outside world. This boundary is further reinforced from the inside by Amish religious views rejecting the pursuit of worldly profit, and a lifestyle which eschews modern vehicles in favour of horse and buggy, and which spurns the use of electricity and telephones. Finally, the Amish are unmistakable because of their eighteenth-century style of clothing and colloquial German dialect. Buck concludes, albeit tentatively, that tourism thus contributes to the sustained cultural vigour of the Amish people themselves (Buck, 1978, 234).

As with Greenwood's paper, there were always aspects of Buck's account which seemed problematic – especially the occasional hints that there was more contact between the two communities than Buck suggests. Exactly who were the tourist middlemen and culture brokers, and who was putting on the staged 'Amish' performances? There are tantalising references to 'teacher guides' (ibid., 230), 'specialists' (ibid., 233), a 'Mennonite guide' (ibid., 231) and one reference to the 'New Order Amish' – people who have modified their traditions (ibid., 223). Amanda North, another anthropology graduate from Queen's, has just begun a Ph.D. study of the Amish. I asked her to consider Buck's paper and its applicability to the Amish today. Her provisional opinion, after an initial period of field-work, is as follows.[2]

Boundary maintenance is no longer so evident. There seem to have been two main developments over the last decade. First, tourist numbers are increasing and they are no longer satisfied with the staged attractions by non-Amish along Route 30, and in fact staged weddings, funerals and barn raisings no longer exist. They now want to see, meet and experience real Amish. Second, the Amish themselves have also been growing in number, and demographic pressure has necessitated the finding of additional sources of jobs and income. Many Old Order Amish now allow tourists to visit their houses and farms (although not all – some lanes have 'tourists not welcome' signs posted). This has stimulated the growth of cottage industries geared to the tourist market.[3] Signs now advertise fresh produce, furniture, souvenirs, teas and 'shoofly pie' available on many of the farms. North suggests that up to 800 Old Order Amish farms could now be involved in supplying the tourist market. In sum, they are beginning to rely on tourism as their farms can no longer support them and economic diversification has become necessary. Without tourism young Amish would have to seek work outside the community, which would be far more strongly disapproved of by the elders.

Alongside these developments, a significant change in attitudes towards tourists has taken place. Tourists are no longer seen as wasteful pleasure-seekers. Many Old Order Amish are now inquisitive about their tourist guests and seem to enjoy meeting them. Contempt is reserved for the 'English' owners of the businesses along Route 30, who continue to exploit Amish culture for their own personal profit. With regard to the other stated attractions, the 'schoolhouse', 'farm', 'kitchen' and 'museum' are still there, although no Old Order Amish would work in them. In other words, the impression of tourism and its relationship to the Amish now depends very much on where you go in Lancaster County (a point which will be developed further in the next section). Furthermore, North tells me that almost certainly this must have been the case when Buck carried out his research. Even in 1980 Hostetler, another writer on the Amish, had apparently noted some 400 farms providing tourist services. North speculates that Buck could have missed all this by researching only along Highway 30.

Finally, another difficulty with Buck's account is the impression it gives that the area is almost exclusively Old Order Amish. Apparently this is not the case, either now or then. There are also the New Order Amish, the Beachy Amish, and Amish Mennonites (this latter group encompassing a wide spectrum of views from liberal to conservative). Each exhibit differences in dress and lifestyle, as well as attitudes towards tourism. A number of liberal Mennonites, for example, do work in the attractions along Route 30 and as 'teacher guides' to them.

The point of these two examples has been to demonstrate how the lack of a time dimension can, especially in the case of 'one-off' articles, confuse rather than clarify our understanding of the impact of tourism. One possible explanation which might account for the extreme position adopted by Greenwood and Buck is that this was how the local people themselves presented the case to the researcher. The Fuenterrabians were disgusted with attempts to interfere with their festival and convincingly persuaded Greenwood they were intent on abandoning it. The Amish were so strong on tradition that they convincingly persuaded Buck of the absolute boundary which separated them from the outside world. Some societies, just like some anthropologists, clearly tend to focus on either tradition or change, and a false picture easily emerges. M. E. Smith argues that 'one of the tasks of anthropology should be to delineate the conditions under which participants in a given socioculture will identify "tradition" or "innovation" as the dominant characteristic of a sociocultural element' (Smith, 1982, 127). Furthermore, in so far as both of these are perceptions (either of the observer or the observed), then 'reality is cognitively defined' (ibid., 138). Another relevant point she makes in her discussion is that 'the past will always seem more stable than the present because humans are cognizant of a multitude of events in the present while the past is blurred into long stretches of "nonoccurance" only occasionally punctuated by memory' (ibid., 128). Smith argues that 'continuity' should be the focus of our attention, and that this dynamic process can either be manifested as 'tradition' (a perception that a pattern is, basically, repetitive) or 'innovative' (a perception that change has been implemented). Of our two examples here, the Amish are presented in the former light, the Fuenterrabians in the latter.

## 'PERCEPTUAL TIME ZONES' IN THE ANTHROPOLOGY OF TOURISM

The problem here is not so much that circumstances change over time, but rather that several different situations may simultaneously co-exist at any given moment in time. Tourism might be perceived by the local people themselves as having quite a different impact than that suggested by supposedly dispassionate outside observers and experts. In addition, local opinion may vary between communities – and social groups within them – depending on the nature and extent of tourism development in their midst.

So far all rather obvious. How can such difficulties be overcome? One way I would suggest is by greater use of comparative studies within the same general area. There are a number of examples in the literature here with which I will contrast some of my own ethnography from the Seychelles Islands of the Indian Ocean. I will also develop an 'autocritique' of my account of the early effects of tourism in the Seychelles (up until the mid-1970s), published in Emmanuel de Kadt's book *Tourism: Passport to Development?* (1979), in which I presented a rather general overview dealing largely with events on the main island of Mahe – although I nowhere made this clear in my paper.

The Seychelles share much in common with the islands of the

Caribbean: multi-racial, ex-slave, plantation-based societies with a Creole culture. The decision to introduce tourism into the Seychelles was made by the then British colonial government rather than by the local people themselves. This necessitated the building of an international airport in the late 1960s, which was accompanied by a property boom as outside developers bought up the best hotel sites in the islands. Control over construction work, ownership of hotels, key development land, as well as most ancillary service industries, was all in expatriate hands. In my published paper I distinguished three stages in the growth of Seychelles tourism (pre-construction, construction, and post-construction phases), during each of which the structure of economic and social opportunities underwent significant changes.

A number of 'models' of tourism development are summarised in Table 2.1. Whereas Noronha's model – itself a summary of much early tourism research – is unilinear, the other three are exceptional in that they are all multilinear, indicating that different rates of growth and/ or control over development have different implications for the host community. Unfortunately, however, with the notable exception of Cohen, they are lacking the sort of detailed ethnography advocated here. Nevertheless, they provide an interesting range of variables with which to compare the situation I found in the Seychelles during my field-work. First of all, what had happened on the main island of Mahe? In terms of Noronha's scheme they went almost directly from his stage one to stage three. Development happened so quickly that there was very little opportunity for independent local entrepreneurs to capitalise on the new opportunities. Comparing Mahe with the other three models, there were only a few brief years during the pre-construction period which could be categorised in Peck and Lepie's terms as a period of 'slow growth', or in Rodenberg's terms as a period of 'small industrial tourism', or in Cohen's terms as a period of 'organic development'.

The difficulty with my original account is that it suggests that tourism development was taking place in a uniform fashion throughout the islands, which it was not, for reasons I shall return to shortly. On the main island of Mahe the locals played little part in the major developments taking place in their midst, except as construction workers and service labour in the hotels. A convenient ideology had also emerged to justify and support these arrangements. Thus their failure to participate in the new economic opportunities was explained by both expatriates and the local elite as confirming the lack of ability of non-white Seychellois who were seen as inherently lazy, dishonest, over-fond of drink, incapable of deferring gratification, unable to

*Table 2.1* Theories of tourism development

**(1) Noronha, 1975**

| *Stage 1* | *Stage 2* | *Stage 3* |
|---|---|---|
| Tourist 'discovery' of new destination | Local entrepreneurs provide facilities to accommodate growing tourist numbers | Mass tourism follows. Take-over of development by organisations located outside local community |

**(2) Peck and Lepie, 1977**

| *Rate of growth* | *Power base* | *Pay-offs and trade-offs* |
|---|---|---|
| Transient growth | 'Pass-throughs', weekenders, seasonal entrepreneurs, local financing | Stable norms, individual mobility within existing power structure, little economic change |
| Slow growth | Individual developments, local ownership and financing, expanding local commerce | Slow change of norms, stable power structure, expanding local economy |
| Rapid growth | 'Bedroom' communities, summer residents, specialised commerce, outside financing | Rapid change in norms, new power structure and economy |

**(3) Rodenberg, 1980**

| *Type of development* | *Scale of development (accommodation and tourist types)* | *Use of local resources and effect on traditional relationships* |
|---|---|---|
| Craft | 'B & B', family owned and run, cater for 'independent travellers' | Entirely based on local resources, traditional relationships remain largely unchanged |
| Small industrial | Average 21 rooms but up to 100. Economy class hotels catering to 'independent travellers' | Some imports, traditional relationships still important, even if changing |
| Large industrial | 100+ rooms. International standard hotels. Many extra facilities. Cater to package/charter tourists | Large import component. New industrial/bureaucratic type relationships and values |

*Table 2.1* Continued

| (4) Cohen, 1983 | | |
|---|---|---|
| Organic development | Initiated by locals in response to growing demand from tourists. With further development a possible shift from insider to outsider control | Organic development more likely if: <br> – local awareness of tourism potential <br> – isolated from national society <br> – strong and hostile local leaders <br> – little infrastructural development <br> – traditional agriculture, little industrial development <br> – no large nearby urban centres |
| Induced development | Initiated by outsiders in an attempt to attract tourism to a new locality. With increasing development growing opportunities for locals, especially in provision of ancillary services. | Induced development less likely if (as above) |

handle credit, and unfamiliar with modern work practices, etc. On the other hand, the Seychelles People's United Party (then in opposition to the government) argued that this inability resulted from a lack of self-confidence and a 'dependency-complex' stemming from two centuries of colonial rule. My own view is that the most important reason was that the scale of development was financially too great to allow locals access and thus from the very beginning the Seychellois had lost control over the tourist developments taking place in their midst. In other words, their failure to innovate reflected economic domination of the island by expatriate capital and management, foreign ownership of the best hotels and development land, and indigenous Asian control over the import/export and wholesale/retail trades.

This did not mean, however, that there was massive resentment of tourism on the part of the ordinary Seychellois, even though this impression has been fostered in certain quarters (see, for example, Houbert, 1978, 297; for a more balanced review of the pros and cons of the developments see Wilson, 1979, 233–36). If anything, it was quite the opposite. It seemed to me that the majority of islanders were happy to see such developments taking place. I was told how it had ended the long isolation of the islands from the outside world, how it was providing new employment opportunities, and how it was helping break down the traditional social hierarchy based on skin colour, family pedigree and plantation agriculture. Support for this generally positive reaction to tourism is found in the estimated quadrupling of per capita income in the islands during the period 1968–76 (Melamid, 1978).

The developments which were taking place at 'Grand Anse' (name changed), a much smaller island some distance from Mahe, challenge both the idea of the innate inability of the islanders and also the belief that dependency on foreigners had produced a local mentality that could achieve nothing on its own account. Grand Anse had acquired the reputation as a particularly remote and beautiful corner of the islands where the 'old' Seychelles could still be found and to which increasing numbers of tourists wished to travel. However, the government felt that the island would be unable to cope with any large-scale developments and so had refused to issue any licences to international consortia who had expressed an interest in building hotels there. This combination of factors had allowed a number of small-scale local entrepreneurs to emerge in response to the new opportunities generated by the arrival of increasing numbers of tourists. This they did most successfully, all establishing thriving businesses including the provision of accommodation, restaurants, bars, transport, and ancillary tourist services such as boat hire and bicycle hire.

Not that all this success was achieved in a spirit of friendly cooperation. Far from it. Several of them were in direct competition for business, and they utilised a variety of ploys to try to attract tourists. For example, one advertised on Mahe through a night-club owned by his brother, another sent his son out to meet the ferry as it disembarked its passengers onto a smaller boat outside the reef, whilst a third would provide free transport from the jetty on a traditional ox-cart. There was also intense rivalry between them to attract local Seychellois into the bars they had built – the first such establishments on the island (one of the more enlightened aspects of tourism in the Seychelles has been to allow locals the same access as visitors to beaches, bars, hotels, etc.). For example, when one advertised an evening dance with an electric band at four rupees admission, another would suddenly announce a rival dance with an acoustic band at two rupees admission. This would inevitably attract many of the poorer islanders who could then buy more beer with the money saved. Perhaps the most cunning strategy was that employed by a third entrepreneur when he occasionally pre-empted both the others by holding free dances in the afternoon! Many people would attend these and, having spent all their money in his bar, had nothing left by the evening to go on to the other establishments.

Such intense competition had led to considerable hostility between these men, exhibited in Grand Anse in a number of ways: factionalism and fluctuating alliances, not speaking to one another for long periods of time (even though they all lived close together), accusations of *gris-gris* (witchcraft), intense fears of malicious damage to their property, reporting people to the police or other authorities for allegedly breaking some law, and rumour-mongering (in fact, all standard local practices for the management of conflict).

Unfortunately, I do not have space here to consider in detail these men and the factors which may have been responsible for their success. What was interesting was that they were all from different socio-economic backgrounds and different positions on the traditional colour/class/status hierarchies. What they did share in common was knowledge (variously acquired) of what tourists expected, fluency in both English and French (as well as the Creole patois of the islands), and organisational talent. They had shown themselves capable of organising such activities as the cooking of meals for visiting tourist parties, providing boats or guides at a certain time and place, training waitresses and maids (many of whom had never been in a hotel or restaurant before) to operate to alien standards of etiquette and hygiene, maintaining electricity generators, and the handling of cash, credit and accounts, all of which demanded an attitude towards work and standards of service hitherto unknown on the island.

Comparing Grand Anse with Mahe, we can see that although tourism took off in both places at the same point in time – with the opening of the international airport in 1971 – it proceeded along two quite different lines of development. Using the language of our other theorists, tourism at Grand Anse had not yet progressed beyond Noronha's stage 2. In Peck and Lepie's terms Grand Anse had shifted from transient growth to slow growth, although with one important difference; the power structure of the island had undergone significant changes with the emergence of a new local elite based on the achieved status of entrepreneurial success rather than the old birth-ascribed values of colour and class. In Rodenberg's terms Grand Anse was beginning to move from a craft to a small industrial type of tourism – with none of the problems he equates with large industrial tourism. With regard to Cohen's scheme Grand Anse provides us with an example of organic development, although it must be noted that unlike his Thailand example this was only possible because planning permission had been refused to outsiders. However, when individual expatriates did become involved they met a response from the locals quite akin to his Thailand situation (one expatriate was driven off the island by a combination of arson, sabotage and theft against his property).

Thus we find in Seychelles two qualitatively different types of tourism developing simultaneously in two different locations. As with the other research referred to, the critical factors affecting this were scale of development and control over development. With large-scale developers kept out of Grand Anse, the vacuum was filled by local entrepreneurs from a diversity of socio-economic backgrounds who proved themselves capable of providing services and facilities which on Mahe had been assumed impossible by people from some of their backgrounds. It can therefore be argued that, under the right structural conditions, most social environments in the islands seem capable of producing people possessing entrepreneurial talent and the necessary ambition to succeed. And this in spite of the prevailing image of the islanders (see above) propagated by expatriates and the local elite.

In conclusion, my plea in this chapter is to treat with caution much of the tourism research we already possess. I have suggested that we are in serious danger of being misled by much of this research because of our lack of awareness of the time dimension attached to it: either the 'conceptual' time that informs the approach taken by the writer, or the 'ethnographic' time in which the research was carried out, or, lastly, the 'perceptual' time where the study was located. Least you think I am being too negative about all this, I conclude with some suggestions for overcoming these difficulties, several of which have already been advocated during the course of this chapter. These would include an innovative rejuvenation of longitudinal, qualitative field research, focused on the perceptions of the participants as well as those of the observers. Such research would incorporate not only re-studies and monitoring programmes, but also multilocation rather than single-site projects. Finally, I would also encourage greater collaboration and team-work, either within or between the various disciplines involved in tourism research.

## NOTES

1 I would like to thank Amanda North and Stephanie Young, who have both generously allowed me to incorporate some of their material into

this chapter. If any misrepresentation of their views has occurred, the fault is entirely mine. Acknowledgement is also made to the Social Science Research Council who funded my own field work in the Seychelles over a fourteen month period between 1972–74.

2 North: personal communication.

3 Particularly Amish embroideries, some of which are made by Hmong refugees from Vietnam, who are employed by the Amish.

# 3 Tourism, culture and the sociology of development

*Robert E. Wood*

## INTRODUCTION

International tourism has been widely promoted, in the words of a joint World Bank-UNESCO report, as a 'passport to development' (de Kadt, 1979). A lively literature debates the merits and shortcomings of this claim, focusing largely on tourism's contribution to economic growth, and, more recently, on its distributional impact. A cost-benefit calculus underlies most summary statements in the field, with a recognition that tourism brings both benefits and costs, and that public policy can affect the balance significantly.[1]

This economic juncture between tourism and development will not be explored in this chapter. Whatever the balance sheet, practically all the world's countries have opted to promote international tourism. Rather, my focus will be on a related, but considerably more controversial, concern that researchers in these two fields have shared: the fate of Third World cultures. Do the processes of modernisation and development necessarily entail the 'passing' of the 'traditional' societies of Asia, Africa and Latin America and a global process of cultural homogenisation in the direction of the West? Are tourists missionaries – or shock troops – of Western modernity, destroying indigenous cultures in the process of seeking them out?

For many, concern with these questions has not been disinterested, perhaps nowhere more so than among South-East Asianists. As Gloria Davis has put it: 'For those of us who work in Indonesia and are emotionally committed to it, change is a threat. The hope is that Indonesia will remain different and it is this hope which suggests the topics we study and colours our facts' (Davis, 1979, 308). Davis' apparent assumption here, shared with many researchers in the fields of both tourism and development, that change will lessen differentness, is one that I will question, but her commitment to the continued integrity of the cultures of South-East Asia resonates with the personal concerns of many.

On the surface, the evolution of research on tourism's impact on culture would seem to parallel the economic research mentioned above, with its cost-benefit calculus. As I shall summarise below, the literature on tourism's cultural impact has moved from a brief period of stressing its benefits, to a much longer period of stressing its costs, to a contemporary emphasis on how tourism inevitably carries with it both cultural benefits and costs which to a significant degree can be managed through public policy. Recent reviews of the literature typically commend the field for recognising that tourism has 'both good and bad sides' and for reaching a 'more balanced view of the impact of tourism' (Nash and Smith, 1991, 15).

In contrast, it will be a central contention of this chapter that this kind of normative cost-benefit framework has become increasingly inadequate to summarise and integrate the research on tourism's cultural consequences in South-East Asia. Calls for researchers to move beyond simplistic normative categories have been around for some time (e.g. Cohen, 1979b; Wood, 1980, 564–65; Nash, 1981, 466; Crick, 1989). These calls have at least in part been attempts to bring the field more into line with positivistic canons of 'value-free' scientific research. What I want to stress in this chapter, however, is the way in which research generated within this normative problematic has increasingly come to undermine the bases of that normative problematic itself. In Kuhnian terms, the normal science has increasingly called into question the paradigm itself. There may remain a place for normative assessments of tourism's impact, but they will have to be made in a far more careful, explicit and positioned way than has characterised most of the literature to date.

This challenge to the normative problematic has grown out of evolving work on culture and development over the past several decades. Accordingly, the first part of this chapter summarises the changing approaches to culture found in the sociology of development and tourism studies up until recently. The second part of the chapter analyses several current research directions that have helped both fields move beyond naive normative problematics and that suggest productive routes forward.

## CULTURE IN EARLY STUDIES OF DEVELOPMENT AND OF TOURISM

International tourism in the Third World was quite limited in the 1950s and 1960s when the development paradigm, that came to be known as modernisation theory, took shape. Nonetheless, tourism growth was easily assimilated to the modernisation perspective, as the following statement by a South Asian modernisation theorist indicates:

> The barriers to modernization are many. Some of these stem from traditional folkways and mores, such as familism or casteism, or attitudes such as fatalism or otherworldliness. These traits develop over centuries and the socialization of the young takes place in terms of these values. However, today a new breeze is blowing over the continents, what with advances and mass media and international exchange of ideas and people. *Every year, more and more tourists from industrial countries descend on the far corners of the earth.* People in the modernizing nations experience this and other changes in their environment. *Consequently*, everywhere they are seen raising their level of aspiration both for themselves and for their children. The success of modernization depends very much on how a high level of aspiration among the population is transformed into a new kind of motivation.
>
> (Varma, 1980, 3–4, emphasis added).

This statement conveys particularly clearly the basic approach to culture taken by early modernisation theorists. Culture was tradition, an inheritance from a deep-rooted but undifferentiated past. It took form above all in values, deeply inculcated in the process of socialisation and translated directly into individual behaviour; culture in general was perceived to be a barrier to development, something that had to be changed by contact with the modern world. Fittingly, the lead article in the first issue of *Economic Development and Cultural Change* was entitled 'Non-Economic Barriers to Economic Development' (Hoselitz, 1952).

As Myron Weiner (1969) has noted, modernisation theorists tended to confuse two separate concepts of tradition: one defined analytically as the opposite of modernity, and one defined empirically as whatever is inherited from the past. Early modernisation theorists clearly tended to equate the two. Traditional culture in the Third World thus formed a radical contrast to modernity. More than this, traditional culture and society was seen as having great staying power, requiring a powerful antidote. In this context, probably no work was more influential than Max Weber's *The Protestant Ethic and the Spirit of Capitalism* (see Eisenstadt, 1968), which suggested what James Peacock (1986) has called a 'sledge-hammer reform model' or what Winston Davis (1987) calls a 'sociology of pain', the need for exceptional motivation and sacrifice to break through the barrier of tradition.

Despite the search for a functional equivalent to the Protestant ethic – what David Apter (1987, 23) has called the 'Holy Grail' of early modernisation theorists – these theorists generally had little doubt that traditional culture would give way in the face of Western modernity. For Daniel Lerner (1958), this meant the inevitable 'passing of traditional society'. For Marion Levy, modernity was the 'universal solvent' which would inevitably dissolve traditional culture (although for Levy this did not by itself ensure successful modernisation) (Levy, 1966, 741–66; 1972, 3–11). In terms of culture, virtually all early modernisation theorists were convergence theorists. Few of them actual specialists in the regions they generalised about, they saw little to regret about the passing of non-Western ways.

Despite glowing pronouncements from the tourism industry and from various international organisations about the benefits of tourism – for example, the UN General Assembly's unanimous resolution for International Tourist Year of 1967 that 'tourism is a basic and most desirable human activity deserving the praise and encouragement of all peoples and governments' (Burkart and Medlik, 1974, 57) – the dominant theme of early studies of tourism's impact in the Third World was the threat posed by tourism to traditional cultures. This point should not be overstated; some early studies (e.g. Forster, 1964) were impressively nuanced. Still, the overall thrust was to detail the ways in which the various forms of tourism tended, as Valene Smith put it in her introduction to the first edition of *Hosts and Guests*, a pioneering anthology of tourism studies, 'to be more negative than positive in impact' (Smith, 1977, 14).

While the evidence behind this 'negative' conclusion cannot be reduced to a single model, Erik Cohen (1988a) has usefully laid out the paradigmatic case, centring on the concepts of authenticity and commoditisation, drawn particularly from the influential work of Dean MacCannell and Davydd Greenwood. MacCannell's (1976) *The Tourist: A New Theory of the Leisure Class* brought the issue of 'authenticity' to the centre of tourism analysis, while Greenwood's (1977) analysis of the 'cultural commodification' and consequent 'destruction' of the Alarde festival of the Basque town of Fuenterrabia has probably been the single most widely-cited and influential English-language case study of tourism's 'negative' effect. Cohen argues that common to these and similar analyses are the assumptions that tourism commoditifies culture and in the process destroys its authenticity, both for locals and for tourists. Real authenticity is subsequently replaced by 'staged authenticity'.

Students of tourism's impact – Valene Smith, Davydd Greenwood, Dennison Nash (1977), Jacques Bugnicourt (1977a, 1977b), Turner and Ash (1976), anthropologists writing for *Cultural Survival Quarterly*, Third World critics and their Western sympathisers (e.g. Bird, 1989; Ron O'Grady, 1990) – held a very different normative outlook from modernisation theorists, but shared a number of basic assumptions. Most notably, critics of tourism's cultural impact generally shared with modernisation theorists assumptions about the incompatibility of traditional and modern cultures and the greater force of the latter. What modernisation theorists welcomed, most early students of tourism's impact lamented, but both made similar assumptions about the nature of the process of cultural change.

## CRITIQUES AND REFINEMENTS: DEVELOPMENT STUDIES

That modernisation theory came under blistering attack from *dependistas* and others in the late 1960s and the 1970s is well known. What is less recognised is the degree to which the 'normal science' of the modernisation paradigm had modified its basic tenets by that time. Hardly had the opposition between traditional and modern society been laid out, than was it subjected to progressively serious modification. Area specialists quickly began to dispute broad generalisations about the anti-developmental qualities of 'their' traditional cultures (see, for example, Singer, 1956; 1972). Others noted how tradition could be reconstructed and manipulated and could coexist with development and modernity (Gusfield, 1967; Apter, 1971). Still others more explicitly began to make a case for how 'traditional' cultures and social structures could promote development (Rudolph and Rudolph, 1967). Virtually all modernisation theorists began to take pains to dissociate their views from a model of unilinear evolution, as the various ways the modernisation process could unleash countertendencies became evident to them (for example, Geertz, 1963b; Huntington, 1968; Eisenstadt, 1966). Among those who emphasised the importance of values, there was a softening of earlier emphasis on value change as a prerequisite of development (compare Inkeles, 1983, 6 with Inkeles and Smith, 1974, 313; see also Banuazizi, 1987). In the hands of sophisticated writers like Clifford Geertz, modernisation themes of the Protestant ethic and cultural change were translated into highly nuanced studies of enduring complexity (e.g. Geertz, 1963a; 1963c).

Like any paradigm, modernisation theory has suffered from the 'idiot disciple' syndrome. Long after the more sophisticated modernisation theorists had abandoned the earlier formulations about culture and development, less sophisticated adherents continued to simplify and popularise them. One example involves a study of those pioneering tourists, the Peace Corps volunteers of the 1960s. Summarising the philosophy behind the Peace Corps, two evaluators wrote, in a passage clearly influenced by early modernisation theory:

> Change is a threat. The citizen of the underdeveloped world tends to be inflexible, to resist that which is new. If, in fact, the character patterns of people in developing countries had already evolved sufficiently to make change a positive value . . . there would be little need for a Peace Corps.
>
> (Hapgood and Bennett, 1968, 27–28)

But while more sophisticated practitioners in the modernisation school had moved beyond this kind of blaming-the-victim explanation of underdevelopment, the basic vocabulary of tradition and modernity was retained, alongside a strong tendency towards narrowly conceived culturalist explanations of underdevelopment that ascribed causal primacy to culture while at the same time reducing its role to the way values either aided or impeded a separate phenomenon known as 'development'.[2]

Despite its harsh tone, a significant part of the *dependista* attack on modernisation theory reiterated the internal critique that had already been generated within the modernisation school. The *dependista* critique went considerably farther, of course. Dependency theorists (and Marxist, world systems, and other theorists who coincided with and followed them) effectively banished the tradition-modernity distinction from the discourse of the sociology of development. They did this by arguing that what modernisation theorists called 'traditional' was not simply *compatible* with modernity. It *was* modern, in the sense of being a creation of, or an adaptation to, the modern world capitalist system (Frank, 1966).

Not only did this view explode the distinction between tradition and modernity, but it challenged the identification of modernity with development. In fact, the combination of what modernisation theorists considered 'tradition' (now seen as the outcome of the incorporation of the periphery into the world capitalist system) and 'modernity' (now seen as capitalist imperialism) produced not development but 'underdevelopment'.

Dependency and related theorists paid more attention to culture than is sometimes supposed. The work of James Scott (1976) and the moral economy school found a sympathetic audience among dependency theorists, who wrote fairly extensively on cultures of resistance. Cultural forms of dependency and domination were explored. Dependency theorists were quick to note affinities between the critical literature on tourism's cultural impact and the concept of 'underdevelopment' (Grynbaum, 1971; Wood, 1979). Nonetheless, the overall thrust of the sociology of development in the 1970s and 1980s was distinctly anti-culturalist, in the sense of denying any privileged place to culture in the analysis of development and underdevelopment.[3] By the early 1980s, Clifford Geertz (1984, 516) lamented, the role of culture in development studies had been reduced to choosing between conceptualising culture as mystifying ideology or else as a kind of formless trapping of 'real' social relations.

Normal science in the 1980s did to many of the certainties of early dependency theory what earlier normal science had done to the certainties of early modernisation theory. In fact, it is now widely agreed that a failing of both perspectives was the attempt to make universal generalisations, and a corresponding lack of sufficient attention to explaining variation. In the process the sharp cleavage between the perspectives has been somewhat modified, and several recent reviews of the sociology of development conclude that the classic opposition between them has been transcended. In the words of Evans and Stephens, the earlier sociologies of development have evolved into a 'new comparative historical political economy' (Evans and Stephens, 1988a; 1988b; for a similar view see Mouzelis, 1988). Several first-generation modernisation theorists have reappeared to celebrate the 'exhuming' of modernisation theory (e.g. Levy, 1986). While there has been a growing sentiment that culture is the 'missing concept' in the sociology of development (Worsley, 1984; Harrison, 1988; Weiner and Huntington, 1987), this widely shared sentiment has yet to be actualised in a shared research agenda. And to the degree that the outlines of such an agenda can be discerned, in part in recent tourism research, the approach to culture is very different than that found in modernisation theory.

## CRITIQUES AND REFINEMENTS: TOURISM STUDIES

As with the sociology of development, the general drift in the sociology of tourism has been away from universal generalisations and towards an interest in documenting and explaining variation in the cultural consequences of tourism. Beginning in the early 1970s, detailed studies of tourism's impact in the Third World began to appear which challenged the 'mostly negative' critique that dominated the field. Traditional cultures, it began to be argued, were adaptive and resilient; neither their dissolution nor their degradation in the face of mass tourism could be assumed. Tourism could even strengthen traditional cultures by augmenting local pride and making the continuation of traditional crafts and activities economically viable.

While earlier authors had touched on these themes, the first major statement of them – at least for South-East Asia – was Philip McKean's (1973) doctoral dissertation on the impact of tourism in Bali. Although unpublished, its findings and general argument subsequently reached a wide audience through several influential articles (McKean, 1976; 1977a; 1977b; 1982). It was quite influential among Balinese policy-makers themselves.

On the opening page of his dissertation, McKean laid out his basic argument: that 'the traditions of Bali will prosper in direct proportion to the success of the tourist industry'. By 'traditions' McKean basically meant 'the arts: dance, music, architecture, carving and painting'. McKean emphasised the active responses the Balinese had developed to tourism. These were cultural, economic and organisational. The cultural responses, to which McKean devoted the most attention, were based above all on distinctions made between audiences: divine, local and tourist. McKean documented in detail how different versions of dances were presented to tourists, and how attempts were made to keep away tourists from the divine and local versions (it should be kept in mind that his fieldwork was carried out in 1970 and 1971, when the number of tourists was still a small fraction of what it is now). He did acknowledge that in some localities repetition of certain dances had diminished their power and significance for local people, but argued that there remained many sacred alternatives untouched, and perhaps indirectly reinforced, by tourism.[4]

McKean did not provide a great deal of economic data, but his basic economic argument was that a significant proportion of the money earned from tourism had been ploughed back into cultural groups and activities, thereby both preserving and revitalising traditional culture. He also detailed the organisational response of both the Balinese and the Indonesian government to the growth of tourism, suggesting on balance that these responses had contributed to the benign cultural impact of tourism in Bali (for a similar view, see McTaggart, 1980).

McKean's work had many virtues. His stress on the active responses of tourist 'hosts', in contrast to the passive image in much of the previous literature, was extremely important. He also took pains to stress the ever-changing quality of Balinese culture, avoiding the tendency to romanticise the past and to equate change with the 'degradation' or 'loss' of traditional culture. Nonetheless, by pitting his work against the 'pessimistic hand-wringing' of others about the likelihood of tourism 'destroying, ruining, or "spoiling" the culture of Bali' (McKean, 1973, 1; 10), McKean remained within the original normative problematic of tourism studies: whether tourism's impact was good or bad, whether one should be optimistic or pessimistic, whether culture would be ruined or preserved. His analysis, as did a number of the individual essays in *Hosts and Guests* (Smith, 1977), which appeared shortly afterwards, strained against the limits of this original problematic, but continued to be framed by it.[5]

Despite the partial eclipse of cultural concerns in the sociology of development during this period, there were again a number of basic similarities between the development and tourism literatures. Both challenged the cultural homogenisation theses of the earlier period. But in doing this, both also developed critiques based on normative assumptions that were rarely explicitly articulated. Tourism researchers assumed (as some still do) that the distinction between 'positive' and 'negative' cultural effects was self-evident. In like manner, concepts of 'dependency' and 'underdevelopment' were used pejoratively without clear elaboration of the normative assumptions underlying them.

Ironically, work in each field contained something of a critique of the other's assumptions. The *dependista* critique of the concept of 'tradition' and 'traditional society' raised serious questions about the normative problematic of tourism studies. If traditional cultures were no more, what did preservation of tradition mean? And if the fundamental quality of Third World societies was captured in the concept of underdevelopment, in whose interest would cultural preservation be? At the same time, the tourism literature's emphasis on active cultural strategies constituted an antidote to the critical development literature's tendency to see Third World peoples as overly passive in their encounter with the capitalist world system.

# NEW DIRECTIONS IN TOURISM AND CULTURAL STUDIES

Reversing my earlier order, I now turn to recent work in tourism studies that may be characterised in the first instance as 'post-normative', in the sense that it has moved beyond the original normative problematic (or straitjacket) of the field. I am taking up tourism studies first because I believe that several recent themes to be found there have both reflected and anticipated reconceptualisations about culture that suggest productive routes forward for the sociology of development.

The overdue shift away from the normative problematic in tourism studies is rooted in three new directions in tourism and cultural studies that enormously complicate normative assessments of tourism's impact. First, an increased awareness of the social construction and invention of both tradition and authenticity has undercut the distinction between positive and negative impacts central to the normative problematic. Second, an increased awareness of how tourism both engenders and becomes implicated in a broad range of cultural politics has brought attention to domestic stratification and conflict much more to the fore of tourism studies, exposing concepts of society-wide interest as naive and obfuscating. Third, various 'post-modern' observations about culture highlight the positioned nature of cultural judgements and suggest interesting and productive ways to reframe the questions we ask about the relationship between tourism, culture and development.

## The pre-tourism baseline: tradition and authenticity

The folklorist Ben-Amos has observed that 'tradition' has generally been a term we have thought *with*, rather than *about* (Ben-Amos, 1984, 97). This was certainly true of much of the normative literature on tourism, which judged authenticity by the unexamined standard of tradition. However, in a number of fields – folklore, history, anthropology, tourism studies themselves - the past decade has seen an important shift in our understanding of the concept of tradition itself.

This shift has been aptly described by Handler and Linnekin as a shift from a 'naturalistic' to a 'symbolic' conception of tradition. Naturalistic concepts of tradition have assumed that tradition is an objective entity, 'a core of inherited culture traits whose continuity and boundedness are analogous to that of a natural object' (Handler and

Linnekin, 1984, 273). Even those recent writers who have emphasised the creative side of tradition (Shils, 1981) and its conscious invention (Hobsbawm and Ranger, 1983) have found it difficult to break with this conception, clinging to distinctions between 'real' versus 'fictitious' and 'genuine' versus 'invented' traditions (for a useful critique, see Waldman, 1986). In doing this they have continued to make assumptions about the boundedness and inherent quality of tradition shared by many of the students of tourism discussed above.

Handler and Linnekin insist in contrast that tradition is always symbolically constructed in the present, not a 'thing' handed down from the past. Arguing on both theoretical and empirical grounds, they:

> take issue with the naturalistic conception of tradition. We suggest that there is no essential, bounded tradition; tradition is a model of the past and is inseparable from the interpretation of tradition in the present . . . the on-going reconstruction of tradition is a facet of all social life, which is not natural but symbolically constituted.
>
> (Handler and Linnekin, 1984, 276)

'Tradition,' they conclude, 'is a symbolic process . . . not an objective property of phenomena but an assigned meaning' (ibid., 286).

A similar insight has guided a great deal of recent research on ethnicity; seemingly 'traditional' and 'primordial' identities turn out to be symbolic constructions 'renewed, modified and remade in each generation'; as Hoben and Hefner observe, 'tradition' is often quite 'untraditional' (1991, 18, 23).

This conception of tradition and authenticity dramatically undermines the normative standard against which change is compared and judged in most tourism studies. It won't do simply to recognise, as sophisticated observers like McKean do, that traditional culture is always changing. The point is that the definition of what is traditional in culture, the specification of links between an invented present and an imagined past, is constantly being symbolically recreated and contested. There is no objective, bounded thing that we can identify as 'traditional culture' against which to measure and judge change. What is defined as traditional culture, both for the past and for the present, is constantly being reformulated.

The same general point applies to that tourism keyword, authenticity. As Handler and Linnekin argue, the authenticity of certain activities or symbols:

does not depend upon an objective relation to the past. The origin of cultural practices is largely irrelevant to the experience of tradition; authenticity is always defined in the present. It is not the pastness or givenness that defines something as traditional. Rather, the latter is an arbitrary symbolic designation; an assigned meaning rather than an objective quality.

(Handler and Linnekin, 1984, 286)

A particularly widely discussed application of this perspective is Allan Hanson's (1989) analysis of cultural invention among the Maori, a case made particularly intriguing by the Maori's incorporation of the historical inaccuracies of early anthropologists into their contemporary understanding of their own culture (see also Wilford, 1990). Arguing that the analytic task of the anthropologist is therefore 'not to strip away the invented portions of culture as unauthentic, but to understand the process by which they acquire authenticity', Hanson goes on to conclude, in a passage in which one might conceivably at times substitute 'tourists' for 'anthropologists', that 'inventions are common components in the on-going development of authentic culture, and that producers of inventions are often outsiders (including anthropologists) as well as insiders' (Hanson, 1989, 888, 899).

Parallel points with respect to tourist authenticity have been articulated by Redfoot (1984) and Cohen (1988a). Redfoot argues that authenticity – as well as its widely perceived opposite, inauthenticity – does not inhere in the touristic experience as such, but rather is a variable that depends on the expectations and goals of the tourist. Cohen likewise insists that authenticity is a socially constructed concept, whose criteria vary greatly depending on the tourist or the observer. The question, Cohen observes, 'is whether the individual does or does not "really" have an authentic experience in MacCannell's sense, but rather what endows his experience with authenticity in his *own* view' (Cohen, 1988a, 378).[6]

The same applies to the tourist hosts. Authenticity for them must be judged through their eyes, and the evidence suggests that 'invented' or reshaped 'traditions' may acquire authenticity quite quickly. Greenwood's recent comment that the Alarde, the Basque festival he had in his classic (1977) study declared to be 'destroyed' and without authentic meaning for its participants, appears now to be imbued 'with contemporary political significance as part of the contest over regional political rights in Spain' (Greenwood, 1989, 181), may be a case of this. The observation that touristic space can offer an opportunity for asserting local identities and rights against other groups is one that is increasingly seen in the tourism literature (e.g. Adams, 1990; Bendix, 1989; Brown, 1984; Crystal, 1989; Klieger, 1990; Wood, 1984). In the process the cultural identities and identified 'traditions' of ethnic groups are likely themselves to be transformed, as several studies of the Toraja, for example, suggest (Adams, 1984; Volkman, 1982; 1984; 1987; 1990).

These insights recall David Wilson's insistence that an anthropological approach to tourism 'must be based on a thoroughly empirical research strategy which seeks hermeneutic understanding in terms of the knowledge possessed by the participants themselves – their definitions, goals, strategies, decisions, and the perceived consequences of their actions (intended or otherwise)' (Wilson, 1981, 477). Clearly this should include their on-going symbolic construction of tradition and authenticity. While progress has been made along these lines, the temptation to make etic judgements about tradition and authenticity has continued to prove difficult to resist for some researchers.[7]

## The cultural politics of tourism

'Cultural politics', anthropologist Sherry Ortner has written:

> are the struggles over the official symbolic representations of reality that shall prevail in a given social order at a given time. One could argue that they are the most important kind of politics, for they seek to control the terms in which all other politics, and all other aspects of life in that society, will take place.
>
> (Ortner, 1989, 200)

One theme in an increasing number of tourism studies is the way tourism becomes implicated in the cultural politics of host countries. Awareness of this has led tourism researchers to pay much more attention to cultural and other forms of stratification, and the very different interests both affected by, and pursued through, the growth of tourism. In the process, earlier assumptions of inherent cultural 'interests' have inevitably been undermined. Tourist attractions are inherently symbolic representations of reality. This is achieved most notably through their symbolic packaging for tourists. While the packaging of tourist attractions has most often been analysed in terms of the images presented to foreigners and the way these images cater to foreign tourists' concerns with 'authenticity' and the like, it is evident that these images are increasingly bound up with local cultural politics as well, particularly as domestic tourism expands. In an important and pioneering study, Kathleen Adams (1991) observes that in the Toraja area of south Sulawesi, 85 per cent (170,000) of all tourists in 1989 were Indonesians, and tourism-related icons of Toraja identity adorn everything from the Indonesian 5,000 rupiah note to the official third grade reader on 'tourist objects'. Adams notes that the dominant cultural concerns of Indonesian tourists are quite different from those of foreign tourists. With the extraordinary expansion of domestic tourism in almost all South-East Asian countries, it is clear that the traditional distinction in tourism studies between those primarily interested in tourists and those in 'tourees' no longer makes much sense. South-East Asians are increasingly both.[8]

The cultural politics of tourism among the Toraja have been ably studied not only by Adams but by Eric Crystal and Toby Alice Volkman as well. A full summary of this particularly fascinating case is not possible here; rather, I want to draw out a few of the findings that highlight the inadequacy of the traditional normative problematic of tourism studies and that underline the complexity of tourism's cultural politics.

First, as Volkman (1984; 1990) particularly emphasises, the advent of tourism coincided with a highly dynamic process of cultural change among the Toraja. Toraja identity as such had been consolidated only recently, and widespread Christian conversion and out-migration had accelerated a process of invention of tradition that had been going on for some time. The pre-tourist cultural baseline was thus highly fluid, largely of recent vintage, and strongly shaped by 'external' influences.

Second, not only had these changes in Toraja society involved a transformation of ritual practices – including the relatively recent centrality of mortuary rituals – but economic changes resulting primarily from out-migration had subsequently fuelled a ritual renaissance and 'inflation' that both made ritual practices more central to Toraja identity and led them to become increasingly elaborate and expensive. These ritual practices historically had a strong competitive aspect, and tourism became a new resource in this competition. The number of tourists at a ritual became a measure of its importance, and nobles vied for official designation of houses and villages as 'tourist objects'. Revenues from tourism and from migrant work enabled commoners to stage elaborate ritual celebrations, in violation of earlier hierarchical norms.

Third, tourism has involved the Toraja in a highly complex redefinition of their relationship with other groups in Indonesian society. Dissatisfaction has been expressed with the fact that the Toraja's historic lowland enemies, the Bugis, have reaped many of the economic benefits of Toraja tourism, but this has put the Bugis in the new position of promoting the glories of a people they used to look down upon as savages. The Toraja in turn have shown an increasing preference for Bugis-style houses, despite their touristic unattractiveness. Volkman has described how Toraja ritual practices are in some ways being 'Indonesianised', but at the same time tourism has drawn the Toraja close to the Bataks and Balinese on the basis of perceived shared cultural characteristics (see Adams, 1991).

Where are the good and bad cultural effects in all of this? On what basis can we presume to distinguish between them? It is not a matter of striking a balance, but rather of developing more adequate tools for grasping what is at stake in the cultural politics of a region long famous for its cultural syncretism.

The ways in which tourism can become part of struggles over symbolic representations of reality clearly vary in different cultural contexts. In Erik Cohen's (1982a; 1982c; 1989) accounts of 'hill tribe' tourism in Northern Thailand, for example, it is evident that the unique cultural homogeneity of Thailand – with its overwhelming ethnic Thai majority and with its culturally fragmented 'hill tribes' largely confined to mountainous border areas – drastically limits the symbolic resources available to these minority peoples, in contrast to the much more complex situation in Indonesia, where diversity (even if in unity) is enshrined in the official ideology and where the politics of *agama* provide one among various possible bases of inter-ethnic affinity and alliance. In the Thai 'hill tribe' context, Cohen (1982a) has argued that the jungle guides are the principal agents of cultural change in the tourist encounter, rather than the tourists themselves, and that the cultural change at issue is much less 'Westernisation', as much of the tourist literature seems to assume, as it is 'Thaisation'. As Arjun Appadurai (1990, 295) has observed, earlier preoccupations with cultural homogenisation on a world scale have been increasingly 'indigenised', so that issues of Indonesianisation, Burmanisation, Vietnamisation, and the like, or possibly even Japanisation, may be much more pressing to many South-East Asians.[9]

While these examples involve identities at once ethnic and national, James Fisher (1990, 137) reports that tourism in Himalayan Nepal has promoted a process of 'Sherpaisation' among adjacent ethnic groups, countering the long-term process of sanskritisation emanating from the lowlands. In South-East Asia, a somewhat similar process has been reported by Davis (1979) in her study of Balinese transmigrants to Sulawesi, who have reasserted their Balinese identity in the wake of the fame brought by tourism.

Cultural politics in South-East Asia is most obvious when it is played out in terms of ethnic and religious identities, and tourism's cultural impact is most easily recognised in such cases, since ethnicity and religion are major foci of ethnic and cultural tourists.[10] But emergent class politics also have a profoundly cultural dimension, and tourism is clearly associated with socio-economic differentiation. In an interesting comparative study of two beach resorts in southern Thailand, Cohen (1982b; 1983a) has observed that tourists to such resorts often fail to define the local culture as an 'attraction' at all. But it is questionable to assume, as it has been by some observers, that specifically cultural tourism will necessarily have greater cultural impact than tourism indifferent to local culture (MacCannell 1984; Universitas Udayana and Francillon, 1975, 750). The dynamics of the changing class relations between locals and different sets of outsiders of the sort described by Cohen could in theory at least set in motion cultural changes fully as significant.

**Gender** is another arena of cultural politics closely bound up with tourism. Fisher (1990, 138) reports that traditional gender differentiation among the Sherpas in Nepal has been largely maintained by the exclusion of women from the main tourist jobs generated by trekking and mountaineering. In much of South-East Asia, such economic exclusion is clearly not the rule. But the evaluation of the outcomes remains highly problematic, as seen in the literature on prostitution in Thailand and the Philippines. While few observers defend the profession, the effects of sex tourism on the life chances of 'sex workers' and on the general status of women have been found to be quite complex (Cohen, 1982c; Phongpaichit, 1982; Truong, 1983; 1990). Prostitution has become a highly contentious issue in the cultural politics of gender and tourism, particularly in Thailand.

Recognition of the pervasive reality of cultural politics intersects with the rethinking of the concepts of tradition and authenticity discussed earlier. The implicit notion of a pristine pre-tourist cultural baseline against which to measure tourism's 'negative' impact is exposed as obfuscating at best and in a profound sense, meaningless. Tourism inevitably enters a dynamic context, and in the process contention over definitions of what is traditional and authentic becomes charged with a variety of additional meanings, as the range of interested parties increases. Early formulations in terms of cultural preservation, degradation, elimination and the like, linked to unex-

amined normative assumptions, have proven increasingly inadequate
to comprehend these processes.

### Tourism and 'post-modern' conceptions of culture

The reorientation of cultural concerns in tourism studies has at once
paralleled, been influenced by, and in some ways anticipated the
broader rethinking of the meaning of culture that has often been
characterised as 'post-modernist'. I propose in this section to explore
very briefly a few leads from this post-modernist literature that seem
promising for tourism studies, but I want to do this without taking a
position on the ultimate status of the 'post-modern' label, either as a
description of a supposedly new social reality or as a type of
theoretical orientation – or, for that matter, as a new form of tourism
(see Urry, 1988; 1990). While I believe there are grounds for considerable scepticism about post-modernism's claims both to stand in
opposition to modernism and to supersede it, and while many of its
claims are less original than often assumed, I do want to suggest that
several recent interpretations of ethnography and of culture have
considerable heuristic value for both tourism studies and the sociology
of development.

A common starting point for most 'post-modernist' discussions of
culture is a critique of the assumption that culture is something out
there that is basically organic in structure and has an identifiable
essence. Summarising this view, James Clifford writes:

> A powerful structure of feeling continues to see culture, wher-
> ever it is found, as a coherent *body* that lives and dies. Culture is
> enduring, traditional, structural (rather than contingent, syn-
> cretic, historical). Culture is a process of ordering, not disrup-
> tion. It changes and develops like a living organism. It does not
> normally 'survive' abrupt alterations.
>
> (Clifford, 1988, 235).

In contrast, Clifford (ibid., 9, 10) describes cultural identity as 'an on-
going process, politically contested and historically unfinished', and as
'always mixed, relational, and inventive'. In the modern world any
boundedness and stability that might have characterised culture in the
past disappears in a multivocal world of an 'unprecedented overlay of
traditions', where 'difference is encountered in the adjoining
neighbourhood, [and] the familiar turns up at the end of the earth'
(ibid., 9, 14). For Marcus and Fischer, this means that: 'The cultures of

world peoples need to be constantly *re*discovered as these peoples reinvent them in changing historical circumstances' (Marcus and Fischer, 1986, 24).

Much of Clifford's attention is devoted to the implications of this view of culture for ethnographers, who necessarily invent the cultures they describe, and in the process become participants in the on-going process of cultural invention (much of what he says about ethnographers applies to tourists as well). How ethnographers have hidden this process of invention – both from others and often from themselves – is a favourite target for Clifford's and others' deconstructive devices. But no one is exempt from the predicament of culture, 'a pervasive condition of off-centredness in a world of distinct meaning systems, a state of being in culture while looking at culture, a form of personal and collective self-fashioning' (Clifford, 1988, 9).

Much of the post-modernist ire in this critique has been directed against naturalistic and organic images of culture, but it is not just the relationship among the parts that is at issue. The long tradition of thinking of culture as something deeply internalised, taking form as values and norms that together form a kind of script for individual behaviour, is also being challenged here. Although she starts from a quite different perspective, some of the practical implications of this have been explored by Ann Swidler (1990), who argues that we must jettison the assumption that culture necessarily penetrates or dominates its users. Swidler (1986) proposes a notion of culture as a kind of tool kit of available 'strategies of action'. People are skilled and active users of culture, flexible and strategic in their appropriation of cultural elements. In fact, as Swidler observes, the cases where culture comes closest to dictating action are often the cases where public cultural meanings are least internalised, as in situations where culture functions as a semiotic code or is formally institutionalised as a set of binding myths (see Meyer, 1987; Meyer and Scott, 1983).[11]

A similar perspective informs Unni Wikan's moving book on Balinese women, in which she observes that 'cultural templates penetrate to the innermost of people's souls' (Wikan, 1990, 17), but argues that life is too messy to allow them to dictate behaviour and that much of their power lies not in internalisation but in the anticipation of the reaction of others – particularly others with power Cultural concepts form 'an elaborate apparatus constantly employed by Balinese to orient themselves and interpret themselves to themselves and to one another' (ibid., 116).

Wikan's 'experience-near' anthropology places individuals – and how they use the cultural materials available to them to deal with the inevitable predicaments of life – at centre stage, a strategy even more important as more and more of the world's population inhabits the cultural 'borderlands' discussed by Renato Rosaldo (1989). Tourism often extends such borderlands to new geographical areas and to new parts of life, but it almost inevitably follows earlier processes of migration, urbanisation and the spread of mass communications. Ulf Hannerz (1986) has argued that the least understood cultures today are not those of isolated villages but those of complex cities, in which the notion of culture as shared meaning is obsolete. The implicit message in all of these observations is that we must increasingly see people as active and strategic users of culture, participating in contexts where no single set of cultural interpretations has an inherent claim to truth and authenticity.

## TOURIST AND DEVELOPMENT DISCOURSES

Let us return at this point to studies of the fate of Third World cultures in the face of tourism and development. The basic point is that it is not only the often unexamined and naive normative assumptions that have to be abandoned, but the basic concept of culture that has underlain them. Not tradition but its on-going symbolic reconstitution; not authenticity but its attribution; not inherited identities but relational, improvised and contested ones; not internalised values as much as available templates and strategies of action; not culture but cultural invention and local discourses – the central questions to be asked are about process, and about the complex ways tourism enters and becomes part of an already on-going process of symbolic meaning and appropriation.

Some years ago in an early survey of the literature on tourism in South-East Asia, I lamented (Wood 1980, 565) that the questions posed in this literature often conjured up a billiard ball game, in which a moving object (tourism) acted upon an inert one (the local culture). My complaint was that this treated culture as unitary, passive and inert. But recent work of Michel Picard and others has helped me see a more fundamental problem: the assumption that tourism can be conceived any longer as outside of South-East Asian culture at all.

Obviously, the degree to which tourism becomes, in Picard's (1990, 74) words, an 'integral part' of culture is a variable. In some ways even more striking in this respect than Picard's picture of Bali is Errington and Gewertz's description of a hazing ritual of the Chambri in Papua New Guinea. In the midst of quite aggressive hazing, the male initiates are met with the challenge: 'Are you (man) enough to make carvings and place them in the men's house for the tourists to buy?' For the Chambri, the authors explain:

> the acquisition of money was . . . regarded as requiring the exercise of ancestral knowledge to 'pull' tourists to Chambri and to impel them to purchase artifacts. Hence, the presence of tourists at Chambri was interpreted not as testimony to the transformation of Chambri tradition but to its persistence and strength.
>
> (Errington and Gewertz, 1989, 37)

Picard paints a similar picture for Bali. In his superb analysis of the cultural politics of Balinese dance performances, Picard disputes McKean's earlier optimism that the Balinese could maintain a clear distinction between sacred and tourist performances. Dances commissioned for tourists have been imported back into temples. Sacred dances have become infused with Western theatrical conventions. Official efforts to institutionalise a Western-based distinction between sacred and profane dances fail in the face of people who make no such distinction. Dances created for non-indigenous audiences come to be seen by the Balinese themselves as exemplars of Balinese culture, and the tourist-oriented Bali Arts Festival increasingly defines Balinese identity for the Balinese. Picard labels the outcome a 'touristic culture', a culture that 'is in fact the product of dialogic construction between the Balinese and their various interlocutors, in a context defined by the growing integration of Bali within the overlapping networks of the internal tourist industry and of the Indonesian state' (Picard, 1990, 74).[12] What is defined as contemporary Balinese culture by the Balinese themselves is increasingly a function of their interaction with tourists.

The degree to which this kind of 'dialogic construction' defines cultural identity is variable, but Linda Richter's observation about Pakistan (Richter, 1989a, 149) – that the very lack of international tourist interest contributes to a sense of relative deprivation and a sort of inferiority complex there, at least among the elite – suggests that in the modern world, where tourism is the single largest industry, few people escape its influence entirely.

International tourism neither 'destroys' culture nor does it ever simply 'preserve' it. It is inevitably bound up in an on-going process of cultural invention in which 'Westernisation' is probably in most cases of lesser importance than other new directions of cultural change. It has its own peculiar dynamics which make it an interesting and challenging field of study, but tourism's impact is always played out in an already dynamic and changing cultural context. In this sense it is questionable whether it is useful to conclude, as Valene Smith has done in the second edition of *Hosts and Guests*, that 'the research undertaken in the intervening decade indicates overall that tourism is *not* the major element of culture change in most societies' (Smith, 1989, x). In how many societies can one process of change be unambiguously identified as the major one? Not only is the importance of tourism highly variable, but tourism is seldom a distinct process of change. One of the key themes of recent research is that tourism's impact is generally played out less through direct host–guest interaction than through other social processes.[13]

Several parallel themes can be discerned in recent work in the sociology of development. On the one hand, even most remaining modernisation theorists have moved away from their earlier identification of modernisation with Westernisation and cultural homogenisation (Moore, 1979; Manning Nash, 1984). This reflects less a sense that 'traditional' culture will survive the development process than a recognition that the possibilities for new cultural syncretism are greatly expanded by modernisation. Even the natives read *National Geographic*.[14] As Hannerz has put it, 'the world system, rather than creating massive cultural homogeneity on a global scale, is replacing one diversity with another; and the new diversity is based relatively more on interrelations and less on autonomy' (quoted in Clifford, 1988, 17).

Beyond this recognition there is the understanding that development itself cannot really be conceptualised outside of culture; it is above all a form of discourse that has welded an enormous range of phenomena into a single concept and provided the framework for the exercise of a wide range of forms of power. This cultural process – 'the development of development' – has had both global and local manifestations (Ariel, 1988; Demaine, 1986; Escobar, 1988; Mowlana and Wilson, 1990; Parajuli, 1991; Pieterse, 1991). In a fundamental sense, both today's and tomorrow's cultural tourists seek out not pre-development culture but the outcomes of different discourses and modes of development.

## NOTES

1 For useful reviews of the economic literature, see Eadington and Redman, 1991 and English, 1986.
2 For a useful analysis locating modernisation theory within a broader culturalist paradigm of the period, and suggesting the progressive role of such a paradigm at the time, see Portes, 1980.

3 See, for example, Richard Robison's (1981) 'Culture, Politics and Economy in the Political History of the New Order', in which he accuses cultural explanations of Indonesian politics of 'Orientalism' and subjects them to lengthy critique. But his general theoretical claim turns out to be strikingly limited: only that one cannot explain Indonesian politics by *exclusive* reference to political culture.

4 In a similar vein, Ron Jenkins (1980) described the introduction of a clown caricature of a tourist in some Balinese dances as 'a method for resolving some of the tensions produced by the intrusion of insensitive tourists into village life'.

5 The continuing hold of this normative framework can be seen in Dogan's (1989, 217) observation that 'tourism has produced both positive and negative results in the Third World countries, but their respective levels vary depending on the socio-cultural structure of the country and the level of touristic development'. Despite the limitations of this normative framework, Dogan provides an interesting typology of strategies for dealing with tourism. Greenwood (1989, 181–82) has recently raised questions about the moral assumptions in his and others' early work, but he continues to use normative language in describing different outcomes and responses, and in response to his own question, 'Are [tourism's] cultural manifestations always negative?', he can only answer: 'The anthropological literature on tourism does not yet provide very clear answers.'

6 The concern in the literature with staged authenticity tends to neglect the degree to which tourists insist on it or go to great lengths to find scenes fitting their preconceptions. Consider how many tour buses have screeched to a halt at the sight of a water buffalo in a ricefield, having passed many tractors and other mechanized devices. See Guldin, 1989 for useful discussion.

7 How difficult it is to give up this etic standpoint is suggested by MacCannell (1984). Acknowledging that all ethnic identities are 'constructed', MacCannell defines 'reconstructed ethnicity' as 'the maintenance and preservation of ethnic forms for the entertainment of ethnically different others'. Although he insists that reconstructed ethnicity is not necessarily less authentic than constructed ethnicity, he nonetheless concludes that: 'When an ethnic group begins to sell itself, or is forced to sell itself, as an ethnic attraction, it ceases to evolve naturally.' The naturalistic concept of tradition reasserts itself; how else can one presume to know a culture's 'natural' evolution? It is also worth noting that historically the claim to etic knowledge about authenticity has often been linked to claims by outsiders to know what is best for others; for Bali, see Pollman, 1990, 14.

8 Domestic tourists may differ from foreign tourists not only in motivation but in terms of treatment, as in Malaysia, where a 'double-standard policy' applies different regulations to domestic Muslim tourists and others (see Kadir Din, 1989a).

9 It is worth remembering that Japanese and other Asian tourists have accounted for and will continue to account for much of the expansion of international tourism in South-East Asia.

10 For the original formulation of the concepts of ethnic and cultural tourists,

see Smith, 1979. For a proposed redefinition of the concepts, focusing on tourist orientation rather than the characteristics of object groups, see Wood, 1984.

11 In fact, the area in which tourism's presence and impact is most predictable is in the accommodation sector, where such 'binding myths' operate particularly effectively. For a discussion of some of the sources of tourism's homogenizing tendencies, see Lanfant, 1980.

12 A sense of dismay is evident in Picard's account, but I would argue that the logic of his argument precludes any condemnation of these changes in terms of a departure from what is 'really' Balinese. For example, while the sacred–profane distinction may not be compatible with the way most Balinese have historically conceived the world, it does constitute a 'cultural template' for an increasing number of Balinese today.

13 For an interesting exploration of some of these in the Balinese village of Kuta, where tourism has had a totally transformative effect, see Hussey, 1989. Tourism may not initiate these processes, but it can influence their outcomes. And in more than a few cases it may become such an integral part of culture that the whole concept of 'impact' becomes problematic.

14 Van den Berghe (1980, 390) reports that Bolivian tin miners have fashioned carnival masks based on an illustrated article about Tibetan masks in National Geographic. He calls this new cultural form 'pseudo-traditional', a problematic label. For a discussion of 'creolisation' as a model of cultural synthesis and fluorescence, see Graburn, 1984.

# 4 'Cultural tourism' in Bali

## National integration and regional differentiation[1]

*Michel Picard*

> Regional diversity is valued, honoured, even apotheosized, but
> only as long as it remains at the level of display, not belief,
> performance, not enactment. . . . Most groups may dance their
> way to the national goals, each with its own ethnic steps, as long
> as the underlying ideology, the tune to which the dance is called,
> is what the state has ratified.
>
> (Acciaioli, 1985, 161–62).

## INTRODUCTION

'Culture' is the focus of the touristic promotion of Bali: tourism in Bali
is 'cultural' tourism. Consequently, Westerners, Indonesians and
Balinese alike fear its demise, anxiously asking the question: 'can
Balinese culture survive the impact of tourism?'

This question gives rise to strikingly diverging opinions, all the more
drastic since they are passionate. Thus, as many tourists are wont to
assure you nowadays, Bali is finished – that is, almost. If tourism in
Bali proves to be a commercial success, it is rapidly becoming a
cultural tragedy. The Balinese have been corrupted by tourist dollars
and the entire island is up for sale. Authentic traditions are being
packaged to conform to tourist expectations, legendary Balinese
artistry is being harnessed to create souvenir trinkets, and age-old
religious ceremonies are being turned into hotel floor shows. Accordingly, so the story goes, tourism is on the verge of engulfing Bali, and
the island's culture cannot possibly survive much longer. So hurry up
and see what you still can see now – next year may be too late.

Other observers, who deem themselves better informed, will be
equally prompt to remind you that Balinese culture is more resistant
than one is led to believe in view of the changes occurring on the island
since its opening up to international tourism. They base their convic-

tion on one of the most deeply rooted assumptions about Balinese culture – its dynamic resilience. Indeed, the Balinese have long been celebrated for knowing their cultural boundaries, and they are unanimously praised for their ability to borrow whatever foreign influence suits them while nevertheless maintaining their identity over the centuries. Accordingly, so the story goes, the Balinese are coping with the tourist invasion of their island as well as they have coped with others in the past – that is, they are taking advantage of the appeal of their cultural traditions to foreign visitors without sacrificing their own values on the altar of monetary profit.

Torn between a commonplace tourist opinion and a view held by more sophisticated connoisseurs of things Balinese, one might wish to turn to acknowledged specialists for more qualified evidence. Unfortunately, this would not be of much help either, as the few scholars who have taken more than a passing interest in tourism are still arguing whether it has had a beneficial or a detrimental effect on Balinese culture – for some, tourism has helped preserve the cultural heritage of Bali, while others accuse tourism of debasing Balinese culture by turning it into a commercial commodity.[2]

Faced with these contradictory statements, one suspects the question they seek to answer is misleading. Indeed, the mere fact of talking about the 'impact' of tourism entails something of a ballistic vision, which amounts to perceiving the host society as a target hit by a missile, that is, like a static object, inertly subjected to exogenous factors of change, which experts are expected to assess by means of a cost-benefit analysis.[3] Such an approach is mistaken on at least two grounds. On the one hand, it deals with tourism as if it were an agent external to the society under consideration, instead of trying to understand how it becomes part of the local reality. On the other hand, it deprives the local people from having anything to say and do about tourism, as if they were but passive recipients of some wholesale package decided and manipulated outright by the multinational firms which control the tourist industry in connection with the central state.[4]

On the contrary, I contend that tourism should be conceived not as the irruption of an external force striking Bali from without, but as a process transforming Balinese society from within. What is more, this process should be contextualised, by placing tourism within the opening up of the Balinese social space to the outside world, following the integration of the island first in the Netherlands Indies and then in the Republic of Indonesia. In short, the 'touristification' of Balinese culture should be considered within the context of the 'colonisation' of Bali and its subsequent 'Indonesianisation'.

Seen in this light, Balinese culture is the product of a dialogic interaction between the Balinese people and significant others: not only the tourists, but also the artists and scholars who contributed to composing the touristic image of Bali, not to forget the Dutch officials who endeavoured to fashion Balinese society according to their idea of how it should be, and their Indonesian successors who are following their lead. This confrontation with significant others has rendered the Balinese self-conscious about their 'Balineseness', while compelling them to explain what it means to be Balinese to a foreign audience. Thus it is that the Balinese – or rather, one should say, the Balinese intelligentsia – came to define themselves in terms of what they call 'Balinese culture' (*kebudayaan Bali*), which they liken to a tree, whose roots are their religion (*agama*), the trunk their customary order (*adat*) and the fruits their artistic expressions (*seni*).[5] If the roots stay well grounded, so they claim, the trunk will grow vigorously and will bear beautiful fruits.

Now, in my opinion, since the subjection of the island at the turn of the century, the tree of Balinese culture has seen its trunk wither, while its roots strengthened and its fruits multiplied. This, I hold, is to be ascribed to the growing encroachment of an alien power upon the customary order – at once an immutable cosmic order and a social order instituted by the ancestors in conformity with the former – which rules the life of the Balinese. More precisely, confronted by the irruption of the outside world into their traditional universe, the Balinese intelligentsia had to proceed to a series of conceptual discriminations, to sort out that which belongs to 'tradition' from that which pertains respectively to 'politics', to 'religion' and to 'art' – with the result that the Balinese *adat* has seen its sphere of authority secularised and relativised, by having to relinquish its former 'political' and 'religious' prerogatives while it was acquiring 'artistic' qualities.

If this contention has any relevance, it entails that instead of asking whether or not Balinese culture has been able to withstand the impact of tourism, it would be better to find out what part tourism has played in the process of shaping Balinese culture. To this end, I shall investigate why it is that Balinese culture inspires such concern to tourists as well as to national and regional authorities. To the extent that Bali is a province of the Republic of Indonesia as well as an international tourist destination, Balinese culture is expected to foster both the development of tourism in Indonesia and the development of a national culture. Thus, the question which is being asked in this chapter is: 'What is becoming of Balinese culture as it contributes to concurrently developing international tourism and Indonesian culture?' To answer this question, one has first to know how it happened that culture has become Bali's defining feature.

## THE 'LIVING MUSEUM'

If the name of Bali is famous the world over as a tourist paradise, it is not due solely to the charm of the Balinese or to the beauty of their island, or even to the extravagance of their ceremonial pageants. What appears nowadays to be the 'touristic vocation' of Bali is the result of deliberate decisions made not originally by the Balinese themselves but by others beyond their shores. In order to become a tourist destination, Bali had to fulfil several conditions. First, an island which had long been reputed in the West for its 'plunderous salvage' of shipwrecks and 'barbarous sacrifice' of widows on the funeral pyre had to be turned into an object of curiosity for Westerners in search of the exotic. Second, this island had to be made accessible to potential visitors. This in turn required that it be integrated within the Dutch colonial empire, along with the rest of the East Indies.

Initiated in 1846, the military conquest of Bali was achieved in 1906–8, with the collective suicide (*puputan*) of several royal houses who had chosen a glorious end rather than capitulate to the foreign invaders.[6] The protests raised by their brutality were a source of international embarrassment to the Dutch, who attempted to atone for the blood bath by displaying a commendable image of their colonial policy on the island – an image based on the preservation of Balinese culture and its promotion as a tourist attraction.

As a matter of fact, the Dutch had not waited for Bali to become part of their colonial empire to take an interest in its culture. Orientalists had long seen the island as a 'living museum' of the Hindu-Javanese civilisation, the one and only surviving heir to the Hindu heritage swept away from Java by the coming of Islam. In their perspective, the Hindu religion was the foundation of the Balinese society, the warrant of its cultural integrity and the inspiration of its artistic manifestations. This orientalist vision of Bali was to have long-lasting consequences for the island's future. Indeed, if the Dutch administrators understood little of the society on which they had imposed their authority, they had on the other hand some idea about what it should look like and they endeavoured to conform it to its image. For the orientalists and civil servants posted on the island, it was not enough that the Balinese cultural heritage be rescued from the onslaught of modernisation, the Balinese people had furthermore to be taught by their new lords how to remain authentically Balinese –

such was the aim of the cultural policy known as the 'Balinisation of Bali' (*Balisering*), launched in the early 1930s. Once restored to its pristine splendour, Balinese culture could then be presented to the appreciation of the outside world.[7]

It was in 1908, the same year which saw the fall of Bali's last unyielding royal house under the assault of Dutch superior military might, that the colonial government opened an Official Tourist Bureau in Batavia, with the aim of promoting the Netherlands Indies as a tourist destination.[8] Initially focusing on Java, the Bureau extended its scope to Bali in 1914, as soon as the pacification of the island by the army permitted its replacement by a police force.[9] But it was not until 1924 that tourism took off in Bali, after the Royal Packet Navigation Company (KPM) established a regular weekly steamship service connecting Bali with Batavia, Surabaya and Makassar via the north coast port of Buleleng (Singaraja). Shortly thereafter, the KPM agent in Buleleng was appointed as the Tourist Bureau representative on Bali, while the government began allowing visitors to use its *pasanggrahan*, the rest houses originally designed to accommodate Dutch officials on their periodic rounds of the island. In 1928 the first hotel opened in Denpasar, the Bali Hotel, built by the KPM on the very site of the *puputan* of 1906. Following this, the KPM also turned the *pasanggrahan* at Kintamani into a bungalow hotel to be used by the tourists who came to enjoy the spectacular panoramas around Lake Batur.

The first tourists arrived in Bali either aboard a cruiser that berthed at Padang Bai for one or two days, or more commonly aboard the weekly KPM steamship that called at the port of Buleleng. Passengers on the KPM ships usually disembarked on Friday morning and departed on the same boat back from Makassar on Sunday evening, giving them just enough time to make a quick round of the island by motor-car. The number of visitors increased steadily from several hundreds a year in the 1920s to several thousands towards the end of the 1930s.

Among these visitors, special mention should be made of the small community of foreign artists and aesthetes (e.g. Walter Spies and Miguel Covarrubias) who resided in Bali between the wars. The accounts, paintings, photographs and films which recorded their sojourn on the island contributed to forging a sensational image of native life, an image which would be relayed in due time through the promotional services of the nascent tourist industry. And indeed, Bali has consistently been described ever since as the 'Island of the Gods', as the homeland of a traditional culture insulated from the modern world and its vicissitudes, whose bearers, endowed with exceptional artistic talents, devote an outstanding amount of time and wealth staging sumptuous ceremonies for their own pleasure and that of their gods – and now in addition for the delight of tourists.[10]

After the artists came the anthropologists, who – like the tourists at that time – were mostly American.[11] Their studies comforted the Dutch colonial policy of cultural preservation by endorsing the idea that Balinese society had not really been affected by the integration of the island within the Netherlands Indies. In this respect, they provided academic credit to the image of serene harmony bestowed on Bali by the artists. Their analysis of the 'steady state', which they ascribed to Balinese society, did not include the 'peace and order' forced upon the island by a colonial power.[12] Reading them, one gathers that the Balinese were too busy performing their culture to bother with the presence of a foreign administration. And indeed, once the matters of government had been appropriated by the Dutch, the Balinese were left with not much else to do but to cultivate their arts and celebrate their religious festivals, further elaborating their expressive culture.

Despite the Dutch claim to preserve Balinese culture, the colonial occupation of the island provoked the disintegration of its customary order, while the requirements of a modern administration prompted the formation of a Balinese intelligentsia, which mediated between the local population and its foreign masters. This intelligentsia strove to make sense of the new situation brought about by the opening up of their social space, at a time when the admiration evinced by foreigners for selected aspects of their culture was arousing the Balinese's interest in their own traditions. On the one hand, the Balinese intellectuals started questioning themselves about the relationship between religion, art and customary order, with the aim of bringing to light the foundations of their cultural identity, whereas on the other hand, they were in the novel position of needing to define what it meant to be Balinese in terms comprehensible by non-Balinese.

Thus it is that 'culture' – in the case in point, mostly narrowed down to artistic and ceremonial manifestations – became Bali's defining feature, providing the common ground on which Dutch orientalists and American anthropologists, artists and tourists could encounter each other and the Balinese.

No sooner had culture become the emblematic image of Bali than foreign visitors and residents started fearing for its oncoming disappearance. Indeed, when one reads the accounts of between-the-wars Bali, one realises how deeply their authors were convinced they were witnessing the swan-song of a traditional culture miraculously preserved from the contagious corruption of modernity. In fact it is as if, since the 'discovery' of the island by an avant-garde of artists and anthropologists during the 1920s, the mere evocation of Bali suggested the imminent and dramatic fall from the 'Garden of Eden':[13] sooner or later, the 'Last Paradise'[14] was doomed to become a 'Paradise Lost'. And one could surmise that the appeal exerted by the island of Bali over its visitors rested to a large extent on the premonition of the impending demise of its culture.

Among the perils seen to be threatening Balinese culture, the most conspicuous one was none other than the coming of the tourists themselves. Hence the ambivalent attitude evinced by the colonial authorities with respect to tourism. On the one hand, the conservation of Bali as a living museum was the major asset for the tourist promotion of the island. But on the other hand, if the Balinese cultural heritage was to be preserved, measures had to be taken in order to protect it against the corruptive contact with the modern world brought about by the presence of foreign visitors to the island.

The landing of Japanese troops on Sanur beach in 1942 spared the colonial government the necessity of defining a consistent tourist policy for Bali. When the war was over, the Dutch attempted to promote tourism anew, but with the growing nationalist movement Bali was in turmoil. After the independence of Indonesia, tourism remained very limited on the island, potential visitors being dissuaded by the rudimentary state of the infrastructure together with the political unrest and the xenophobic orientation of the regime that marked the period. Yet, President Sukarno adopted Bali – which had become a province of the Republic of Indonesia in 1958 – as his favourite retreat and made it a 'showplace' for state guests. Eager to use the fame of the island to attract foreign tourists, he undertook the construction of an international airport in Tuban and had a luxury hotel built on Sanur beach. The Bali Beach Hotel was completed in 1966 at a time when the blood bath following the 30 September 1965 coup d'état had closed Indonesia's doors to foreigners.

Only after the New Order (Orde Baru) regime installed by President Suharto began opening Indonesia to the West would tourists start coming back to Bali in significant numbers. More precisely, one can date the launching of mass tourism in Bali from 1 August 1969, the day of the inauguration of the Ngurah Rai International Airport.

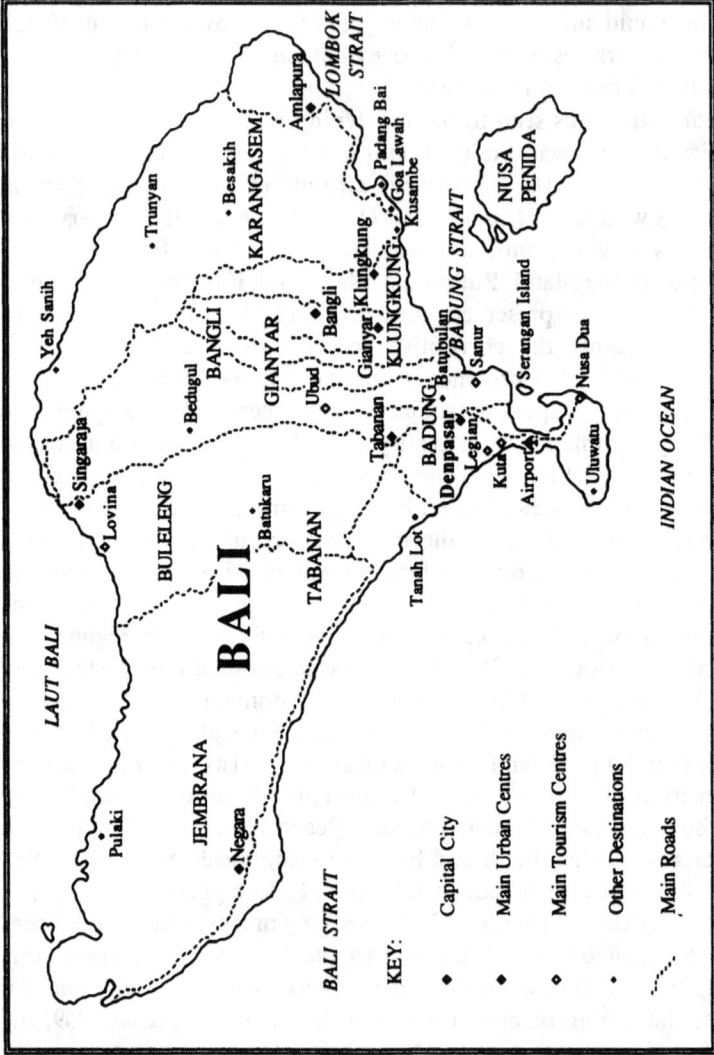

*Figure 4.1* Map of Bali

## THE MASTER PLAN FOR THE DEVELOPMENT OF
## TOURISM IN BALI

Earlier that year, the First Five-Year Development Plan had stressed the importance of international tourism as a factor of economic development for Indonesia, while laying the foundations of a national tourism policy.[15] Banking on Bali's prestigious image as a tourist paradise, inherited from colonial times, the government decided to make this island the 'showcase' of Indonesia as an international tourist destination. Furthermore, Bali was to serve as a model for future development of tourism in the archipelago.

The Indonesian government put in an international tender for a plan to promote the growth of mass tourism in Bali. The plan was to be financed by the United Nations Development Programme with the World Bank as executing agency. A French consulting firm, the SCETO, won the bid and drew up a *Master Plan for the Development of Tourism in Bali*, published in 1971. Revised in 1974 by the World Bank, the Master Plan proposed to confine the bulk of tourists to a luxury beach enclave – a 425 hectare resort at Nusa Dua, on the east coast of the Bukit peninsula, between Benoa and Bualu – while providing for a network of excursion routes linking the new resort with major attractions on the island.[16] With the official promulgation of the Master Plan by presidential decree in 1972, tourism became a top economic priority in the Province of Bali second only to agriculture.

Now, why should tourists be confined to a luxury beach enclave? According to the market study on which the Master Plan was based, these tourists were expected to be wealthy Westerners coming on tour to Bali with the idea of vacationing for a few days on the beach. Yet, for prospective visitors Bali was not just another tropical island with beaches of white sand bordered by palm trees, it was the 'Island of the Gods', a place teeming with temples and ceremonies, vibrating with music and dance. But if they expected to find in Bali a traditional culture preserved up until now from the undermining attacks of modernity, the tourists themselves were active carriers of this modernity spreading across the planet, so that their presence might well smother what they strove to embrace. Therefore, the problem faced by the French consultants was to develop tourism in Bali without spoiling Balinese culture.

Consequently, the consultants tried to shield Balinese culture as much as possible from the frontal impact of tourism by keeping the tourist resorts well away from Balinese residential areas. But – given the fact that the chief attraction of Bali, which differentiates it from other exotic destinations, lay in the possibility of contact, however fleeting, with a living traditional culture – they also deemed it necessary to create tourism excursion routes through those areas providing the most typical manifestations of the Balinese way of life.

The rationale underlying the Master Plan was thus to warrant a sustainable development of tourism on Bali by ensuring the preservation of the resources upon which its success was seen to depend – primarily the cultural traditions which had made the island famous the world over. Nevertheless, the consultants did not seem to have much confidence in the success of their plan, as witnessed by this statement voiced on the very conclusion of their study:

> The cultural manifestations will probably have disappeared, (that is, at the term of the Master Plan, by 1985) but Bali can still retain its romantic image and still be thought of as a green and sumptuous garden.
>
> (SCETO, 1971, Vol. 2, 161).

## THE DEVELOPMENT OF TOURISM IN BALI

As a matter of fact, tourism did not quite develop in the way that had been expected by foreign and Indonesian experts in the late 1960s. After a promising start, it fell well below target. It was only after the mid-1980s oil market collapse, when Indonesia embarked on an economic about-face aimed at promoting non-oil exports and private investments, both local and foreign, that the government decided to take specific measures destined to boost international tourism. And indeed, since 1986, after Garuda had finally agreed to open Bali to foreign airlines, which until then had to land in Jakarta, tourist arrivals in Indonesia – and especially in Bali – registered a real boom. Thus, the number of foreign visitors to Indonesia multiplied from 86,000 in 1969 to 1,626,000 in 1989 (yielding US\$ 1.28 billion in tourism receipts), while foreign visitors to Bali grew from fewer than 30,000 to around 700,000 during the same period.[17]

Since 1989, Indonesia has entered its Fifth Five-Year Development Plan, which forecasts 2.5 million visitors and US\$ 2.25 billion in tourism receipts by 1993. With this plan, the promotion of international tourism has reached a new momentum, backed by 'Tourism Awareness' (*Sadar Wisata*) campaigns culminating in 1991, which was declared 'Visit Indonesia Year'. Bali is now seen as a distribution point for the rest of the country and, in order to bring in ever more tourists,

the Ngurah Rai International Airport is being expanded to accommodate Boeing 747 jets. By 1993, 1.5 million foreign tourists are expected
to visit the island, while hotel capacity should increase from 13,000 to
22,000 rooms.

These forecasts were clearly pessimistic because 2,177,000 foreign
visitors entered Indonesia in 1990, a figure likely to reach 2.4 million
during 'Visit Indonesia Year 1991' in spite of the dampening effect of
the Gulf War. Visitors to Bali are expected to come to around 1.5
million, taking into account both foreign and domestic tourists.
Despite this steady increase in the frequentation of the island, though,
the occupancy rates are decreasing drastically, due to the recent boom
in hotel construction. The number of hotel rooms increased radically
to 25,000 by the end of 1991. According to experts, the situation is not
likely to improve before 1995.

It was not only in terms of scale but also in terms of clientele that the
development of tourism in Bali had thwarted the experts' forecasts.
The Master Plan had been designed to attract and accommodate
tourists of the upper-income range, who were expected to stay in
expensive luxury hotels. But it turned out that a considerable proportion of the arrivals were not of the target group but comprised young,
low-cost travellers or vacationists, eager to see more of Bali than the
luxury resorts. Thus, nowadays the tourist industry in Bali
encompasses two broad categories of facilities and services, catering to
quite distinct groups of visitors: package-tour group high-spending
tourists on the one hand, individual low-spending tourists on the
other.

The luxury resorts are concentrated on the beaches of Nusa Dua
and Sanur, where most of the hotels are owned and operated by large
corporate bodies, of Indonesian or foreign origin. The implementation
of Nusa Dua in particular has involved a substantial loan from the
International Development Association, budgetary allocations of the
government, as well as access to cheap credit from state banks. While
these resorts employ local staff – though mostly of the low-skilled type
– they constitute capital-intensive enclaves, with only limited links to
domestic Balinese economy.

Largely unanticipated by planners, and therefore almost completely
unplanned, there has been a growing share of 'budget' tourists. As the
Balinese have been prompt to adapt to this unexpected clientele – for
years derogatively dubbed 'hippies' – new resorts have developed. In
contrast to the luxury resorts, in areas such as Kuta,[18] Ubud, Batur,
Lovina or Candi Dasa, most of the owners and employees of tourist

accommodations and services are Balinese, and the links with the local economy are close and numerous.

Despite the unquestionable importance of this clientele, the Director-General of Tourism is still giving top priority to the up-market visitors, whereas the regional government holds a more balanced view, being eager to give the local population an opportunity to get involved in the tourist trade and to reap its benefits. As to the foreign analysts, their opinions tend to diverge on the respective economic pros and cons of these tourist sub-sectors. Some have stressed that smaller-scale enterprises offer a greater opportunity for profit and control to the Balinese than do enterprises on a larger scale, whereas others insist that the declining per capita expenditure for visitor arrivals to Bali, due to the growing share of 'budget' tourists, is not offset by its lower import leakage rate.[19]

In any case, this rather neat circumscription of the tourist resorts is rapidly changing with the growing popularity of the island and the boom of hotel investments stimulated by the prospect of the 'Visit Indonesia Year'. In 1988, alleging the pressure of demand, the Governor of Bali created fifteen tourist areas, thus in effect lifting the restrictions imposed by the Master Plan, which prohibited the building of large hotels and equipments outside of Nusa Dua, Sanur and Kuta. Then, in 1990, an agreement was signed between the Directorate General of Tourism and the United Nations Development Programme to review the Master Plan, whose term had expired in 1985. Finally, just as the 'Visit Indonesia Year' programme was about to be launched, the Director-General of Tourism decreed a one-year moratorium on new hotel construction in the overcrowded beach front of southern Bali. At the same time, environmentalists claimed that if expansion continued, the island could face a critical shortage of water. Furthermore, tourist industry officials themselves admitted that increasing mass tourism would destroy the island's touristic appeal. Meanwhile, the districts which had seen themselves at a disadvantage in comparison with the southern belt, are busy discovering and promoting picturesque customs or spectacular sceneries, fiercely competing with each other to seize a bigger portion of the tourist pie.

While for the last two decades tourism has been the most visible factor of economic growth in Bali – not to mention its conspicuous repercussions on the environment – its actual contribution to the regional economy is difficult to assess accurately. Studies on this issue are scarce, and their results are unreliable, being all too often based on faulty statistics and inadequate methodology. The latest study conducted by Balinese economists of Udayana University in Denpasar estimated that foreign tourists' spendings contributed to nearly 33 per cent of Bali's GDP in 1987, and predicted that the role of tourism was soon to exceed that of agriculture in the economy of the island.[20]

Most experts tend to agree that, on balance, tourism has conferred considerable economic gains on Bali – even though their equitable distribution within the population and between the districts, as well as the growing encroachment of foreign interests, remain a matter of concern. The Balinese authorities, however, appear to display an ambivalent attitude toward the consequences of tourism for their society and culture.

## CULTURAL TOURISM

To tell the truth, the Balinese authorities did not really have a say in the decision of the central government to trade in their island's charms in order to refill the coffers of the state, and they had not been consulted about the Master Plan. Behind a facade of official assent – attested by its ratification by the Regional Assembly – the plan advocated by French consultants, finalised by World Bank experts, and imposed by Jakarta technocrats, gave rise to undisguised criticism in Bali. According to its detractors, the Master Plan might be a plan for the development of tourism, but it clearly was not a plan for the development of Bali. Witness the fact that it was based on a market study of anticipated growth in tourist arrivals to Bali and not on an assessment of the development needs of the island. To judge from written evidence, the Balinese authorities objected to the Master Plan on three specific points:

1 the plan did not pay sufficient attention to the consequences of tourism on Balinese society and culture;
2 the geographic concentration of the tourist resorts in the south of the island, and the very design of the Nusa Dua enclave in particular, did not provide for consistent regional development;
3 imposed from above, the plan did not allow the regional government to conduct its own tourism policy in Bali.

Faced with a *fait accompli*, the Balinese authorities attempted to turn to their own advantage the decision of the central government to make their island the showcase of Indonesia as an international tourist destination. They adopted the slogan 'the tourists must be for Bali and not Bali for the tourists' and made their position clear on each of the following points:

1  tourism in Bali should be 'cultural', that is, it should foster Balinese culture, which is the main attraction of the island in the eyes of tourists;
2  tourist resorts should be spread evenly throughout the island, so as to permit the active involvement of the Balinese population in the tourist trade and to allow for the equitable distribution of its economic benefits;
3  tourism should be used by the Balinese as a means to further their own ends: in particular, they should take advantage of the prestige of their island abroad as well as of its economic importance for the country, to obtain full recognition of their cultural identity from the central government and to improve their position within the Indonesian nation.

While this last point was not mentioned as such by the Balinese authorities, it clearly appears – at least in retrospect – as the one in which they invested most effort, whereas the first two have been more a matter of rhetoric.

Some clarification is in order here, concerning what I call the 'Balinese authorities'. Besides the personnel of the regional government proper, these authorities include the 'intelligentsia' at large – such as academics and journalists, bureaucrats and technocrats, entrepreneurs and professionals who make up the Balinese 'public opinion'. In particular this means those Balinese who are *authorised* to speak in the name of their society and who are thus in a position to monopolise legitimate discourse on Bali. While not necessarily voicing a unanimous opinion on every topic, the members of this intelligentsia share a common outlook concerning the place of Bali within Indonesia, in contrast to what might be regarded as the Balinese literati. Whereas the latter are primarily still enclosed within their traditional frame of reference, the former bestride two worlds: the society into which they were enculturated and the increasingly intrusive wider world. Thus these opinion-formers, most of whom live in Denpasar, comprise the modern Balinese élite. They mediate between the villages and central government by speaking on behalf of the Balinese to Jakarta, and by conveying the instructions of the capital to the province. In the remaining part of this chapter, these are the people I shall refer to as 'the Balinese'.

In response to the Master Plan, the Balinese authorities proclaimed their own conception of the kind of tourism they deemed the most suitable to their island – namely what they termed 'Cultural Tourism' (*Pariwisata Budaya*). This conception was formulated a few months after the publication of the Master Plan, in October 1971, when the Governor convened a 'Seminar on Cultural Tourism in Bali' (*Seminar Pariwisata Budaya Daerah Bali*), under the joint aegis of the regional agencies for tourism, religion, culture and education.[21]

The proceedings of this seminar reveal that the view of tourism held by the Balinese authorities is blatantly ambivalent, the driving force of a modernisation process which they welcome as ardently as they fear. Tourism in their eyes appears at once as the most promising source of economic development and as the most subversive agent for the spread of foreign cultural influences in Bali. On the one hand, the artistic and religious traditions, which have made the name of Bali famous world-wide, have served as the main tourist attraction, thus turning Balinese culture into its most valuable 'resource' (*sumber*) for the island's economic development; but on the other hand, the invasion of Bali by foreign visitors was perceived in terms of 'cultural pollution' (*polusi kebudayaan*). Accordingly, the Balinese regarded tourism as a 'challenge' (*tantangan*) that should be taken up with caution: 'how could tourism be developed without polluting Balinese culture?' Such was the task assigned to Cultural Tourism: to take advantage of the power of Balinese culture to attract tourists, while using the economic benefits of tourism for the preservation and promotion of Balinese culture.

Thus one sees that, from the 1930s to the 1970s, the problem facing the authorities responsible for designing a tourist policy for Bali – the Dutch colonial administration, the SCETO consultants and World Bank experts, the Balinese government – has been defined in terms of a dilemma: *tourism relies on culture, but tourism is a threat to culture.* Yet the solution favoured by the Balinese differs in significant respects from those adopted by their foreign predecessors – instead of trying to keep the tourists at bay, they welcome them.

The rationale underlying this choice is that, insofar as tourism is being developed on their island, the Balinese may as well capitalise on it to further their own economic development. This objective requires the local population to participate in the tourist trade and reap its benefits, which in turn implies that the tourists must be allowed to travel freely and spend their money throughout the island. But this presupposes in turn that the threat hanging over culture due to tourism should be removed, as the whole idea of Cultural Tourism rests on the claim that the interests of Balinese culture must concur, in the long run, with those of the tourist industry.

Moreover, the Balinese appear to be genuinely proud of the fame of their culture abroad, and are eager to show their cultural traditions at their best to the tourists. In this respect, they link the success of tourism to the state of their culture, and thus bind their culture to tourism, to a larger extent than did the Master Plan.[22] By so doing, they turn to their own advantage Jakarta's decision to promote their island as an international tourist destination in order to acquire hard currency. Through tourism culture has been transformed into the island's main economic resource and by the same token Balinese culture has become a major bargaining point with central government.[23] Clearly, should the touristic exploitation of Balinese culture depreciate it, it would diminish the appeal of Bali as a tourist paradise. If such was the case, not only would the tourist industry have ruined Balinese culture, but it would have sown the seeds of its own destruction as a result. Accordingly – so the Balinese say – once the central government has chosen Bali as the main tourist destination in Indonesia, it is in its own interest, as well as in the interest of the tourist industry, to preserve and promote Balinese culture.

Now, the question that arises immediately is whether or not the Balinese government had the means to conduct the tourist policy of its choice? Once the Master Plan had been approved by presidential decree in 1972, it became effective, whereas the doctrine of Cultural Tourism retained only a normative character.[24] Moreover in 1979, the central government issued a regulation entitled the *Delegation to Regions of Some Governmental Responsibilities in the Domain of Tourism*, which delegated to the provinces a very limited sphere of decision-making.[25] According to this legislation, the following areas remained under the control of central government: research and planning; development of tourist destinations, tourist products and their marketing; participation of the population; regulations and measures of control; infrastructure and manpower. Thus, it is painfully clear that the regional government has no legal authority to conduct its own tourist policy.

Under these conditions, it might not really be surprising that, instead of the adoption of the concrete measures which one could have expected, the doctrine of Cultural Tourism led to a confusing profusion of discourses, while arousing impressive fervour among the Balinese public opinion. But one should beware of dismissing all this enthusiasm as mere verbal gesticulation, as but an implicit admission of powerlessness on the part of the Balinese authorities. For, by defining Balinese cultural identity in reference to the 'challenge' of tourism, these discourses strengthen the social links that bind the Balinese people together in defence of their culture, while their authors can pretend they are actually speaking in the name of Bali. And furthermore, to the extent that it stresses the preservation of Balinese culture, the doctrine of Cultural Tourism is able to enlist the support of literati and other tradition-minded Balinese, because, as Adrian Vickers puts it: 'Nobody on Bali would seriously think to challenge the idea of Balinese culture. Even those people who oppose tourism and see themselves as defenders of tradition are supporters of the idea' (Vickers, 1989, 195).

## From 'cultural pollution' to 'cultural renaissance'

The Balinese doctrine of Cultural Tourism was elaborated and propagated throughout the 1970s by means of a series of surveys and seminars dealing with the development of tourism and its consequences on Balinese society and culture.

In 1972, the Udayana University launched a research programme in order to assess the 'sociocultural impact' (*dampak sosial budaya*) of tourism. Six reports were published between 1973 and 1978, whose results reveal not so much the actual implications of tourism for the Balinese as their perception generally shared among the intelligentsia.[26] It emerges from these surveys that Cultural Tourism amounts for the Balinese to a trade-off between cultural values and economic values. Indeed, even though the authors of the reports do not actually proceed to a formal cost-benefit analysis, the balance sheet of their research plainly shows that, by and large, they consider the economic impact as *positive*, whereas the cultural impact is on the whole deemed *negative*.

How could the Balinese acquire economic values without losing their cultural values, in other words: *how could they maximise the economic benefits of tourism while minimising its cultural costs?* Such was the issue discussed at no less than five seminars held between 1977 and 1979, some convened by the Directorate General of Tourism alone, others jointly with the Directorate General of Culture.

It should come as no surprise that spokesmen of the Directorate General of Culture would tend to stress the cultural costs of tourism, calling for measures to preserve the integrity of Balinese cultural values, while spokesmen of the Directorate General of Tourism would be more inclined to laying emphasis upon the economic benefits of tourism and would insist on boosting its development. Accordingly it is tempting to regard these seminars as the scene of a confrontation between the advocates of culture and the partisans of tourism. However, such an interpretation would be mistaken, as it would fail to register the basic agreement underlying the doctrine of Cultural

Tourism, that is, the simultaneous recognition of the necessity both to develop tourism and to preserve Balinese culture and, above all, the claim that these objectives are compatible.

This is clearly illustrated by the title of the seminars jointly organised by the Directorate General of Culture and the Directorate General of Tourism – 'Promotion of Culture and Development of Tourism' (*Pembinaan Kebudayaan dan Pengembangan Kepariwisataan*). From the proceedings of these seminars, it emerges that the solution of Cultural Tourism consists in promoting culture and tourism simultaneously, so as to ensure that the development of tourism results in a reciprocal development of culture. Consequently, in order to make sure that the interests of culture do concur with those of tourism, the cultural and the tourist policies should be coordinated by a supervising institutional body. This was rendered effective in 1979, by the signing of an agreement between the Director-General of Culture and the Director-General of Tourism, resulting in the creation of a Commission of Cooperation for the Promotion and Development of Cultural Tourism (*Komisi Kerjasama Pembinaan dan Pengembangan Wisata Budaya*). The objectives of this commission were defined as follows: 'To increase and extend the use of cultural objects for the development of tourism, and to use the proceeds of tourism development for the promotion and the development of culture' (Proyek Sasana Budaya Jakarta, 1979, 6).

Thus it is that, in less than a decade, between 1971 and 1979, the doctrine of Cultural Tourism succeeded in merging the 'promotion of culture' with the 'development of tourism', to the point of entrusting the fate of Balinese culture to the interested care of the tourist industry. By the same token, it managed to reconcile the interests of their respective spokesmen. For this to happen though, the opposition between tourism and culture – which had given rise to the doctrine of Cultural Tourism in the first place – had to be denied.

Since the agreement defining the respective roles of culture and tourism has been signed, the enthusiasm initially aroused in Bali by the motto of Cultural Tourism has waned, while the surveys and seminars on tourism have been few and far between. Not that the concern for tourism among the Balinese has diminished, far from it, but tourism has become part of their cultural landscape. In fact, the Balinese nowadays appear more interested in making the most of their culture in the interest of tourism rather than attempting to assess the impact of tourism on their culture.[27] And for seemingly good reason. The fears initially raised by the coming of tourists have given way to a public expression of satisfaction. Indeed, the reversal of opinion regarding the consequences attributed to tourism is spectacular: formerly accused of being a cause of 'cultural pollution', tourism is now extolled as an agent of the 'cultural renaissance' (*renaissance kultural*) of Bali. As for justification to back this favourable reappraisal of tourism, one finds continually asserted in the media that tourist money has revived the Balinese interest in their artistic traditions, while the admiration of foreign visitors for their culture has reinforced the Balinese sense of identity. So much so that by patronising Balinese culture tourism is said to have contributed to its preservation and even to its revitalisation, to the extent that it has turned it into a source of both profit and pride for the Balinese.

Such is the present-day official position on Bali, after having been upheld by the Governor appointed in 1978 by President Suharto as a replacement for the Javanese Colonel who had been imposed on the Balinese a decade earlier to restore Jakarta's control over the island after the turmoil which had marked the establishment of the New Order. The new Governor accumulated all the required credentials to assert his authority – both among the Balinese and *vis-à-vis* the central government: he was a Balinese, a *Brahmana* as well as a Professor Doctor, a recognised expert on Balinese religion and culture, he had been the Head of Udayana University in Bali before becoming the Director-General of Culture in Jakarta and, last but not least, he was a protégé of President Suharto. For the Balinese, concerned by the growing Javanese influence on their island, the appointment of a Balinese Governor was perceived as a sign of national reconciliation as well as the recognition of their cultural identity on the part of the Indonesian government. The concern manifest until then in Bali has been transformed into self-assurance, the former defensive attitude of the Balinese becoming self-assertive.

If one relies thus on the declarations of the Balinese authorities, one might surmise that, after an initial period of adjustment during which the rapid spread of tourists on the island would naturally arouse legitimate fears, Cultural Tourism has achieved its mission successfully. Yet, before rejoicing with the Balinese, one should ascertain the evidence presented as proof of this alleged 'renaissance' of Balinese culture.

## BALINESE CULTURE AS 'SENI BUDAYA'

From the fear of 'cultural pollution' to the claim of 'cultural renaissance', what is meant by 'Balinese culture' has undergone a significant shift. Whereas it was previously a matter of 'cultural values' (*nilai budaya*) it has become mostly a question of 'cultural arts' (*seni budaya*). When tourism was charged with 'polluting' Balinese culture, what was at stake was the profanation of temples and the desecration of religious ceremonies, the monetisation of social relations and the weakening of communal solidarity, as well as the slackening of moral standards seen to result from the pervading mercantilism. Now, whether they denounce the risk of commercialisation incurred by their culture or praise the renewed creativity of the artists, the Balinese appear mainly concerned by what can be marketed and staged for the tourists. Accordingly, 'culture' is not understood as the anthropologists' broadly defined conception of 'the total range of activities and ideas of a group of people with shared traditions', but is narrowed down to those aspects of culture that are subject to aesthetic appreciation, namely artistic expressions. And this indeed is precisely what the Balinese authorities have in mind when they talk of 'cultural renaissance', that is, what they call 'cultural arts' (*seni budaya*), in accordance with the slogan devised by the Directorate General of Tourism: 'tourism preserves the nation's cultural arts' (*kepariwisataan melestarikan seni budaya bangsa*).

Nowhere is this conception of Balinese culture as *seni budaya* so clearly illustrated as in the 'Bali Arts Festival' (*Pesta Kesenian Bali*), which was one of the very first initiatives taken by the new Governor. Launched in June 1979 at the recently opened Arts Centre (*Werdi Budaya*) of Denpasar (another creation of the Governor, when he was Director-General of Culture), this month-long annual manifestation has since its inception been regarded by the Balinese authorities as the best evidence of the island's cultural renaissance. Thus, one could read in a booklet issued in 1981 by the Bali Government Tourist Office to present both the Arts Centre and the Arts Festival:

> A popular misconception is that Balinese Dance and Drama has lost much of its lustre: that gamelans are rusting in their pavilions and dancers leaving the stage for a life on the juice blender. The truth is that Bali is undergoing a cultural renaissance with bigger and brighter temple festivals, revived art forms and more orchestras than ever before.
>
> (Wijaya, Pemayun and Raka, 1981, 1)

The Arts Festival is a perfect illustration of what Cultural Tourism is about, as it was conceived from the start by the Governor as a means of cultural promotion while at the same time furthering the development of tourism on the island. Thus, among the slogans heralding its opening, one could read: 'Via the Bali Arts Festival we build up Cultural Tourism' (*Melalui Pesta Kesenian Bali kita tingkatkan Pariwisata Budaya*). Yet, it would be mistaken to consider this event primarily as a tourist attraction, as over the years it has proved so popular with the Balinese that they make up nowadays the major part of its public.[28] Thoroughly publicised by the regional as well as by the national media, the Festival is first and foremost a showcase where the Balinese celebrate their culture on a grand scale.

The Arts Festival provides an opportunity for the regional government to maintain the deeply rooted tradition of patronising the arts, particularly the performing arts. For example, among the various stage performances exhibited each year at the Festival, the star attraction – and the one provided with the largest budget – is indisputably the series of dance-dramas called *sendratari*, which are presented on weekends at the large outdoor *Ardha Candra* theatre, reputed to accommodate 6,000 spectators.[29] As a rule, the *sendratari* are created by teachers and students belonging to the Conservatory of Music as well as to the Academy of Dance.[30] In some respects, these institutions have taken over the role formerly exerted by the courts – the creation of styles and the establishment of norms for their execution, the training of dancers and musicians, and the organising and financing of performances. With the difference, which is crucial, that contrary to the courts, always anxious to maintain their own distinctive style, the regional government is deliberately centralising, homogenising and standardising the Balinese performing arts.

The same could be said as well about the plastic arts and, for that matter, about all forms of cultural expression administered by the Ministry of Education and Culture (*Departemen Pendidikan dan Kebudayaan*, known as *Dep Dik Bud*), through its Directorate General of Culture (*Direktorat Jenderal Kebudayaan*). Indeed, one could contend with good reason that Balinese culture, as it is celebrated by the Arts Festival, concerns everything that falls within the competence of the *Dep Dik Bud* – in Indonesia, 'culture' (*kebudayaan*) is what the *Direktorat Jenderal Kebudayaan* says it is.

## BALINESE CULTURE AS REGIONAL CULTURE 'KEBUDAYAAN DAERAH'

If the culture presented as evidence of the 'cultural renaissance' of Bali turns out in fact to be mostly *seni budaya*, at least one could surmise that the Bali Arts Festival is celebrating the Balinese 'cultural arts'. Well, yes of course, what else could it be?[31] Yet this assertion requires qualifying: the culture displayed at the Festival is Balinese in the sense that it is one of the 'regional cultures' (*kebudayaan daerah*) which compose Indonesia. This is to say that Balinese culture as *kebudayaan daerah* should not be identified with the Balinese as an ethnic group (*suku bangsa*) – like, say, the Dayak peoples or the Atoni – but with Bali as a province (*propinsi*) of Indonesia – like Kalimantan Tengah or Nusa Tenggara Timur. But while Dayak groups are spread over several provinces, and while the Atoni are included with other ethnic groups in one province, the situation is peculiar in the case of Bali, whose name refers simultaneously to an island, a province and an ethnic group.[32]

Now, as one *kebudayaan daerah* among others, Balinese culture is considered not for what it means to the Balinese people but for what it can contribute to the Indonesian 'national culture' (*kebudayaan nasional*). Regional cultures are seen as a 'resource' (*sumber*), providing 'cultural elements' (*unsur-unsur kebudayaan*) to the development of the Indonesian national culture in the making, just as the participants in these cultures are Indonesians in the making. These cultural elements – regarded as the 'peaks' of each regional culture (*puncak-puncak budaya yang ada di daerah-daerah*) – are expected to provide 'nuances of colour' (*aneka warna*) to the national culture.[33] This conception of Indonesian culture(s), inscribed into the national motto 'Unity in Diversity' (*Bhinneka Tunggal Ika*), is best exemplified in such creations as the 'Beautiful Indonesia in Miniature Park' (*Taman Mini Indonesia Indah*), an outdoor museum erected in Jakarta in the early 1970s, where each of the twenty-seven provinces is represented by a 'traditional house' (*rumah adat*). The point here is that the locus of 'tradition' has become the province, in effect creating a provincial *adat*.

As far as Bali is directly concerned, I shall briefly mention two examples which I find relevant for the present discussion. In 1983 – the year when the end of the oil bonanza started forcing the government to give international tourism a push – the Minister of Foreign Affairs proposed the idea of 'Cultural Diplomacy' (*Diplomasi Kebudayaan*). The aim was to bank on the country's cultural riches in order to promote the image of Indonesia abroad as a 'nation of high culture' (*bangsa yang berkebudayaan tinggi*). Given its prestigious reputation, the province of Bali was particularly requested to contribute its 'cultural peaks' to represent Indonesian culture to the world. Accordingly, the cultural shows of Balinese dance regularly sent on tours were regarded as 'artistic missions' (*misi kesenian*), expected to further international tourism in Indonesia while at the same time promoting

Indonesia's cultural image. In this respect, the recognised 'peaks' of Balinese culture are supposed to 'reflect' (*mencerminkan*) simultaneously the identity of Bali (*identitas kedaerahan*) and the identity of Indonesia (*identitas keindonesiaan*). Thus, Cultural Diplomacy aims not only at the outside world, invited to admire the 'cultural peaks' of Indonesia, but also at the Indonesians, asked to identify with the accepted cultural manifestations of their nation's various regions.[34]

In 1984, within the framework of the Fourth Five-Year Development Plan, was launched the 'Project for the Research and Investigation of the Cultures of the Indonesian Archipelago' (*Proyek Penelitian dan Pengkajian Kebudayaan Nusantara*). The Balinese culture was one of the five 'regional cultures' to be selected, along with the Javanese, Sundanese, Malay and Bugis cultures. At the official inauguration of the so-called *Proyek Baliologi*, held at the Arts Centre of Denpasar, the Minister of Education and Culture declared that the Balinese cultural values should be 'preserved' (*dilestarikan*) and 'developed' (*dikembangkan*) in order to 'support' (*menunjang*) the national culture, while reminding the Balinese people that they should beware of the pitfalls of 'ethnicism' (*sukuisme*) as well as of 'provincialism' (*provinsialisme*). Accordingly, he called upon the experts on Balinese culture – first of all, the Balinese themselves, but also their colleagues from the outside – to select among the available Balinese cultural traditions the 'peaks' worthy of being 'raised' (*ditingkatkan*) to become integrated into the cultural heritage of Indonesia.[35]

Thus, the conception of Balinese culture as *kebudayaan daerah* implies its decomposition into discrete cultural elements, to be sieved through the filter of the national ideology and sorted out: those deemed appropriate to contribute to the development of the *kebudayaan nasional* should be salvaged and promoted, whereas those deemed too primitive or emphasising local ethnic identity should be eradicated. As an example of Balinese cultural element deserving to be elected as fully Indonesian, the Minister of Education and Culture mentioned the *subak* (the customary irrigation society), while conversely rejecting the *tajen* (the customary cockfights) as unworthy of the national culture.

## TOURISTIFICATION AND INDONESIANISATION

Even though one should beware of endorsing a view of ethnic cultures as susceptible to being instrumentally manipulated outright by the government, one notices that 'Balinese culture' is placed in a similar position with respect both to tourism and to Indonesia: that is, as a 'resource', whose function is to contribute with its 'cultural peaks' to the development of international tourism in Indonesia as well as to the development of the Indonesian national culture. For this to be feasible, though, Balinese culture had to be deprived of its anthropological singularity, in order to become commensurable to the other regional cultures of Indonesia, as well as to the other tourist destinations with which it is in competition.[36] The touristification of Bali and its Indonesianisation combine their implications to classify Balinese culture within a set where it becomes an item among others. In this respect, the locus of diversity between regional cultures as well as between tourist destinations tends to be merely aesthetic.

## NOTES

1 This chapter is based on observations gathered during numerous trips to Bali since 1974, and more precisely on research undertaken in the island during 1981 and 1982. The field work was accomplished under the auspices of the *Lembaga Ilmu Pengetahuan Indonesia* and benefited from the institutional patronage of Prof. Dr I Gusti Ngurah Bagus, Head of the Department of Anthropology at the Universitas Udayana. I would like to thank Kunang Helmi and Vivienne Roberts for their assistance in conveying my French thoughts in English.

2 For examples of the first opinion, see Lansing, 1974; McKean, 1973; McTaggart, 1980; Maurer, 1979; Noronha, 1979a. For the second one, see Francillon, 1989; Hanna, 1972; Maurer and Zeigler, 1988; Turnbull, 1982.

3 This interpretation is not unlike that of Robert Wood, who writes of 'a billiard ball model, in which a moving object (tourism) acts upon an inert one (culture)' (1980, 565). On the question of 'the sociocultural impact of tourism' and its implications, see Picard, 1979 and 1987.

4 Of course, this somewhat blunt statement does not do justice to the various authors mentioned above, especially to McKean, whose work played a pioneering role in the study of tourism in Bali. I have dealt at some length with McKean's thesis in Picard, forthcoming.

5 The reader should note that these terms are not Balinese but Indonesian. Indeed, the Balinese language does not have a word for 'culture', or for 'art' either. What is more, in Indonesian, *agama* officially defines 'religion', considered to be universal and monotheistic, whereas *adat* applies to 'tradition' understood in the sense of the customary order handed down from the ancestors and thus specific to a particular ethnic group. The problem is that in Balinese not only do these terms originally bear a markedly different meaning, but even more so, their respective semantic fields overlap to a considerable extent. Thus, the same process which compelled the Balinese to externalize their culture resulted in dispossessing them of their own words.

6 For a Western view of the Dutch conquest of Bali, see Hanna, 1976, and for a Balinese view, Agung, 1989. Baum, 1986 provides a romantic approach of the *puputan*.

7 This is but an over-simplification of a highly complex and poorly documented history. For a survey of the Dutch colonial policy on Bali, see Schulte Nordholt, 1986. On *Balisering*, see te Flierhaar, 1941.

8 On the Official Tourist Bureau, see *Picturesque Dutch East Indies*, 1925.

9 The Tourist Bureau published its first guide book to Bali in 1914. See Official Tourist Bureau, 1914.

10 See for example Covarrubias, 1937; Gorer, 1936; Krause, 1920; Powell, 1930; Yates, 1933; De Zoete and Spies, 1938, etc. On the creation of the image of Bali as a tourist paradise, see Boon, 1977, and Vickers, 1989.

11 The most famous ones were of course Margaret Mead and Gregory Bateson. See Bateson and Mead, 1942 and the collection of articles assembled in Belo, 1970.

12 See the much commented on article by Gregory Bateson on 'the value system of a steady state' (1949).

13 This was the title of a famous brochure published by the KPM Line in 1936.

14 The title of the first book written in English on Bali, published in New York in 1930 (Powell, 1930).

15 While the rationale for justifying the launching of this tourism policy was in terms of its expected economic benefits – among which, curbing the huge national balance of payments deficit was the most pressing – one should not underestimate the political objectives of the operation. Tourism was seized upon as a means to refurbish Indonesia's international image after the troubled Sukarno years and the massacres that had followed the 30 September 1965 *coup d'état*. Political legitimacy was no less important at home than abroad, and the spectacle of thousands of businessmen and vacationists visiting Indonesia was well suited to assuaging elites and developing a clientele, while supporting the New Order's claim to have earned the confidence and respect of the world. To some extent, the way the Indonesian government used international tourism was not unlike the way it had been used earlier by the Dutch colonial government: in both instances, tourism turned out to be one of the most effective means to restore a respectability badly discredited by the turmoil that had given birth to the new regime. For a similar assessment of the politics of tourism in Marcos' Philippines, see Richter, 1989a. On the Indonesian tourism policy and its evolution, see Department of Information, 1969: Vol. 2B, Chap. VIII, 168–80, and Prajogo, 1985, 48–87.

16 On the Master Plan, see IBRD/IDA, 1974; Noronha, 1973; Pacific Consultants, 1973; SCETO, 1971.

17 Surprising as it may sound, there are no reliable figures concerning the total number of 'foreign tourists' – that is, visitors who are not Indonesian citizens, usually dubbed *wisatawan mancanegara* (abbreviated '*wisman*') nowadays, as opposed to 'domestic tourists', who are called *wisatawan nusantara* (abbreviated '*wisnu*') – visiting Bali. The only figures regularly published by the Bali Government Tourist Office (*Diparda Bali*) concern foreign tourists entering Indonesia directly via Ngurah Rai International Airport, who were reported to number 436,358 in 1989. To this figure one has to add the foreign visitors to Bali having entered Indonesia through another international airport, who are estimated as being about 60 per

cent of the direct arrivals, thus making up a total of roughly 700,000 foreign tourist arrivals to Bali in 1989. These figures do not take into account the steadily increasing numbers of domestic tourists visiting Bali. Indonesian visitors to the island were estimated by the Tourist Office at over 300,000 in 1989 – which amounts to an overall estimation of 1 million tourists to Bali in the late 1980s.

18  Despite its dubious image, more and more classified hotels have opened on Kuta Beach in the past few years, thus steadily upgrading the clientele of this resort.

19  For the former opinion, see Rodenburg, 1980, and for the latter, Gibbons and Fish, 1989.

20  Nehen *et al.*, 1990. See also Bendesa and Sukarsa, 1980; Daroesman, 1973; and Jayasuriya and Nehen, 1989, for earlier surveys on tourism and economic growth in Bali.

21  See Seminar Pariwisata Budaya, 1971. Actually, the Balinese had not waited for the publication of the Master Plan to assert their position on tourism. As early as January 1968, the Deputy Governor of Bali had organised a 'First Workshop on Tourism in Bali' (*Musyawarah Kerja Pariwisata Daerah Bali I*), at the outcome of which he declared that 'Bali should be developed on the basis of its culture, which is rooted in the religious character of the Balinese community', while calling for a tourism policy 'which would preserve and promote Balinese culture in its most authentic form so as to attract tourists' (Musyawarah Kerja, 1968, 1).

22  Far more anyway than what is actually the case. Strictly speaking, 'cultural' tourism concerns only a tiny minority of tourists, mostly those who stay in and around Ubud, who want to see Bali the way it is described in their guide book – the 'authentic' and 'unspoiled' Bali – instead of finding themselves caught in a 'tourist trap'. Even though the reputation of Ubud as a 'storehouse of the arts' (*gudang kesenian*) is largely a tourist creation, it still holds strong, and this not only among tourists but among Balinese as well. But most tourists barely venture out of their beach resort, be it Nusa Dua, Sanur or Kuta – to go shopping in Celuk, Mas or Ubud, to see Lake Batur and the famed temple at Tanah Lot, to watch a 'Barong and Kris Dance' at Batubulan or, for the luckier ones, to go see a cremation. As the authors of the Master Plan had rightly asserted, Bali is for them essentially a tropical paradise, whose cultural image confers some extra glamour to their holiday, compared, say, to Hawaii or to the Maldives. Thus, the Balinese claim that the tourists are really eager to discover the cultural wonders of their island is more an expression of wishful thinking – besides being an ideological stance of the utmost importance – than a statement of factual evidence.

23  Seminar Pariwisata Budaya, 1971, 11: 'If you want the golden eggs, don't kill the goose that lays them!'

24  During the closing ceremony of the seminar, the Governor had announced that its conclusions would be the subject of regulations, in order to permit the regional government to monitor the development of tourism on the island. In 1973–74, three decrees were issued – regulating the performance of sacred dances, the activity of guides, and the access into temples – to be followed by a 'Regional Regulation on Cultural Tourism' (*Peraturan Daerah Tingkat I Bali no. 3 tahun 1974 tentang Pariwisata Budaya*). Like

many others though, these regulations were 'statements of intention without teeth' (Noronha, 1979a, 200), in that they could not be enforced.

25  *Peraturan Pemerintah R.I. n° 24 tahun 1979 tentang Penyerahan Sebagian Urusan Pemerintahan dalam Bidang Kepariwisataan kepada Daerah Tingkat I.*

26  For a circumstantial appraisal of these reports, see Francillon, 1979.

27  The main seminar on tourism held in Bali during the 1980s is a case in point. Whereas the previous ones dealt with 'the promotion of culture and the development of tourism', the seminar organised by the regional government in 1987 focused specifically on 'the promotion and development of tourism' (Pemerintah Daerah, 1987). And the one and only paper dealing with culture, given by the Head of the Regional Service of Culture, was mostly devoted to specify what the Balinese culture should be in order to contribute more effectively to the development of tourism.

28  This is also the result of a deliberate policy, as the date of the Arts Festival – the last three weeks of June and the first two weeks of July – has been officially chosen in order to coincide with the long term holidays of school children and students in Indonesia.

29  For a presentation of the various manifestations of the festival, see the album issued by the regional government: Sudhyatmaka Sugriwa, 1991.

30  The Conservatory of Music (*Konservatori Karawitan Indonesia, KOKAR*) was founded in 1960 through the initiative of a few Balinese artists. Later on it became the High School of Music (*Sekolah Menengah Karawitan Indonesia, SMKI*), to be placed under the formal responsibility of the Ministry of Education and Culture. The Academy of Dance (*Akademi Seni Tari Indonesia, ASTI*) was created in 1967 and was integrated into the Ministry of Education and Culture in 1969. Its name has recently been changed into the College of Arts (*Sekolah Tinggi Seni Indonesia, STSI*).

31  Even though the qualification of the *sendratari*, the chief attraction of the Arts Festival, as Balinese is debatable. An acronym composed of the – Indonesian, not Balinese – words *seni* (art), *drama* (theatre), and *tari* (dance), the *sendratari* was conceived and first performed in 1961 at Prambanan in Java as an example of official state art. The idea was originally to design a spectacle suited for domestic and foreign tourists, by mixing various regional traditions into an Indonesian dance form. Inspired by the instant success of the new creation, a Balinese choreographer adapted it to the local taste to celebrate the first anniversary of the Conservatory of Music in Denpasar. The *sendratari* proved immediately popular with Balinese and tourist audiences alike, a popularity which has continued to this day, judging by the enthusiastic mobs it regularly draws to the Arts Centre. The Bali Arts Festival emphasises thus precisely an art form initially imported from Java and designed to appeal to the taste of Indonesian audiences – and which departs accordingly to a considerable extent from the traditional standards of dance and drama in Bali. For detailed information on the creation of the Balinese *sendratari* and its evolution, see de Boer, 1989; and for a critical assessment of the upheaval brought about by its advent onto the Balinese stage, see Picard, 1990, 52–56.

32  Sellato, 1990, discusses the situation with respect to Kalimantan.

33 See for example the brochure issued by the Director-General of Culture on the Cultural Policy in Indonesia (Soebadio, 1985).
34 For an illustration of the way Balinese culture is expected to contribute to Cultural Diplomacy, see Geriya, 1988.
35 See the collection of papers published under the title 'Contribution of the Balinese cultural values to the development of the national culture', in Bagus, 1986.
36 What is being said here for Bali holds true to a certain extent for other regions of Indonesia, at least since 1978, when the Directorate General of Tourism officially designated ten provinces to become 'Tourist Destinations' (*Daerah Tujuan Wisata*), while launching the slogan 'Bali Plus Nine'. In the long run, all the provinces of Indonesia should eventually become 'Tourist Destinations', and to this end they are all expected to dig up their natural and cultural resources and to promote them as tourist attractions, susceptible to define each one of them as unique and distinctive. For a similar view concerning Tanah Toraja, see Volkman, 1990.

# 5  Tourism and culture in Malaysia[1]

*Victor T. King*

## INTRODUCTION

This chapter provides a general overview of some of the relationships between tourism and culture in Malaysia. Despite the fact that tourism has developed rapidly in Malaysia during the past decade, there has been little attempt to examine sociologically some of the actual and probable consequences of tourism development for Malaysian culture and society. The exceptions are the insightful articles by such observers as Kadir Din (1982; 1989b). Generally academic studies have concentrated on the simple issue of whether tourism has negative or positive effects on local cultures. The dominant approach has been to conceive of culture as a homogeneous entity which suffers impacts from tourism. This process, in turn, produces effects evaluated as either beneficial or disadvantageous.

Evelyne Hong's well-known study (1985) is characteristic of this perspective, and an important issue which I wish to address is whether, following Hong, tourism development in Malaysia has resulted in 'cultural deterioration'. It is also one of her main propositions that the response to 'cultural corrosion, the loss of traditional pride and values and the destruction of a whole way of life' should be to preserve cultures and to redirect tourism in terms of 'local needs and priorities' (Hong, 1985, 26, 84; cf. Junaenah and Fatimah, 1989). This position is also taken by Bella Bird, in her analysis of the impact of tourism on Langkawi Island, although hers is a more balanced and detailed case study (1989).[2]

In order to examine the assertion that tourism undermines and degrades Malaysian culture, it is necessary to investigate the scale of tourist activity; the length of stay; whether the main tourist sites are dispersed or focused; the kinds of leisure activities which are available and the sorts of tourists encouraged to visit Malaysia. More importantly we have to begin by addressing the specific problem of what is meant by Malaysian culture, and how we might conceptualise 'culture' in a general sense.

An examination of Malaysian culture also requires us to consider the sorts of images which tourists, especially foreign ones, are encouraged to construct of the country and its people, or those images which serve to reinforce established views and prejudices. In this connection, I shall analyse a range of both domestic- and Western-produced tourist promotional literature using John Urry's concept of 'the tourist gaze' (Urry, 1990). As Urry says, part of the tourist experience is 'to gaze upon or view a set of different scenes, of landscapes or townscapes which are out of the ordinary' (ibid., 1). The tourist gaze is 'constructed through signs' (ibid., 3). Turner and Ash also remark that usually 'foreign cultures . . . are reduced to a few instantly recognisable characteristics' (Turner and Ash, 1975, 140). Some assessment is made of this literature as to whether it is likely to assist in encouraging greater cultural understanding between Malaysia's 'guests and hosts'.

## TOURISM AND CULTURE

We can agree with Urry that tourism is socially grounded 'imaginative pleasure-seeking' (Urry, 1990, 13) and that, following Nash, a tourist is 'a person at leisure, who also travels' (Nash, 1981, 462). But we also know that tourism is not a unitary phenomenon, and, therefore, its effects will be various. The academic literature on tourism has established the different kinds of tourism, and tourist interests, motivations, personalities and social types (e.g. Cohen, 1972; 1979a; Graburn, 1983). Certain sorts of tourists will probably be attracted to particular destinations, although some tourists will attempt to pursue and satisfy a combination of needs and objectives.

We have no shortage of categorisations and terminologies (Furnham and Bochner, 1990, 35–38). Some are simple distinctions between, for example, the 'recreationist', for whom 'the recreational activity itself is the main element', and the 'vacationist' for whom 'the journey as such constitutes the main activity of the trip' (Campbell, 1966; cited in Pearce, 1987, 7). In personality terms, we are told that there are 'psychocentrics', 'who tend to be anxious. self-inhibited, non-adventuresome and concerned with the little problems of life', and the 'allocentrics', who are 'self-confident, curious, adventurous and outgo-ing' (Plog, 1973; cited in Pearce, 1987, 15). More recently Urry has presented us with the useful ideal-types of 'mass consumption' and 'post-Fordist consumption'; he argues that there has been a discernible shift in tourism towards post-modernist concerns, with increasing importance played on 'play, pleasure and pastiche', and a move away from the undifferentiated, standardised, regulated kinds of tourism exemplified by the British working-class holiday camps and seaside resorts.

For the purpose of understanding the ways in which Malaysia has been promoted as a tourist destination, I can see some value in all the above discriminations. Yet, from the available literature, we do not really know much about tourist motivations and objectives with regard to Malaysia. What we do know is what Malaysia promotes and the different kinds of tourist 'assets' on which visitors are encouraged to gaze. For this reason, I have relied on Valene Smith's general categorisation of types of tourism (Smith, 1978, 2–3), and, although I would not agree fully with some of her characterisations, I think she does provide a useful guide for considering what Malaysia offers to different sorts of tourist.

First, there is 'ethnic tourism', with its concern for the 'quaint customs of indigenous and often exotic peoples' (ibid., 2). Wood more accurately defines the focus of interest of 'ethnic tourism' as 'the cultural practices which define a unique ethnicity' (Wood, 1984, 361). One can see this kind of tourist activity in relation to some of the native populations of East Malaysia, such as the Ibans of Sarawak. But, at the moment, tourism in Malaysia is not significantly directed towards 'off-the-beaten track' holidays among 'exotic' tribal peoples.

Second, 'cultural tourism' is characterised by the tourists' generalised desire for local colour, festivals and costumes. This kind of tourism, although it overlaps with ethnic tourism, is especially prominent in Malaysia. The Malaysian Tourist Development Corporation (TDC), in its advertising campaign for Visit Malaysia Year 1990, leaves us in no doubt about the importance it attaches to culture in Malaysian tourism.

> Malaysia has a wonderful *pot-pourri* of different races comprising three main groups – Malays, Chinese and Indians – in Peninsular Malaysia, and numerous indigenous groups . . . in Sabah and Sarawak . . . Visitors from all over the world can . . . expect to always feel at home and welcome in this vital, colourful and kaleidoscopic nation of ours.
>
> (TDC, 1990a, 1)

The third category is 'historical tourism', for the education-oriented visitor who wishes to see objects – buildings, architecture and museum collections – rather than people and to hear about and imagine the past. Malaysia's promotion of Melaka, in particular, and some of the sites of Kuala Lumpur and Penang, dwells on this aspect of the country's tourism resources. In this regard the colonial experience, for example, is repackaged as 'heritage' and incorporated into a generalised notion of Malaysian culture.[3]

Fourth, there is 'environmental tourism' which, as Smith notes, is often ancillary to ethnic tourism. In Malaysia the attractions of nature are specifically promoted in the East Malaysian territories – the tropical rainforest and the national parks such as Kinabalu in Sabah, and Niah and Mulu in Sarawak. The Malaysian TDC advertises East Malaysia as an 'adventureland'. 'Green holidays' are also a feature of certain parts of Peninsular Malaysia: Taman Negara and the east coast states are cases in point. Again the Malaysian promotional literature for 1990 draws our attention to:

> a naturalist's paradise with more butterflies than you can find anywhere else on earth . . . more orchids . . . more unique events in nature like the giant leatherback turtles arriving each year to lay their eggs on one of the world's most beautiful beaches.
>
> (TDC, 1990b, 2)

Finally, there is 'recreational tourism' – that which is preoccupied with sun, sand and sea. The TDC again remarks 'What Malaysia has in abundance are beautiful, empty beaches' (ibid., 33). In one of the Corporation's brochures 'recreation' goes with 'relaxation', and the same ideas were promoted in other earlier official images of Malaysia as a 'vacationland'.

In true Urryan post-modernist spirit, Malaysia's recent promotional campaigns offer diverse attractions, moving away from the earlier concentration on urban-based and beach tourism (Malaysian Government, *Mid-Term Review of the Fifth Malaysia Plan* 1989, 266). In this respect two symbolic categories much beloved by structuralist anthropologists are emphasised: nature and culture. Indeed, the juxtaposition and opposition between the wild or untamed and the civilised are quite deliberately constructed, although much more subtly in the Malaysian official literature than in the guides and brochures for Western audiences. Furthermore, in Malaysian-based publications, there seems to be a search for harmonious relations and mediation between nature and culture. This is not so much the case in the Western materials.

The Postguide edition on Malaysia, for example, suggests that 'Visitors (to Sarawak) can experience the jungle and its inhabitants in situations almost untouched by modern civilization' (1988, 101). The

Insight Guides to Malaysia directly exploit the dangers and uncertainties of the jungle; less than a half-hour drive from Kuala Lumpur 'is wilderness without any trace of civilisation' (1989, 60) and 'there are many more dark corners of the jungle that remain totally unexplored' (ibid.,).[4] Most compelling are the frontierlands of Sarawak and Sabah. We read that 'The mystery of Borneo spun a golden thread through the history of the "civilized" world' (ibid., 255).

What is stressed then is the unknown, a world removed from the everyday experiences of the potential visitor. An article in *Time* magazine boldly proclaims that for Asia as a whole the 'primary allure . . . has always been its otherworldliness' (1989, 37), and *Silk Cut Travel, Faraway Holidays* maintains more specifically that 'Sabah is still a world apart' (1989, 72).

The main point about this variegated Malaysian tourist gaze is that only some activities are likely to have direct relevance to local culture; others may have only an indirect or partial relationship with it. There is a further complication. One of the problems in examining Malaysian culture is to discern precisely its main constituents. At one level Malaysian culture is a construct of Malaysian officialdom to serve national purposes and to assist in the promotion of tourism. What is referred to, in a unitary way, as Malaysian culture is, in fact, an *ad hoc* assemblage of beliefs and practices held by diverse populations. It is, as the tourist brochures state, a pot-pourri, a medley, with no shared dominant cultural themes. Some values have indeed been elevated to national status, but they remain the preserve of certain segments of Malaysian society; they do not form the basis of a distinctively Malaysian culture. On the contrary, there are all kinds of cultural cleavages and differences between the various ethnic groups and regions.

Of course, this variety can be an asset, and it is this very diversity which is the Malaysian cultural product. The Tourist Development Corporation tells us that the different cultures and regions are 'bonded together by a unity built on diversity and a strength built on complementarity' (TDC, 1990a, 14).[5] This sense of interconnection and harmony is expressed in different ways: 'it is not uncommon to see mosques, temples and churches sharing a common neighbourhood' (TDC, 1990b, 9). Two especially common images in the official tourist material are the variety of festivals and the wide choice of cuisine (ibid., 28). In more obviously upbeat mood the commercial tour company and airline brochures delight in diversity. Thomas Cook's *The Faraway Collection*, for example, instructs us to '(s)avour the swirl of colour, sound and sensation' (Thomas Cook, 1990, 116).

An immediate problem is that this portrayal of Malaysian culture has the potential to attract and excite, but it does depend primarily on presenting what Malaysian culture is not, in that it has no shared dominant beliefs and practices. Yet, in terms of one of my main concerns, the absence of a unified Malaysian culture and the presence of a multitude of different cultural forms suggest that these latter will react to and interrelate differently with tourism development. Again, there will be no simple answer to the question 'Does tourism distort, degrade, and destroy culture, or does it fortify, enhance and reproduce it?'

What is more, even if we dissect the obvious constituent parts of Malaysian society – Chinese, Malays, Indians, Ibans, Kadazans and so on – and assume that each ethnic grouping carries a particular culture, and therefore that each will be likely to respond to tourism in different ways, this still assumes that culture, at some level of analysis, and when attached to defined groups, is a monolithic, homogeneous, bounded entity which can be acted upon by outside forces and either strengthened or undermined. This is precisely how Hong views the problematic of tourism in Malaysia. She is concerned with 'impacts' and, specifically, 'adverse socio-cultural effects' (Hong, 1985, 26), as is Bird in her discussion of the impact of the influx of tourists on Langkawi Island society (Bird, 1989, 45–54).[6] This assumes that culture, however defined, is passive and self-reproducing. It celebrates pre- or non-European 'tradition', which, in some sense, is believed to be 'authentic' and should be preserved.

This is too simplistic. It does not recognise that what we call 'culture' may not be held or internalised to the same degree or in the same way by different individuals. In other words, culture is symbolically constituted, changed and recreated; it can be used or discarded, segmented or homogenised; it is dynamic and adaptive (cf. Wood, 1980); it is an *ad hoc* assemblage of sets of practices, objects, meanings and symbols, although some elements may be more coherently interrelated than others. Above all it is not the passive plaything of Turner's and Ash's 'golden hordes' (Turner and Ash, 1975). Tourism does not necessarily result in 'obscene obsequiousness and cultural inferiority' on the part of the hosts (Hong, 1985, 60).

If we accept that the definitions of both tourism and culture are problematical, then any analysis of the relations between them is equally problematical. I maintain that the interrelations between tourism and culture are complex; they are not generalisable and they have to be demonstrated in given cases. It is also difficult to separate out the effects of tourism from other processes and events which are

part of such agencies of contact as business and commerce, educational exchange and the mass media (Hofmann, 1979, 36; Jafari, 1986,
129–37; Kadir Din, 1982, 473; Nash, 1981, 466). Furthermore, the
assumption that there is something authentically 'traditional', untouched by the outside world, which should be preserved by promoting
alternative kinds of appropriate tourism, is mistaken (cf. Cohen,
1988a, 371–86). Malaysian communities, however remote, have been
brought into relationship, to varying degrees, with wider economic,
political and cultural systems before, during and after the European
colonial period; some outside cultural influences, including those from
the West, have been adopted and reproduced in Malaysian cultures.
What is referred to as 'traditional' in Malaysian cultures is a symbolic
attribution; it is that which has been assigned and signified as
authentically and essentially long-established, as something which is
bound up historically with given ethnic identities.

## THE CONTEXT OF MALAYSIAN TOURISM

I shall sketch out the main parameters of the relationship between
tourism and culture to demonstrate that Hong's pessimistic appraisal
needs some qualification. This exercise will hopefully provide a
research agenda for future students of tourism development in
Malaysia.

The first point to address is the extent or scale of tourism in
Malaysia. In comparison with some other parts of South-East Asia,
Malaysian tourism is much less developed, and there is a lower level of
awareness of it. The country began seriously to promote its tourist
resources much later than Singapore, Thailand and Indonesian Bali.
The Malaysian Tourist Development Corporation was established
only in 1972. Major promotions had to wait until the late 1970s, and a
separate Ministry of Culture and Tourism was created as recently as
1987, with the successful Fascinating Malaysia promotion commenc-
ing in 1988.[7]

In 1963 just under 27,000 tourists were recorded for Malaysia, in
1970, 76,000, and by 1976 there were still only approximately 1.2
million tourist arrivals (Hofmann, 1979, 17–18; Robinson, 1976, 430;
Wood, 1979, 276). By 1980 it had reached the 2.25 million mark, in
1985, 2.9 million, and from 1988, following the establishment of the
new Ministry, fairly strong growth to 3.67 million in 1989 (Economist
Intelligence Unit (EIU), 1990, 71). As a result of Visit Malaysia Year in
1990, estimated visitors were set at 4.02 million, but this figure has
been greatly exceeded; it increased to 7.4 million arrivals (*Malaysia*

*Tourism News*, 1991). Therefore, during the 1970s and much of the 1980s, Malaysia was not inundated by tourists, nor, until recently, has tourism contributed much to the country's GNP. As Suhaini has said '(t)ourism, as an industry, is still a relatively novel idea to Malaysia' (Suhaini, 1990, 31). An interesting adjunct to this is that Malaysia should be in a potentially more favourable position to avoid some of the mistakes of other countries where the effects of tourism are more advanced.

Second, it is misleading to assume that Malaysia at present is in danger of losing indigenous cultural forms under the influence of Western tourist values. Malaysian tourism is not primarily, in Turner's and Ash's general characterisation of contemporary tourism, 'an invasion outwards from the highly developed metropolitan centres into the "uncivilised" peripheries' (Turner and Ash, 1975, 129). About 75 per cent of the tourist traffic into Malaysia comes from neighbouring ASEAN countries, and this has been a relatively constant feature of Malaysian tourism during the last two decades (Wood, 1984, 357–58; *Malaysia Tourism News*, 1991). In other words, most visitors share cultural and ethnic traits with segments of Malaysia's population. The bulk of arrivals in 1989, about 62 per cent, came from Singapore, with 7 per cent from Thailand, and smaller numbers from Brunei, Indonesia and the Philippines (EIU, 1990, 71–72; Sub-committee on Tourism (SCOT), 1990, 51). If we include other non-Malaysian Asian populations from further afield, which at least share certain values and practices in common with some Malaysians, we have about another 4 per cent (Hong Kong, Taiwan and India).

Of the obviously foreign arrivals about 4.8 per cent (just under 190,000 visitors) came from Japan, and their 'cultural threat', if that is the right concept, should not be overestimated. As Suhaini has said '(a)s reserved as his Malaysian counterpart, the Japanese tourist is the least likely to cause offence here' (Suhaini, 1990, 32). Finally, Westerners comprised only about 9 per cent of tourists to Malaysia in 1989. These were mainly from three countries – the United Kingdom (120,000), Australia (109,000) and the USA (66,000) – with smaller numbers from West Germany, France and New Zealand (EIU, 1990, 72–73).

Third, Malaysia is a large country with a range of tourist attractions. The tourist infrastructure, though improving, is still not comprehensive. There is, for example, a shortage of well-developed multicentre packages. Visitors therefore tend to focus on only a few destinations. Over 90 per cent of the tourists go to Peninsular Malaysia. Not many find their way to Sarawak and Sabah.

One of the earliest general surveys of tourism in Malaysia, although it was confined to the Peninsula and concentrated mainly on economic issues, was that by Norbert Hofmann (1979). In the late 1970s Hofmann indicated that

> (t)he main tourist resorts are the two islands of Penang and Langkawi, the West Coast towns of Kuala Lumpur, Ipoh, Melaka and Port Dickson, the hill resorts (Genting Highlands, Maxwell Hill, Fraser's Hill), the East Coast states (especially the coastal areas of North Pahang, Trengganu and Kelantan), and finally the newly developed area of Southeast Johor, Desaru.
>
> (Hofmann, 1979, 2–3).

Of these the west coast centres of Kuala Lumpur, Melaka (Malacca) and the hill resorts were particularly important, and, for foreign tourism, Penang (Kadir Din, 1982, 458–59).

If we examine British tourist brochures for 1990–91, we find that the main tourist attractions are still Penang, Kuala Lumpur and Melaka, and to some extent the hill resorts. Increasing attention, however, is being paid to east coast beach holidays at Kuantan, Cherating, Tanjung Jara, Tioman and, along with Langkawi on the west coast, Pangkor Island. The Borneo states of Sarawak and Sabah received only about 280,000 foreign visitors in 1989 and these too are highly concentrated; they focus on Kuching and its environs, the national parks of Niah and Mulu, the Kota Kinabalu region and the nearby Kinabalu National Park. The developed and cosmopolitan urban centres of the west coast, and especially Penang and Kuala Lumpur, take the lion's share of tourism (EIU, 1990, 74). Singaporeans, the main market for Malaysian tourism, also have specific interests, which are not so much cultural (Wood, 1984, 358); they go to Malaysia mainly 'for shopping trips, to visit friends or relations, to eat out or just to fill up their car tanks with Malaysia's lower priced petrol' (ibid., 71). Aside from Kuala Lumpur, Penang, Melaka and other west coast towns, and of course Johor, there is a significant level of Singaporean attention to the Genting Highlands for sports, cool air and gambling.

Finally, foreign visitors to Malaysia are generally short stay. Malaysia is frequently marketed as one element of a wider 'tourist circuit', including the neighbouring ASEAN countries of Thailand, Singapore and Indonesia. Many tourists do not spend a full holiday there, but only part of it, in a package which includes other destinations. The average stay is four to five nights, and is mainly urban-based (SCOT, 1990, 39). Western tourists commonly go on organised excursions, or to the beach and national parks; they rely on tour guides and move mainly in their own social and cultural circles. The beach resort enclaves, especially on the west and east coast islands, and in such places as Club Mediterranee at Cherating, usually involve only superficial contact with local communities, if indeed there is any noticeable contact at all (cf. Furnham and Bochner, 1990, 149; Wood, 1984, 359). Many of the tourists who go to these destinations are 'passive holidaymakers' (Hofmann, 1979, 7); they do not become socially and culturally involved. Suhaini suggests that 'by and large, the ordinary Malaysian has little contact with . . . the much advertised tourist' (Suhaini, 1990, 33).[8] This is not to say that the effects of tourism are therefore not felt outside the main resorts; they obviously are (cf. Wood, 1980, 569).[9] But we need to be careful in evaluating effects which, in the Malaysian case, would appear to be particularly directed and focused.

The more active kinds of ethnic tourism are again only a small part of Malaysian interests, although this is growing with the emergence of small tour companies offering specialist adventures. There has also been only a limited development of various 'village-stay' holidays on the east coast, where visitors get a flavour of rural life by staying in local communities (Kadir Din, 1982, 466).

An examination of the scale and distribution of tourism, the kinds of tourists visiting Malaysia and their origins and ethnic identities, leads me to suppose that there are several significant limitations to cultural contacts and exchanges. Therefore, the overall perception or suspicion of cultural degradation should require some qualification.

## MALAYSIAN CULTURE AND MODES OF REPRESENTATION

I intend to look now at the depiction of Malaysian culture in the tourism literature. In comparison with the brochures of commercial tour companies and some of the popular non-Malaysian tourist guides, the recent Malaysian official publications are usually sober, informative and straightforward expressions of what Malaysia has to offer. Of course, the TDC's *Visit Malaysia Year 1990 Consumer Brochure* (1990a) and *Malaysia Travel Planner* (1990b) dwell on the theme of exoticism. Malaysia is 'fascinating' and 'vibrantly unique'; it is a 'tropical wonderland', with 'diversity and colour'. But the promotion of culture, at least in this medium, is rather uncontroversial and neutral. I shall suggest a few reasons for this. The fact that Islam is the national religion, and that Malaysia has to be conscious of ethnic divisions and sensibilities, lead to a more cautious and circumspect treatment of culture. Nevertheless, the Malaysian government is in no doubt about its importance for tourism: the *Mid-Term Review of the Fifth Malaysia Plan* remarks on the establishment of the Ministry of Culture and Tourism that '(o)f paramount importance was the propagation of Malaysian culture as a touristic asset' (Malaysian Government, 1989, 262). This 'asset' is seen as constituting an important market niche.

With the globalisation of tourism each country and region tries to establish its own place in the international tourist market. However, Malaysia does not have its eye on only the overseas visitor. The creation of a Ministry combining both tourism and culture has a national purpose as well. Its task is to engender a local awareness of cultural matters and national identity and heritage, and to enhance national pride and commitments. It is designed as much to encourage domestic tourism because '(d)omestic visitors account for more than 8 mn (million), or over half, of all hotel bednights' (EIU, 1990, 69). Malaysia has to be especially careful in its domestic characterisation of its diverse ethnic groups and their cultures, and, in a multi-ethnic society, in which the government conceives of a national culture, and in which Islam plays a significant part, the tendency is to emphasise relatively uncontentious cultural elements (Collins, 1990). As Wood says generally of the role of the state in marketing 'cultural meanings', the choice of which parts of a country's cultural heritage to develop for tourism constitutes a statement about national identity which is conveyed to both tourists and locals' (Wood, 1984, 365). The official promotion of culture for tourism is therefore interesting as much as for what is left out as for what is included, and for what is defined as 'traditional' and 'authentic'. We should also bear in mind that Malaysia is in competition, as well as in cooperation, with neighbouring Singapore and Thailand. Clearly Malaysia has avoided the brash, racy image of Thailand with its nightlife. It also emphasises its more 'authentic' cultures, its heritage, rural life and natural beauty in contrast to Singapore. The modern, urban image of Singapore is contrasted with the judicious blend of the old and the new, and culture and nature in Malaysia.

Therefore, in cultural terms, Malaysia dwells on its diversity of cuisine and festivals, its handicrafts, its traditions and heritage, and the charm, friendliness, hospitality and warmth of its population. Major festivals from each of the main ethnic groups are selected; each cuisine is described. Perhaps most importantly Islam is distanced in official promotions (Kadir Din, 1989a, 557–58). The only aspects of the religion which are given attention are mosques, the festivals, royal towns and palaces of the Sultans, and Hari Raya Puasa, the ceremony to mark the end of Ramadan (TDC, 1990b, 36; cf. Bird, 1989, 4–5). In the more detailed tourist brochures covering each state, it is noticeable how much information is provided on the historical dimensions of Islam. In short, it is not a major object of tourism promotion, except in a very narrow sense (cf. Hofmann, 1979, 38ff). The state of Perak is 'rich in history, folklore and heritage' (TDC, 1989b, 2); Perlis is '(u)nblemished, wholesome, serene' (TDC, 1990a, 2); Kelantan '(t)o many, . . . is the cradle of Malay culture' (ibid., 74), but it has little to do with Islam; Malay culture is mainly about non-Islamic sports, pastimes and traditional crafts and skills: martial arts (*silat*), kite-flying, top-spinning, metal-smithing, boat-building, shadow theatre, weaving, and dance and music.

This promotion of culture presents a distinctly neutral imagery, as well as distancing Islam; its strength depends on diversity and colour. On the other hand, the mystery, allure and seduction is confined very much to Malaysia's natural resources: beaches, islands and forests.[10] The imagery and atmosphere encapsulated in Turner's and Ash's 'lotus-eating' – 'a permanent state of blissful drowsiness' (Turner and Ash, 1975, 151), associated with forbidden fruit and the celebration of the natural and primitive   is expressed in the TDC's characterisation of Malaysia's islands and beaches. Great play is made of the legend of Mahsuri in promoting Langkawi Island, which is 'steeped in history, its past full of wronged maidens and lovelorn princes' (TDC, 1990a, 61). A whole series of ideas are brought together here: romance, love, tragedy, myth and mystery.

Nevertheless, the official literature does find it difficult to resist the rural context of much of Malay culture, which also parallels some of the stereotypes in the commercial brochures. Malays, on the east coast especially, live in 'quaint *kampongs*', and in 'a fishing community culture that is truly idyllic' (ibid., 15). There is, in this characterisation, an attempt to create a harmonious combination of nature and culture, although in its development programmes, the Malaysian government is very much concerned with rural modernisation and the transformation of Malay communities into 'modern' ones.

Turning to the brochures and guides for Western audiences, most of these demonstrate the use of a pervasive structural principle in organising the 'signs' which depict 'Malaysianess'. Dualistic imagery abounds, as we have seen in the preoccupation with nature and culture. There are, for example, the oppositions between the exotic and the familiar, East and West, tradition and modernity, urban and rural, mediated by the notion of a country 'in transition'. It is seen most vividly in the descriptions of Kuala Lumpur and Penang, and expressed in clothes, music, dance and architecture. Kuala Lumpur presents 'a blend of Eastern culture with a mix of Western influence' (*Quantas Jetabout*, 1991, 6); it 'rocks to electric guitars and sways to ancient flutes' (Insight Guides, 1989, 15).

Unfortunately this Western imagery confirms the worst prejudices of the colonial literature on Malaya and Borneo; and in Peninsular Malaysia, rural Malays were invariably contrasted with commercially-minded, urban-based Chinese.[11] The imagery of the native, non-Chinese populations dwells on the contrast between tradition and modernity, and the evolutionary movement of more backward, rural people from simple life-styles to complex ones. Nowhere is this seen as vividly as in the current characterisations of tribal peoples of Borneo and the Orang Asli (Negritoes) of the Peninsula. The idea of the 'noble savage' close to nature – of the exotic, the unknown, the timeless – is deep-rooted. The Insight Guides tell us that 'Longhouse dwellers lived in the midst of a verdant environment strewn with twisting vines, capricious butterflies and luminescent insects. Like the wild life around them, they primped their bodies in natural elegance' (1989, 117). Jungles and people are 'ageless', and the overpowering images of Borneo peoples are of traditional war-dancing, bloodthirsty, belligerent headhunters, who live in longhouses and whose women are bare-breasted.[12] The *Holiday Which?* guide says 'You'll spend an interesting day among shrunken heads, blowpipes and tattooed men in sarongs, earrings and striking head dresses' (1990, 45). As one can see, despite the sense of excitement and danger, the tourist is unlikely to spend too long in this 'primitive' world. Package tours now include a trip and an overnight stay in an Iban longhouse along the Skrang river, with facilities for tourists. We are told reassuringly by *Silk Cut Travel, Faraway Holidays* that 'it is reminiscent of family camping holidays!' (1989, 73).

As for the Orang Asli, *Kuoni*, in its description of its 'excursions' through Malaysian culture (overnight stays in longhouses, a drive through a Malay *kampong*), suggests that we might even 'catch a glimpse of the aborigines who have inhabited Malaysia for 7,000 years, out on a hunting trip armed with blowpipes and poison darts' (1989, 153). The Insight Guides give us more detail of the 'Stone-age existence' of the aborigines: 'Naked save for a breech cloth, a man, dark as stained mahogany, stands with feet apart upon a crude bamboo raft which floats silently downstream' (1989, 54).

The images conveyed of rural Malays present some differences from the above. Malay life is rural, removed and quiet, but also leisurely.

Collins guide states that '(t)he Malays . . . have learnt the fine art of sparing oneself' (1989, 26), and the Insight Guides link spare time to Malay traditional skills – 'leisure nurtured . . . arts' (1989, 233). The *Which?* guide notes that '(m)uslim women . . . sit on the ground lethargically, their wares strewn around them' (*Holiday Which?*, 1990, 49), and Insight Guides remark that '(i)n between harvests and fishing seasons, men pass their free afternoons lounging in a communal open-air pavilion' (1989, 98). We learn that the *kampong* is 'another world, far from the noise and bustle that characterise the towns and cities' (Collins, 1989, 76). The stress is on lack of change, indeed sometimes resistance to change, on continuity and stability (Postguide, 1988, 31); time is unimportant – it is a 'vague concept'.

On the other hand the Chinese are always part of the bustle and hum of urban life. The impression given is one of noise and chaos, contrasted with the serenity and calm of Malay life. Although tourists can still find much that is 'traditional' in urban cultures, there is a noticeable concern with movement and change.

In this connection it was Hofmann who remarked over a decade ago that we need to encourage the provision of objective information in tourist guidebooks (Hofmann, 1979, 41). In reading many of the popular guides, as well as the commercial literature, it is obvious that some of the images promoted establish highly misleading characterisations, which are unlikely to assist in any genuine cultural understanding between foreigners and locals. This is not the case with much of the official literature, but the stereotypes of the major ethnic groups in Malaysia are, I would argue, potential barriers to effective communication. They encourage foreign superiority, a simplistic view of local cultures, and often intolerance and impatience with supposedly more backward, primitive ways of life. Bird says specifically of Langkawi that during her stay she 'noticed a remarkable lack of meaningful cultural exchange between most foreign visitors and the local people' (Bird, 1989, 51).

Having said this, we still have to get the contact between hosts and guests into proper perspective, and, as I have demonstrated, some communities and some aspects of culture are distanced from contacts with, and the potential influences of foreign tourists. By way of conclusion, let me return to the issue of encounters and exchange.

## CONTACTS BETWEEN GUESTS AND HOSTS

Most foreign tourists in Malaysia go principally to the already highly urbanised parts of the country, which are populated to a significant degree by Chinese and to some extent Indians. These Malaysian peoples have adapted and transformed their cultures in urban environments. Chinese cultural forms in Malaysia have been subject to fluid, cosmopolitan commercial situations for a considerable period of time, and it is unlikely, given the strength of Chinese cultural identity and their concern to enter into exchanges with foreigners in order to realise profit, that tourism will have any particular effect upon them, as distinct from other influences of modernisation. The same can be said for the Indian urban commercial sector.

The potentially most vulnerable cultures are those of the rural native populations. But to date much of the tourism has been concentrated elsewhere, and if foreign tourists do venture into the countryside, most do so in organised excursions, stopping briefly to gaze, buy and photograph. Cultural images of Malays and Ibans and others are often presented to them in staged performances in hotels or at special venues, deliberately separated from everyday life.

Furthermore, Islam, as a religion, is not advertised as a tourist asset, except in terms of mosques, art forms, and royal pageants and parades (cf. Bird, 1989, 4–5). Of course, unlike the Balinese religion, for example, Islam is not given to visual, active ceremonial display, and therefore does not lend itself to the sorts of image-creation which are thought to be attractive to potential visitors. Instead non-Islamic elements of Malay culture are promoted, especially from the east coast of Peninsular Malaysia.

Nevertheless, there is evidence of some tensions between foreign tourists and certain Malay communities which are accessible and on the tourist circuit (e.g. ibid., 52–54). One can also begin to discern problems emerging between the tourist promotion of Malay culture and the proscriptions of Islam. For example, recently the Kelantan government banned the staging of Malay dances, because, where they involve female performers, they raise the question of *aurat* (parts of the body which should not be exposed according to Islamic law) (*New Straits Times*, 1991b, 3). This development is perhaps not surprising, especially when tourist guides try to generate interest in Malay culture; the Insight Guides, for example, talk of 'gay rounds of flirtatious folk dances' (1989, 78). The Ministry of Culture and Tourism is said to be monitoring the possible effects on tourism of this religious ban. It is interesting that specific examples referred to by Hong of the negative impact of tourism on Malaysian culture relate especially to Islam – the general permissive atmosphere for female workers in hotels, restaurants and bars, the immodesty of uniforms and costumes, and the exposure to forbidden foods. It is this issue of Islamic proscriptions, especially for females, which is clearly a subject for debate in Malaysian tourism. Indeed, Kadir Din has already addressed a number of these issues generally, and notes that 'mass tourism as an industry characterised by hedonism, permissiveness, lavishness, servitude, foreignness, with a lack of cross-cultural understanding and communication, obviously diverges from what tourism ought to be in an Islamic framework' (Kadir Din, 1989a, 551). Yet my main point remains: these effects are still relatively localised, and Islam is not a significant object of the tourist gaze.

Briefly, if we examine longhouse tourism in East Malaysia, we again need the same qualifications concerning tourist–host contacts. Most foreign tourists are taken on arranged packages to a few specially organised and equipped 'show' longhouses, among the Ibans in the Skrang area, and Bidayuh houses near to Kuching (Kedit, 1980). The ethnic tourism industry there is still limited. Communications and tourist infrastructure are poorly developed. There is, however, evidence that the effects of tourism are gradually spreading in Malaysian Borneo as tourists go further afield in search of the 'traditional'. It has been noted that some German tourists have stopped going to the Skrang river because the communities there are not considered 'traditional' enough (Hon, 1989, 287). Yet one wonders again what this notion of 'tradition' comprises, which German visitors desire to gaze on and experience. Loose and Ramb note that the intrusive visitors to more remote longhouses do cause conflict and often place excessive demands on local people (Loose and Ramb, 1990, 325). Nevertheless, given this contact, the cultural effects on local communities are often not specified in the literature, and I am forced to argue that the consequences for longhouse societies and cultures are not yet sufficiently marked to warrant the conclusion that Borneo peoples generally are suffering unduly deleterious effects from tourism, as distinct from other processes of modernisation.[13]

Thus, I return to my opening statement. I do not see much evidence that tourism, rather than other processes of change, is as yet having a generally detrimental influence on Malaysian cultures. There are claims that it is. There are anxieties about the actual and potential conflicts between Western values and Islamic ones, and the possibility of deterioration in Muslim moral values. This is clearly an issue, and will continue to be so, especially for the east coast Peninsular states. Yet despite the claims and rhetoric, and despite the effects of tourism on specific local communities which are particularly exposed to tourism or near to the major resorts and tourist sites (e.g. Bird, 1989,

6),[14] I remain to be convinced of the generally pessimistic, critical view of the relationship between tourism and culture in Malaysia.

## NOTES

1 I am grateful to the British Academy for its support in preparing this chapter, although the opinions expressed here are my own.

2 Yet Bird's generalisation that '(t)ourism is acknowledged by anthropologists as having a particularly disruptive influence on vulnerable traditional societies, such as some of those existing in Malaysia' (Bird, 1989, 4), does need qualification.

3 The *Quantas Jetabout* brochure refers to culture and society in Penang as 'a fascinating blend of Malay, Chinese, Indian and British' (1991, 9).

4 The *Thomson Worldwide* brochure also plays on the theme of the untamed jungle and '. . . the power that nature holds' (1990, 106; cf. Collins, 1989, 37).

5 The official brochures for each state in the Federation continue this theme. The TDC's Perlis brochure, for example, refers to a 'congenial mix' of cultures and peoples (1989a, 2).

6 There is a concern in this approach with the assumed corrupting effect of the West: foreign tourists exhibit loose morals in sexual attitudes and behaviour, appearance and dress. This is then assumed to have a 'demonstration' effect on local values and behaviour. The assumption is often never demonstrated in detailed empirical evidence.

7 The close relationship perceived by the Malaysian government between culture and tourism is seen directly in the creation of this Ministry.

8 Bird, despite her critique of tourism development in Langkawi, notes that for the 'luxury class' tourists '(t)heir exposure to islanders is limited'; even for the 'budget tourists' or 'travellers' who meet local people and stay in local accommodation 'generally, language barriers exist'. Overall, she concludes that '(t)he nature of the encounters between tourists and locals is usually brief and fairly superficial' (Bird, 1989, 47, 48, 50).

9 Wood has argued that 'the development of an international tourism industry has consequences that extend far beyond the immediate sites of host–tourist interaction and rest on dynamics that increasingly involve a restructuring of the relationship between the state and local culture' (Wood, 1984, 354). These processes can be seen especially in such countries as Indonesia where local cultures such as those of Bali and Toraja have achieved a particular prominence and identity in the context of national culture. However, Malaysia has yet to experience these consequences of tourism, although there are signs that they might be beginning to occur with regard to certain minority cultures of East Malaysia.

10 Interestingly, the theme for Malaysia's tourist promotion in 1991 is 'Back to Nature' (*New Straits Times*, 1991a, 4).

11 Some tourist guides are aware of this problem of stereotyping and provide a much more realistic depiction of local cultures. See, for example, Crowther and Wheeler, 1988 and Loose and Ramb, 1990.

12 See, for example, Collins *Illustrated Guide*, 1989, and Insight Guides, 1989.
13 Cohen, in his examination of 'hill tribe tourism' in Northern Thailand over a decade ago, noted then that

> the effects of tourism on the people are as yet fairly limited, both in terms of their intensity and of their geographical scope. This is so, owing not only to the relatively small scale of the tourist industry but also to its nature: it is sightseeing tourism, rather than resort tourism. Tourists have only short, often fleeting and superficial contacts with highlanders.
>
> (Cohen, 1983b, 322)

14 Kadir Din raises the issue of guest–host encounters in Malaysia, and the importance of tour guides, intermediaries or 'cultural brokers' in the interaction and communication process (Kadir Din, 1982, 467–71). However, we really do not have much detailed ethnography on cultural exchanges and their effects, and Kadir Din has called for more research on this topic (ibid., 475).

# 6 Peter Pan in South-East Asia
## Views from the brochures

*Tom Selwyn*

## INTRODUCTION

This chapter presents two alternative readings of tourist brochures
advertising holidays in South-East Asia (together with some brief
references to destinations elsewhere).[1] Two sets of brochures are used:
the first collected in 1990 from travel agents in Camden Town,
London; the second drawn from the World Travel Mart at London's
Olympia exhibition hall in 1991. The chapter builds on the innovative
work on tourist brochures by Dann (1988 and forthcoming).

The two readings are constructed with reference to elements of
'structuralist' and, more loosely, 'post-structuralist' traditions
respectively, and the chapter starts by defining how these terms are
used in the present context. Following this, evidence will be given from
the first set of brochures which will allow initial readings to be made,
and an overall theoretical orientation to be established. Excerpts from
the second collection will then be used to refine and develop the
argument. The chapter ends with a conclusion which suggests ways in
which the analysis helps carry forward an understanding of contemporary tourism in South-East Asia and elsewhere.

## THE TOURIST AS 'STRUCTURALIST'

Dean MacCannell tells us that he was inspired to write *The Tourist* as
a reaction to Levi-Strauss's claim that structuralist readings of the
modern world were impossible. The latter's argument had been that
modernity thrived on – indeed was defined by – the 'smashing up' and
fragmentation of structures. Uneasy with this formulation,
MacCannell set out to find, in his own words, 'structures of modernity'
(MacCannell, 1976, 4). The character he discovered working away at
making such structures was the tourist. Tourism itself, or, to be more

precise, leisure, was taken by him to be the arena in which the fragmented modern may recover his or her sense of structure or, to borrow terms from Louis Dumont, 'orientation to the whole' (Dumont, 1970, 10).

We may begin by exploring MacCannell's notion that the tourist, in some senses 'alienated' by the conditions of contemporary life, goes on holiday in order to recreate, frequently with the help of representations from the imagined *pre-modern* world, the structures which life in the post-modern world has appeared to demolish.

MacCannell's view of the 'alienated modern', in search of Durkheimian experiences of the social, rest upon the same sort of assumptions made by Berger, Berger and Kellner in their well-known book, *The Homeless Mind*, written about the same time as the original article upon which MacCannell based *The Tourist*. For them the mechanistic nature of work, the separation of work and home, the anonymous rationality of modern bureaucracy, and other features of life associated with late capitalist modes of production, all contribute to the formation of a 'consciousness' which is rootless or 'homeless' (Berger, Berger and Kellner, 1973-4, 163).

MacCannell argues that during the 'benign' period of a holiday, this 'homeless' tourist can, in fact, retrieve some sort of holistic orientation from the scattered fragments of everyday life. The evidence he uses for this claim is the 'classical' guided tour of Paris (to be found in any of the older guide books of the city and in the itineraries of many contemporary tour guides). He argues that guide books and tour guides customarily present tourists not just with museums, galleries, shopping areas, and so on, but with all sorts of other things as well. These include factories, building sites, the stock exchange, every conceivable example of transport and transportation network – such as roads, railways, railway stations, bridges, the Seine, and so on – markets, *pissoirs* and sewers. The point of all this, MacCannell argues, is simply to 'present society and its works' in a way that is fun. Moreover, in this benevolent context the rough edges of everyday concrete social relations are smoothed over by a combination of the experience of being at leisure and the explanations of the tour guide. Thus he can conclude that 'society is renewed in the heart of the individual through warm, open, unquestioned relations, characterised by a near absence of alienation when compared with other contemporary relationships' (MacCannell, 1976, 55).

All of this strongly calls to mind Barthes' (1983) essay *The Eiffel Tower*. Barthes argues that the tourist symbol (one is tempted to say monument) serves as a vantage point from which the tourist can feel him or herself at the centre of centuries of French history. In a single sweeping view various different parts of Paris can be linked up. The different functions and characteristics of the city – religious, sexual, materialistic, gastronomic, intellectual, as symbolised by Sacré Coeur, Pigalle, La Bourse, Les Halles, the Left Bank – all appear joined as parts of a single body, and can thus be experienced as being united within connecting parts of a whole.

The inference of Barthes' and MacCannell's work is that the 'homeless' tourist 'comes home', in the very precise sense of recapturing an experience of the social, by going away on holiday.

The lineage of these ideas stretches back in a number of directions, including work on myth and totemism by Levi-Strauss (1962; 1978; 1985) and religion by Durkheim (1976). As MacCannell says: tourists are 'motivated by an elementary impulse analogous to the one that animates the Australian's awe for his Churinga board' (MacCannell, 1976, 42). It is this in-built 'totemic' quality of tourism, together with the propensity of the structure of 'tourist language' (in brochures and elsewhere) to resemble the language of more traditional myths, which forms the basis of the claim here that part of the tourist project may, indeed, as MacCannell claims, be described as 'structuralist'.

## THE TOURIST AS 'POST-STRUCTURALIST'

The change in emphasis from 'structuralism' to 'post-structuralism' in the anthropology of tourism may be associated with the work of several writers, especially those who have been concerned with tourism and cultural 'commoditisation' (cf., for example, Greenwood, 1977; Ireland, 1989; O' Rourke, 1987). There is also the more general work on Western consumer culture itself by such authors as Eco (1986) and Baudrillard (1988), and on 'post-modernism' and 'post-structuralism' by Jameson (1985) and Harvey (1989).

For Baudrillard, consumerism has become the paramount cultural form in the contemporary world. The needs of individuals have been reduced to those which coincide with the needs of a system dedicated to an almost unlimited production of consumables. In this view tourists become consumers of cultural goods and are hardly distinguishable from other types of consumers in high streets and supermarkets. The world itself becomes a tourist supermarket. For Eco, consumers, particularly North American ones, now have unlimited access to reproductions of every conceivable kind of representation, including models of historical, fictional or religious subjects, which claim the attention of the tourist in the museum souvenir shop primarily as commodities and only secondly (if at all) as images carrying significant historical, religious or metaphorical meanings. Indeed in this view the boundaries between history, religion and fiction become blurred. In one sense, as Eco observes, this blurring of the boundaries leads to an apparent 'democratisation' of knowledge: historians, theologians and novelists become purveyors of souvenirs to which the tourist as consumer has immediate access. The harbinger of this new 'freedom' appears as none other than the brochure writer who, together with other marketing experts, can build into the tourist itinerary a little history here, a touch of religion there, and mix the result up with a rich and spicy sauce of fiction. At all-inclusive prices too!

Both Jameson and Harvey have discussed what they term the 'schizophrenic' nature of post-modern experience. Crucially, for Jameson,

> the schizophrenic does not have an experience of temporal continuity, and is condemned to live a perpetual present with which the various moments of his or her past have little connection and for which there is no conceivable future on the horizon. Schizophrenic experience is an experience of isolated, disconnected, discontinuous material signifiers which fail to link up into a coherent sequence.
>
> (Jameson, 1985, 119).

One of the consequences of this 'disconnected state' is that

> the schizophrenic will clearly have a far more intense experience of any given present of the world than we do, since our own present is always part of some larger set of projects which force us selectively to focus our perceptions.
>
> (ibid.)

These observations suggest a line of thought in which the 'post-structuralist' tourist appears not only as consumer but also as 'schizophrenic' in the rather particular sense Jameson uses the term in relation to experiences which are at once 'intense' and 'disconnected'.

## SOUTH-EAST ASIA (AND ELSEWHERE) IN CAMDEN TOWN 1990

The Cosmos brochure *Distant Dreams* consists of details of seven long-haul destinations with lists and descriptions of the attractions, hotels and itineraries in each place. The attractions are sub-titled in a consistent style throughout under the headings: 'shopping', 'activities', 'nightlife', 'eating out' and 'sightseeing' together with annual temperature charts and sprinklings of photographs. The front cover shows a couple, embracing and alone, in a blue sea. In the background are palm trees, a sandy beach and blue sky.

The first location described inside is Thailand which, we are told, has long been known as 'the land of smiles', where 'the people ("many of whom today speak English") combine Buddhist charity and gentleness with a fun loving energy, making for a unique blend of Western and Eastern values'. 'Everywhere', the text explains, 'you're surrounded by reminders of the country's serene cultural past. Like the spires of Bangkok's countless golden "Wats" or temples . . . and the Buddhist statues, large or small, that invariably appear in hotel lobbies and rooms, perhaps even forming part of a lampshade.' Under the subtitle 'nightlife' we are informed that 'the Patpong Road area of Bangkok is particularly renowned, even notorious, for its lively range of bars, massage parlours and nightspots of all imaginable kinds, from the chic to the raucous'. Lobster and seafood are recommended as good value while food prices generally are said to be 'incredibly cheap . . . ranging from a few pence for a simple dish at a food stall, to a good meal for two persons costing no more than five or six pounds'.

The two-page introduction to Sri Lanka contains two key photographs: him and her, practically alone, in the surf backed by palm trees, and a dazzling little tableau of tropical fruit. In some of the cooler spots on the island 'like Nuwara Eliya, the feel of a British colonial past lives on, while, in the mountains to the north, ruined fortresses and cities like Sigiriwa and Anuradhapura display Sri Lanka's ancient Buddhist heritage. Elsewhere, its variations have a timeless nature . . . (while) . . . the people are friendly, hospitable and ever ready with a disarming smile. . . . Seafood is a real delight . . . and most traditional dishes combine rice with blends of spices such as coriander, chili or cumin'. Once again 'prices are incredibly low' (although not quite as cheap as the 'real bargain paradise' of the Dominican Republic).

At this point it is useful briefly to make cross references to three brochures advertising destinations in the Mediterranean and the Canary Islands.

Speedwing's brochure on Eilat consists of a list of hotels and their specialities. In King Solomon's Palace Hotel, for example, 'you can eat somewhere different almost every day of the week! The main restaurant, King Solomon's Table, offers three different dining possibilities: a traditional buffet dinner, a delightful Italian section or an authentic Chinese section'. The assurance is given, however, that 'most dishes are kosher, which means their food conforms to Jewish dietary laws. You won't be served pork or shellfish, and meat and dairy dishes are never combined at the same meal. . . . The culinary delight is undoubtedly the Israeli breakfast – the most spectacular morning meal in the world'.

Mark Warner's *Summer 90* catalogue operates holiday camps for an 18–30ish age group, including families, in five Mediterranean resorts. Much of this brochure is spent describing who goes on Mark Warner holidays ('People Like You') and what they receive ('More Choice', 'Freedom', 'Glorious Food', 'Great Value', and so on).

Redwing's *Summersun: Go Canaries 1990* brochure has three aspects of importance for the argument here. The first is the large quantity of photographs showing buildings; the holidays offered by Redwing in the Canaries are 'apartment holidays', rather than the hotel or 'club' holidays of Cosmos, Speedwing or Mark Warner. The second, which follows directly from the first, is that there are quite a number of photographs showing families, or groups of families. This is to be expected since the apartments are obviously built for families. The third is the large number of photographs showing, literally, masses of people, often in rows, under beach umbrellas, on the beach. Another detail of interest is that many of these photographs are slightly blurred. The front cover shows, exceptionally for this brochure, a young woman, quite alone, sitting on a sand dune. It also contains a number of references to the landscape of the island of the following kind: 'We regard Lanzarote as the most spectacular of all the Canary Islands. Like the other Canaries, it rose from the Atlantic sea bed during gargantuan volcanic eruptions, back when our ancestors thought popping your head out of the swamp was a holiday!'

To return to South-East Asia, to consider Redwing's *Go Places* (1989/90) brochure, which opens with the assurance that '(a)s one of the U.K.'s biggest tour operators, we have tremendous buying power, as well as all the right connections.' What, then, does the company buy and sell? In their introductory essay on Thailand they tell us:

> One of the very early episodes of Star Trek saw Captain Kirk and his crew on a distant planet peopled by a beautiful gentle race of people where life was given over totally to pleasure. Kirk and Spock had a hard time on the philosophy front, trying to convince the aliens that there ought to be more to life than the pursuit of pleasure. Well for 'distant world' read Thailand, the pleasure centre of the world.

The piece proceeds to list some of the qualities of the product: 'The country is spotlessly clean'; 'one can wander about without being continually pestered by beggars and touts'; Thailand is 'like a Greenhouse all year round'; 'the climate, the food, and the stunning beaches are all part of the magic of Thailand, but it's the people that add the icing to the cake'; 'The people are the most sensual and overtly sexual on earth'; 'To come to terms with the unique character of the Thai people, you must regard them all as Peter Pans. Eternal children who have never grown up.' Then the silly jokes and 'the lights are on but there's nobody at home demeanour will make more sense. When you see a girl in a bar with strategically torn slits in her shorts, dancing suggestively with a live snake, then instead of thinking of her as a harlot, picture instead a little girl trying to shock an adult out of pure bedevilment' . . . and so on . . . and then, a little further on . . . 'even some of the religious festivals are childlike'. 'As a long haul Wintersun destination it's better in every respect than the Caribbean . . . Thailand is very "Sunmed", the highest accolade we can think of.'

In the section on Bangkok, there appears the following: 'Bangkok has to be experienced to be believed. The truly nice thing is that in spite of all the blatant sex, the knowledge that in this City you can buy anything, and the general feeling of being right in the heart of the mysterious East, one can walk around in total safety.' A few pages later, amongst the pages devoted to Pattaya beach, comes the following: 'If you can suck it, use it, eat it, taste it, abuse it, or see it then it is available in this resort.'

At this point an initial reading of the material presented so far may be made.

### Reading the brochures I: a 'structuralist' view

We may begin by abstracting four themes from the material presented so far in rather the same way that Levi-Strauss located 'themes' in myths (Levi-Strauss, 1964; 1966). These may conveniently be grouped under the headings 'Sites', 'Beaches and boundaries', 'Smiles of local friends' and 'Food'. They may be considered in turn.

#### Sites

The sites, or attractions, recommended in the brochures fall into four categories. There are the classical, often religious, shrines and monuments in Cosmos's Thailand and Sri Lanka, Speedwing's Eilat (King Solomon's tin mines) and Mark Warner's Turkey (the temple of Artemis at Ephesus) and so on. There are the natural sites which are, in turn, 'breathtaking' (Speedwing), 'most spectacular' (Redwing), 'incredible' (Redwing): generally fantastic. Then there are the monuments left over from the British colonial period, to which both Cosmos and Redwing draw attention. Finally, there are the 'raucous' bars and massage parlours of Cosmos's Thailand, the packed disco pubs of Redwing's Lanzarote, and, of course, the site which is arguably the most enduring and powerful of all: the naked or near-naked human body. As Redwing says of Lanzarote's official naturist beach: 'if you want to see all the sights and tan your own, then leave your swimsuit in your beach bag'.

We may further break these categories down into two sets of contrasting parts. First, the mystical, religious or metaphysical on the one hand; the immediately experienced and physical on the other. Second, wild and exotic natural sites on the one hand; more familiar monuments built by British colonial administrators or contemporary property developers and their cement mixers on the other. These sorts of patterns of preoccupations, and the language with which they are cast is, we might agree, quite familiar to us from a mainstream of anthropological studies on the structure of myth and totemism. We may make the argument more secure by considering the other themes.

*Beaches and boundaries*

If we look at the beach images presented in the brochures we find remarkably consistent preoccupations with categories and groups of people and boundaries between them. The Redwing brochure, for example, which is perhaps the clearest in this regard, opens with a lone figure on a sand dune, shorn of any social or natural context, save the dune itself. Inside the brochure the images alternate between nuclear families in or around their apartments and the blurred rows of masses of people on the beach. One plausible reading of this series of images and their juxtaposition might be that the isolated 'single' is translated, courtesy of Redwing, into, first of all, a member of a family group and, second, into a member of a social mass. Mark Warner does not deal in masses at all, but the theme of 'singles' coming together in 'clubs', which become 'excellent company' and are then displayed as happily consuming food together, carries a similar message: this company, like Redwing, takes the isolated modern individual and offers him or her back, as it were, as social self. This pattern is repeated in various ways in other brochures sufficiently clearly for us to suggest that the brochures do concern themselves in a broad sense with individuals and social groups, and the way that they are brought into relationship with one another.

## Smiles of local friends

The third theme concerns local people. If they show up in photographs at all, which is rare, it is either as salespersons or in the highly stylised form of, for example, Cosmos's classical Thai dancers. They achieve reference, slightly more frequently, in the written texts. References to their easy-going natures or their religious practices are sometimes remarked on, as we have seen. But if there is one quality which they always seem to achieve, it is their friendliness. Thus, Cosmos's Sri Lankans are 'friendly, hospitable and ever ready with a disarming smile', while Speedwings's local Eilat residents are 'remarkably welcoming, friendly and good-humoured', and so on.

## Food

A fourth theme is food. In all four brochures there are repeated references to the 'tremendous choice' of food, its 'tremendous value', and its 'tremendous quality'. Furthermore, in all brochures food is presented as a focus for social groups and categories. The form that this focus takes may vary. Eilat, for example, is presented as being a part of a broader Jewish commensal environment, while for Mark Warner's clients the food table appears, as it always has done in Club Mediterranee promotions, as a, if not *the*, centre of 'club' life. For Redwing the difference in the types of establishments offering food and drink (which 'range from the cheap and cheerful up to "Oh a gold one! That will do nicely, Sir"') suggest a clientele experienced in the subtleties of finely graded class and status systems.

## Summary

Let us try and draw some of the threads together.

We may start with the 'homeless tourist' himself or herself, the isolated modern, the 'single' who appears on the front covers of both the Redwing and Mark Warner brochures. This tourist is offered a journey 'out there' to a tropical paradise, the beaches of which are presented as sites for various activities such as sports but seem, primarily, the foci of social attachments and expressions of social solidarity.

In some respects the 'liminality' of the beach image is self-evident.

Beaches are divorced from social, economic or political contexts (beaches could be anywhere). Their association with physical 'freedoms' call to mind Turnerian notions of anti-structure and communitas. However, the brochures do not present their destinations as *just* beaches, for the theme of nature and the apparent 'freedoms' of the beach are consistently presented in relation to images of a built environment which appears either as attraction, accommodation or both. Indeed, the *culture* of this built environment (hotels, apartments, bars, restaurants, colonial forts, and so forth) suggests, in the fairly precise ways outlined, that the 'holiday' is celebration both of 'ourselves' in a relatively free and unstructured position and of 'our' social and cultural values which belong to the world back home: of families, of 'great value' and 'great choice', of finely graded status systems, and so on. This awareness of some of *our* key values is further juxtaposed with an appearance, however stylised and shadowy, of *their* values. If we also place this beside one of the central themes of at least two of the brochures mentioned here (as well as others not mentioned) – namely *them* as friendly, welcoming and hospitable – then there is an appearance of a relationship between *us* and *them* which is to some extent constructed in a language of hospitality and exchange between groups which are at once different and related. Moreover, the emphasis placed on ancient sites – including sites of volcanic eruptions which were explicitly associated with swamps out of which our ancestors popped their heads, and, more particularly, religious sites – suggests that *they* have histories and traditions which, while at one level may be different from ours, may at another serve as mirrors and models of our own. At least they may call up memories of what might have been our own in some imagined past. Indeed, there could be a suggestion here that the emphasis on such religious and natural sites beckon the 'homeless tourist' with metaphorical means of recovering other aspects of a 'lost self' buried, so to speak, back home, under more compelling day-to-day demands.

All of this is to suggest that the use of an analytic language and way of looking at the material – which is reminiscent of 'structuralist' approaches in other contexts – is, in certain limited and specific senses, revealing about the nature of tourism and its attractions. It has been argued that the brochures contain several discernible common themes. There is a pre-occupation with the construction of individuals and groups, and also with relations between groups; with nature, often wild and exotic, and with human nature caught up in a play of 'freedoms' associated with notions of beach and paradise while simultaneously being constrained by the culture and ideology associated with the architecture of a resort's built environment of hotels, apartments and shops. In general terms, these themes are familiar from other more traditional myths of the kind anthropologists are customarily more familiar with, and, certainly, the brochures do seem to be in the business of selling myths.

The analysis so far has sought to build upon MacCannell's original insights and to confirm their fundamentally fruitful nature – even for thinking about locations and destinations well beyond the geographical and social boundaries of tourist Paris.

## Reading the brochures II: a 'post-structuralist' view

We may now proceed with a contrasting reading of the brochures, beginning with the observation that one clearly dominant theme in the material presented here is that of 'commoditisation', the gathering of everything, from sites to emotions to persons, into the cash nexus. One way of proceeding is to have a look at some of the parameters of the process as it appears in the texts.

### The omnipotence of the instantaneous

One obvious fact about a tourist brochure is that it gives its reader (viewer?) a sense of having immediate and instant access to all the 'commodities' it represents. From the instant sex in Patpong Road, to the instant society engendered by the Mark Warner holidays, to the ubiquitous images of immediately available food, the invitation is to make instant choices: to suck, fuck and then quickly move on to the Dominican Republic. Perhaps another Redwing production, the company's *Go Greek* brochure, sums it up best. On the front cover is a picture of two elderly Greek men sitting under a potted plant. One is pointing with some animation at a picture in a newspaper that the other is reading. The reader is an orthodox priest and the newspaper is the *Sun*. Such a juxtaposition seems designed loudly to celebrate the triumph of the instant judgement and the instantly available breast in the face of two millennia of religious thought and practice.

### Boundary fragmentation

Despite earlier arguments in this chapter, the version of the commoditisation process found in the brochures fragments and, in many senses, abolishes boundaries. Boundaries between 'high' and 'popular' culture, for example, are swept away in settings in which Buddhist statues of Thai deities turn up as lampshades in hotel bedrooms. Sexual *rites of passage* are similarly abandoned in contexts of instant sexual availability. In a significant sense, boundaries and frontiers between countries are erased in the very experience of choosing a holiday from alternative 'destinations'. The prospective tourist may be transported from Sri Lanka to Miami simply by turning pages and encountering again and again the same blue sea, golden beaches, and coconut palm. Perhaps most significant is the removal of any sense of boundary between *types of information*. Thus information about food, temples, volcanoes, timetables and out-of-season tariffs jostle more or less indiscriminately for space. By rendering self-evidently different sorts of messages (a list of a resort's monthly temperatures beside a list of its religious festivals, for example) into alternative 'bits' of 'information', intellectual distinctions and judgements about the relative value of things becomes blurred. As Theodore Roszak says 'for the information theorist it does not matter whether we are transmitting a fact, a judgement, a shallow cliche, a deep teaching, a sublime truth, or a nasty obscenity. All are "information".' In the process of transmission, however, 'the meaning of things communicated comes to be levelled, and so too the value' (Roszak, 1986, 14). For him, such 'information overload' fulfils the same political function in the post-modern world as the withholding and censorship of information did in the modern world. 'Data Glut' becomes a form of censorship.

### Intensity and the abolition of continuity

References to the work of Jameson and Harvey have already been made. Jameson's notion of the 'schizophrenic' nature of post-modern life was emphasised, and it is this which we may pick up now.

It was argued earlier that the brochures indicated that in some senses tourists are engaged with the history of their 'destinations'. Following Jameson, I would now like to argue that in other (and perhaps increasingly dominant) senses the brochures indicate a disengagement between tourist and 'destination' as a place located in time and space. Like Poe's Arthur Gordon Pym, whose canoe was swept by a hurricane into a heavenly (but, for him, fatal) whirlpool (Poe, 1927, 426), the tourist is caught up, without much choice in the matter, in a current of increasingly dazzling and unrelated sensations. The brochure reader is conducted from the 'majestic ancient cities of Polonnaruwa and Anuradhapura' (Cosmos on Sri Lanka) to 'breathtaking' and 'spectacular' natural sites (or, on the same lines, the

Israeli breakfast which, we will recall, is 'the most spectacular morning meal in the world') to the 'most sensual and overtly sexual people on earth' to 'the most awe inspiring sight ever to be experienced' (the view of the statue of Ramses II as described by Cosmos). The point is that each attraction or site is presented in terms of the extreme intensity of the experience it offers. Temples, breakfasts, temperatures (Thailand is 'like a Greenhouse' while Eilat 'radiates a warm, welcoming glow'), sexual encounters, visits to 'breathtaking' natural sites, and the rest, are linked principally by the superlatives with which they are described.

*Summary*

We have come a very long way indeed from MacCannell's tourist. In the present reading, sites are no longer signifiers which, linked together, form coherent structures within which individual tourists find historical and biographic meaning, but instead they are centres of physical and emotional sensation from which temporal and spatial continuities have been abolished. We might put it this way. For Francis Bacon, travel formed part of a 'larger project', to pick up Jameson's phrase, of scientific discovery and the making of diplomatic relationships (Bacon, 1597). For Barthes and MacCannell, tourism also formed part of a larger project in which the tourist became an active myth-maker at the intersection of the resort's structures of time and space and his or her own identity and biography. By contrast, and in a manner reminiscent of the language of Jameson's schizophrenics, the language of our brochures appears to propel the post-modern tourist into experiences whose discontinuous intensity seems to rule out the possibility of tourism being part of any larger project associated with other, and possibly more sober, spheres of his or her own life, work and thought.

## SOUTH-EAST ASIA AT OLYMPIA 1991

The second set of brochures to be considered was gathered at the World Travel Mart at Olympia in December 1991. One, amongst several, benefits to be gained from comparing this collection with the 'Camden' set is that it will enable, in the concluding remarks, some speculative comments to be made about how the style and content of brochure presentations are developing over time.

What, at least, is clear is that both the 'structuralist' and 'post-structuralist' language of the earlier set of brochures has been carried through into the second. Arguably, however, the latter, in the particular form in which it appears in the brochures, is gaining ground.

*Tours and totems*

In the Discovery Tours (Sabah) brochure *Borneo, Sabah, Malaysia* the traveller is offered several tours. Each is described by a brief text illustrated by a picture. One of these, the 'Penampang Cultural Tour', promises travellers the chance to 'get to know the rich cultural heritage of the Kadazans'. Its itinerary consists of the World War Two War Memorial at Putatan, the 'House of Skulls' ( 'residence of Monsopaid, the famous headhunter'), the pre-historic 'megaliths amid the paddy fields', and St Michael's Church in Sabah. The text is accompanied by a photograph of a megalithic monument. Whatever this tour is about it does seem that one central preoccupation is with death, the manner of its coming and its representation. The centrality of the megalithic stone pillar, with its eminently totemic appearance, surrounded by the textual references to the war grave cemetery and the headhunter's house, suggests that the structure of the tour is built around the juxtaposition of the ritual, symbolic and cultural diversity occasioned by death and the existential fact of its universality.

A second tour, adjacent on the page to the above, visits Kinabalu Park. The traveller is invited to 'enjoy the scenic countryside and breathtaking view of the mountain ranges'. He or she is conducted into the 'cool temperate forest' (and have an optional 'canopy walk on top of the forest') and then move onwards to the 'Japanese-style hot sulphuric spring water' before exploring a bat cave and 'buying tropical fruits at the Kundasang market on the way back'. The idiom here is reminiscent of the ritual language of south and central India described by Beck (1969) and Babb (1973). In the contexts they describe, symbols of hot and cold, particularly when opposed to, or brought into relation with, each other, stand metaphorically for ideas central to the rituals they discuss. In the present context the juxtaposition of the heat of the spring and tropical fruit market with the coolness of the forest, waterfalls and bat cave suggests a sensual (rather than, say, an intellectual) link between tourists and the landscape of the tour. It is, precisely, this *link* that is important here: later on we shall explore a contrasting type of promotional language in which the focus of sensual feelings becomes the tourist himself (occasionally, herself). Here at Kinabalu Park, the focus is the *relationship* between tourist and surroundings.

The counterposition of these two tours arguably reveals a series of preoccupations which calls to mind those which inform Australian aborigine totemic rituals as these have become interpreted, by authors from Durkheim to Levi-Strauss, within a mainstream of 'structural' anthropology. In these rituals symbolic unions between the sensual and intellectual promote senses of social solidarity, identification with territory and union with ancestors and deities. Bearing in mind Durkheim's notion of the social and religious primacy of such 'elementary forms', the identification of a comparable language in these tourist brochures amounts to an encounter with a powerfully effective promotional rhetoric.

*Ordering the plural*

Several of the brochures emphasise the closeness of the relationship between traditional and modern, frequently linking this to a comparable closeness between ethnically diverse populations. In Garuda International's brochure *Java* the reader is informed that although 'Java is an island steeped in history and traditions', there is 'an acute awareness that old ways cannot survive without adaptation; that such things as computers, satellite and jet communications (and so on) all have their places in a world that is changing fast'. Although most of Api Tour's (Borneo) *Borneo Adventurama* is taken up with descriptions and photographs of Borneo's natural attractions (including a close-up photograph of a green turtle laying eggs, many photographs of orchids and orang-utans, and so on), the opening double-page spread describes the city of Kota Kinabalu. Accompanying the text are eight photographs. Three of these are of religious buildings – the state mosque, the main Buddhist temple and the Catholic cathedral. There is a photograph of the Sabah museum – a modern building said to 'embody the spirit of Sabah' because it combines architectural references to the ethnically plural nature of Sabah. There is also a photograph of the 'ultra-modern' Sabah Foundation building and two shots of the city from the air. In Premier Holiday's *Asia* catalogue, the attraction of Japan is said to be that it provides an 'intriguing contrast between the imperial and traditional past and the ultra-modern'.

This emphasis on symbolically unifying the traditional and modern, the religious and scientific, and the socially plural, calls to mind Barthes' *Eiffel Tower* essay (see above) in which the diverse parts of Paris are linked up in the tourist eye view from the tower. The argument of both Barthes and Api Tours seems to be that one central component of a tourist attraction is its capacity to symbolise unity in diversity.

Reference to unity and 'wholeness' appear throughout in several guises. *Malaysia Incentive*, for example, informs readers that Malaysia is 'a thriving nation of Malays, Chinese, Indians, Eurasians and the many indigenous races living happily together to create a cultural mix that is both invigorating and colourful with its year-round festivities', while the *Java* brochure speaks of Java as 'an island of happy, smiling faces'.

One theme which consistently appears concerns the quality of the relationship between tourist and resident. Musi Holiday's *Great Mahakam River Tours*, for example, promises the tourist an 'encounter with ancient tribes' and includes, in each of the four itineraries listed, tribal 'welcome ceremonies'. In the CPH Travel Agencies (Sarawak) brochure *Borneo Unexplored*, the traveller is invited into the communal hall of an Iban longhouse on the Sarawak river. The brochure reports that this hall is 'the main reception area for guests where you shall be cordially invited to observe or partake in a simple *tuak* (rice-wine) ceremony'.

### Probing frontiers

The possibility of a close relation between tradition and modernity, tribal host and tourist guest, is, not surprisingly, complemented with repeated references to one of the features of several of the destinations covered in these brochures: their 'unexplored' nature. Thus the front cover of *Borneo Unexplored* consists of a photograph of four men in tribal costume (including feather headdresses) paddling a dugout canoe, while Bob Bates, founder/president of Trans Niugini Tours (offering 'Unspoilt environments, primitive cultures') is reported by his company's brochure as saying that 'Papua New Guinea is something of a "last frontier" for that small number of international travellers who visit our country each year'.

The evidence presented so far is sufficient to suggest that the tour companies referred to are all concerned to cater for tourists in search of, and indeed motivated by, the kind of 'structuralist' paradigms outlined by MacCannell. Texts and illustrative material alike systematically probe relations between the natural and cultural, between the unexplored (and geographically liminal) and the familiar, between self and other, between individuals (or parts) and wholes. The emphasis on cultural and spiritual 'meanings' in 'host cultures' is complemented and reinforced by references to symbolic exchanges between 'hosts' and 'guests'. The 'tourist as structuralist' seems well served by these tours for, in the sense that tourists enter into symbolic transactions with their 'hosts' which involve food, drink, greetings, and even, as in the *Discovery Tours* brochure, styles of representing the dead, MacCannell's 'alienated modern' cannot help but feel invited into a universe which seems intellectually and emotionally warm and encompassing.

One way of introducing a change in focus, from 'structuralist' to 'post-structuralist' language, may be introduced by way of the idea of 'incentive travel' for, arguably, this is a determining idea in the construction of contemporary promotional language.

## Incentives for the deserving

In their brochure *Malaysia Incentive*, the Tourist Development Corporation (TDC) of Malaysia defines incentive travel as follows: 'Incentive travel is more than just providing an ideal tourist destination. It is about hospitality, time, creative planning, value-for-money, and above all, first-class service all the way'.

In *Explore Malaysia*, a supplement of the trade journal *Tourism Asia*, Madam Kee Phaik Cheen, Penang's executive councillor for tourism, is quoted as saying that Penang should become a centre for 'incentive travel'. The journal reports a visit to Penang of an official of the US-based Society of Incentive Travel Executives (SITE) who is reported to be 'already sold on Penang'. The journal goes on to report that 'at stake is a very lucrative market' (i.e. tourism by American corporate executives and their wives on incentive travel deals) 'which earns US$5 to US$15 billion every year'. As Madam Kee puts it: 'Penang quite naturally now wants its share'.

Incentive Asia Destination Services *Malaysia* brochure takes up Madam Kee's challenge, asserting 'Incentive Asia Destination Services has the ability to look at a destination and its people, draw inspirations from them, and put their fascinations into sharp focus for deserving high achievers'. They promise to 'Meet your expectations' with 'satisfying experiences', claiming to 'take great pains to get to know our clients and their expectations . . . (going on to) . . . turn fantasy into reality and reality into fantasy'. 'Our commitment', they say, 'stems from a sincere desire to make our clients feel utterly good at the end of their experience'.

All Nippon Airways' *Club Ana* brochure follows several of these themes. They explain: 'As today's business world becomes increasingly international, it is creating a whole new breed of business traveler.

These people are savvy, sophisticated and they want, expect and deserve the best in international travel services. Making sure we provide them is the reason behind our having completely rethought the conventional concept of the "class" system. We've gone beyond the traditional ideals of luxury and privilege to create a world of refined elegance, where sumptuous comforts serve to set a new standard in airline travel.'

Already the interlocked themes of first class service, luxury, privilege, the interchangeability of reality and fantasy, and the absolute primacy of the traveller's own good feelings are apparent.

Accompanied by a profusion of superlatives, these become most pronounced in the language used to describe some of the region's luxury hotels.

### The coronation of the tourist

'Life at the utterly beautiful Bali Oberoi is enjoyed quietly, luxuriously and in absolute tranquility', claims the brochure of the Oberoi Hotel in Bali. Guests are offered 'fresh fruit, magnificent seafood, spicy Indonesian delicacies and first class international cuisine' and told that 'the choice is yours 24 hours a day'. As the brochure says 'the Oberoi, Bali provides a unique yet ideal . . . incentive destination for your senior executives'. The 700 staff at the Lanka Oberoi, Columbo, Sri Lanka are said to be 'genuinely concerned that the guests are content', while the brochure promoting the chain as a whole (*Oberoi Hotels International*) assures readers that 'wherever in the world you find Oberoi, you'll find luxury and comfort' adding 'Because you deserve the best the world has to offer.' The two floating restaurants on the Nile owned by the chain are introduced by the legend: 'Cleopatra couldn't have done it better or with more *élan*. And she certainly didn't have finer gourmet cuisine or more solicitous service than you'll have as you are wined and dined afloat the Pharaohs.'

### The view from the throne

Having placed the tourist at ease in his or her hotel, the brochures move on to guide the tourist eye towards the world outside. The Bali Oberoi brochure begins this task as follows: 'When writer and anthropologist Margaret Mead visited the island of Bali she said "it was like journeying in a dream" . . . and she was right. Bali is the very essence of dreams. A fantastic, magical Garden of Eden, remote from the turmoils of the world; bypassed by time and strife and affliction'.

The style of this sort of writing takes its cue from the idea, familiar to the anthropology of tourism (Gottlieb, 1982), of the tourist as 'king (or queen) for a day'. Here, however, the promise is made to extend the power of the tourist/king/queen beyond the boundaries of the hotel into the world beyond its walls. 'We understand how you want Bali to be . . . and it is!'

What does the tourist want the world outside the window to be like?

In describing Pelangi Beach Resort, Langkawi, Premier Holiday's brochure *Asia* answers as follows: 'In a world where time seems to stand still . . . the hotel is situated beside a glorious sandy beach in 28 acres of lush tropical gardens. Designed like a traditional Malay village, the resort will appeal to those seeking an original and authentic location with deluxe facilities. Due to limited accessibility, Langkawi is still, thankfully, uncommercialised and reflects a true picture of Malaysia.' The picture illustrating Pelangi beach is of a middle aged British couple in a cycle rickshaw, both wearing garlands of jasmine petals. Unusually for travel brochures, their names, Denis and Margaret Thatcher, are widely known from other contexts.

Singapore Tourist Promotion Board's brochure *Singapore* is amongst the most specific in describing what sort of world the tourist is seeking. The following is a selection from their extensive list of Singapore's attractions. Haw Par Villa is a 'high-tec fun park designed to bring Chinese legends alive'. It caters for 'theme party organisers in search of the mystical and the magical'. Alkaff Mansion is a 'stately home once owned by one of Singapore's founding families which threw open its elegantly restored doors . . . to greet visitors to a unique dining and entertainment experience'. 'Imagine', the brochure writer asks the reader 'sitting on the verandah of a stately colonial mansion, sipping a refreshingly chilled cocktail as the tropical sun paints the sky crimson as it sets.' The Empress Place was formerly a colonial government building. Carefully restored it is now an art museum. The brochure comments: 'it is this fascinating combination of the old with the ancient which has seen the Empress Place rapidly gain in stature as one of Singapore's more unique theme party venues'. Another attraction listed is Bugis Street. 'Long remembered as an impromptu outdoor cabaret with food to set the taste buds tingling, Bugis Street closed its shutters in 1985 to make way for Singapore's Mass Rapid Transit development. But like all good things, its spirit could not be kept down, and Bugis Street is ready to burst back on the night scene in a US$6.8 million reconstruction of Asia's most talked about tourist spot.' Other attractions on the point of development include Telok Ayer Market, Raffles Hotel, Tang Dynasty Village, Marina Village

International and Singapore's 'discovery island' of Sentosa. Each of these (together with others) is being developed by private companies and development corporations.

The Tourist Development Corporation of Malaysia's *Malaysia Incentive* pledges 'full assistance and support to all incentive planners who decide to make their clients' dreams come true in Malaysia'. They claim successfully 'to have handled incentive programmes for such corporations as Ford Europe, Roolag Group, Switzerland, BP Australia, L'Oreal of Belgium, Renault of Italy, Kameyama Candles of Japan, Philips of the UK, Arnotts of Australia, Cannon Group UK and Travelstrength of Australia to name but a few'. Each page of their brochure is introduced with a headline. Thus Malaysia is a 'Strategic Stop' which is 'Dazzling Even After Dark' and has 'Endless Possibilities'. 'Gift Items to Look Out For' are carefully itemised and illustrated on four whole pages, following which some ideas described as 'Party Bestsellers' are listed ('choose from these theme parties which are proven best-sellers: Jungle Adventure, Kampung (Village) Night, Colourful Malaysia, Out at Sea, Chinatown, Trishaws Aplenty, Arabian Nights, Old British, Penang Bridge Extravaganza, to name a few'). The tourist is invited to 'Take Your Pick'. 'Sample Itineraries' include 'City Sensations', 'Historical Splendour', 'Idyllic Hideaway', 'Peak Excitement' and 'Wild Adventure'. The brochure concludes with some 'Fascinating Facts of Malaysia' ('Malaysia is a tropical wonderland situated in the heart of South East Asia . . .' and so on).

## CONCLUSION

Encounters with the 'other' have always provided fuel for myths and mythical language. Contemporary tourism has developed its own promotional lexicon and repertoire of myths and the purpose of this chapter has been to suggest ways of looking at these that will allow understanding of the nature of modern tourism itself and also, perhaps, the framework within which it takes place.

Langholz's claim that modern advertising has taken the place of traditional myth (Langholz-Leymore, 1975) seems borne out in the case of tourist brochures in the fairly specific ways which have been described. Langholz's own analysis, however, was based exclusively on the 'structuralist' tradition of Levi-Strauss, his antecedents and followers. Now we are able, with some 'post-structuralist' insight, to take the analysis further. Thus, having considered the present material closely, it seems plausible to suggest that the 'structuralist' lexicon will, into the foreseeable future, continue to be put to the use of advertising holidays. Feelings of belonging to a group, of having relations with, and of sharing elements of histories and biographies with the 'other', of resolving the pain of (social, economic, cultural) difference with a myth of the omnipresence of the local smile, and so on, are powerful allies in any advertiser's armoury. Indeed, it is precisely *because* this type of language links with dispositions which are so 'elementary' (to borrow from Durkheim, 1976 and Bourdieu, 1977) that its employment in advertising is unlikely ever to be terminated.

However, the economic and political framework in which all development, including tourism development, takes place has had a decisive influence on the language of advertising in general, our brochures in particular. The language of the 'New World Order' as it has been termed, is, above all, individualistic, and the representations considered here elevate the individual – with his or her pleasures, fantasies, senses of power, and so forth – to a central position in the pantheon of symbols used by the brochure writers.

One lesson to be learnt from many of the brochures (it is particularly clear in the case of Singapore) is that the key players in the development of tourism are increasingly the large development corporations and large tourist companies who, as Redwing puts it, can exercise their 'tremendous buying power'. But what they sell to contemporary tourists seems, from the 'post-structuralist' view, to be not so much any real individual 'freedom' (to use one of their words) in any recognisably real world, but more a sort of space in a world of 'Peter Pans' in which 'eternal children . . . never grow up'.

And, insofar as they are about fantasies about individual omnipotence in a world of eternal children, the brochures clearly deal in 'myths' of a rather different kind from those more generally familiar to the anthropologist.

## NOTE

1 An earlier and substantially shorter draft of this chapter appeared under the title 'Mity Post-nowoczesne w prospektach tunystycznych' in *Problemy Turystyki*, 13, 3/4, Warsaw: Institute of Tourism (Selwyn 1990).

# 7 Packaging dreams
## Javanese perceptions of tourism and performance

*Felicia Hughes-Freeland*

The effect of tourism on cultural reproduction is a subject increasingly addressed by social anthropologists. This chapter considers this subject with reference to the Special Region of Yogyakarta, one of the 27 provinces which make up the Republic of Indonesia. It will concentrate on how tourists and tourism were being perceived during field-work carried out in 1989, and what this perception implies for the effect of tourism on visual performance (dance-theatre genres). The research analysed tourism as one among many styles of contemporary patronage in the performing arts in Central Java, and the results indicate that it is of limited value to isolate tourism as an object of analysis. Its significance resides in the connections and disconnections it constitutes in the general processes of social change.

## 'OUR TOURIST WORLD IN YOGYA'

When I arrived in Yogyakarta in February 1989 there was a flurry of activity to prepare for 'Visit Indonesia Year' (1991–92). Indeed, 1989 had been dubbed 'Tourism Consciousness Year' (*Tahun Sadar Wisata*). The first indication of this was a demonstration by the Student Tourism Consciousness Movement (*Gerakan Mahasiswa Sadar Wisata*) against the plans to develop local nightlife to attract more tourists. They voiced fears that the opening of discotheques and massage parlours to attract more tourists would bring moral degeneration to the region.

The printed media regularly carries reports of the perceived ills of tourism; moral and environmental corruption are the most commonly anticipated effects of the intensification of the tourist industry. These generalised negative perceptions of tourist development in the areas of moral and environmental destruction are countered by equally general expectations of the anticipated benefits. Overall, tourism is expected to bring material profit, and this is perceived as a good thing. Negative fantasies are thus matched by the positive fantasy that tourism will put *rupiah* (or dollars) in one's purse. The economic arguments about the contribution of tourism to inflation such as one hears in Bali, or underdevelopment, have yet to alter these general assumptions about the connections between tourism and gain, although as we will see, particular individual experiences reveal these expectations to be false. There is a sense in which the material expectations of tourism resemble latter-day cargo cults.

Environmental and moral climates thus are sporadically conceived to be at risk from tourists. These perceptions may have a general validity, although they do raise questions about particulars. This leads to my first main point. The stereotype of the tourist as wealthy Westerner which lies behind the negative and positive evaluations of tourism is quite distinct from the actualities of tourism in Yogya. There are overseas tourists, but there are also domestic ones. In 1988 nearly three times as many domestic tourists as overseas ones stayed in Yogya. When asked about the perceived negative moral effects of overseas tourists, the director of a tour company responded with another question: 'If you go to the government brothels or massage parlours, how many foreign tourists do you see there? None! All the clients are Indonesian!' Similarly, development along the south coast has chiefly been the provision by local government of numerous car parks and monumental gates and walls which Westerners would certainly not regard as environment friendly. The visitors who enjoy these improvements are mostly Indonesians. The vehicles that park in the Parangtritis car parks are either coaches carrying school children on study-trips, or mini-buses which arrive on Sundays or auspicious days in the Javanese calendar (the eves of Tuesday or Friday Kliwon) to visit the south sea and its legendary goddess. The thousands of visitors who flock to the beach on the eve of the Javanese New Year are Indonesians, not foreigners. A kite festival held in August 1987 resulted in tailbacks of over 7 kilometres: the aspiring visitors were Indonesians, not foreigners.

A second point concerning the category of tourist needs to be mentioned here. The overseas tourist category includes not only people on various kinds of holiday (recreational, cultural, environmental, questing) but also people living temporarily in the region for reasons of work. This means that a foreign lecturer teaching in Gadjah Mada University or a foreign consultant working on the Kali Progo irrigation project will be perceived as a tourist (Bakdi Soemanto, 1989). Indeed, when I attended the anniversary of the death of Sultan Hamengku Buwono IX at the royal tombs at Imogiri, the local press reported that a 'tourist' had gone alone to take notes. What we have here then is an overtly articulated classification of, among others, the anthropologist, which contrasts with the analytical dimensions of anthropological field-worker as field-worker (Crick, 1985) while endorsing the view that professional status and local categorisation may be highly discrepant.

*Turis* therefore is coming to replace the formerly ubiquitous *londo* (Dutch person) as something to yell at Caucasian foreigners. Identifications, however, become further confused in the local eye as greater numbers of overseas tourists come from closer to home. In April 1989, the monthly tally of tourists in Yogya revealed that the Dutch had been ousted as the 'greatest number of overseas tourists according to nationality' by the Japanese. This seems to be a growing trend in other regions of touristic Indonesia.

The tourist therefore is a more diverse category than might be expected, and includes domestic and overseas tourists. The latter are from many nations, but the Caucasians are more readily interpreted as tourists, regardless of whether they are in Yogya for business or pleasure. When negative assertions are made about tourism, however, the implication is usually that it is the overseas 'Western' tourists who are causing the damage, be it moral or environmental.

I suggested above that people in Yogya have not yet started to blame tourism for economic ills as is now the case in Bali. However, people in Yogya have a certain amount of first or second hand knowledge about tourism in Bali, and this predisposes them to certain anxieties. Although Indonesia has the second smallest tourist industry in ASEAN (only the Philippines receives fewer tourists), the majority of the 1.06 million overseas tourists who visited Indonesia in 1987 went to Bali. The Special Region of Yogyakarta has a comparable population to that of Bali (*circa* 3 million in 1989), but in 1988 it received an estimated 70 times fewer overseas tourists than Bali.

Perceptions are not, however, necessarily congruent with statistics. Fewer overseas tourists will attract more attention than many: the unexpected stands out more than the familiar. The general publicising of the government's aim to increase the number of overseas tourists during the fifth Five-Year Development Phase from 1,660,000 in 1990 to 2,500,000 in 1993 (Garuda Indonesia Airways in-flight magazine, Vol. 9, 1989) and the designation of Yogya as 'Second antique region after Bali' has created a certain amount of panic about imminent invasions. Apart from numerical increases, the government tourist office in Yogya has the specific objective of increasing the length of stay from an average of three days to twelve days. As it was national policy to intensify tourism-consciousness during 1989, there was a certain caution in criticisms and comments in discussion of this developmental objective, although one could note a polarisation of opinion among the less circumspect. My own research interviews were often turned into impromptu consultancy sessions by the interviewees to find out what I had to say on the subject of effective promotions and packages. Travel professionals complained both of the paucity of local investment and the delay in confirming the amount for the coming year: this meant preparation of promotional material would be too late. It seemed that the amount of propaganda about tourism promotion was inverse to the local investment in it.

The year to develop tourism consciousness in Yogya therefore served to make people conscious not only of the need to make tourists welcome, but of some of the potential results of the intensification of the industry.

## PERFORMANCE AND TOURISM

Apart from concern about effects of tourism on environmental and moral spheres, there is also a more generally articulated concern for cultural preservation. The cultural sphere is more often regarded as being at risk from Western films and music, and, more recently, from the influence of Jakartan culture, than from tourism as such. However, it is useful to go into this area which is commonly identified by Westerners as one most vulnerable to the ills of tourism (Graburn, 1976). I will discuss this with specific reference to the performing arts of Java, which I will illustrate with examples from Yogya.

Research into the patronage of performance in 1989 concentrated on two performance traditions perceived to be opposed according to local classifications. One originated from the Sultan's palace of Yogyakarta, the other I tracked down to remote villages, usually in deprived mountainous regions at the boundaries of provincial administrations, spatially and conceptually. The palace genre is called Golek Menak dance drama, and uses movements characteristic of the round *golek* puppets. This dance drama was the brain-child of the late Sultan Hamengku Buwono IX, although its development took off only at the end of his life. Golek Menak can be performed as a full-scale drama, or as a dance duet.

Golek Menak is one among many palace performance genres which are identified as 'high and noble' (*adiluhung*), and which have been associated with a system of honour and service, not a system of commercial exchange. Performers of palace genres have in the past danced for honour, not cash, and it is this particular aspect of contemporary styles of patronage which I was interested in, as well as formal changes in the genres and their power to carry valued references and identifications.

The second genre has been relegated to villages for a number of reasons, including religious politics and reformist Islam in Yogya (*Muhammadiyah*). *Tayuban* dancing still occurs at feasts for rites of passage and village thanksgivings. It requires the hiring of two professional dancers and musicians who entertain the men of the village all night. *Tayuban* was performed in the princely houses of Yogyakarta until the 1920s, but it has been regarded as a rural phenomenon since the creation of the Indonesian Republic, and has been scarce since the political traumas of the mid-1960s. It persists in peripheral regions in Yogya, although by 1989 the only surviving traditionally trained dancers were living in villages in the mountains on the southeastern borders of the Special Region of Yogyakarta. Yogyakartans think that traditional *tayuban* is extinct, but it is still frequently practised in the adjoining provinces of Central and East Java.

The significance of *tayuban* for my discussion here is that it is conceived to be both the origin and the opposite of women's dance as performed in the palace. It is only one of many genres associated with the rural and the traditional, which are ranked as being inferior and less refined than the performance culture of the palaces. The contrast tells us something of the way in which culture has been classified in Java: the 'high and noble' culture of 'within' the palace is contrasted with the 'rough' culture of 'outside'. Using this indigenous 'inside/outside' contrast, I will discuss first of all the 'inside' palace traditions and then the 'outside' variety, which I will term 'regional' (a translation of *daerah*). The discussion of these two spheres of performance will raise some points about how tourism articulates with the negotiation of cultural reproduction, particularly in the context of national development programmes.

### Performance of the palace

Quintessentially 'inside' performance is claimed to originate in the Sultan's palace (*kraton*). Many tourists flock here every Sunday to see the 'palace dancing'. Despite being open to tourists, the palace is less of a museum than the palace of the Susuhunan of Surakarta 60 kilometres away, and continues to live, although the nature of its future life is in question. Indeed, it seems that the present Sultan is hoping to transform the palace from being a centre of culture in Java to a centre of international culture (see further, Hughes-Freeland, 1991).

Its present life within a republican context paradoxically is due to its role as a tourist object. As soon as Indonesia was declared independent in 1945, the then Sultan-cum-freedom-fighter opened up the palace to the first generation of domestic tourists. For them, the *kraton* was a shrine of nationalist endeavour and noble past. This is still expressed in current visits: in December 1988, following the death of the ninth Sultan, 7,982 overseas tourists went to the palace, and over 130,000 domestic ones (statistics of Tepas Pariwisata Karaton Ngayogyakarta, the palace tourist office).

The Sultan's palace therefore has been a tourist object since republican Indonesia came into being, but the place of palace performance has been discontinuous. It was not until 1973 that palace performance was brought back into the palace proper from the 'branch' to which it was assigned when the Sultan was busy with his roles as government minister and vice-president in Jakarta. It was in 1973 that the Sunday practices were instituted. Their structure was based on the form of daily practices which used to take place in the palace during the reign of the eighth Sultan until his death in 1939.

The first dance package in the palace was the 'dinner dance' (*andrawina*), where groups of overseas tourists would eat lunch and watch palace dances in the elegant shade of the palace pavilions. This soon stopped. Yogya princes today mutter about being cheated by tour operators and claim that they are still owed money; this is hotly denied by veteran tour operators. The dinner dance package was revived in 1989 by one of the present Sultan's brothers and at least four princely compounds have now been restored and spruced up in order to cater for small groups of twenty or so overseas tourists to provide a sufficiently luxurious setting for visitors to enjoy a concert and an evening meal. Local tourists also consume such events, but on a larger scale, and not on a regular basis. For instance, I heard of one group of 200 chemists dining and watching dance in the Yogyakartan residence of Mr Probosutedjo, President Suharto's half brother. There is a tendency for more people to open their homes for dance and dinner concerts. Many of Yogya's well-known painters and designers are setting up exclusive concert venues in their homes. These are intended to appeal to the tourists' desire for a sense of authenticity and exclusive access.

Many visitors to the palace and princely residences think that they are watching palace dancers, but this is a misapprehension. Until the installation of the new Sultan in March 1989, palace dance was performed by the best dancers among those training at the many associations of Yogya. In 1988, however, the central Javanese palaces sponsored a concert in Japan which was performed by so-called 'palace dancers'. Although they were the members of the many dance associations, they were identified in this way because the palace had invited them as individuals, rather than going through the organisations. A similar procedure took place to assemble a company to perform in the USA as the centre piece of the Indonesian-American Cooperation (KIAS), a promotion running in the USA from 1990 to the end of 1991.

Palace dancers therefore are not people who perform in the palace and belong to it, but people who are invited by the Sultan to perform in his name. Much 'palace' or 'classical' dance in Yogya is done not by palace dancers as such, although the dancers may be palace dancers on particular occasions. The dancers at the Sunday morning palace practices from 1973 to 1989 were hand-picked from all the associations.

Tourism alone is not accountable for the proliferation of venues where palace or classical dancing may be seen by tourists. Before independence princes and nobles used to put on dances to entertain guests. The Kanoman residence which now hosts tour groups was the home of palace performance from the 1950s till 1973. An independent association developed out of that group, and continued to train and perform in the same place, and this group is arguably one of the most palace-oriented of the many training venues in Yogya for classical palace dance. Its objective was not to provide entertainment for tourists, but to teach the first generations of Indonesians about Javanese traditions. Its main rival, founded in 1962, developed a different objective. In 1970 it was recognised by the Association of Tourism Promotion, and became the first venue in Yogya to provide dancers and dances in the 'palace' style for tourists. It continues to draw overseas tourists as well as a large number of dance students which it trains to performance standard. It is difficult to verify how many dance associations there are today; one estimate for 1986 refers to 62 classical dance associations in the city of Yogya alone.

The format for the Sunday morning sessions in the palace was basically unchanged from 1973 to 1989. At the end of 1989, a number of groups drawn from the leading classical training venues were assigned a rota to take turns filling the Sunday slot. The object was first to provide a costumed show – formerly, practices were not costumed, although make-up and some costume would be used for

Sunday after the Sultan's monthly birthday on Pon Saturday in the Javanese calendar – and second, to give the different organisations a chance to perform.

This is often given as a reason why dancers in the classical sphere perform for tourists. One recently formed group performed at a princely house every night for a year. The performers earned Rp 2,000 (about 75p in 1989) and were fed. The number of performers for such a show could be as many as 25 people – dancers, musicians, and make-up helpers.

When I asked about the delicate question of money, I was always told that the money was not the point; it was the 'opportunity to perform' which mattered. Also, the honour factor was clearly involved. Discussion revealed that many dancers perceived that hotels, particularly the Ambarrukmo Palace Hotel, would pay more. However, those who belonged to this particular association in the south who took the trouble to go to the Ambarrukmo, which is located some 6 kilometres to the northeast of Yogya, soon discovered that the minimum fee for dancers there was less than anywhere else: a dancer could earn between Rp 1,600 and Rp 2,200 for an evening's work in 1989. The smallest tip in Yogya was given by the palace up to 1989: Rp 25 for dancers to take part in the Sunday practices, Rp 200 for teachers.

An important point relating to the imagined economic effects of tourism as demonstrated in the sphere of performance can be made here. Since independence, the palace has been a place for tourism-in-the-name-of-nationhood, and although in 1973 overseas tourists were recognised as a source of revenue for the palace and classical dancing has until now been the most commonly consumed kind of performance by overseas tourists in Yogya, with the exception perhaps of the 'Ramayana Ballet', the economic conditions of performance have not yet changed. Performers of classical dance cannot live from dancing even when they perform for tourists who pay for exclusive shows.

Palace culture has become state prestige culture, and dancers in this context continue to be regarded with honour (or honorariums) and not wage payments. This means that classical performance in the tourist sphere has not yet been commercialised in such a way as to change a performer's status into a viably professional one. The lack of commercialisation in the performing arts of Yogyakarta has been discussed by Indonesian analysts (Soedarsono, 1989). It has been suggested to me that there is a deep cultural resistance to paying for performance, because it should be part of an event, not something one pays to see. This remark was made by a man who works in the tourist industry and is interesting because it assumes that commercialisation can succeed only when Javanese audiences change their habits.

Dance education which started in the 1960s has played an important part in defining changes, and provided the opportunities and personnel to transform palace dance into the classical sphere. What remains unchanged are the heated aesthetic and factional disputes about purity, style and appropriateness in the various cultural circles. The extent to which these developments have resulted in a truly classical tradition or a kind of kitsch has been discussed (Lindsay, 1985), and is beyond the scope of this chapter, but the important point here is that this debate is not exclusively the result of touristic developments. Tourism may provide the opportunities to develop new venues for performance which hots up the competition, but the questions about change within the classical sphere cannot be accounted for by tourism development only, or blamed on tourism. To do so is to fall into the trap of oversimplifying traditional culture (Crick, 1989, 311–12).

Dancer and historian Soedarsono has perhaps fallen into the trap of reifying tradition when he divides traditional performance in Yogya into five categories: ritual, pseudo-ritual, festival, commercial and tourist art/performance (Soedarsono, 1989). He deplores the pseudo-ritual tendency which he argues is motivated by entertainment criteria rather than simply 'traditional' appropriateness, and which may 'look' traditional, but is not fulfilling the requirements of the entire context. For instance, classical-looking dances may be performed at wedding receptions with inappropriate themes and tape-recorded accompaniments. Or else dances may be done for anniversaries which are not Javanese: Javanese anniversaries are in multiples of eight, not '25 years' or one calendar year (ibid., 110).

As an influential cultural figure in Yogya, a performer and an academic, Soedarsono has played a considerable role in determining dance directions in the Province. He has done much to develop new classical performance, and has questioned the contemporary relevance of the long and complex forms such as Bedhaya (a dance for women which can last for up to two hours) and Wayang Wong (dance drama) which used to serve as high ceremonial entertainment in the palace. Soedarsono has taken the position that special dances need to be created for the tourists, rather than offering truncated versions of traditional genres, and makes a distinction between the discriminating powers of 'cultural tourists' and the needs of the more general visitor. His vision is to create performances which can pull the large audiences he has witnessed watching the hula in Hawaii (ibid., 46). Whether one agrees or not with Soedarsono's distinction between ritual and pseudo-ritual according to criteria of replication, which is a questionable definition of tradition, the interesting point to emerge from his invective against pseudo-ritual is that performance standards are at risk not from tourism, but from contemporary Javanese practices.

A recent development in Javanese understandings of overseas tourists in particular has been the discovery that they do not necessarily like their dances short and sweet. Members of the palace troupe who performed in the USA last year reported with astonishment that the audiences liked the long Bedhaya dance best of all. It seems that there is a now a tendency to attribute to some overseas tourists the capacity to take on a full-scale performance (unlike many modern Javanese), and to produce performances according to traditional standards instead of catering for imagined overseas tastes.

Soedarsono's view that there is a need for special dances made for tourists as in Bali is influential, but not exclusively so. Furthermore, in Bali a clever witty dance created for a tourist venue may catch the fancy of the Balinese and make its way to the front of the temple, becoming part of the least sacred class of performances which are allowed to be taken to tourists also. In Yogya one comes across new 'traditional' dances produced by different groups working in the classical Yogya tradition. These are usually described as 'revived' or 'rediscovered', and reference will be made to a Prince, a date, an old manuscript extricated from a palace archive. There is, however, another kind of dance brought to the town from the outlying regions, which brings us to the performances from the 'outside' of the palace.

## Regional performances

The classical dance genres in Yogya have tended to monopolise claim to being 'the local culture' if only because the tourist centre coincided with the kingdom's centre. Now there are changes.

Companies running tours to remote regions arrange 'regional' performances *en route*. If you go to Borobudur temple or the volcanic Dieng plateau you might stop at Sleman or Wonosobo for coffee and be entertained by *kuda lumping* and *jathilan* (hobby horse dances) or *lengger*, a genre related to *tayuban*. Heads of settlements as yet unvisited by tourist coaches or minibuses speak of reviving local performance traditions such as *tayuban* should they happen to be situated near routes leading to temples. Such revivals, they say, would be fun for the community and would create a new source of income.

Enterprise in the field of regional performance promotion in the

tourist context has been in the hands of tour professionals or
government officials. Tourist development, like all development in
Indonesia, comes from the top, and there has been little local
enterprise. One notable exception is the case of the Prambanan horse-
dance troupe which was set up by the community head in 1970 and
which earns for the participant locals a better income than most
classically trained dancers in Yogya can expect to earn. An ingenious
system which summons the performers from their fields at short notice
means that the headman can be very flexible. If a performer arrives
and finds all the costumes gone, it means he is too late. Earnings are
shared if someone consistently misses out.

Regional or non-classical performance is on the increase. Tourism
patronage to date has tended to provide opportunities for existing
local groups to put on more shows, rather than creating more groups.
A more significant cause of the growing importance of regional genres
is their incorporation into the curricula of State performance
academies.

Classical dance groups performing at hotels tend to be graduates of
dance academies who have set up their own groups. Such groups are
now bringing to the hotels the recently introduced regional styles of
performance they are being taught at college. One entertainments
manager told me that he had recently hired a *tayuban* group set up by
a dance lecturer at the Academy of Indonesian Arts (ISI) to provide a
change for the tourists. In such performances, dance graduates take on
the roles of traditional dancers and invite the guests to dance. Apart
from the origin of these graduate *tayuban* dancers, touristic *tayubans*
differ in two major respects from traditional ones. First, the old-style
*tayuban* dancer was a professional and could earn a living by dancing;
one night's performance could earn her a personal fee of anything
from Rp 20,000–Rp 50,000 (in 1989); the modern dance graduate is
lucky to get Rp 10,000. Second, there are male dancers who invite the
female tourists to dance, a supplement to the traditional pattern of the
male guests being handed the dance scarf by female dancers. This kind
of entertainment is on the increase, and it will be interesting to see if
the gender symmetry feeds into non-touristic *tayuban*.

There is a certain irony in the way in which *tayuban* is being
developed: as the traditional performers are being squeezed out by
decades of disapproval and broadened work opportunities, the new
performers from the academies are being allowed to take on the role of
dancing girl in performances which are also coming into the prestige
areas of national culture. This is one example of a regional 'outside'
tradition which is being promoted as an alternative to classical forms

for receiving guests at state events. Touristic guests are an extension of this category.

## TOURISM AS ONE ASPECT OF CULTURAL DEVELOPMENT

As we have seen, domestic tourists make up an important part of the number of tourists who come to Yogyakarta. The fact of people, their cash, and their 'influence' moving more frequently and in greater numbers around different regions is not a phenomenon concerning 'outside' influence in the contrastive sense. This movement of people might be compared to the kind of 'pilgrimages' which have been described as a crucial stage in the emergence of the imagined community of nationhood (Anderson, 1983). Local tourists in Indonesia may be changing local culture, but while local culture is being developed and preserved, this is according to principles which are designed to consolidate the Indonesian nation.

It is policy in Indonesia today to develop and preserve traditional cultural practices. Although such policies are the domain of the Ministry of Education and Culture, the implementation cuts across many more departments and levels in the administration, particularly the Ministry of Telecommunications and Tourism. However, although this policy is implicated in tourism development, both cultural policies and tourism development are part of national development policies. It would be wrong therefore to isolate tourism development from other cultural policies and to somehow claim that tourism automatically implies (a) a unique source of change, and (b) change from outside.

Although there are two contrasted spheres of performance, they are both included in development policies, with a certain reference to tourism. If we examine how cultural administrations define their objective, we are better able to understand how tourism is understood to be one and only one aspect of an elaborate programme of development, both practical and ideological.

Cultural projects and funding are administered by the offices of the Ministry of Education and Culture. Some projects centre on reviving lost performance genres, be they from 'inside' or 'outside'. It is revealing to see in what terms the objectives of such projects are defined. For example, a project carried out in Yogya between 1984 and 1985 centred on a regional drama from the Bantul district called *krumpyung*. The objectives of this project were two-fold:

1 To care for and to watch over the preservation of the values and

vitality of the traditional arts so that these can be passed down to future generations, so that in the long term the values embodied in these arts will still be protected and developed in order to instil feelings of pride towards the traditional arts as an inheritance from our ancestors which has high values.

2 To make an entertainment and attraction which has the special characteristics of the traditional arts of the Special Region of Yogyakarta in the eyes of tourists. (From Pendidikan Dasar dan Kebudajaan [Department of Basic Education and Culture], 1984–85).

A report of a performance given as a follow-up to the project in 1987 lists the desired results. These were as follows:

1 To provide an opportunity for creative participation of artists in this show in the context of making the traditional art of *krumpyung* everlasting.
2 To provide an opportunity for the people to be entertained and to gain appreciation of popular art, particularly *krumpyung*.
3 For documentation (photos, video).
4 The art of *krumpyung*, with its traditional characteristics, would make a good treat for tourists. (From Pendidikan Dasar dan Kebudajaan [Department of Basic Education and Culture], 1987–88).

While these reports form a genre in their own right, the ordering of interests does demonstrate the way in which the tourism factor is not the chief motivation of such projects. Rather, cultural development is to do with nation building. If it also results in a product that can attract tourists to the region, all well and good. However, I do not think *krumpyung* so far has become a tourist attraction. If anything, it has yet to enter the regional drama competition and festival circuit, which is a major arena for performance development.

Even an overt act of entrepreneurship in the field of tourism can have a more complex cultural significance. For example, in the 1960s, a centre for short shadow plays was set up in Yogya. The founder claims that this centre not only satisfied a demand from foreigners for Javanese shadow play shows, shortened from nine to two hours in length and held during the afternoon instead of at night; it also made local people realise that the shadow play had something to offer. Foreign interest legitimised and thereby maintained or recreated local interest in things close to home.

This continues to be the case. Studies on 'tradition' are increasingly aware of the fluid processes of change over time, and how 'tradition' describes ideas rather than historical continuities. Tourism may alter

the conditions under which performances may be enacted as traditions, but one could argue that Dutch colonials watching the famed
three-day-long dance dramas of the 1920s and 1930s in Yogya were
not in essence different from the people thronging the palace on
Sundays in the 1990s. Performance is an inevitable part of prestige
hospitality in Yogya, and is a complement to food and drink. The
guests today may not be invited individually, but they were extended
in 1991 a national invitation to 'visit Indonesia'. The political status of
both kinds of guest of course is an aspect which could also be
compared, but my point here is that tourism today is not threatening a
hitherto hermetically sealed traditional cultural world.

The diversification of performance training in academies is also not
caused by the development of tourism as such. As we have seen, even
were the tourist industry to be interpreted as an incentive for
performers, most performers discover that one cannot live by dance
(even for tourists) alone. The search for generic variation and novelty
is the result of cultural policy and institutional. In the past there were
no professional performers in Java (perhaps with the exception of the
*tayuban* dancer and the shadow puppeteer); people performed specific
dramatic forms for specific occasions or reasons. The academically
trained dancer who invests his or her identity in that work is the
product of modern republican educational institutes. Many still dance
as a 'hobby', in the Javanese way, but the search for more genres may
be explained as the result of a new category of full-time dancer as
much as the demand of a tourist market.

Outside the training institutions, in the bureaucratic hierarchy of
Culture and Education Offices, professional interests and ambition
also motivate the quest for new 'forgotten' forms. I was recently
informed by an official for cultural promotion in a district in Central
Java that he had found a lost local performance tradition, and was
planning to revive it. *Buginul*, he said, is not a very interesting kind of
performance, 'but everyone else is reviving *tayuban*, and I've had
enough of that!' Once revived, the new tradition would be shown in
competitions and festivals which are an important arena for cultural
promotion functioning in the name of development, and tourism too,
as a second thought.

What the tourist industry does is to provide a rationalisation for
diversification. Indeed, if anything, the tourist industry is providing a
contemporary style of rationalisation for continuing to maintain and
develop classical and regional performance traditions. It is possible
that the creative energies of the young participants might well have
turned elsewhere, were it not for these new kinds of audiences and

opportunities, even if these are perceived as being more materially beneficent than has been the case.

There is another side to touristic entrepreneurship, however. When a princely residence was reallocated on the death of the previous incumbent, the main pavilion where performance takes place was restored, and the people who used to live in the main courtyard were instructed to move to cramped quarters at the back of the compound. The Kanoman, as it is now called, was opened on 29 December 1990 and dinner-dance packages are presumably now taking place. This kind of 'development' is causing people to understand more specifically that tourism has short-term negative effects, but there is little that people can do to seek redress or compensation. In this instance, the effect of tourism is not on the performance as such, but on the security of tenants; the objective to provide performance venues precipitates these situations. Tourism can also provide an incentive to trample the 'little person'.

Returning to performance concerns, I would suggest here that there is another way in which local perceptions of the needs of tourists have come into play, and which may determine styles of production in the long term for Javanese and Indonesian performance genres and options.

A very beautiful covered theatre opened at Prambanan in 1988. This new theatre complements the newly-restored open stage which is used for the 'Ramayana Ballet' productions mentioned previously. The management of the closed theatre is currently under experimentation. The director proudly showed off the sophisticated computerised lighting system and demonstrated the acoustics. My research assistant, a student of the drama faculty at the Academy for Performing Arts, quickly became interested in the potential of this stage. The director had been filling the performance schedule with a classical Ramayana performance by a number of dance groups, who normally perform every Thursday for a month. He said that it was necessary for groups to come before the performance to rehearse with the lighting, but that this was causing problems. Pramabanan is 12 kilometres outside the city, a problem for audiences as well as performers. It makes it difficult for many of the associations in Yogya to arrange time and transportation for this rehearsal. Although the fee of Rp 400,000 per performance might sound attractive and make the journey worthwhile, nothing is paid for rehearsals.

In the long term the new theatre and the scope it offers to performers for experimentation might cause interested parties to develop the quality and scope of their stage management. Fancy lighting to date has been the prerogative of modern drama, cabaret and pop concerts; traditional performance relies on simple illumination rather than lighting. The new theatre is in the round, with tiered seats, a unique performing space in the region. It would not have been built without an intensive tourism policy. The director hopes to diversify the range of performance and it will be interesting to see how or if it has any effect on performance in Yogya over the next decade, and whether or not this effect is evaluated negatively or positively by local or outside opinion. It is of interest in this connection that in 1989, a leading Indonesian playwright W. S. Rendra chose the open theatre at Prambanan to stage his comeback to his home town. The performance was for locals, not tourists, and represents another divergence between touristic aim and potential uses.

## CONCLUDING REMARKS

It has been seen that tourists in Yogya are domestic as well as from overseas; in general people expect to profit from tourism, although the micro example for performers to date shows how payments take the form of honoraria which are insufficient to live on. Profit is clearly going to the middle persons who may be Indonesians or overseas operators; where local entrepreneurs are troupe leaders, any profits at this stage are being used to make new costumes. Reliable data on such finances have been difficult to determine so far. One often has to depend on gossip which is motivated by envy. A different kind of economic result of performance tourism which has been noted is that the creation of dance venues for tourists can also jeopardise the security of tenants.

Performance traditions are changing, as they always have done. Tourism is often given as a reason for promoting or developing particular forms or genres, but it has had little effect in itself on the 'regional' genres. The classical sphere has been more affected by the influence of tourism because it has been easier to control by means of packaging in response to specific demands than have the regional forms thus far. There is little evidence to suggest that definite policies towards the performing arts have been adopted by the official bodies responsible for tourist development in Yogyakarta. If anything, the justification or rationalisation that tourism provides has become assimilated into broader-based factional cleavages which engage in competition for cultural control within the region. Any artistic promotion in the name of tourism is invariably linked to plans for local development in its widest sense, and tourism is often the last consideration to be listed in reports about such plans.

Mobility was impossible before the creation of a more far-reaching communication network. My own research benefited from dirt tracks having been, or in the process of being, upgraded into tarred roads. Very often, at the end of such a tarred road, there would be a community head who had initiated the road building, asking me for suggestions so that other tourists would also go along that road.

Media communications also play an important part in the dissemination of socio-cultural alternatives. There is a feeling in Central Java that certain traditions, often performance ones, are lost because electricity arrives. What this often means is that television has entered the village, and when this happens, culture dies, or so the logic goes. Although the situation is much more complex than this, it is important to recognise that just as roads facilitate mobility, electronic media networks break down cultural boundaries. As a guide in Tanah Toraja is reported to have said, 'Tourism is not important in our lives – we see the world on television every night' (Smith, 1989, 9). This suggests that the changes which tourism is used to explain have already been set in motion by developments of communication networks.

The examples of diversification of genres and resources and the production of classical dance in its longer form indicate that more realistic insights into tourist requirements may prevent the trivialisation of Javanese performance culture which seemed inevitable ten years ago. At the same time, changing institutional formations and changing rationales are part of national development, of which tourism is only a part. It is also perhaps fair to say that tourism provides the state with an invaluable function: it can be blamed for unanticipated consequences or failure of domestic policy. As well as being able to refract fantasies for the future, tourism can take the blame for problems in the present.

# 8 Open-ended prostitution as a skilful game of luck
## Opportunity, risk and security among tourist-oriented prostitutes in a Bangkok soi[1]

*Erik Cohen*

## PROLOGUE

Tourist oriented prostitution in Thailand first developed during the 1960s. It was popularised by the R & R vacations of American soldiers serving in Vietnam. After the war Thailand became an increasingly attractive destination of sex-tourism. This type of tourism peaked during the 1970s and early 1980s. The threat of AIDS and the efforts of the Thai government to change the touristic image of the country apparently led to a gradual decline in its salience and scope (Mills, 1990). However, perhaps more significant sociologically are the subtle changes in the atmosphere of the relationship between tourist-oriented prostitutes and their clients which accompanied these recent developments.

This chapter reports on the culture of 'open-ended', tourism-oriented prostitution during its heyday in the early 1980s, as it was observed in the hinterland of one of the major tourist entertainment areas in Bangkok. The ludic character of the encounter between tourist-oriented prostitutes and their clients at that time stemmed partly from the fact that the risks involved in engaging in prostitution, even if they may have been substantial, were relatively low, particularly in the area of health; low in comparison to those faced by prostitutes in the domestic sector, and certainly low when compared to the subsequent period, when AIDS became a factor of growing significance in the practice of prostitution in Thailand, as well as in the consciousness of tourist-oriented prostitutes.

The body of this chapter hence captures the culture of tourist-oriented prostitution during a specific period of Thai history. It thus contributes to the comparative study of prostitution in general and specifically to the study of relations between prostitution and society. Some of the more recent developments, on the background of the threat of AIDS, will be briefly sketched out in the postscript.

## INTRODUCTION

Rural to urban migrants from depressed areas of Thailand, and particularly the north-east (*Isan*), move into Bangkok in ever greater numbers in search of employment and income, for their own subsistence or for the support of their relatives back home. Prominent among these are large numbers of young women, many of whom hope to make enough money in the city to be able to support not only themselves, but also their parents, siblings and children. They soon realise that the employment opportunities for uneducated and unskilled workers are severely limited. In fact, it appears that in recent years the opportunity structure facing unskilled in-migrant women in Bangkok has even contracted: as the price level of basic necessities rose continually in the metropolis, wages on the depressed labour market remained low, even as many recent in-migrants were unable to secure a job. Moreover, even if they can find employment as domestics or in a factory, the earnings of unskilled labourers will usually not even reach the 1982 legal minimum wage of 64 Baht (approx. US$3) a day. Indeed, many of those who work earn less than 1,000 Baht (US$50) a month. This is hardly sufficient for their own upkeep, not to speak of support for dependants. Many of the women, finding employment opportunities unsatisfactory, turn to hawking and ped- dling, a sector which is notorious for its apparent ability to absorb practically unlimited numbers of self-employed sellers (Geertz, 1963c, 29). But even here it becomes increasingly more difficult to establish oneself, and marginal hawkers are frequently driven out of business.

Many migrants are thus caught in a predicament from which there is apparently no exit. Under such conditions prostitution provides one of the few ways out: despite the very large number of women in Bangkok engaging in prostitution in its various forms, conservatively estimated at 300,000 (Phongpaichit, 1981, 14–15), this occupation still offers to most women an income considerably greater than anything they could hope to earn in another line of work. Massage women, for example, according to Phongpaichit (ibid., 19) reported incomes which range 'from $75 to $750 a month, with over half earning $150 to $300, and another quarter earning more than that'. Brothel women probably earn less, but even those – insofar as they are not 'bonded' (ibid., 17) – earn more than they could make elsewhere.

Prostitution existed in Thailand long before the country became a popular destination of sex tourism. Tourism, however, had a crucial impact on the trade. Not only did the number of women engaging in prostitution grow considerably, but the nature of the occupation changed with the emergence of the new clientele. The interaction with white, foreign, male tourists (*farangs*) engendered a new subculture of prostitution (Cohen, 1982c). It is this which I seek to capture in the concept of 'open-ended' prostitution and analyse on the basis of my study of an urban lane (*soi*) in the hinterland of one of the principal tourist areas of Bangkok, conducted during the summers of 1981 and 1982, as part of an on-going longitudinal urban anthropological study

I lived in a slum in the *soi* for two months at a time, and conducted observations and in-depth interviews with inhabitants and informants. In the *soi* live several hundred Thai women who derive their livelihood from tourists and other foreigners, mainly as bar and coffee shop women. Many of these have rooms in the slum. I conducted extended conversations with several dozen women and collected some biographies. Family background, education, work-experience in and outside prostitution, and attitudes and relationships with *farangs* were the principal topics of investigation. I also talked to a large number of *farangs* in and outside the *soi* (Cohen, 1984a; 1986).

Despite the reputation of Bangkok as a world centre of sex-tourism, most prostitutes work in brothels and massage parlours with a predominantly local clientele. Tourist-oriented prostitutes, operating from bars and coffee shops, constitute a small portion of the total number of women in the trade, but one of considerable economic importance. They are in no small degree responsible for tourist spending, thus contributing to national foreign currency earnings. They are, in a sense, the elite of the trade: their life-chances, work conditions and income are incomparably better than those of most women working with a local clientele. Indeed, the circumstances of their work enable them to deny that they are 'prostitutes' (*sophenee*) and to define themselves as 'working with foreigners' (*tham ngan kap farang*) or with 'guests' (*tham ngan kap khaek*); these occupational self-conceptions closely resemble the designation 'hospitality women', by which their counterparts in Manila are known (Neumann, 1978; van der Velden, 1982). The women profess to be insulted when they are called 'prostitutes'; some of their *farang* customers and boyfriends also vehemently oppose that designation.

The young women do not differ much in background and education from those working with a local clientele, but are, on the average, older than those working in brothels. They are mostly in their twenties or early thirties, of rural background, predominantly from the northeast. Most have children from an earlier, disrupted marriage or cohabitation with a Thai man. They have usually already lived in Bangkok for a few years, having worked as domestics, factory workers or hawkers prior to turning to their present occupation. They have not generally worked as prostitutes with a local clientele, prior to engaging in tourist-oriented prostitution. Those I talked to worked in bars and coffee shops for a couple of days up to – mostly intermittently – a few years. They are a highly mobile group, frequently changing their habitation and moving in and out of the trade. Some of this mobility is related to the special character of 'open-ended' prostitution, to be explained below.

The young women usually live alone or with another woman in a rented room. Several houses in the *soi* cater exclusively to the women. Most of their free time interaction is with other females in the trade. They tend to form closely-knit peer-groups of women living in the same house or yard and working in the same bar or coffee shop. Members of such groups assist and support one another in times of need or crisis, financial or emotional. They often claim to be 'sisters', even if they are not really related. Peers are their main reference group and much of their conduct, attire and aspirations can be understood in terms of their relations and competition with peers. However, despite the mutual dependency, the women are also suspicious of one another – an ambiguity which runs through many kinds of primary relations in Thai society.

Some women have Thai boyfriends who live with them when they are not in the company of a *farang* customer. These Thai men exploit the women, but do not usually control them, protect them or hustle customers, and hence cannot be described as pimps.

Most women work in a few dozen bars and several big coffee shops not far from the *soi*. With the exception of those who serve as go-go dancers in bars, the women are not employed by the establishments, but operate on their own. Bar women, however, are not free to leave the premises at will. Customers who take out a woman from a bar (but not from a coffee shop) have to pay 'take out money'[2] to the bar; the women are, however, free to keep any money they receive from their customers. The bar and coffee shop women thus differ from prostitutes working in brothels, massage parlours and similar establishments, who frequently receive only a fraction of their customers' payments – the bulk of it going to the owners, procurers, taxi-drivers and so on (Khin Thitsa, 1980). Bar and coffee shop women are thus essentially independent operators. Their independence is a crucial precondition for open-ended prostitution, increasing both the chances and the hazards of their trade.

The women who work in bars derive their income from three principal sources: go-go dancing, for which they are paid a fixed sum of about 700–1,300 Baht (US$35–60) a month; drinks with customers, for which their cut is usually 10 Baht (US$0.50) per drink; and prostitution, which usually pays about 150–250 Baht for a single-shot, 'short time' and 350–500 Baht for a night; but being 'open-ended' the relationship may be extended beyond that, and eventually bring in many times more. Of the three sources of income, prostitution is the one the women are most interested in; go-go dancing and hustling for drinks, though in themselves financially not unimportant, seem secondary sources of income – a stabilising counterpart to the uncertainty of prostitution; indirectly, they are also ways to attract customers and start a liaison. Coffee shop women, in contrast, neither dance nor drink with the customers, but derive their income exclusively from prostitution. Still, their trade is considered more lucrative and convenient, and many bar women switch after some time to a coffee shop, or move to coffee shops after the bars close for the night.

The women use the various services in the *soi* which cater to their needs, such as general stores, stalls, restaurants, seamstress shops and beauty parlours. Those living in the slum rarely depart beyond its limits except for work. They live seemingly frugally, and indeed spend little on food and other basic necessities. But, once they have money, it passes quickly through their hands on clothing, cosmetics, drink, gambling and, in some cases, drugs. Almost all have family obligations and support their children, parents or younger siblings from their income – although the actual remittances seem to be smaller than they claim.

Few women remain in tourist-oriented prostitution long enough to make a career out of it. However, many women do stay in the trade longer than they had originally intended (cf. Phongpaichit, 1981, 18–19); a few are in their mid-thirties, an age which is considered old for a prostitute in Thailand (Khin Thitsa, 1980, 14). While I have not systematically examined their patterns of mobility and the factors influencing their eventual success or failure in the trade, the latter seems to depend essentially on their ability to exploit changing opportunities, while at the same time building for themselves a basis of economic and emotional security, which will enable them to overcome the uncertainties inherent in their situation.

## THE DYNAMICS OF OPEN-ENDED PROSTITUTION

Prostitution has been conceived of by sociologists as an emotionally neutral, indiscriminate, specifically remunerated sexual service.

Prostitutes were pictured as meeting their customers in temporarily limited, usually brief, well-defined encounters. Even though a prostitute may build up a permanent clientele, each encounter is typically a discrete, separately remunerated affair, during which a specific sexual act is performed. Repetitive encounters with the same customer are ordinarily not supposed to create a continuous relationship, nor to lead to any emotional involvement on the part of the woman; indeed, professional prostitutes develop psychological defence mechanisms which control such involvement (Rasmussen and Kuhn, 1976, 279). Though prostitutes may differ considerably in their income, depending upon the nature of the establishment in which they work, the class of their customers, their attractiveness and the kinds of services they provide, remuneration is routine and usually fixed or agreed upon in advance; there are few uncertainties in the situation, and if there are, these relate primarily to the dangers of venereal infection or physical attack upon the prostitutes, rather than any extraordinary rewards or benefits which may accrue from their customers.

I suggest the term 'open-ended' prostitution to characterise a kind of relationship between a prostitute and her customer which, though it may start as a specific neutral service, rendered more or less indiscriminately to any customer, may be extended into a more protracted, diffused and personalised liaison, involving both emotional attachment and economic interest. The tourist-oriented bar and coffee shop women living in the *soi* illustrate such 'open-ended' prostitution, but the concept is also applicable to tourist-oriented prostitutes in some other developing countries, and especially the 'hospitality women' of Manila (van der Velden, 1982).

My analysis departs from the difference between the opportunity structure facing the tourist-oriented prostitute in bars and coffee shops and that facing brothel and massage parlour women working with a local clientele. Whatever the size and distribution of the earnings of brothel and massage parlour women, they derive from essentially routinised and brief encounters with clients; hence, given the type of establishment in which they work, their earnings depend primarily on the number of customers they serve.

Bar and coffee shop women probably earn, on the average, less than massage parlour women in the first-class establishments, but more than women working in brothels. They operate on a buyer's market – the number of women in bars and coffee shops usually much exceeds the number of prospective customers. There is also less turnover of customers: while a brothel or massage parlour woman may have intercourse with several men a night, bar or coffee shop women rarely have it with more than one, and in off-season periods they may go for days without a customer. The important point to note, however, is that their opportunities are differently structured than those of brothel and massage parlour women, owing to the much less routinised character of their relations with customers. The range of their incomes is considerably greater than that found in other types of prostitution. The earnings of a prostitute may also fluctuate widely – between utter pennilessness one day and considerable riches the other. It is this extreme variability and uncertainty which endows the occupational culture of open-ended prostitution with some of its distinguishing features.

The woman who meets a customer in a bar or coffee shop in most cases retires with him initially for a 'short-time' or a single night. That initial encounter is normally of a purely mercenary character (Cohen, 1982c, 415); but it is significant that the woman frequently underplays the commercial side (cf. van der Velden, 1982) and often 'stages' affection for the customer (Cohen, 1982c, 415–16). Such an approach facilitates the extension of the initial brief encounter into a more permanent liaison.

If the customer desires the woman to stay, and he is agreeable to her, she may simply stay on; the customer then continues to pay the bar the daily 'take out' money. The relationship in such a case often changes from a purely mercenary one into a mixed liaison, consisting, on the part of the woman, of both economic interests and emotional involvement; in some cases, it may even be transformed into a love relationship (ibid., 416–17). If the couple stays together for more than a week or two, the woman usually leaves her job in the bar or coffee shop for the length of her partner's stay; in some cases she returns to the bar, but abstains from relations with other men; and she usually demands the same of her partner. The fact that she does not 'work', however, can be used by her to put moral pressure upon her partner to reimburse her for her losses.

It is important to note that most short liaisons are generally not purely contractual economic relationships. Khin Thitsa writes that '(a) woman costs for the night about US$12.50; for a week's rental (i.e. seven days and seven nights service) the bargain price of $50 is offered' (Khin Thitsa, 1980, 15); while correct in substance, this statement is somewhat misleading: in some instances the couple may agree that the woman will receive a given sum a day. But the woman's reward is rarely stated in such fixed, commercial terms; rather, it depends on and fluctuates with many factors, such as the *farang's* wealth and generosity and the woman's skill and willingness to extricate money from him.

If the partner is a well-to-do, short-term tourist the woman may 'live it up' during his stay: move with him into a luxurious hotel, eat in the best restaurants, receive expensive gifts of clothing or jewellery and enjoy a holiday in a fashionable seaside resort, such as Pattaya. Upon his departure, she may receive a considerable amount of money. If he is less wealthy, she may just savour the agreeable relationship as long as it lasts. In any case, the woman tends to become tense prior to her partner's departure, both in anticipation of the size of her remuneration and of the emotional impact of the rupture of her liaison and of the return to her ordinary routine in the bar or coffee shop.

In fact, in many cases the liaison does not explicitly terminate with the *farang's* departure, but is expected to continue even after separation: addresses are exchanged, promises of continual love and of return and renewal of the liaison are made. Afterwards, letters are exchanged, through which the relationship lingers on for a while, but then usually peters out as both partners get otherwise involved. Some liaisons, however, continue intermittently for years, the *farang* returning regularly to see his girlfriend. Some women get invited for a visit abroad – indeed, a surprisingly large number of those in the *soi* have visited various European countries. A smaller number of women get married; some of these remain abroad and get out of prostitution altogether. Others, however, return after a short while as their marriage breaks up, and resume their previous occupation. Still others go abroad, and either willingly or unwillingly engage in prostitution there.

The prolongation of a liaison beyond the actual departure of her partner has both an economic and an emotional significance for the woman. It gives her the feeling that there is someone who cares for her and on whom she may depend in times of need, in her insecure and frequently changing predicament. An ex-boyfriend, like a Thai boyfriend, is thus a haven of emotional security, even as the woman passes from one temporary liaison to another, a process which she frequently finds emotionally taxing (Cohen, 1982c, 421). Many women therefore maintain a lively correspondence with their past boyfriends, telling them of their problems and often asking for financial support to help them out of real or contrived troubles. Some, indeed, have developed considerable dexterity in corresponding with a number of men, from whom they solicit, and receive, support (Cohen, 1986). Indeed, one way for a prostitute in her thirties to insure her future is to build up a coterie of boyfriends who visit her regularly and to all of whom she serves intermittently as a mistress.

## THE CULTURE OF SEXUALITY AND OPEN-ENDED PROSTITUTION

Traditional Thai culture emits contradictory messages, which facilitate conflicting interpretations of the nature of Thai society and the extent of change in contemporary Thailand (Cohen, 1984b) This generalisation is well illustrated in the current debate surrounding the status of women in Therevada Buddhist ideology. Khin Thitsa (1980), taking up a theme first developed by Kirsch (1975), argued that the inferior position of women in Buddhism preconditions them to become prostitutes:

> With the low value attached to the female body and the female spirit by Buddhism, woman has been sufficiently degraded already to enter prostitution. If historically woman has served men helping him as wife, minor wife or mistress, it is not such a big step to become an actual prostitute. Indeed, the traditional emphasis on polygamy in Buddhist society encourages the widespread practice of prostitution in modern Thailand
>
> (Khin Thitsa, 1980, 23)

This position has recently been severely criticised by Keyes (1984), who emphasised the elevated position of women in Buddhism, and argued that the urban secularised image of woman as sex symbol is a completely new cultural pattern, unassociated with any tempering Buddhist message'. It follows that impoverished rural-to-urban migrant women are forced, under the pressure of circumstances and against their better cultural convictions, to adopt this novel image, as they enter prostitution in their struggle for survival. If Kirsch and Khin Thitsa's position is adopted, prostitution is thus just a contemporary form of an ingrained cultural pattern; if one adopts Keyes' position, however, it is a novel form of sexual relations, based on an essentially Western 'market mentality' which tends to commercialise everything, including sex.

My material on open-ended prostitution holds forth the possibility of mediating between the conflicting views of Kirsch and Khin Thitsa on the one hand and Keyes on the other: whatever the Buddhist ideal of womanhood, there is little doubt that the actual standing of women in the traditional Thai social hierarchy is fairly low; this lowly standing may well inculcate young rural Thai women with a diffuse service-orientation, which facilitates their acceptance of such inferior roles as prostitution. At the same time, however, the fact that they fail to realise the cultural ideal of womanhood, as described by Keyes, fills them with shame and a feeling of 'loss of face', particularly in cases where women who had been married before feel forced by circumstances to enter prostitution. This sensation, however, is tempered by another cultural principle, that of individual freedom of mobility: as Kirsch (1975) pointed out, the fact that Thai women are in daily life less subject to religiously inspired restrictions facilitates their involvement in entrepreneurial activities. I suggest that open-ended prostitution is one area in which such entrepreneurship finds expression: it demands no initial capital, and, if one is willing to take risks and dare one's 'luck', holds forth the promise of considerable opportunities. One way to interpret the women engaging in open-ended prostitution, then, is to see them as risk-taking, small-scale entrepreneurs. The culturally patterned role of the women as daring entrepreneurs, relieved from some restrictions incumbent upon men, fits remarkably well the structure of opportunities in open-ended prostitution.

However, the uncertainty, insecurity and impermanency involved in the trade call into play the contrary cultural theme of hierarchical dependency of a lower status person on a higher status person or patron (Hanks, 1975, 198–200). In the context of open-ended prostitution, this means that the woman will seek to establish a permanent relationship with a man towards whom she could play the role of a mistress. While the attitude of individualistic entrepreneurial opportunism induces in the women a tendency to trade-off sexual attraction for money, the contrary attitude of hierarchical dependency induces a tendency to combine the quest for emotional attachment and material benefits in a master/mistress relationship.

In my earlier work (Cohen, 1982c) I have conceptualised four types of relationships between the women and *farangs*, based on the mix of economic interests and emotional involvement which they embody:

1 mercenary – based on an emotionless 'economic exchange';
2 staged – also based on 'economic exchange', but accompanied by faked or staged emotions on the part of the woman;
3 mixed – based on both 'economic exchange', as well as emotional involvement on the part of the woman; and
4 emotional – based primarily or exclusively on emotional involvement or 'love' (Cohen, 1982c, 414–17).

This is an essentially etic typology, i.e. one constructed by an external observer with the help of general theoretical concepts taken from Blau's (1967) exchange theory. Whatever its adequacy, it disregards the emic conception of the Thai woman–*farang* man relationships, i.e. the manner in which it is interpreted in the Thai culture. I shall now attempt such an emic reinterpretation of the typology. Such an analysis is intended to examine to what extent the prevailing conception of tourism-oriented prostitution is essentially a Western or also a Thai one, i.e. whether, under the impact of exogenous factors, the women adopted a Western view of their trade and their relationships with their customers, or whether they reinterpreted the traditional Thai cultural codes in a new context.

An analysis of the women's own conceptions and attitudes to the four relationships indicates that each is the subject, for different women, and perhaps even on different occasions for the same woman, of *both* a Western and a Thai emic interpretation.

1 Mercenary: This type comes closest to the kind of prostitution prevalent in the modern West (Cagnon, 1968, 592–93). Indeed, many of the women interpret this type of relationship in essentially Western terms, as a clear-cut economic exchange in which a specific sexual service is provided for money. However, this type of relationship is frequently fictitiously assimilated to the culturally more acceptable gift-relationship: the woman refuses to quote her price explicitly, preferring to leave remuneration to the generosity of her customer (Cohen, 1982c, 411). Her remuneration thus becomes a kind of gratuity. Though remaining an essentially economic transaction, its implicit character has several advantages for the woman: it enables her to dissociate herself from the ordinary prostitute and thus to enhance her self-image as one who 'works with guests'; simultaneously, it is also a display of Thai opportunism: by appealing to her customer's generosity, she may extricate from him a much larger sum than she would ever dare to ask for explicitly. Finally, it also helps to 'open up' the initial brief encounter into a more protracted liaison.

2 Staged: While the mercenary relationship is a purely sexual affair, without any display of emotions, in the 'staged' relationship, the woman fakes feelings, emotions or sexual attraction to the customer, which she does not, in fact, experience. Staging, however, may also be emically understood from two contrasting perspectives: from a Western perspective as a trick played upon the customer as a means to attract him, bolster his ego and attach him sexually to the woman, thereby enhancing her material rewards (cf. Rasmussen and

Kuhn, 1976, 279); or from a Thai cultural perspective as a playful display of personalised service (cf. de Gallo and Alzate, 1976), expressing a culturally induced motive to please her sexual partner, as she would an unloved Thai man to whom she is wife or mistress. While like Amittatapana in the story quoted by Keyes (1984), she may do so in order to receive greater material benefits from an emotionally unrewarding relationship, she thus *also* acts out a Thai cultural theme – an obligation of those lower in the social hierarchy to please those higher up on it.

3  Mixed: This type, involving both material interests and a genuine emotional attachment on the part of the woman, is also subject to both emic perspectives: it may be approached from a Western perspective – in which case it will be based on the assumption, generally taken for granted in Western cultures, that economic remuneration and emotional attachment are *substitutive* (hence the maxim that 'love cannot be bought'). In that case, the greater the woman's involvement, the *less* she will look for material rewards from her partner as an inducement to continue the relationship. From the Thai cultural perspective, however, economic remune-ration and emotional attachment are often seen as *additive*; women tend to assimilate their 'mixed' relationships with *farangs* to the cultural model of the relationship of a Thai mistress to her master. Such a perspective induces the woman to react emotionally to her partner in accordance with the amount of material benefits she receives from him, interpreting these as a token of her value, attractiveness and desirability to him, as well as of his generosity. The woman in such cases is in a state of emotional dependence on her partner, rather than in love, in the Western sense – but her feelings cannot be said to be faked.

4  Emotional: In this type, material benefits cease to be a significant factor in the relationship, which depends primarily or exclusively on the mutual infatuation of the partners. Here too, however, two emic perspectives can be distinguished. From a Western perspective, the woman may well perceive such a relationship as an instance of the imported cultural model of 'romantic' love. But she may also view it from a Thai perspective as an acting out of the culturally approved pattern of selfless devotion of the wife to her husband.

While my materials indicate that each of the various types of relationships is, indeed, emically interpreted differently by different women and on various occasions by the same woman according to each of the two cultural models, I have no precise data on the relative incidence of each interpretation. My hunch, however, is that the traditional Thai interpretation is more ingrained and more common than the modern Western one, especially among recent arrivals on the scene.

Relationships between Thai women and *farang* men are thus a fertile area for cross-cultural misunderstanding. A relationship which appears to a Westerner highly Westernised, may be acceptable to the woman because it fits a Thai cultural pattern. Precisely in the more protracted and intimate relationships, the differential interpretation may suddenly lead to an acute crisis, as the cultural gap separating the partners dawns upon them. Moreover, it is doubtful whether the alternative emic models of interpretation of the various types of relationships penetrate the consciousness of the women themselves, or that they distinguish them clearly; there are cases in which they interpret a relationship equivocally in terms of both models, switching precipitately, in moments of conflict, from one emic perspective to the other. Such ambiguity adds to the bemusement of their uncomprehending *farang* partners.

## RISK AND LUCK: THE GAME ELEMENT IN OPEN-ENDED PROSTITUTION

Open-ended prostitution is a non-routine occupation. By the same token it involves a strong element of chance – in the sense of both risk of life and limb and opportunity for success and riches, which is significantly greater than in more routine forms of prostitution, such as brothels or massage parlours. This element of chance, which cannot be completely reduced and mastered through knowledge and skill, takes on emically the character of 'luck' (*chok*; cf. Mosel, 1966, 193–95; Zulaika, 1981). Work in open-ended prostitution thus becomes a skilled game of hazard or 'luck'. This forms an important ingredient in the motivation and attitude of the women toward their trade.

Safety and security is one of the reasons for prostitutes to work in establishments or to attach themselves to pimps. The open-ended prostitution of bar and coffee shop women is devoid of many of the safety arrangements found in other establishments: the women are on their own, and once they depart with a customer, they are essentially at his mercy. In this situation they face three kinds of risk:

1 Material: The most common risk is that the customer may exploit the woman, i.e. make use of her sexual services and then abandon her or refuse to remunerate her. The women are helpless against

such exploitation, and mostly take it in their stride as part of their job.

A more devious risk is the demand for payments, made by corrupt policemen, in exchange for the women's liberty. This risk is faced especially by coffee shop women: the coffee shops are frequently raided by police, mostly in token attempts to erase nominally illegal prostitution (Hail, 1980, 14). Instead of going to jail, many women prefer to pay off the police, usually to the tune of 500 Baht (about US$25). The women, scared of being arrested, therefore carry with them to work a sum of money – but then they are exposed to another kind of risk, that of theft: cases are known in which *farang* men took women to remote locations, and after intercourse, robbed them of their money.

2  Physical safety: The women are defenceless against attack by disturbed or dissatisfied customers. They may suffer physical attack, and, in extreme cases, even pay with their life, as did one woman in a hotel room in the summer of 1982 – a case which provoked widespread apprehension and fear among the women in the *soi*.

3  Health: Venereal disease is widespread among prostitutes in Bangkok (Khin Thitsa, 1980, 13; Suthaporn, 1983), although it is apparently lower among those oriented to tourists than among those working with a local clientele. Still, many tourists do infect themselves during their sojourn and transmit the disease from one woman to another. Women who are new to the trade are often terrified of VD, whereas the older ones take it as part of their occupational risk. Many women go regularly for VD check-ups, and carry 'VD cards'. Some bars actually demand such regular checks. Still, the checks are not wholly dependable and infected women continue to engage in the trade, thus contributing to the spread of VD.

The challenge facing a woman engaged in open-ended prostitution is to develop those skills which enable her to maximise her opportunities, while minimising these and similar risks. These consist primarily of the ability to discriminate dangerous and unpromising from safe and generous clients; the skill to attract the latter; the capacity to create the most advantageous relationship with them – which often means transforming a single encounter into a more permanent liaison.

Skill and chance are obviously in an inverted relationship: the greater one's skill, the more control one has over the situation, and hence the smaller the element of chance. However, whatever the degree of skill, an irreducible element of chance always remains (Mosel, 1966, 195; cf. also Zulaika, 1981). This is greater for the less skilful, smaller for the more skilful women. It is this element which is emically conceived of as 'luck' and plays a prominent role in the occupational culture of the women; in comparison, the development of skills, though not unimportant, plays a secondary role: many women depend in their work on their natural endowment, for which, indeed, they are appreciated by their customers. There is none of the professional training found, for example, in American prostitution (Heyl, 1977). To the extent that there is some development of skills, it is distinctly amateurish and informal. It comes mostly from contact with more experienced women, who advise the newly arrived ones on how to deal with customers.

The principal area of skill in which the need for training is most often perceived by the women is that of foreign languages, which in practice means English, the *lingua franca* of the trade. Many women profess a desire to learn English which, they claim, will enable them to find more and better customers. Many indeed begin to teach themselves the language, mostly with the aid of Thai books for self-instruction. Few, however, persist in their study, finding that it overtaxes their learning capacity, which was stunted by their inadequate and limited rural education. None of the women attended the English conversation club in the *soi*, a medium of instruction very popular among the young Thai middle class. Most women after some time in the trade do acquire a basic sprinkling of English, but their conversation is severely limited to a few routine topics. Indeed, communication with customers is usually conducted in a simplified 'foreigner talk'; an additional constraint is the visiting non-Anglophone *farang's* incompetence in English. The point to note is that the women are aware of the importance of English for their job, but are still unable or unwilling to study it systematically and persistently.

Another area of skill, in which the women are more proficient, is the care of their attire, toilet and general appearance. Even a casual observer will notice the fast transformation in the appearance of a newly arrived woman in the first week or two after her arrival on the scene. Girls, especially if they came recently from their village, usually start work in their rural finery, use little make-up and do their hair in a rural or provincial style. Soon, upon earning some money, they acquire the working outfit of tourist-oriented prostitutes: tight jeans, T-shirts (often imprinted with some English word, such as 'Watermelon') and high-heeled shoes. They put on make-up and paint their nails. Later on, gold jewellery, frequently received as a present from their boyfriends, is added, and constitutes the most conspicuous symbol of their occupational success. On the whole, however, the appearance of most women resembles that of the urban Thai lower-middle class, but is a shade louder. Older women, who have experience in the trade, but whose charms have suffered with age, develop considerable dexterity in improving their appearance when preparing for work – so much so that they are hard to recognise in their nocturnal work attire, for one who knew them in their diurnal leisure appearance in the *soi*.

Girls who specialise in late night work in the coffee shops often put on fancy or outlandish attire – such as provocative clothing, complex hair-dos or fingernails painted in a variety of colours. However, it is important to note that though such attires are purportedly intended to enhance a woman's attractiveness to prospective customers, they also tend to become part of a game which the women play among themselves: clothing, toiletry, hair-dos and especially gold jewellery are a subject of much interest and concern for the women; self-care takes up much of their free time and is a principal subject of conversation in the small, tightly-knit groups in which most women spend their leisure time. I suggest that, in their endeavour to out-do one another, a tendency to an 'attire hypertrophy' develops, which may well be detrimental to the chances of a woman's success with *farang* customers, but serves the game of one-upmanship which the women play with one another.

In contrast to brothel and massage parlour prostitution, the women in open-ended prostitution enjoy considerable discretion in the choice of their customers. Since open-ended prostitution is both risky and promising, the women's skill in the selection of the right customer seems to be crucial for their success. As far as can be established, the women are in fact motivated by two kinds of consideration in this respect: the attractiveness of the customer, and his seeming affluence and generosity. Pecuniary considerations, however, in many instances take precedence over sexual ones, and the women frequently decline to stay with a customer who is sexually gratifying but fails to remunerate them sufficiently. If they dislike a customer, however, they may decline to go out with him, even if promised a considerable amount of money. They therefore tend to prefer pleasant, affluent-looking, recently arrived tourists, who are known to be safe and generous with money.

Owing to the open-ended character of the form of prostitution practised by the women, their success depends on their skill at a 'soft sell'; rather than hustling the customer to buy a more expensive service – a skill taught to American brothel prostitutes (Heyl, 1977) – the woman learns how to extricate money from her customer by appealing to his generosity and compassion, rather than by outright demands for payment, and to attach him to her by subserviently attaching herself to him.

The women develop a great dexterity in keying (Goffman, 1974) their personal stories so as to stress their poverty and financial problems – e.g. their need for money to pay the rent or hospital bills for themselves or their relatives, or to support their children, parents or younger siblings. Some indeed straightforwardly fabricate non-existent financial needs rather than ask their *farang* boyfriends expressly for remuneration. Entreaties for help, indeed, do not stop with the departure of the *farang*, but usually constitute the principal *raison d'être* of the women's correspondence with ex-boyfriends (Cohen, 1986).

There are certainly considerable differences between the women in their skills in attracting customers and profiting from the relationship. These find expression in the wide discrepancies in the economic and personal success of similarly endowed women, some of whom have accumulated significant amounts of money in their bank accounts, enjoy a steady stream of support from ex-boyfriends or marry rich and attractive foreigners, while others remain poor and lacking any security for the future.

The importance of skills is generally perceived by the women themselves who say appreciatively that a woman is *keng* (clever, skilful) at doing this or that. Still, they are even more aware of the fact that skilfulness in itself is not a sufficient guarantee of success, owing to the irreducible element of chance in the trade – 'luck' (*chok*). Open-ended prostitution is thus, from the emic perspective of the women, essentially a 'skilful game of luck', for success in which one has to be both *keng* and have *chok*. I suggest that in open-ended prostitution in Thailand, a greater emphasis is given to luck than in the more professional prostitution in the West. If this is correct, then the readiness of the Thai women, trusting their luck, to take incalculable risks becomes more comprehensible.

While Therevada Buddhism is lenient towards prostitution (Keyes, 1984), it does not approve of it. Neither does luck have a place in orthodox Therevada theology. Still, in Thai folk religion, Buddha (and other supernatural beings) are frequently supplicated for luck and good fortune (cf. Piker, 1968, 387). Indeed, the women working in open-ended prostitution are not only frequently devout, but regularly supplicate Buddha or other supernatural beings prior to going to work, for good luck, success and protection – whether at their house altar or at an altar erected in the bars. Though they might be ashamed of their trade, they certainly do not see it as so radical a deviation that it places them outside the fold of religion and denies them religious succour and protection. Indeed, as McDowell commented, 'In Thailand, the prim and the prurient meet and merge, and Buddhist monks may be invited to extend their benediction to a girlie bar' (McDowell, 1982, 500–4).

To enhance their luck, the women also appear to employ a good deal of love magic (*sanee*) (Thongthew-Ratarasarn, 1979), though precise information on the subject was elusive.

While the quest for luck in open-ended prostitution, by means of religious ritual, is an indicator of a perceived absence or disruption with tradition, if not of continuation, it does not yet explain the source of the game element in the trade and the playful willingness to take risks. Therevada Buddhism certainly does not approve of games of luck and gambling.[3] Whatever the standing of gambling in official Buddhist ideology, however, it is a fact that Thais are enthusiastic gamblers – as illustrated by the popularity of the national lottery and in the widespread betting common in the traditional Thai sports of cock-fighting, fish-fighting and Thai-boxing (*muay*). Indeed, many women in the trade are inveterate gamblers: card-playing sessions in the *soi* are a favourite past-time and sometimes last for several days, involving considerable sums of money. The women's profligacy in gambling stands in sharp contrast to the frugality of their daily life-styles. They frequently risk all their money in a single gambling session, after which they have to sell or pawn their jewellery and other possessions, or borrow money from their friends to meet basic necessities.

The attitude of many women to their job also resembles that to a game. Most women claim that they dislike their job, and complain of 'boredom' (*beua*). Rather than relating to it neutrally as 'work', whose reward is in the earnings, they seek to make it an enjoyable, gratifying activity (*sanuk*; cf. Phillips, 1965, 59–61). They prefer partners with whom they have satisfying, enjoyable relationships – a 'good time'. Their attitude to their job also includes an element of excitement and indefinite hope, characteristic of that found with gamblers: there is always, in the background, a vague expectation of winning the big prize or making a killing – whether by catching a wealthy and generous customer, becoming a mistress to a permanent boyfriend, or even finding a husband who will take the woman away from the prostitution scene altogether. The highest prizes in this game of luck are those which enable the player eventually to *leave* the game. For most who leave, however, the departure proves to be merely temporary: lovers go away and marriages disintegrate, and the women return to their previous job, recognising, as Keyes (1984) pointed out, 'through their own experience of the loss of lovers . . . the truth of Buddha's teaching about suffering'. Still others, though economically secure, cannot permanently forego the excitement of the game itself – and when they have the opportunity (for example, during a visit from abroad or the absence of their boyfriend), they return to their old haunts, to 'butterfly' (*chauchu*); it is neither the quest of money nor sex which brings them there, but rather the excitement of the game itself: particularly the desire to find out whether they are still attractive to *farangs* and capable of making a killing. More than anything else, such women exemplify the character of open-ended prostitution as not just 'work', but as a 'skilful game of luck', played for excitement and not only merely for gain.

## CONCLUSIONS: THE STRUCTURE AND DYNAMICS OF OPEN-ENDED PROSTITUTION

The preceding presentation and analysis leads to three significant conclusions concerning the structure and dynamics of the occupational culture of open-ended prostitution – as practised by tourist-oriented prostitutes in Bangkok.

There exists a high degree of fit between the opportunity structure facing the women who work in bars and coffee shops, and their occupational culture. In contrast to the more limited but also more evenly distributed opportunities in brothel or massage parlour prostitution, these women face greater but much more uneven and fluctuating opportunities. The difference ensues from differences in the institutional structure of brothels and massage parlours as compared to bars and coffee shops, the different position of the women in these establishments and the differences in the nature of the customers.

1 Brothels and massage parlours are closed institutions, and the women are prohibited from leaving with their customers, at least during work hours; hence they are limited to routine, mostly short-time sexual intercourse and consequently are also more routinely remunerated than the more independently operating bar and coffee shop women.
2 Bar and coffee shop women, owing to their relative independence, do not have to share their income with the establishment and various intermediaries; however, they also do not enjoy the protection which such establishments provide to their employees.
3 Bar and coffee shop women work most with *farang* customers, who, being predominantly on vacation and free from normal obligations

and impediments, are more willing to spend money and to get involved in an adventure than the more sedate customers of brothels or massage parlours, who are either locals or resident *farangs*, encumbered with various obligations or impediments. The number of vacationing *farangs*, however, fluctuates owing to seasonal and global economic factors, a circumstance which causes considerable fluctuation in the women's income.

The work situation of the women thus features both considerable opportunities as well as much uncertainty, and even risk. It is this combination of opportunity and risk which poses a series of dilemmas for the women; the occupational culture of the women can be seen largely as an attempt to resolve these dilemmas.

1 Opportunism versus security: The highly skewed and fluctuating opportunity structure facing bar and coffee shop women induces in them a marked opportunism;[4] but such opportunism increases the risks of their trade and induces its opposite – a search for security through protracted liaisons. The great majority of these are temporary – they last at most for the length of a tourist's stay; some, however, are more protracted, extending through correspondence and repeat visits for several years, and leading, in some cases, to a master–mistress relationship. Open-ended prostitution is thus an optimising strategy which combines opportunism with the quest for security under conditions of a highly skewed and fluctuating opportunity structure.

It should be noted, however, that these two concerns, maximal exploitation of opportunities and achievement of security, reflect in a conerete, localised form the two poles of one of the principal pairs of contradictory Thai cultural codes: the emphasis on individual independence, on the one hand, and on structural hierarchy on the other (Cohen, 1984b).[5] Opportunism in open-ended prostitution is the women's version of the wider cultural tendency to individualism, while the emphasis on security is their version of integration into a social hierarchy, their waiving of insecure independence for secure dependence, finding its fullest expression in the wider Thai society in the diadic kinship or patron–client relationship, and in the concrete case of the women, in the establishment of a mistress–master relationship. The hierarchical principle characteristic of much of Thai society is thus extended to the *farang*, who comes to play the patron's role and finds himself burdened, often to his uncomprehending astonishment and dismay, with a series of social obligations which automatically fall to his part. While even Thai patron-client relations are frequently unstable, relations with *farang* clients are even more so – since the impermanency of the patron's presence facilitates the woman's involvement in new relationships during his absences.

2  Work and game: Etically seen, open-ended prostitution, like all full-time prostitution, is work – the woman has to attend daily to her job, wait long hours for a customer, conduct repetitive and boring conversations with unattractive and often uncomprehending foreigners; emically, however, it is more of a game in which the women compete, with skill and daring, and what they consider 'luck', for the prizes which the prospective customers offer. While such an attitude may be foreign to the neutral, professional, Western prostitutes, it very much reflects, in the concrete area of prostitution, a wider Thai cultural attitude emphasising preference for activities which are pleasurable or fun (*sanuk*) (Phillips, 1965, 59–61), and an aversion to purely neutral, reward-oriented 'work'.

3  Economic interest and emotional involvement: Open-ended prostitution is predicated upon an extension of the initial mercenary encounter between the woman and her customer into a more protracted relationship. Thereby, however, the nature of the relationship is frequently changed into a 'mixed' one, involving on the part of the woman both economic interests and emotional involvement; though such a development agrees with the woman's tendency to assimilate the relationship to a patron–client one, it also generates, from the *farang's* point of view, considerable ambiguity and leads to misunderstandings and conflicts.

This review of the contrary tendencies in open-ended prostitution leads to our concluding question: the extent to which open-ended, tourist-oriented prostitution signifies social change in Thailand, as for instance Keyes (1984) recently argued, or, conversely, is just another novel expression of pervasive and persevering Thai cultural trends.

I deal with this question in terms of my general approach to the study of change in Thai society (Cohen, 1984b), which departs from the view of Thai culture as informed by conflicting cultural codes which vie with one another for preponderance; their relative ascendancy is expressed in the expansion or contraction of their respective domains, i.e. the extent to which they shape conduct in different institutional realms. Exogenous factors, such as 'modernisation', penetrating from the West, rather than completely transforming Thai culture, influence the balance of forces between the cultural codes – for example, they may encourage individualism at the expense of submission to hierarchy, but such individualism will typically manifest a peculiar 'anarchistic' quality (Ayal, 1963, 48), rather than a tendency to methodical, systematic realisation of self-interest, as in the West. In the case of the women, this quality is expressed in their marked opportunism. Whether one chooses to interpret this shift towards individualism as 'continuity' or 'change' depends on whether one is able or not to recognise the familiar Thai cultural 'physiognomy' in the new situation. This ability ultimately depends on the observer's world-view and paradigmatic or theoretical approach to the study of Thai culture and society (Cohen, 1984b).

The concept of change is thus not an absolute, but depends on one's frame of reference. Open-ended prostitution at first view involves considerable change; a more detailed analysis, however, reveals a surprising degree of cultural continuity – though it could be claimed that the balance between the traditional cultural codes has, in open-ended prostitution, shifted so much to the individualistic (though opportunistic) pole, and structural hierarchical checks have been so weakened, that the 'physiognomy' of Thai culture has been distorted out of recognition. Moreover, a clear break with the past and a definite, indisputable 'change' has taken place in those cases where the Women themselves substituted a modern Western emic perspective on their job for the Thai one; that such a substitution exists has been shown by our analysis of their differential emic interpretations of the various types of relationships with *farangs*. Our data, however, are insufficient to determine whether the shift to a Western perspective dominates the scene of open-ended prostitution, or whether the majority of the women still interpret their relationships with *farangs* in terms of a more traditional Thai emic perspective.

## POSTSCRIPT

While the basic cultural codes of Thai society hardly changed in the decade or so since the data for this chapter were collected, the immediate context of tourist-oriented prostitution changed considerably. The changes appear to have reduced the ludic element in tourist-oriented prostitution, and brought its character closer to that of a serious gamble and away from that of a game.

Two principal factors seem to have influenced this change in the last decade. On the one hand, through the expansion of sex tourism, tourist-oriented prostitution became increasingly routinised with the growth in mass tourism. The expectations of short-time sex tourists as to sexual services available in Thailand became standardised, and so did the behaviour of the Thai women responding to these expectations. Conseqeuntly, the open-ended character of the relationship was attenuated and the leeway for playing the game was narrowed. Fixed prices for short-time services became the overwhelming practice, while the frequency of the other, more ambiguous and open-ended types of relationship seems to have fallen off.

On the other hand, a new element gained gowing salience on the prostitution scene: AIDS (Cohen, 1988c). From a seemingly remote problem facing drug addicts (Usher, 1988a; 1988b), homosexuals (Acosta, 1988; Senftleben, 1988, 63) and prisoners in Thai jails (City Desk, 1987), AIDS became a serious threat to women engaging in prostitution (Cohen, 1988c; Jensen, 1990; *Far Eastern Economic Review*, 1992, 29–30). However, the threat only penetrated slowly into the consciousness of the male tourist seeking sexual services, and even more slowly into that of the Thai women engaging in prostitution. The Thai authorities at first equivocated regarding their AIDS policy (Cohen, 1988c; Mills, 1990). Only after the threat of AIDS came into the public limelight, mainly through the activities of individuals and non-governmental organisations, did the Thai authorities start an information campaign on the dangers of AIDS (Otaganonta, 1991; Techawongtham, 1991b; *Far Eastern Economic Review*, 1992), while individual campaigners and organisations sought to bring the threat, and the means of self-protection, to the awareness of the women engaging in prostitution (Techawongtham, 1991a; Rattanawannathip, 1992b). The success of such efforts was limited at first, since many of the women had difficulties comprehending the threat of AIDS as an affliction with no initial visible external signs, while their culturally-conditioned orientation to the present induced them to discount long-range dangers to their health. It appears, however, that the specific efforts to reach this population have gradually borne fruit, and that prostitutes in general, and the tourist-oriented ones specifically, are presently much more aware of the threat of AIDS, and better prepared to protect themselves, than they were a few years ago.

The authorities on their part seek to gain control over the threat of AIDS by institutionalising prostitution; they recently introduced a controversial prostitution law, which obliges prostitutes to carry health certificates (Rattanawannathip, 1992a; Usher, 1991). However, while it helps to protect the customer, this law hardly helps to protect the prostitutes themselves.

The principal implication of these developments for the main theme of this chapter is that the risk element in tourist-oriented prostitution has grown significantly, not only in objective terms but also in the consciousness of the prostitutes. Their sense of risk may even have been augmented by the widespread tendency to ascribe the introduction of AIDS to Thailand, and its dissemination, to foreigners (Senftleben, 1988, 62–63). This tendency, in turn, made prostitutes much more apprehensive and wary of *farangs* than they have been in the past. Indeed, some well-known massage parlours even closed their doors to foreigners at the peak of the AIDS scare in 1987 (*The Nation*, 1987, 2).

Fear of AIDS and apprehension that *farang* clients may be its bearers made tourist-oriented prostitution a much more serious business than it has been before – it became more of a gamble, but less of a game; its ludic character was thus dampened by the dangers unknown a decade ago. It still remains to be seen to what extent better means of self-protection and safer sexual practices will further modify the culture of tourism-oriented prostitution in the future.

## NOTES

1 This chapter is based on the first two stages of an urban anthropological study of a *soi* in Bangkok conducted in the summers of 1981 and 1982, under a grant from the Harry S. Truman Research Institute for the Advancement of Peace at the Hebrew University of Jerusalem, whose support is gratefully acknowledged. Thanks are due to Walter Meyer for his helpful comments on an earlier draft of this chapter.
2 For the origins of this arrangement, see Gittings, 1967, 34.
3 For example, the Thai Thitthatham Mikatthaprayot tract (Present or This Worldly Utilities) in its instructions to people on how to improve their economic welfare, expressly urges them to avoid indulgence in gambling (Pudyodyana, 1971, 320).
4 Such opportunism is a general feature of Thai socio-culture and a trait of Thai 'anarchistic individualism' (Ayal, 1963, 48). Cf. for example Batt's (1974, 29) rendering of the Thai cultural viewpoint: 'Opportunities strike unexpectedly and one must be prepared to seize them (*ty okad*) when they arise . . . .'
5 Both these characteristics and their interrelationships have been amply documented in the literature; see especially Ayal (1963), Hanks (1962), Hanks and Phillips (1961), Phillips (1965), and Rabibhadana (1975).

# 9 Tourism policy-making in South-East Asia

*Linda K. Richter*

## INTRODUCTION

It has been said that there are two things one should never watch being made, sausage and public policy. That may be good advice from an aesthetic point of view, but when it comes to tourism policy, not watching is a luxury we cannot afford. That is particularly true in South-East Asia which has seen tourist arrivals double and tourism receipts triple in the last decade (Hawkins, 1990, 10). While the area still receives less than 11 per cent of all tourists, the impact of tourism on these nations is immense and often disturbing. Tourism is the leading source of foreign exchange in Thailand, a major source of foreign exchange in Malaysia, the second largest industry in the Philippines (Scott, 1986, 21), and the third highest source of foreign exchange in Singapore (Waters, 1987, 104).

Even in nations like Cambodia, Myanmar (Burma), Vietnam and Laos, where tourism receipts are minuscule, ambitions for tourism's playing a major development role are quite high. It is on the agenda in every South-East Asian nation except oil-rich Brunei. Reporting about tourism varies widely, however, and academics are seldom privy to debates over the basic features of a nation's tourism policy. Still, making sense of the clues we do have is very important if this critical policy area and its spillover effects are to be understood.

There needs to be a common context in which to understand the salient policy discussions and to project probable policy directions. Several approaches can be used. An industry analyst might reasonably examine the tourism policies of these nations in terms of transportation, accommodations, destination development, investment and labour policies. Planners, consumer groups, environmentalists, labour unions and business groups would dissect the policy issues differently.

From a political science perspective, the organisation of power around tourism policy issues, the political motivations surrounding decisions affecting tourism, and the decisions regarding who will be the political constituencies for tourism policy are particularly germane (Bachrach and Baratz, 1963, 632–42). Thus, Part I of this chapter will describe four key policy decisions affecting tourism and will then compare South-East Asian nations in terms of the ways they have made such tourism policy decisions. These policies proved to be useful when applied to South Asia as indicators of the course tourism would take (Richter and Richter, 1985, 201–17).

In Part II, the focus will be not on decisions already taken but on key policy areas in which decisions will need to be made. In fact, my argument is that most nations will need to confront these new challenges in terms of tourism policy within the next decade. Specific instances of how these issues will affect South-East Asian countries will be noted. However, it should be recognised at the outset that information will vary greatly from nation to nation. Ideally, such efforts should be followed by individual studies that prove more definitively the policy-making milieu in each nation, but that represents a stage of the research not yet under way.

The advantage of the approach outlined is that it moves the comparisons back a bit from day-to-day decision-making to a level of analysis that nonetheless highlights *patterns* of policy-making that should alert the reader to the strengths and weaknesses of policy formation in that nation. Additionally, it will provide a preliminary basis for comparing policy-making dynamics across the region.

Finally, consideration of South-East Asia as the focus for this policy exploration, while appearing to constrain the conclusions of the analysis, actually offers one almost a microcosm of nation-states in general. South-East Asia includes democracies (the Philippines and Malaysia), a government whose parameters are set by the military (Indonesia) and strong, almost authoritarian, civilian leadership (Singapore). It also includes socialist states like Laos and Vietnam, a monarchy like Brunei and military dictatorships as in Myanmar and in Thailand. Also in Myanmar, Cambodia and the Philippines major insurgencies exist.

Buddhism, Christianity, Hinduism and Islam as well as animist beliefs are a part of the religious diversity of the region, while the nations range in size from Singapore and Brunei with populations of 2.6 million and 300,000 respectively to major powers like Indonesia with 180 million, Vietnam with 65 million, the Philippines with 60 million and Thailand with 58 million. Economically, the range is from impoverished Laos to affluent Singapore and Brunei, while topographically the region includes both mainland and island nations.

Thus while specific tourism situations obviously pertain locally, the nations examined are remarkably diverse and as such their experiences may be worth consideration by policy analysts beyond the region.

## PART I: THE POLICY FRAMEWORK FOR TOURISM DECISION-MAKING

Most nations turn to tourism as a means of economic development, though a few leaders see it as a personal political tool (Richter, 1980; Pi-Sunyer, 1979) or as a means of encouraging political integration or social change (Richter, 1984b; Kadir Din, 1989b). Whatever the impetus, many of the same key policy decisions need to be determined. In Part I, I will consider four such decisions, each offering a continuum along which nations theoretically may be put at any given point in time. These four continua offer a skeletal look at how policy-makers approach tourism politics.

### Public–private ownership issues

The first continuum is a public–private one. To what extent is tourism policy a government-directed and government-owned sector and to what extent is the ownership of tourism in the private sector (see Table 9.1)?

As Table 9.1 illustrates, all South-East Asian nations have government-owned airlines, though at least two, the Philippines and Thailand, are prepared to privatise their airlines. Indeed, regardless of political system and current level of government-owned tourist infrastructure, all of the nations are moving to encourage greater private and foreign enterprise. Thus it is that even socialist countries like Vietnam are contemplating a number of joint tourism ventures with former arch-enemies. The recent peace agreement in Cambodia may facilitate further deals. Even the xenophobic leadership of General Saw Maung in Myanmar is welcoming foreign investment, though finding few interested in equity deals in a dictatorship as grim as his.

### Centralisation–decentralisation continuum

The second continuum examines South-East Asian nations according to the degree of centralisation–decentralisation that is exhibited. Each nation is considered in terms of ten indices of centralisation. Because data are lacking at this juncture for many key elements, no attempt is

Table 9.1 Public–private ownership and direction

| Public | Myanmar | Philippines | Singapore | Thailand | Vietnam |
|---|---|---|---|---|---|
| **National government ownership of infrastructure** | | | | | |
| Airlines | Myanmar Airlines has a grim safety record; is government-owned. | Government-owned Philippines Airlines is for sale. | Singapore Airlines is government-owned. | Thai International is in the process of being sold to the private sector. | Air Vietnam is government-owned. 2nd gov't airline under consideration. |
| Hotels and Inns | | Government owns many resorts, duty-free shops and hotels which it is trying to sell. | | A few tourist establishments are government-owned. | The government owns some large older hotels and some government agencies have been building 'mini' hotels. |
| Buses | Transportation is government-owned, poorly maintained and downright dangerous. | | | | |
| Trains | | Philippine National Railways. | | | |
| National parks | | | A statutory National Parks Board was set up in 1990. There are several small parks and two more under development. | Weak controls threaten national parks. | |
| National agencies for tourism development and promotion | Myanmar Hotel and Tourism Services. A declared priority of the regime, but foreign investors will need to publicise since the government is broke. | Department of Tourism. | Singapore Tourist Promotion Board. | Tourism Authority of Thailand. | The Overseas Finance and Trade Corporation develops joint ventures for tourism. |

| | | | | | |
|---|---|---|---|---|---|
| Regional/local public agencies with tourism tasks | Most cities have tourism programmes. | | | N.A. | Saigon Tourist is the tourist authority for the South where most tourism is concentrated. |
| Regulatory climate of public bodies | Liberal investments and tax holidays to attract foreign exchange. | There is less central control than during the Marcos era. Prostitution is widespread though illegal. | Some controls on zoning to preserve the last of the ethnic historical buildings and some parks. | Room and restaurant taxes are high, but licensing nil. Prostitution is illegal but widespread. | 85% of foreign investment is in the South. |
| *Laissez-faire* regulatory environment | Alcohol only permitted in clubs for foreigners. | Licensing exists but is not onerous. | No. | $100 exit tax in 1982. Relatively unregulated. | Government requires hotels to join hotel associations, but control is relatively slight. |
| Mostly private promotion | Yes. | Yes. | Yes. | Yes. | Yes. Golf courses and foreign-owned hotels are being built. |
| Mostly private control | | Yes. 43.9% of hotels are owned by multinational chains. | Yes. | Yes. | Government liberalised to allow much private enterprise in tourist infrastructure. |

*Private*

*Sources:* Primarily from Richter, 1989a; *Asia Travel Trade*, 1990; *Asia Yearbook*, 1989; *Contours*, 1984–91; Singh, 1989, 56, 189, 192–99; Elliott, 1983

made to rank the nations themselves along these continua (see Table 9.2). Some generalisations can, however, be suggested.

Most of the nations do continue to have a national cabinet-level portfolio for tourism and play a substantial and increasing financial role in the planning and promotion of tourism. As Table 9.2 demonstrates, the regulatory climate is relatively weak to non-existent except for Singapore; but there are signs that critical interest groups are belatedly emerging in those nations like Thailand, the Philippines and Indonesia where social and cultural impacts of mass tourism have been most strongly felt. Local authorities have some tourism role in most societies, but most act as tourism boosters. Only a few areas like Bali or in some temple complexes such as those in Chiang Mai did there appear to be local leaders attempting to regulate tourism or to constrain its negative impacts.

It should be noted that in developing nations tourism policy will generally be centralised. However, in wealthy mini-states as different as Singapore and Brunei the size of the political system also encourages a centralised approach.

## Domestic or international tourism

A third decision area is focused on market. What kind of tourist is sought? In most of these nations the tourism policy is clearly designed to attract international tourists, because the countries are so poor that a significant domestic tourism base does not exist. This is particularly true in Myanmar, Laos, Cambodia and Vietnam. However, the situation is more complex in the other South-East Asian nations where the buying power of many of the élite and middle class can exacerbate the trade balance if those resources are spent abroad instead of within the country.

Malaysia is a good case in point. Malaysians spend much more in other countries than foreign nationals spend in Malaysia (Wong, 1989; in Kadir Din, 1989b, 191). This has led to a two-pronged tourism policy: (1) to develop modest facilities within the nation for domestic tourists coupled with a stiff customs duty on purchases made abroad; and (2) a major effort to attract international visitors. Malaysia has particularly tried to target Muslims from the Middle East, appealing to their desire to visit a religiously 'clean' Islamic nation. So far it hasn't worked. Islamic travellers, characteristically young males, overwhelmingly prefer the secular and sexier attractions of Thailand (Kadir Din, 1989a, 548–49) to the more conservative ambience of Islamic Malaysia. Malaysia has also embarked on a five-star hotel-building spree for the IMF-World Bank conference. This is reminiscent of the ill-fated construction frenzy the Marcos regime launched in the Philippines for a similar conference in 1976 (Richter, 1980).

Related to the issue of domestic or international tourist is the scale and type of clientele sought. This could be characterised as a policy decision for class versus mass tourism. For the sake of this chapter this issue has been subsumed in Table 9.3, but could represent a distinct continuum in and of itself. Most of the nations aspire to hosting luxury international and business travellers, with some – like the Philippines, Thailand, Malaysia and Indonesia – recognising a need for medium-level facilities for their domestic tourists. In all South-East Asian countries male business and convention travellers are particularly sought. Group tours and middle-class charters are also welcome. Important to Singapore and the Philippines are tourists (*balikbayans*) of Chinese and Philippine ancestry. They bring gifts, are influential, and have longer lengths of stay than other tourists (Richter, 1982).

Not generally welcome in South-East Asia as they are in Europe, North America or East Asia are budget travellers, campers and students. Malaysia contends they are welcome, but the facilities promoted do not confirm that. Golf courses, not camp-grounds, Hyatts not budget motels, man-made amusements not national parks are in the expectations of most planners and policy-makers. Only because they now lack the luxury infrastructure they seek do countries like Myanmar, Laos, Cambodia and Vietnam still welcome the foreign individual traveller (FIT) and then only on highly structured itineraries and often with required guides as in Myanmar (Wigglesworth, 1990).

**Integrated versus enclave tourism**

A fourth basic policy question has to do with the degree of integration of tourists and tourism facilities into the overall society. Some cultures lend themselves to that more easily than others. In Islamic societies, particularly, governments have sometimes favoured – as in the Maldives, Morocco or Indonesia – efforts to isolate tourists from the mainstream of their Islamic societies (Richter, 1989a; 1989b). In Indonesia much of the sun and sand tourism has been confined to resort areas like Nusa Dua, Sanur and Kuta Beach on the Hindu island of Bali.

The cultural advantages may seem to warrant such exclusion. Pattaya, Phuket and Chiang Mai are whole towns in Thailand largely

Table 9.2 Indices of centralisation–decentralisation

| Centralised | Myanmar | Philippines | Thailand | Singapore | Vietnam |
|---|---|---|---|---|---|
| National plan | | Yes. There have been several, but the first comprehensive post-Marcos plan is now formed. It is supposed to diffuse tourism. | Tourism plan is part of National Economic and Social Development Plan done every 5 years. | Tourism Product Development Plan ($1 billion) | N.A. |
| Government-controlled airlines | Yes. Myanmar Airlines. | Philippine Airlines. Private, then government-owned and now being privatised. | Thai International is in the process of being privatised. | Singapore Airlines. | Yes. |
| Ministry of Tourism counterpart | Myanmar Hotel and Tourism Services. | Department of Tourism – is now in the process of being incorporated with another department. | Tourism Authority of Thailand. | Singapore Tourist Promotion Board. | |
| National Licensing or Inspection of Tourism Facilities | N.A. | Yes, but being transferred to local control. | No. | Yes. | |
| Government-controlled/owned accommodations | | A few were deliberately public, others by default; now being sold. | Very few. | N.A. | Some. |

| | | | | | |
|---|---|---|---|---|---|
| National currency and investment controls on tourism | Yes. | Tax on travel tickets for outside Philippines. | Board of Investment oversees imports and concessions. Foreigners may take out all profits. Generally weak on regulations. There are tourism police units. | Yes. | N.A. |
| Regulatory environment | Strong in terms of control of visitors; must buy a package tour and have a guide. | Moderate. | | Strong environmental controls. | N.A. |
| Active local interest groups | Anti-government groups repressed. Overall political organisation weak. | Unions, religious groups are critical. | Beginning to be some opposition, like the new Thai Network on Tourism (TNT). These are primarily environmental and religious. Unions weak. | | N.A. |
| Private ownership of most infrastructure | | Yes, but much is foreign. | Yes. There are few limits to foreign ownership or to exchange leakage. | Yes. | |
| Local control of tourism planning | No. On the other hand, the government's effective control does not extend to 40% of the country in rebel hands. | Some. The plan does require more training of indigenous workers at managerial level. | Most of it is under local or private control. Most jurisdictions have very slight controls. AIDS testing of prostitutes is now being pursued locally. | Almost none. Sentosa Island, for example, is being developed totally from the centre. | No. |

*Decentralised*

*Sources:* Richter, 1989a; *Asia Yearbook*, 1989; Waters, 1987; 1989; *Asia Travel Trade*, 1990

Table 9.3 Tourism policy priorities: the market – domestic or international

| | Brunei | Cambodia | Indonesia | Laos | Malaysia |
|---|---|---|---|---|---|
| Q Who are the focus of tourism infrastructure development? | N.A. | International luxury and business tourists. | International luxury tourists. | | Increasingly more domestic tourism; international luxury tourists. |
| Q Who are the focus of tourism promotion? | This is hard to say. There are fewer than 10,000 per year. Most are probably business travellers. | International. | Luxury tourists; business travellers; domestic tours. | Promotion is nil but international tourists are the ones sought. | International luxury tourists, business travellers. Promoted to Muslims as 'clean Muslim destination'. |
| Q Who are the focus of efforts to regulate tourism facilities? | N.A. | | International tourists. | | International tourists. |
| Q About whom are most tourism statistics collected? | Foreign tourist data are occasionally available. | International. | International. | International. | International. |

| | Myanmar | Philippines | Singapore | Thailand | Vietnam |
|---|---|---|---|---|---|
| Q Who are the focus of tourism infrastructure development? | International moderate to luxury tourists. | International luxury tourists. | International luxury tourists. | Domestic or international tourists. 8.7 million domestic tourists in 1987. | International moderate to luxury tourists. |
| Q Who are the focus of tourism promotion? | Promotion is nil but international tourists. | International luxury tourists; business travellers; *balikbayans*. | Business and convention travellers. | Business and luxury escapist travellers primarily, but some domestic promotion. | Students/FIT; former Vietnam War participants; international. |
| Q Who are the focus of efforts to regulate tourism facilities? | N.A. | Luxury tourists. | | Some regulatory efforts to protect safety/health of international tourists. | N.A. |
| Q About whom are most tourism statistics collected? | International. | International and *balikbayans*. | International. | International, but domestic statistics developing. | International. |
| Class versus mass | Anyone, but directions are towards up-market travellers. | Moving partially away from class towards a variety of travellers. | Luxury tourists. | Class 3–5. Gradually more attention to students and moderate FITs. | Spartan, but aiming at luxury clientele in future. |

*Sources:* Waters, 1986; 1987; 1989; Kadir Din, 1989b; Richter, 1989a

given over to tourism, and where sex tourism figures quite prominently. The bulk of Thailand, however, can be kept rather removed
from tourism excesses in this way. With such a strategy, however, the
economic and social investments in tourism largely by-pass most of
the society. The tourist industry becomes the major beneficiary of
roads, energy and water development, medical and transport facilities.

As Table 9.4 illustrates, large-scale enclaves of tourism are generally
confined to the World Bank-fostered Nusa Dua area and Sanur Beach
strip development on Bali, the resort enclaves in the Philippines and
the tawdry towns of Pattaya and Phuket in Thailand. In such locales,
not only are scarce resources and incentives diverted to fuel tourism
development, but in many cases the resorts are ill-equipped to provide
for and monitor the environment they are affecting. As the experience
of Malaysia illustrates:

> Many of the newly developed island resorts such as Langkawi,
> Pangkor, and Tioman, do not have proper waste disposal
> facilities and as a result of this, waste materials discharged from
> the hotels are dumped into adjacent pits and the sea, causing
> water and air pollution problems.
>
> (Kadir Din, 1989b, 196)

At the same time, tourism's importance overall may operate to
encourage tougher environmental standards even in the face of a
government ideological rhetoric that extols *laissez-faire* policies.

## PART II: THE CRITICAL FUTURE ISSUES FOR TOURISM POLICY

The issues discussed up to now are central to the early decisions taken
with regard to tourism development. If the industry is to develop,
these issues may well determine priorities. However, it will be
important to consider the more far-reaching and strategic policy
decisions which will determine how tourism development impacts the
nation's future.

Except in Cambodia, Vietnam, Laos and Brunei the basic framework for tourism development in South-East Asia has been determined. It will continue to evolve, but most planners probably expect
changes to occur at the margins rather than at the core. They may be
wrong, but this appears to be the thrust of their five-year plans, budget
projections, infrastructure and investment patterns.

The substantive politics for the next generation of tourism policies

Table 9.4 Integrated or enclave tourism

| Integrated | Myanmar | Philippines | Singapore | Thailand | Vietnam |
|---|---|---|---|---|---|
| Q Is tourism transportation also used by non-tourists? | Rarely. | Yes, airlines, ferries, luxury buses, jeepneys. | Yes. | Yes, trains, aeroplanes, not local buses as a rule. | Rarely. |
| Q Are roads, energy plants and water facilities used by tourists and non-tourists alike? | Yes, except for rare resorts. | Many resort facilities have private water and energy facilities. | Yes. | Yes. | Yes. |
| Q Are tourist attractions used by non-tourists? | Yes, in terms of temples. | Not usually, except for churches and museums. Rich locals use hotels for parties. | Yes. | Primarily the temples, national parks. | Yes, particularly for educational field-trips. |
| Q Do domestic and international tourists mix? | No. | Rarely. *Balikbayans* (Filipinos visiting from overseas) do. | Not much domestic tourism because the country is so small. | Business travellers. Domestic travel tends to go South. | Almost no domestic travel exists. |
| Q Are some international tourist facilities expressly forbidden to non-international tourists (e.g. gambling casinos)? | N.A. | Floating Casino and other casinos largely limited to foreign exchange. | N.A. | Thai government has turned down some casinos but Thai investors are planning to place these just over the border in Myanmar. | N.A. |
| **Enclave** | | | | | |
| Q Are isolated resorts or resort towns a major component of tourism in that country? | Inle Lake. Tourism resorts planned by Thai investors. | Yes, there are many but in terms of numbers still small. | Nothing is isolated in Singapore, but Sentosa Island is a major tourism initiative. | Yes. | No. |

Sources: *Asia Travel Trade*, 1990; Richter, 1989a; Waters, 1987; 1989; 1990; Singh, 1989, 50, 192; Rodenburg, 1988; *Contours*, 1989

are just beginning. This chapter argues that the issues of the near future remain largely ignored by the industry and the tourism establishment, but that they will play a crucial role in the contribution tourism can make to national well-being. The critical issues are essentially four.

## The distribution issue

The distribution issue is essentially what American political scientist Harold Lasswell described as 'Who gets what, when and how?' (Lasswell, 1936), to which Michael Parenti added 'and who already has what?' (Parenti, 1977). And as I have argued elsewhere, 'who cares?' (Richter, 1991, 189). The latter dimension includes the reaction to perceptions of power and privilege as well as the absolute reality. Planners and politicians occasionally weigh aloud the distribution of economic and political benefits of tourism infrastructure and employ- ment opportunities but the initial projections of profits, risks, advant- age and disadvantage are typically more closely held views. More importantly the **distribution of political power over decision-making in tourism tends to mirror the distribution of political influence generally** (Ashford, 1978). Add to that the often needed capital investment from outside the nation and it is clear that **negotiations will more closely follow private economic advantage than some ideal of balanced development.** Thus, arguments for investing in areas where a critical mass of services already exists may be much more persuasive than diffusion of economic opportunity. This is especially true if the stratum of political influentials is narrow, as it is in countries like those in South-East Asia.

There is no clean slate on which to forge tourism policy even in countries without a major tourism industry, for the patterns of power are likely to be in place. In Malaysia, for example, where ethnic power is sharply delineated, the Chinese entrepreneurial advantage is extremely pronounced in capital-intensive sectors of the industry just as it has been in the economy at large. Malay involvement has been nurtured by the government but it remains largely confined to areas like travel agencies, which require little capital but need government licences (Kadir Din, 1989b, 189). In Bali, tourism development has concentrated earnings rather than percolating them through the economy in a geographically balanced way (Rodenburg, 1980).

Still tourism does affect a broad stratum. Some contend '1 in every 16 people on earth works in tourism,' (Edgell, 1990) and thus is directly impacted. But it is the nature of that work, its predictability, the type of people employed and the clout they can organise that will determine the political power of those affected.

As I argued elsewhere, employment effects are only one facet of the distribution issue:

> those displaced by mega events, impoverished by land specula-
> tion in tourist areas, inconvenienced by tourism development or
> hurt by tax breaks that disproportionately help the hospitality
> industry . . . have not been the focus of much research attention.
> That is changing. . . . The public – at least in many pluralist
> countries – are asking sharper and more focused questions about
> who really benefits. . . . **The labour, church, women and envir-
> onmental groups are now mobilizing in countries like Thailand
> to challenge the government to develop tourism with more care
> and sensitivity. Often those charged with developing tourism do
> so at the behest of those with the greatest political and economic
> resources.**
>
> (Richter, 1991, 190)

This was particularly true and tragic during the twenty years of the Marcos administration in the Philippines (Richter, 1980). Those who lose in economic, political, social or cultural terms may not be prepared to resist the policy. That will depend on another key political dimension – how power is organised around tourism.

**The political organisation of power**

The emergence of a tourism issue, its ability to get on the political agenda, the framing of the issue by those with power, the number of claimants for political influence and the manner in which issues will be resolved is reflected in the basic framework of the policy environment which was discussed earlier. The new element is the increasing fragmentation of power we are witnessing even among some of the most tightly controlled nation-states, such as those in Eastern Europe. The effect on tourism policy is still uncertain and may vary from system to system.

On the other hand, tourism policy in most countries has been an élite-driven policy, chosen by the powerful for political and economic advantage on both personal and regime levels. It is characteristically at the beginning a chosen policy, something governments choose to embark upon, not something forced on them like agricultural or educational policies (Hirschman, 1975, 385–402). Vietnam, Laos, Myanmar and Brunei are in that category. The first three may see few other economic alternatives, while Brunei's affluence – like Saudi Arabia's – makes tourism seem more trouble than it is worth.

In most of South-East Asia, however, especially major centres in Thailand, Bali in Indonesia, Penang and Kuala Lumpur in Malaysia and Manila, Baguio and Cebu in the Philippines, tourism is no longer a chosen policy but a pressing one. Though tourism is still élite-driven as tourism policy is almost everywhere, there are now.many more claimants to power in decisions about the industry. Some, like labour unions, women's groups, religious organisations, environmental groups and health agencies are challenging the statistics extolling tourism's contribution to development. Sector alliances within the tourism industry are also making distinct bids for influence over policy. In South-East Asia this is particularly true of the airline and accommodation sectors. Local political leaders may also constrain national policy planning with both positive effects as in Ubud, Indonesia, or disastrous effects as in Pattaya, Thailand.

Even countries like Thailand, with superbly regarded public-owned airlines, are rushing to deregulate and privatise. As the public–private mix in the industry shifts toward the private sector, it becomes politically difficult to maintain or increase government controls for environmental, social, health and safety purposes.

Policy-makers may find it increasingly frustrating to lose the monopoly over policy direction that was once the norm in most of the region and to find it necessary to negotiate the issues with an increasing number of political claimants with more dramatically opposed points of view to reconcile.

## The political climate

Tourism in and of itself and tourism as a government-encouraged activity have always evoked mixed reactions. However, until the 1980s, government policy-makers could safely ignore the carping of a few and could assume that the industry offered rich rewards at best and was benign at worst. A few academics and writers would quarrel with that assumption – indeed some critics go back several centuries (Feiffer, 1985) but it wasn't until the late 1970s and 1980s that the case studies of tourism began to multiply (Jones, 1986; Powers, 1986; Singh, 1989; Richter, 1982; 1989a).

The complex positive and negative spillover effects have led to a polarisation of attitudes about tourism that have made policy-making more controversial, more acrimonious and more volatile than ever before. The disinterest and ignorance many had about tourism policy, when such policies began, appears to be replaced by a heightened interest and level of politicisation but an absence of consensus. To date, in South-East Asia, proponents of more tourism appear to enjoy much more power and influence than critics, but that is changing. The level and intensity of the criticism has been accelerating.

For example, in Thailand, surely one of the most successful South-East Asian nations in terms of tourism receipts, many groups are beginning to question and criticise tourism's impact on the society. The Ecumenical Coalition on Third World Tourism (ECTWT) based in Bangkok has publicised the sexual exploitation of Thai children and women as has the *Bangkok Post*. The ECTWT has also sponsored workshops on alternative tourism and has published *Contours*, a quarterly magazine detailing the environmental, economic and social costs of tourism in Thailand and other developing nations. Underground film-makers have captured the seaminess of the Thai tourist industry in films like 'Business on Bodies'. The Catholic Bishops of Thailand have issued a pastoral letter on tourism celebrating tourism's potential for good and decrying its disastrous impact as now organised in Thailand. Even the American ABC show '20-20' has featured the abuse of women and children through sex tourism. Similar critics are emerging in the Philippines and Indonesia and throughout the region the environmental impact is also attracting concern (see *Contours*, 1984–90; Richter, 1982; 1989a; Roekaerts and Savat, 1989, 35–70).

More importantly, tourism policy does not succeed simply because supporters outnumber detractors in numbers, clout or resources if the disenchanted truly turn on the industry and its backers. Tourism is a very fragile industry ultimately dependent on at least the acquiescence of the host population and the security of its visitors. When either of those ingredients cannot be guaranteed, tourism is really more of a high stakes crap game than an economic panacea. As the Philippines has repeatedly discovered, violence directed at tourist establishments can cripple the industry (Richter and Waugh, 1986). Tourists caught in literal or figurative crossfire of non-tourism related origins are equally unlikely to travel. Their situation also leads to political advisories against travel from their own country and the type of publicity that promotion efforts cannot overcome for months and without enormous costs. A dramatic case in point has been the recent Gulf War's impact on travel not only in that region but throughout the world.

## The sustainability issue

The final issue that this chapter contends is neglected in tourism policy-making is in many ways the most important, for though all are inter-related, how it is handled will make the critical difference in whether tourism contributes to the preservation or degradation of the increasingly vulnerable planet. Whether tourism can be compatible with the increased scarcity of agricultural land, water supply, energy resources and cultural preservation will be tested as cruelly in South-East Asia as any place on earth. The signs are not encouraging.

The pressures are coming both from increased travel to the region by outsiders and by increased domestic and intra-regional travel. That travel is primarily escapist or business travel, with culture holding much less lure than good business facilities and luxury relaxation. Short-term promotional policies have blinded policy-makers to the larger looming question of how access to fragile cultures and environments can be rationed to preserve long-term value (*Contours*, 1991, 26–27). Such concerns need to focus debate on who can travel and under what conditions. At a time when governments should be planning the most intensive and environmentally sound investments, they are building land-, water- and chemical-intensive golf courses for Japanese tourists and a tiny stratum of their own citizens (*Contours*, 1990, 22). Are golf courses to be built for the most affluent or highest bidders or will a new ethic see the long-term health of the industry focused on the least intrusive, the domestic tourist, or according to some other criterion? (Teh, 1989, 60).

More nations should be grappling with the need to attract more wholesome clienteles, and to cope with the health and security factors unrestrained tourism has brought (Kadir Din, 1988a, 563–66). For too long governments were eager to overlook AIDS and other side effects of sex tourism in their eagerness to keep tourism income flowing. That may be changing in Thailand, (Cohen, 1988c, 467–86) but there is no indication that governments or the industry have refined their tourism goals much beyond 'bring us more'. Those that have, like Bhutan, have opted to restrict tourism only to the most wealthy and even that country is moving to greater numbers.

What *has* happened, however, is a growing recognition by many beyond the industry of the complex interdependence of issues related to tourism and the increasing inability of either the industry or the local political jurisdictions to cope with them. In some cases this has led to a realisation that tourism issues need to be coordinated at a policy level high enough to consider the public interest broadly. In the

US, for example, a small step was made in that direction when, in 1981, the National Tourism Policy Act was passed.

It was designed to create mechanisms of coordination and consultation with different sectors of the industry, with government agencies whose regulations could impact tourism and with representatives of state tourism programmes as well as academia. The intent was excellent, but the vast bulk of US tourism is domestic (over 90 per cent) and the federal government's role is diffuse and limited (Richter, 1985). In other countries such coordination could prove more effective. At this juncture, however, I know of no South-East Asian nation that has attempted such coordination of the policy process though several have tourism plans like Thailand and the Philippines. Malaysia and the Philippines also have national umbrella organisations with major private tourism sectors represented (Waters, 1989; Richter, 1982).

Bilateral or multilateral tourism accords are also needed. The bilateral accords are typically low-stake agreements, but particularly in cases where relations have been characterised by hostility and distrust they can be what the UN calls 'confidence-building measures' upon which more significant agreements may be built. ASEAN already has in place a permanent subcommittee on tourism that has sought to facilitate intra-regional tourism and greater air access. It remains to be seen if it can move toward inclusion of Myanmar, Cambodia, Laos and Vietnam in its planning and whether it can offer the critical leadership needed on coastal and marine issues, environmental controls, and a common front against investment from outside the region that exploits basic resources.

The environmental planning in Western Europe that is now moving to integrate the badly polluted nations of Eastern Europe offers an example from which South-East Asia may be able to learn.

To be fair, most of the environmental problems in these nations are not due to tourism. Myanmar and the Philippines, for example, have allowed fire sale prices for their teak and mahogany in an effort to earn foreign exchange. Only 5 per cent of Philippines' coral is undamaged (*Manila Chronicle*, 29.1.90). What they are reaping is erosion and ecological tragedy. In fact, tourism may help to build a political constituency for conserving historical sites, protecting forests and preserving wildlife. However, even then it can threaten the environment in three ways. First, it can 'love' a site until it is ruined. Yosemite National Park in the US, the Galapagos Island off South America, Kuta Beach in Bali, Pagsanjan Falls on Luzon in the Philippines are only a few such sites reeling under the tourist pressure that threatens to spoil the very attractions the tourists came to see (Richter, 1989b, 29–30).

Second, the desire for tourist infrastructure with its resultant land speculation near major points of cultural or scenic interest means that zoning laws, density planning, water, electricity and sewage control get neglected at the very juncture when political authority is most needed (Gelston, 1989, 57; Thorne and Munro-Clark, 1989, 154–71).

Third, in an effort to make resort sites all things to all tourists rather than designed for an appropriate niche in the market, most sites develop elaborate pools, dynamite coral for sandy beaches, and create championship golf courses without regard to terrain, availability of water, and so on. Local political jurisdictions seeking foreign exchange and domestic spending are not likely to curtail travel nor be in a position to withstand the tourist industry's demand for access. This is especially true when foreign investment is encouraged. The appeal of large, glamorous hotels, affluent tourists and the prospects of wealthy visitors are hard to resist.

Though some profess to see governments like Indonesia moving toward more vigorous environmental control, even they acknowledge it will come at the price of a stronger, more authoritarian state (Cribb, 1990).

For most of the region the impetus is likely to be toward less public control, more deregulation or continued lack of regulation, and a continuing assumption that the private sector has the answers to tourism development. In many respects it does if short-term profit maximisation is the objective but it is not accountable for the *public interest*. Sustainable tourism will need incentives for the industry to make the long-range commitment to the destination that management contracts and piecemeal development do not encourage. Governments in the region both singly and in concert will need to consider how to protect the environment they share not only from physical erosion but from cultural and spiritual decay as well (Catholic Bishops of Thailand, 1990).

## CONCLUSION

This chapter has tried to provide a framework for assessing where the nations of South-East Asia are with respect to fundamental policy decisions *vis à vis* tourism. The prevailing direction of current efforts, regardless of the state of the industry or political ideology, is in the direction of private enterprise be it home-grown or foreign. In most, the market is geared toward the affluent at home or abroad and at best the regulation is geared toward consistency of quality and safety for tourists over quality of life for residents.

This chapter also sought to chart a proposed agenda for future policy-making by focusing on four issues that nations need to confront soon if tourism is to be a palatable policy for economic development. Unfortunately, as this brief survey noted, there is little evidence that nations perceive these issues as urgent or that political jurisdictions recognise or are prepared to address them. There are indications, however, that the various and increasingly attentive groups concerned about tourism may encourage greater government involvement in its future directions.

# 10 The economics of tourism in Asia and the Pacific

*M. Thea Sinclair and R. W. A. Vokes*

## INTRODUCTION

The economics of tourism is a generally underresearched area owing, in part, to the lack of widespread recognition of the importance of tourism until recent years. Research has, however, been undertaken on specific economic aspects of tourism as well as in such related areas as tourism development policies (Richter and Richter, 1985; Sinclair, 1991). This chapter will examine existing work on the economics of tourism and its past or potential application to Asia and the Pacific (excluding Australasia and Japan) in six main categories: the supply of tourism, the demand for tourism, capital utilisation and employment, price determination, income generation and the balance of payments. The examination will concentrate on the macroeconomic level and will not be exhaustive; it will, nevertheless, indicate the type of research which could usefully be undertaken in the future.

## THE SUPPLY OF TOURISM

Study of the supply of tourism is complex owing to the fact that tourism is a composite commodity, consisting of inputs supplied by a variety of agents including travel agents, tour operators, airlines and hoteliers (Sinclair and Stabler, 1991). Little attention has been paid to the economics of tourism supply relative to the large amount of research on tourism demand. The structure of the tourism industry has been examined within the literature, and attention has been paid to the degree of horizontal and vertical integration in the industry. Horizontal integration consists of joint ownership of the same type of enterprises (for example, hotel chains) and vertical integration consists of ownership linkages between firms and their output purchasers and/or input suppliers (such as airlines and hotels). Some evidence about the types and extent of horizontal and vertical integration in Asia and the Pacific is available. Dunning and McQueen's report for the United Nations Centre for Transnational Corporations (UNCTC, 1982) showed that the number of hotel rooms which had some form of multinational participation as a percentage of the total number of hotel rooms in the destination country, in 1978, was 6 per cent for Bangladesh, 34 per cent for Hong Kong, 10 per cent for India, 11 per cent for Indonesia, 6 per cent for Malaysia, 10 per cent for Pakistan, 44 per cent for the Philippines, 28 per cent for the Republic of Korea, 33 per cent for Singapore, 21 per cent for Sri Lanka and 10 per cent for Thailand.

The types of integration which occur between tourism enterprises include joint ventures involving equity participation, leasing arrangements, management contracts and franchise agreements. In the context of high demand for tourism in the Asia Pacific region in the late 1980s and early 1990s, equity participation was an increasingly important means by which international hotel management companies obtained good sites for hotels, and the terms of management contracts became more favourable to the destination country owners. Hotel companies have attempted to target hotels in gateway cities, particularly Bangkok, Hong Kong, Jakarta, Kuala Lumpur, Seoul, Singapore and Taipei, as a precondition for participation in secondary cities and resorts (Hunt, 1990).

Hotel companies may engage in different types of integration with enterprises in the same (and different) countries. For example, in 1990, Holiday Inn had hotel management contracts with hotels in Thailand and also had a franchise agreement, with Nimmanaradi Development Company, to construct a hotel in Chiang Mai, the agreement allowing the company to use the Holiday Inn name for its hotel. An example of a joint venture is that established, in 1991, between Hilton International and the Industrial Bank of Japan and Nippon Fire and Marine. The Japanese development company is responsible for providing Hilton with services including the provision of finance for new developments and acquisitions, and the location and evaluation of new hotel sites. The joint venture, known as Japan Hilton Projects Development, will enable Hilton to increase the number of luxury hotels in Japan and the Asia Pacific region. An indication of the involvement of major hotel companies in Asia is given in Table 10.1. The companies participate in hotels in a range of Asian countries, thereby decreasing their net level of risk and increasing the stability of their overall earnings.

Although large multinational hotel companies dominate the luxury hotel sector, some indigenous hotel groups have developed, as Table

Table 10.1  Major international hotel companies' existing and projected hotels in Asia (excluding Australasia and Fiji), 1990.

| Hotel company | No. of hotels in Asia | Number of hotel projects and countries in which situated | |
|---|---|---|---|
| Holiday Inn International (UK) | 37 | 21 | China 8, Indonesia 7, Thailand 2, Bangladesh,Guam, Macau, India |
| Hyatt International Hotels and Resorts (USA) | 23 | 3 | Bali, Bangkok, Jakarta |
| Sheraton Hotels International (USA) | 20 | 8 | Indonesia 4, Thailand 3, Saipan |
| Hilton International (UK) | 16 | 3 | Bali, Kyonju, Beijing |
| Ramada International (Hong Kong) | 10 | 8 | China 3, Thailand 2, Indonesia, Japan, Malaysia |
| Inter-Continental (Japan) | 10 | 2 | Bali, Yokohama |
| Westin Corporation (Japan) | 7 | 1 | Shanghai |
| Mandarin Oriental Hotel Group (Hong Kong) | 8 | 3 | Delhi, Kuala Lumpur, Macau |
| Regent International (Hong Kong and Shanghai) | 5 | 4 | Agra, Delhi, Bali, Jakarta |
| Hong Kong and Shanghai Hotels (Hong Kong) | 5 | 2 | Thailand |
| Shangri-La International (private Asian) | 14 | 10 | Philippines 3, Bali 2, Bangkok, Hong Kong, Jak-arta, Singapore, Taipei |
| New World Hotels International (Hong Kong) | 9 | 9 | Indonesia 2, Thailand 2, China, Macau, Malaysia, Philippines, Vietnam |

*Source*: Based on Hunt, 1990

10.1 shows. **The Thai Dusit Thani Group**, with a chain of hotels in Thailand at the beginning of 1991, is a further example, and is considered to be a market leader in the country's luxury hotel market. The Dusit Thani Group has established franchise agreements with hotels in different regions of Thailand, and provides them with marketing, advertising, promotion and centralised reservation services, including bookings by foreign tour operators. The Group also had management contracts with five hotels in Indonesia in 1990, has entered into negotiations on hotel and tourism development projects in neighbouring countries, notably Laos and Vietnam, and is clearly keen to expand in the Asia Pacific region. Other international hotel companies wish to participate in Indochina despite the possibility of excess supply, as occurred in China (with over 40 joint venture hotels open since 1982 and 40 under construction: Hunt, 1990).

Different types of integration have different costs and benefits for tourist destination countries at different stages of development and in different contexts (Sinclair *et al.*, 1992; UNCTC, 1982). For example, Indian hotels can draw on some domestic hotel management expertise but might find franchise agreements useful for marketing purposes, whereas management contracts might provide the Republic of Korea with the specialist skills required for the expansion of its hotel sector. The terms of the different types of contractual relationships can vary greatly between enterprises in the same and different countries (UNCTC, 1982), and between different macroeconomic contexts, and can involve widely differing degrees of control of the destination country enterprise. Joint ventures involving foreign and local equity participation may be a means of increasing the foreign partner's provision of capital and commitment to tourism development in the host country; involvement by local residents may also tend to decrease adverse environmental impacts, as Parnwell points out in Chapter 15 of this volume. However, in Indonesia, for example, the majority of capital invested in the hotel sector appears to have come from domestic sources (Booth, 1990), and the foreign partner may view the investment as a means of improving its real estate portfolio. Thus, careful examination and regular monitoring of the alternative owner-ship and contractual options available, as well as those which are most commonly utilised, would be a useful policy for tourist host countries.

Little is known about the sensitivity of tourism supply to its major determinants. Supply can vary considerably over relatively short time periods, as is shown by the Tourism Authority of Thailand's calculations that the number of hotel rooms in the country increased from 46,100 in 1980 to 168,600 in 1990. However, estimates of the sensitivity of tourism supply to key variables are rarely available. The relevant variables include 'promotional privileges', for example those available for the construction of hotels in Thailand prior to 1982 and, from 1987, in such forms as tax deductions on equipment and some total tax exemptions. Quantitative estimates of supply sensitivity would be useful for policy purposes. In the case of Thailand, hotel construction appears to have been highly responsive to such incentives with the result that predictions of 'room to expand' in 1989 (Handley, 1989) were replaced, as soon as 1990, by forecasts of an 'oversupply of rooms ahead' (*Bangkok Post*, 1990), while the 1991 context was one of 'room rates under pressure' (*Bangkok Post*, 1991). The supply of accommo-dation has thus been an intermittent constraint on the growth of tourism in the Asia Pacific region; further potential constraints in the form of infrastructure provision and the availability of skilled labour are discussed below.

## THE DEMAND FOR TOURISM

During the 1980s, East Asia, South-East Asia and the Pacific experienced the fastest growth in regional tourist arrivals in the world, at an average of 9.2 per cent per annum, while South Asia also experienced an above average annual growth of 4.2 per cent (World Tourism Organization, 1990). Demand is, however, concentrated in particular destinations, including Singapore, Thailand and Malaysia, as well as Fiji in the South Pacific. Research on the demand for tourism has attempted to estimate the responsiveness of demand to changes in significant determinants, such as exchange rates. Knowledge of the sensitivity of demand to changes in key explanatory variables is important because of the repercussions of changes in demand on the host economy, including variations in foreign currency earnings, GNP, employment and tax revenue.

Two main approaches have been used to model the demand for tourism: the single equation approach and the system of equations approach. Tourism demand within the single equation approach can be measured as tourist expenditure or receipts, the number of tourist arrivals or departures, or the number of overnight stays by tourists. It is generally accepted in the literature that tourism demand depends upon income, relative prices and/or exchange rates, and may also depend upon transport costs between the origin and destination countries and on other variables including marketing expenditure or 'shocks' such as political crises or major sporting events. Expenditure on campaigns such as the Visit Thailand Year of 1987 appears to have had a considerable positive effect on tourist arrivals, and this form of promotion was subsequently followed by the Visit Malaysia Year of 1990, the Visit Indonesia Year of 1991, and the unsuccessful Visit India Year 1991 (McDonald and Schuman, 1991). Estimates of the effectiveness of marketing expenditure would be useful, since national resources are used to finance such campaigns.

The relationship between tourism demand and its determinants may be estimated using multiple regression analysis, and the elasticity values, showing the short-run and long-run sensitivity of tourism demand to changes in the variables, can be calculated. Demand elasticities for tourism in Singapore were calculated by Gunadhi and Boey (1986), who found that tourism demand was highly sensitive to increases in the disposable income of the tourist origin countries, whereas the responsiveness of demand to changes in prices and exchange rates varied between the countries. Shopping prices in Singapore were also a significant determinant of demand by Australian and Japanese tourists. Such information is of relevance to policy-makers who are evaluating the merits of exchange rate changes or anti-inflationary measures, and research on the determinants of the demand for tourism in other countries in the Asia Pacific region would be useful.

The system of equations models, used to estimate tourism demand, have an explicit theoretical basis in consumer demand theory. The models have been used to explain the allocation of a tourism expenditure budget between different countries, and to estimate the sensitivity of a country's share of the budget to changes in relative prices and expenditure. The model has been applied using the Almost Ideal Demand System model (Deaton and Muellbauer, 1980a; 1980b) to explain the distribution of US tourists' expenditure among different European countries (O'Hagen and Harrison, 1984; White, 1985), and of expenditure by tourists from the US and some European countries among Southern European countries (Syriopoulos, 1990), but has not been applied to countries in Asia and the Pacific.

The application of the approach might provide useful information about the sensitivity of the shares of the tourism expenditure budget of major origin countries, which are received by individual countries within a destination region, such as the ASEAN countries. Malaysia, for example, is known to wish to increase its share of the ASEAN countries' foreign exchange receipts from tourism above its 1990 percentage of approximately 13 per cent, compared with 28 per cent for Thailand and 35 per cent for Singapore (Aznam, 1990). The system of equations approach might also shed light on tourists' perceptions of different countries as substitutes (and hence competitors) or complements. In the latter case, two or more countries may be visited during one trip, as is common for tourists visiting Malaysia, as well as Thailand, Singapore and Indonesia (see King in Chapter 5 in this volume). An example of an attempt to develop complementary tourist destinations is Thailand's plans to sell holidays in Thailand as complements to holidays in the surrounding countries of Indochina (particularly Vietnam and Laos). The Visit ASEAN Year 1992 is a further example of an attempt to increase the demand for complementary destinations.

The system of equations approach lacks the flexibility of the single equation approach, since it does not permit the inclusion in the model of variables which are determinants of tourism demand in some countries but not others, such as political changes. Unanticipated political changes, for example the assassination of Rajiv Gandhi in India, and instability, including violence in Kashmir, Sri Lanka and the Philippines, are known to have adverse effects on tourism demand, at least in the short run. Some of the results obtained from past applications of the system of equations model have been surprising, possibly owing to the past application of the model on a static basis, rather than a dynamic basis which could take account of time lags in the adjustment of demand to changes in relative prices or income. Single equation models, in contrast, have shown that specific time lags in adjustment can be significant for particular tourist origin nations, such as the USA, as was indicated for the case of the demand for tourism in Fiji (Broomfield, 1991).

## EMPLOYMENT AND CAPITAL UTILISATION

Tourism is often assumed to be advantageous because of its employment creation potential. Barang (1988), for example, pointed out that the tourism industry in Thailand was a source of direct employment for 460,000 people, and of indirect employment for an additional 1 million, and Carver (1987) noted that each nine tourists in the country were estimated to create one job. However, many jobs within the tourism industry are gender-specific and require a considerable level of skill, such as familiarity with a number of foreign languages, and many countries in the Asia Pacific region are faced with a shortage of the required skilled labour (see Hitchcock, Chapter 16 in this volume). Thailand had only one hotel school in 1988 and has relied on foreign labour to meet its skill shortages, particularly at the management level (Barang, 1988). Indonesia is a further example of a country whose tourism industry has experienced a considerable shortage of skilled labour (Schwarz, 1989) and which requires additional training facilities (Booth, 1990), as do the South Pacific island economies (Yacoumis, 1990).

The view that the tourism industry does not require high capital expenditure or skilled labour has been challenged by some authors, for example Diamond (1974; 1977). However, few attempts have been made to measure the degree of capital-intensity of the sector. The small number of estimates of the incremental capital:output ratios (ICOR) for tourism and other sectors of the economy which have been made (for countries within and outside the Asia Pacific region) indicate that the relative capital-intensity of tourism varies between countries, and between different stages of development of the tourism

industry. The provision of the airport and road infrastructure necessary for international tourism may involve particularly large-scale
capital investment during the initial development of the tourism
industry.

Inadequate infrastructure can act as a constraint on tourism growth
in countries ranging from the small South Pacific islands, with their
incipient tourism industries (Yacoumis, 1990), to the large, traditional
tourist destination of India (McDonald and Schuman, 1991). Infrastructure constraints include poor ground and air transport. The
quality of air transport varies greatly between the different carriers of
the Asia Pacific countries, and destinations such as the South Pacific,
other than Fiji and Tahiti, as well as resorts including Penang, Phuket
and Langkawi, have experienced the considerable problem of poor
access to tourist origin markets. Fiji and Tahiti, in contrast, are
examples of countries which have benefited from their positions as
gateways on the international airline route network, which is of key
importance to the growth of tourist arrivals.

## PRICE DETERMINATION AND THE ENVIRONMENT

Within a competitive economy, prices are determined by the interaction of supply and demand. Producers wish to cover both their
variable costs (such as the operation of a hotel) and their fixed costs
(which are incurred irrespective of the degree of utilisation of the hotel
or other asset). They also wish to obtain a profit margin which enables
them to continue to operate over the long run. Over the short run,
prices sometimes fall below the level which enables firms to finance
their fixed costs, with the result that the smaller firms in the market go
out of business. 'Price wars' sometimes enable larger firms within the
market to increase their market share.

Governments in tourist host countries sometimes intervene in the
market with the objective of attaining minimum prices. Officially-
determined prices have been established for accommodation in hotels
of different categories in Thailand in an attempt to ensure hoteliers an
adequate profit margin. Such policies are rarely consistently successful
as hoteliers, dependent upon overseas tour operators to ensure them a
high occupancy rate, provide tour operators with substantial discounts
below the official prices. Overseas tour operators usually reserve
'blocks' of hotel rooms by means of annual contracts with hoteliers,
and pay the hoteliers after the clients have left. If tour operators
experience lower demand for their holidays than they anticipated and
do not wish to use the rooms, they make use of a 'release back' system.

The hotelier is informed that the rooms will not be required – often seven to 28 days before the date of the tourists' arrival in the case of major international tour operators – and the hoteliers rarely receive compensation.

Contracts between hoteliers and tour operators vary over time and between different destinations according to the level of demand for and supply at the destination. In 1988, in a context of high growth of demand, luxury hotels in Bangkok increased their room prices by 10–20 per cent and dropped some of their contracts with tour operators in order to accommodate individual tourists paying higher prices for the accommodation (Barang, 1988). However, by 1990 luxury hotels were offering considerable discounts for tourist groups, and real decreases in room rates for all categories of hotel accommodation resulted from the increasing supply of accommodation in both hotels and unregulated serviced apartments, guest houses and condominiums. The issue of power and related policy within the tourism industry, discussed by Richter in Chapter 9 in this volume, is of relevance here, in that large international tour operators can often exert considerable bargaining power over individual hoteliers, whose negotiating position depends not only on the macroeconomic context, but also on their degree of organisation.

There is increasing concern about the adverse effects of environmental pollution upon tourism demand in the Asia Pacific region, especially in countries such as Thailand (Taylor, 1991a). Such concern stems, in part, from increasing awareness of the income generation which can result from environmental conservation, examined by Cochrane in Chapter 17 in this volume, in the context of Indonesia and Malaysia. Market prices, which are based on private costs and benefits, do not take account of environmental effects. Nevertheless, Pearce *et al.* (1989), among other authors, have shown that market prices can be modified to include not only private costs, but the cost of environmental damage and the use of non-renewable resources.

Different methods can be used to tackle pollution affecting and/or resulting from tourism. Environmental regulations, such as those introduced in Malaysia and discussed by Kadir Din in Chapter 18 in this volume, are one possible means. However, enforcement is sometimes lax, for example owing to the lack of clear demarcation of the responsibilities of different government agencies, as in Thailand (Elliott, 1987; Taylor, 1991a; Parnwell, Chapter 15 in this volume). Moreover, unregistered accommodation is often exempt from the regulations. Other means of confronting adverse environmental effects include the setting of taxes or charges appropriate to cover the cost of environmental pollution or to reduce excess demand and its associated environmental costs. Tourism-related taxes also provide a useful source of government revenue which could be used to meet such objectives as wider distribution of the income earned from tourism.

Neither tourism-related taxes nor regulations appear to have been used to tackle effectively the adverse environmental impacts associated with the 'over-development' of major tourist resorts, which can decrease the demand for tourism and/or lead to changes in clientele. Examples include the rapid, unplanned development of Pattaya in Thailand, which has resulted in an excess demand for infrastructure, especially water, as well as causing the pollution of coastal waters. The lack of controls on construction in Phuket, Thailand, has made the area a less attractive destination for tourists, resulting in lower demand by the higher expenditure groups, and development in Ko Samui has also been criticised for its adverse effects on the environment.

## INCOME GENERATION

Tourism's role as a catalyst to income generation has received extensive attention within the literature on the economics of tourism (Archer, 1977; 1989), and studies of the income generation effects of tourism in some of the countries in Asia and the Pacific have been undertaken. Tourism expenditure within a destination country can generate income, in a context of less than full employment, via the multiplier process, whereby the increase in local income resulting from tourist expenditure results in an increase in expenditure, generating further increases in income and expenditure, in an on-going income generation process. Leakages from each stage of the income generation process occur in the form of payments for imports, savings, taxation, national insurance contributions and remittances. Leakages in the form of import payments are particularly important in small, developing, island economies. The income multiplier is the ratio between the total income generated and the initial change in tourist expenditure, higher multiplier values indicating a higher ratio of income generation to expenditure, although the absolute value of income generation also depends upon the magnitude of the initial tourist expenditure. The multiplier model has the limitation of failing to provide information about the distribution of the income generated by the tourist expenditure.

Two models have been used to calculate the multiplier values associated with tourist expenditure. The first is the Keynesian income

multiplier model, which can take account of non-proportional relationships between the different variables. The second approach is the
input–output methodology which requires more data than the Keynesian multiplier model, but provides more detailed information
about the interrelationships between the different sectors of the
economy at a given period of time. Varley (1978) used the input–
output methodology to estimate the income generation effects of
tourist expenditure in Fiji on gross domestic product and gross
national product, as well as on specific sectors of the economy,
ranging from sugar cane production to retailing and wholesaling and
government services. Fletcher and Snee (1989) provided multiplier
values relating to tourist expenditure in Western Samoa, Palau and
the Solomon Islands, and Yacoumis (1990) cited multiplier values for
Tonga and Vanuatu. Tourist income multipliers were estimated for the
Cook Islands by Milne (1987), Hong Kong by Lin and Sung (1983),
the Philippines by Santos *et al.* (1983), Sri Lanka by Attanayake *et al.*
(1983) and Singapore by Toh Heng and Low (1990) and Khan *et al.*
(1990) (discussed in more detail by Walton in Chapter 11 in this
volume). The different studies show that tourist expenditure creates
considerable multiplier effects, particularly in the larger economies.

Varley emphasised the importance of examining the linkages
between tourism firms in the destination country and their input
sources, since large amounts of scarce foreign currency can be lost
from host countries if inputs are imported. Island economies including
Palau, Western Samoa and the Solomon Islands (Fletcher and Snee,
1989) usually have more problems in supplying such inputs locally
than larger countries such as Thailand (Carver, 1987). Varley (1978)
pointed out the apparent lack of responsiveness of local fruit and
vegetable production to higher prices in Fiji. Hitchcock, in Chapter 16
in this volume, notes that the extent of local purchasing can decrease
over time, and imports increase, as occurred for rice consumption
during the growth of tourism in Komodo in Indonesia. National
governments and international organisations have undertaken a variety of surveys and projects, designed to explore ways of increasing the
linkages between tourism enterprises and the local economy (Arndell,
1990).

Domestic tourists are more likely to purchase from smaller enterprises which tend to sell relatively high proportions of locally produced inputs, are labour intensive and retain most of their profits
within the country (Milne, 1987). Domestic tourists are usually less
geographically concentrated in a small number of resorts than foreign
tourists (Booth, 1990). Intra-Asian travel, which is predicted to have a

faster rate of growth than tourist arrivals into the Asia Pacific region from Europe and North America (Goldstein, 1990), has similar characteristics. Moreover, intra-regional tourists' spending levels may approximate those of tourists from industrialised countries (Toh Heng and Low, 1990).

## THE BALANCE OF PAYMENTS

International tourism has become renowned as a source of increasing receipts of foreign currency (English, 1986; Lee, 1987; World Tourism Organization, 1988; Walton, Chapter 11 in this volume). In some established tourist destinations, tourism has been the main source of foreign currency, for example in Thailand since 1982 (Elliott, 1987); even in a less established destination such as Indonesia, tourism was the fourth largest source of non-oil receipts in 1988 and was predicted to become the second largest source before the year 2000 (Schwarz, 1989; Booth, 1990). Tourism can aid economic growth by providing foreign currency receipts to finance the purchase of essential imports, increasing local income and employment directly and indirectly, increasing government revenue from taxation and stimulating investment.

Destination economies experience currency outflows in the form of payments for imports, as well as remittances of expatriates' wages, profits, interest and dividends. They also incur the adverse effects of decreases in income and investment during periods of falling tourism demand. Tourism is highly sensitive to 'shocks' such as the Gulf War, which caused a 30 per cent fall in American and European tourist arrivals in Thailand in the month following the outbreak of the war (Taylor, 1991b). The variability over time in tourism earnings need not be a problem if decreases in tourism receipts are offset by increases in receipts from other exports. The instability of receipts from different types of exports can be measured by calculating the value of deviations from a trend or moving average fitted to the values of receipts over time. Estimation of the instability values for receipts from tourism and from merchandise exports between 1960 and 1985 indicated that tourism receipts were more unstable than merchandise export receipts in the large economies of India and Thailand but less unstable in the island of Fiji, prior to the *coup* (Sinclair and Tsegaye, 1990). Examination of the degree of correlation between the variations over time in tourism and merchandise export receipts indicated that tourism earnings failed to have a net stabilising effect on the export earnings of India, Singapore and Thailand, while the net instability of foreign currency receipts in Fiji increased.

The instability of tourism receipts may be decreased by the promotion of arrivals from a wider range of origin countries. The Tourism Authority of Thailand is attempting to encourage greater inflows of tourists from the Asia Pacific region and, at the beginning of the 1990s, tourists from Australia, Japan, South Korea and Taiwan constituted Thailand's fastest growing sources of tourist arrivals. The Malaysian authorities have also attempted to diversify their sources of tourist arrivals (Aznam, 1990). The Malaysian Tourist Development Corporation has established overseas offices in origin countries identified as sources of growth: France, Germany, Hong Kong, Indonesia, Taiwan, Thailand and Singapore. An additional American office has been opened in Los Angeles in an attempt to stimulate the west coast market. The ASEAN countries are also attempting to increase the level of intra-ASEAN tourism.

## CONCLUSION

Examination of the economics of tourism in Asia and the Pacific indicates that a considerable amount of research remains to be undertaken. Tourism's contribution to the balance of payments has received attention, and some studies have estimated income and employment multipliers relating to tourist expenditure. However, until 1991, little research had been carried out on the economics of tourism supply, capital utilisation, price determination or environmental impacts. Even in the area of the demand for tourism, on which a large body of literature is available, there are few studies of Asian and Pacific countries. The general absence of such research is surprising, given the major contribution which tourism makes to the economies of the countries concerned and the relevance for policy-making which such studies would have.

An aspect of tourism demand of particular importance, but which has not been examined in detail in this chapter, is the role of domestic and intra-regional tourism. The general absence of research on domestic tourism is reflected by the limited availability of relevant statistics and its lack of perceived importance. Available data for intra-regional tourism demonstrate that many of the countries in the Asia Pacific region receive the majority of their foreign tourist arrivals from geographically proximate countries. Domestic and intra-regional tourism avoids many of the problems associated with long haul tourism, for example the large amounts of capital required for investment in luxury accommodation and infrastructure. Tourists from within the region usually stay in smaller-scale establishments which are predominantly owned by residents of the destination country, and consume a higher proportion of locally produced goods. They also tend to travel to more geographically dispersed areas of the destination country, thereby facilitating wider distribution of the income from tourism. The promotion of domestic and intra-regional tourism would thus permit a larger proportion of the returns from tourist expenditure to be retained within the Asia Pacific region.

# 11 Tourism and economic development in ASEAN

*John Walton*

## INTRODUCTION

During the last decade ASEAN countries, perhaps with the exception of Brunei, have given increasing attention to developing the international tourist industry as a means of promoting economic growth and development within their economies, especially since it is claimed to generate large foreign exchange earnings and is also a substantial employer of labour.

In terms of natural features generally considered attractive and to be of importance to the international tourist the ASEAN countries compare favourably with other areas such as those in the Caribbean. However, until recently the development of the tourist industry in ASEAN countries has tended to lag behind many other countries. The earlier lack of emphasis on tourism development can be attributed, to a large extent, to the rich natural resource endowments of the ASEAN countries and the large export earnings from primary products including oil, timber, rubber, tin and a large variety of other tropical products. Moreover, the distance from the major tourist supply areas of the United States and Europe may also have been a disadvantage, although the rapid development of wide-bodied jet airliners has to a large degree offset this problem, while the rapid growth of incomes in the Asia Pacific region has substantially increased the potential supply of tourists.

The down-turn in the world economy, particularly in the 1980s, following the oil price shocks of the 1970s, prompted the governments of ASEAN countries to promote their tourist industries on a more vigorous scale than previously, especially when their traditional sources of foreign exchange receipts became less reliable.

The emphasis on the development of the tourist industry has opened up considerable debate and discussion in relation to its impact on the economy and society in general. This debate has of course been discussed at length in other countries with longer histories of tourism, and whilst many issues will undoubtedly cover a common ground from which ASEAN countries may be able to learn and benefit from past experiences, it is also true that individual ASEAN countries have unique features or situations which may require specific or individual solutions.

The aim of this chapter is to portray an overall picture of recent trends and patterns of development of the international tourist industry in ASEAN whilst at the same time examining some of the issues which appear to arouse concern from within the region. Brunei is excluded since tourism plays a relatively insignificant role in its economy and the government has shown little commitment to its development. The focus is primarily directed to economic issues since other equally important areas involving social, cultural and environmental considerations are covered in detail in other chapters.

From an economic point of view the crucial question is how much economic benefit does the international tourist industry bring to an individual country? Benefits are usually seen in terms of income or value-added generated, foreign exchange receipts and also employment generation. There may be other benefit or externalities less easily quantifiable, such as improved infrastructure. Conversely it may be argued that international tourism imposes costs on a society.

## INTERNATIONAL TOURISM AND ECONOMIC DEVELOPMENT: POTENTIAL BENEFITS

The main economic benefits claimed for the international tourist industry as an agent of economic development as well as its associated problems can be summarised as follows.

1 It is claimed that international tourism can aid economic development by generating foreign exchange and alleviating balance of payments problems. It is argued that it is a sector less subject to trading restrictions or barriers, unlike many commodity exports. For instance, Thailand's cassava exports have been subject to restriction by the European Community, Indonesia is subject to OPEC oil quotas, etc. However, it should be noted that restrictions also exist within tourism, e.g. Indonesia, Philippines and Thailand introduced exit taxes in the 1980s to deter their nationals from travelling overseas.

2 It is a growth sector with relatively high elasticities of demand compared with primary products and their lower elasticities. There-

fore, as the world's most rapidly growing industry, tourism can be viewed as an important growth sector and also help to diversify the economy.

3 Because it is labour intensive it can be a significant provider of employment opportunities.

4 Since areas suitable for tourism – beaches, areas of natural beauty, etc. – are often situated away from the main centres of economic activity, it can help overcome regional disparities in income and employment.

5 It has high intermediate or indirect effects and therefore has important linkages or carry-over effects with the rest of the economy e.g. demand for locally produced food, handicrafts, etc.

6 It provides additional sources of revenue for the government through taxation, e.g. sales tax, corporation tax, etc. The Prime Minister of Malaysia recently stated that every dollar of tourist income provides the government with 35 cents, with which it is able to build clinics, roads, etc. (*The Star*, 2.7.90). This is of course an overstatement since the net effect is likely to be much less once investment incentives and tax concessions are taken into account.

7 It is claimed that international tourism may promote a better image of the country abroad, which in turn may lead to more foreign investment and exports.

## NEGATIVE ASPECTS

The negative aspects generally relate to socio-cultural problems which are of course difficult to quantify, but there are economic issues also.

### Economic

1 Exploitation by foreign firms and large foreign exchange leakages. The most obvious and most quoted example in ASEAN is the Japanese tourist whose tour is pre-paid in Japan, and who travels on Japan Air Lines, is transported to a Japanese hotel in a Japanese car and probably consumes a large proportion of imported food.

2 It is argued that the inflationary effect of tourist expenditure will increase prices for local inhabitants.

3 Tourism displaces workers in local industries.

4 It is claimed that investment is diverted to tourism which could be used for more worthwhile development projects. This particular claim, which may have validity in certain instances, is, however,

often misconstrued by individuals unaware of the process of economic development. In other words, it is necessary in the first instance to develop industries which are potentially large income or wealth creators so that the surpluses from future income streams can then, through taxation, be channelled to welfare projects such as hospitals and schools.

**Socio-cultural**

1 Destruction or degradation of cultural or geographical areas through overcrowding and overdevelopment leading to resource depletion, pollution, etc.
2 Habits of visiting foreigners (e.g. alcohol, drugs, sexual behaviour, crime, etc.) are detrimental to the domestic population.
3 General disruption of traditional societies and cultures.

In economic terms international tourism is an invisible export, or an export of a service. However, it differs from other exports in the sense that the consumer visits a country to receive or collect the tourist service. This places international tourism in a rather unique position and also tends to generate more controversy concerning its potential benefits and disadvantages. Apart from the various social and cultural implications associated with the foreign visitor, many problems arise when attempting to determine accurately the economic impact of international tourism. For instance, the value of a manufactured article or primary product, when exported, can readily be measured with a high degree of precision, whereas the expenditure pattern of the foreign tourist – which may involve spending on a large variety of goods and services in a wide variety of locations, sometimes in the informal sectors of the economy – is much less easy to quantify.

Although the tourist industry is claimed to be the world's largest industry, it is a complex amalgam of industries including hotels, restaurants, shops, transportation, sightseeing, entertainment and recreation. Within individual industries some may offer their goods and services exclusively to the tourist, whilst others may be only partially involved (for example, restaurants may also provide a service to local residents). The array of goods and services is diverse and the division between satisfying international, local and non-tourist demand is often the subject of arbitrary judgement; it is understandable, therefore, that margins of error may be considerable when attempts are made to measure the economic impact of the international tourist industry.

Within the ASEAN context a recent change in the measurement of tourism receipts illustrates the potential difficulties in obtaining accurate data. In the Philippines, prior to 1988, tourism receipts were calculated from data derived from the balance of payments account. However, in the belief that this seriously understated the actual amount of tourist expenditure a sample survey of tourist expenditure was conducted, the result of which suggested that average expenditure was more than three times that indicated by the balance of payments data. As a consequence, a new method was adopted which multiplies estimated average expenditure by the number of tourist arrivals. This change in methodology estimated tourist receipts for 1988 as US$1,456 million as compared with the balance of payments estimate of US$405 million (Philippine National Economic Development Authority, 1988, 233).

## THE ECONOMIC IMPACT OF TOURISM IN ASEAN

Perhaps because the serious commitment to tourism development by ASEAN governments is a relatively recent occurrence there have been few studies to assess the economic impact of tourism on the ASEAN economies.

Due to the multiproduct nature of tourism, input–output analysis has generally become the major instrument in assessing the economic impact of tourism within a specific country. Input–output (I–O) tables are able to reveal the interrelationship of one industry (or more correctly in our case the component industries of tourism) with all the other sectors of the economy.

Thus, in the case of tourism, it is able to identify and measure linkages between tourist expenditure and other sectors of the economy. As such, the total effect (both direct and indirect) on output, income and employment generated by tourism can be estimated. Since part of the analysis involves the measurement of inputs, it is also able to assess the amount of inputs originating from outside the country (i.e. imports). Input–output analysis, therefore, makes it possible to calculate foreign exchange leakages associated with the tourist industry.

Although input–output analysis is a useful and convenient technique to assess the economic impact of tourism, the conclusions reached are influenced by the quality of statistical data, assumptions used in defining what actually constitutes the expenditure of the tourist industry, and the methodology employed in calculating the multipliers or impact coefficients. Needless to say, these vary considerably within ASEAN so strict comparison between countries is not possible.

Analysis of the economic impact of tourism in ASEAN countries using input–output analysis ranges from little coverage in the case of Indonesia to several studies in relation to Singapore.

In the case of Indonesia no official attempt has been made to measure the impact of tourist expenditure through the use of input–output analysis, although Tucker, Seow and Sundberg (1984) using 1975 I–O tables estimated a foreign exchange leakage of 23 per cent of gross tourism receipts for the year 1980.

In Thailand the Tourism Authority of Thailand (TAT) sponsored the first study on the economic impact of tourism in 1977; however, the 1971 I–O tables were too aggregative and outdated to produce a satisfactory result. A more up-to-date study in 1985 used 1980 I–O Tables to assess the situation in 1983. This estimated a foreign exchange leakage of 34.26 per cent, whilst on the income side 1 million Baht of foreign tourist expenditure generated a direct income of 0.524 million Baht and an indirect income of 1.536 million, making a total income of 2.060 million Baht. Tucker's estimate for foreign exchange leakage was somewhat lower at 22.8 per cent.

For Malaysia, a study based on 1978 I–O tables gives some indication of the impact of tourism within the Malaysian economy. The study assessed a number of industries and was not specifically addressed to tourism. However, by taking the hotel, restaurant and shopping expenditures of foreign tourists it is possible to give an approximation for the tourist industry as a whole, since these three categories account for over 70 per cent of total tourist expenditure. The conclusions reached suggest an output multiplier of 1.79, an income multiplier of 0.73 and a foreign exchange leakage of 22 per cent. The same study also assessed the economic impact of other recently established manufacturing industries, including export-oriented industries such as electrical machinery and textiles. Electrical machinery had an output multiplier of 1.36 and an income multiplier of 0.42 with a foreign exchange leakage of 53 per cent. For textiles the corresponding figures were 1.56, 0.51 and a foreign exchange leakage of 45 per cent. These figures suggest that tourism has a significantly greater economic impact in terms of output and income generation than some of the newly established manufacturing industries in Malaysia; moreover the foreign exchange leakage is much less. Tucker *et al.*'s calculation of foreign exchange leakage for tourism is similar to the above – i.e. 20.4 per cent.

In the Philippines the Asian Institute of Tourism in Manila

conducted a comprehensive study as part of a research project funded by the International Development Research Centre of Canada. This study concluded that tourism in the Philippines in 1978 had an output multiplier of 1.87, an income multiplier of 2.22 and a foreign exchange leakage of 17 per cent. Tucker *et al.* calculated the foreign exchange leakage at 13.9 per cent.

Singapore has been the subject of a number of studies in attempts to assess the importance and economic impact of the foreign tourist's dollar. These include studies by Diamond (1979), Seow (1981) and Schymyck (1983). However, two studies published in 1990 – Khan, Chou and Wong, and Toh and Low – present a more up-to-date appraisal and offer detailed insights into Singapore's tourist industry.

As Khan *et al.* point out the receipts from tourism (as indeed do receipts from other industries) have a magnified impact on the economy in three ways.

1 Direct effect: The initial injection of tourist expenditure creates direct revenue to hotels, shops, restaurants, travel agents, transport operators and other tourist services.
2 Indirect effect: The recipients of the direct expenditure generate additional revenues to businesses or producers supplying them with necessary inputs, e.g. fuel for various forms of transport, food for restaurants, equipment for hotels, construction of hotels, etc.
3 Induced effect: The beneficiaries of the direct and indirect effects spend their increased incomes on consumer and investment goods, which induces further consumption within the economy.

By using input–output techniques multiplier effects are calculated from standard I–O tables and can be used to assess the economic impact of tourism expenditure on income or value-added, output and employment. The same analysis also allows measurement of foreign exchange leakages.

Table 11.1 indicates that every tourist dollar of expenditure creates 94 cents of income or value-added, S$2 worth of output, whilst S$1 million create 33 jobs. It also shows a breakdown into the direct, indirect and induced effects. The fact that secondary effects account for half the total effect demonstrates the strong linkages between tourism and the other sectors of the economy. Using the same methodology Khan *et al.* estimate an import multiplier of 0.38, suggesting a foreign exchange leakage of 38 cents out of every tourist dollar.

Toh and Low, using similar analysis, produce output, income and employment multipliers almost identical to Khan *et al.*: output – 1.96,

*Table 11.1* Output, income and employment multipliers in Singapore's tourism, 1983

| Components | Output | Income | Employment |
|-----------|--------|--------|------------|
| Direct | 1.0000 | 0.4621 | 18.3050 |
| Indirect | 0.4824 | 0.2269 | 6.5372 |
| Induced | 0.5179 | 0.2503 | 7.9058 |
| Total | 2.0003 | 0.9393 | 32.7480 |

*Note*: Output and income multipliers are defined in terms of per S$1 of tourist expenditure. Employment multipliers are defined in terms of per S$1 million of tourist expenditure.
*Source*: Khan *et al.* 1990, 415.

*Table 11.2* Comparison of tourism with other exports, 1983

| | Manufacturing | Exports | Tourism |
|-----------|---------------|---------|---------|
| Output | 1.6255 | 1.4090 | 1.9622 |
| Income | 0.5705 | 0.3953 | 0.9798 |
| Labour | 17.315 | 9.8818 | 33.078 |
| Imports | 0.5904 | 0.7218 | 0.2718 |

*Source*: Toh and Low, 1990, 263.

income – 0.98 and employment – 33.08. Their import multiplier, however, is smaller at 0.27.

Toh and Low also calculate multipliers for manufacturing exports and total exports to enable comparisons to be made between tourism and other sectors.

From Table 11.2 it can be seen that the tourist dollar has a much larger impact than either manufacturing exports or total exports. For instance, tourism creates twice as many jobs as manufacturing exports and three times as many as total exports. Similarly the tourist dollar generated almost S$1 in income or value-added compared with 57 cents in manufacturing and 40 cents in total exports.

In terms of foreign exchange leakages manufacturing exports and total exports have significantly higher import content than tourism (i.e. 59 per cent and 72 per cent as compared to 27 per cent for tourism).

To establish a clearer picture of the tourist industry it is worthwhile to break it down into its main component parts. This can be seen from Table 11.3, which also shows the pattern of tourist expenditure as well as income and employment multipliers for the individual sectors.

The notable feature of tourist expenditure in Singapore is the large

*Table 11.3* Composition of tourist expenditure and income and employment multipliers for individual sectors, Singapore 1986

| Item | % of tourist expenditure | Multiplier | |
|------|------|------|------|
| | | Income | Labour |
| Shopping | 59.6 | 1.0668 | 29.8234 |
| Food & drink (Restaurants) | 14.8 | 0.8718 | 32.9316 |
| Accommodation (Hotels) | 17.3 | 0.9432 | 35.7950 |
| Local transportation | 4.1 | 0.7558 | 16.7248 |
| Entertainment & recreation | 1.6 | 1.0375 | 42.3526 |
| Sightseeing | 1.1 | (included under recreation) | |
| Other services | 1.6 | 1.0129 | 21.3777 |

*Source*: adapted from Toh and Low, 1990.


*Table 11.4* Tourism multipliers: Singapore 1987

| | Output | Income | Employment | Imports |
|------|------|------|------|------|
| Direct | 0.71 | 0.36 | 17 | 0.42 |
| Indirect | 0.30 | 0.15 | 4 | 0.07 |
| Induced | 0.30 | 0.18 | 5 | 0.10 |
| Total | 1.31 | 0.69 | 26 | 0.59 |

*Source*: *ESCAP Tourism Review*, No. 5, 1988.


amount spent on shopping which is considerably higher than in other ASEAN countries. Shopping also has the largest income multiplier of the various tourist sectors, although its employment multiplier is less than food, accommodation and recreation. Tucker calculated a foreign exchange leakage of 31.1 per cent for Singapore.

Although the above studies come out favourably with regard to tourism's impact on the Singapore economy, it should be noted that other studies portray its position less favourably. For instance, a paper presented at ESCAP (Economic and Social Commission for Asia and the Pacific) in 1988 calculated multipliers significantly differently (see Table 11.4).

The above analyses focus on the actual impact on various sectors of the economy, in particular the multiplier effects on output, income and employment, as well as identifying foreign exchange leakages. As such they make an important contribution to understanding the linkages between tourism and other sectors of the economy, and also

*Table 11.5* ASEAN: tourist arrivals and average length of stay

|  | Tourist arrivals ('000s) | | | Average length of stay |
|  | 1980 | 1985 | 1990* | 1989 (days) |
|---|---|---|---|---|
| Indonesia | 561 | 749 | 2,100 | 11.6 |
| Malaysia | 2,251 | 2,933 | 7,400 | 4.5 |
| Philippines | 1,008 | 773 | 1,000 | 12.0 |
| Singapore | 2,562 | 3,031 | 5,300 | 3.3 |
| Thailand | 1,859 | 2,438 | 5,200 | 7.6 |
| ASEAN | 8,233 | 9,924 | 21,000 | |

*Note*: *Estimate
*Source*: National Tourist Boards.

the processes by which tourism may be able to stimulate economic growth. Although the results vary considerably there is still a clear indication that tourism has strong multiplier effects in terms of output, income and employment. Generally these effects appear greater than those associated with export manufacturing industries whilst foreign exchange leakages are substantially less. Thus government policies promoting tourism as an export industry appear to be vindicated.

Although the above multipliers provide information on how a given amount of tourist expenditure interacts with other sectors of the economy they give little indication regarding the magnitude, character, structure and growth trends of the tourist industry in individual ASEAN countries. These characteristics are now examined in more detail.

Apart from the Philippines, where political instability and more recently natural disasters have tended to deter foreign visitors, there has been a rapid growth in tourist arrivals in ASEAN countries (Table 11.5). Singapore and Thailand are the leading tourist countries due, to a considerable degree, to their earlier promotional initiatives. This rapid growth is expected to continue, especially with the more vigorous promotion by government tourist boards, which have set a target of 22 million visitors for Visit ASEAN Year 1992.

Table 11.5 also shows the average length of stay which varies significantly within ASEAN. Singapore with 3.3 days is generally regarded as a stop-over destination whilst in the larger countries with their greater variety of natural tourist attractions and internal travel potential visitors stay for longer periods of time. In the case of Malaysia the average length of stay of 4.5 days is largely influenced by the large number of short-stay visitors from Singapore who have easy land access to Malaysia across the causeway between Singapore and Malaysia.

*Table 11.6* ASEAN: tourist receipts and average daily per capita expenditure

| | Tourist receipts (US$ million) | | | *Average daily per capita expenditure, 1989 (US$)* |
| | *1980* | *1985* | *1990\** | |
|---|---|---|---|---|
| Indonesia | 289 | 525 | 1,860 | 68 |
| Malaysia | 265 | 545 | 1,520 | 47 |
| Philippines | 320 | 507 | 1,650 | 103 |
| Singapore | 1,421 | 1,827 | 4,200 | 182 |
| Thailand | 867 | 1,318 | 4,400 | 103 |
| ASEAN | 3,161 | 4,721 | 13,630 | |

*Note:* \*Estimate.
The Philippines adopted a different method of calculation in 1988.
*Source*: National Tourist Boards.

*Table 11.7* ASEAN: visitor expenditure pattern, 1989 (per cent)

| | *Singapore* | *Malaysia* | *Indonesia* | *Philippines* | *Thailand* |
|---|---|---|---|---|---|
| Shopping | 64.6 | 16.7 | 18.6 | 21.0 | 36.9 |
| Accommodation | 16.5 | 37.3 | 33.4 | 33.2 | 27.1 |
| Food and beverages | 11.9 | 20.8 | 17.8 | 22.1 | 16.2 |
| Local transport and sightseeing | 5.0 | 16.9 | 17.6 | 5.1 | 13.7 |
| Other | 2.0 | 8.3 | 12.6 | 18.7 | 6.1 |

*Source*: *ASEAN Tourist Industry Report*, 1990.

Tourist receipts in Table 11.6 show the substantial growth of income from tourism in the 1980s. Daily per capita expenditure varies a great deal between countries and, whilst it reflects cost of living differences, it is also influenced by special factors. In Singapore the greater outlays on shopping (see Table 11.7) tend to push up expenditure, while in Malaysia the influence of Singaporean visitors once again needs to be taken into account, many of whom will stay with relatives or friends and therefore save on accommodation expenses.

The hotel industry is a very essential part of tourism considering that the definition of a tourist requires the visitor to be involved in at least one overnight stay away from home. In ASEAN Thailand has by far the largest number of hotel rooms (see Table 11.8) and this may be a contributory factor to its success in attracting a large number of visitors in the 1980s. However, only about 30,000 of Bangkok's hotel

*Table 11.8* ASEAN: number of hotel rooms and occupancy rates

|              | 1980    | 1985    | 1989    |
|--------------|---------|---------|---------|
| Indonesia    | 53,358  | 97,136  | 109,600 |
| (%)          | —       | 48.0    | 55.7    |
| Malaysia     | 27,565  | 35,720  | 45,032  |
| (%)          | 64.4    | 49.8    | 66.9    |
| Philippines  | 10,434  | 16,483  | 14,674  |
| (%)          | 68.9    | 51.8    | 76.4    |
| Singapore    | 13,804  | 20,547  | 23,453  |
| (%)          | 86.1    | 65.9    | 86.4    |
| Thailand     | 46,072  | 110,003 | 168,593 |
| (%)          | 80.1    | —       | 87.9    |
| ASEAN        | 151,233 | 279,889 | 361,352 |

*Source*: National Tourist Boards.

rooms are considered to be up to international tourist standards (EIU Report No. 2030), and a high occupancy rate of 87.9 per cent (1989) suggests a shortage of high-class hotel accommodation. A similar situation prevails in Singapore with an occupancy rate of 86.4 per cent in 1989.

Table 11.9 shows a detailed breakdown of the origins of the 16.4 million tourists who visited ASEAN in 1989. With the exception of the Philippines, ASEAN countries rely heavily on intra-ASEAN travel with over 6 million, or 37 per cent, of foreign arrivals being accounted for by ASEAN nationals. The next largest markets from outside ASEAN are Japan, with almost 2 million visitors, and Australia, with 1 million visitors.

Within ASEAN Singapore established an early lead in the promotion of tourism and in 1980 it accounted for 45 per cent of total ASEAN tourist receipts and 31 per cent of tourist arrivals. By 1990 these market shares were reduced to 31 per cent and 25 per cent respectively as other ASEAN countries became more competitive.

On separating from the Federation of Malaysia in 1965, Singapore, without natural resources and largely dependent on its entrepot trade and British military expenditure, quickly looked to other areas of economic activity, including international tourism, to diversify the economy. The Singapore Tourist Promotion Board (STPB) was established in 1964 when international tourist arrivals totalled a mere 90,000. Aggressive promotion during the ensuing period increased arrivals to 2.56 million in 1980 and in 1990 tourist arrivals exceeded 5 million for the first time. The rapid increase in tourists and the concomitant expenditure, together with high levels of overall econ-

Table 11.9 Tourist arrivals in ASEAN countries, 1989, by country of origin

| Destination: | Indonesia* | Malaysia* | Philippines | Singapore | Thailand** | Total |
|---|---|---|---|---|---|---|
| *Country of origin:* | | | | | | |
| ASEAN *** | 642,770 | 2,950,706 | 64,806 | 1,257,038 | 1,129,719 | 6,045,039 |
| Japan | 186,521 | 188,260 | 215,634 | 841,371 | 555,638 | 1,987,424 |
| Australia | 178,456 | 109,461 | 50,529 | 450,235 | 218,856 | 1,007,537 |
| UK | 74,617 | 119,636 | 26,600 | 281,280 | 200,347 | 702,480 |
| Germany | 70,362 | 35,742 | 30,045 | 140,604 | 222,148 | 498,901 |
| USA | 80,196 | 65,957 | 246,586 | 247,996 | 266,735 | 907,470 |
| Korea | 24,106 | n/a | 36,587 | 87,664 | 111,591 | 259,958 |
| Taiwan | 39,840 | 48,978 | 90,146 | 223,806 | 399,704 | 802,474 |
| France | 45,277 | 19,608 | 9,543 | 68,796 | 186,960 | 330,184 |
| Hong Kong | 34,463 | 65,174 | 130,346 | 147,480 | 395,681 | 773,144 |
| Italy | 38,628 | n/a | 8,869 | 55,035 | 92,450 | 194,982 |
| India | 6,317 | 44,215 | 6,348 | 194,068 | 120,032 | 370,980 |
| Others | 204,412 | 306,036 | 273,680 | 834,577 | 909,597 | 2,528,352 |
| Total | 1,625,965 | 3,953,773 | 1,189,719 | 4,829,950 | 4,809,508 | 16,408,915 |

*Notes:* *Estimates 1989 **Tourists ***Brunei Darussalam not included.
*Source: ASEAN Tourism Industry Report,* 1990.

omic growth, appeared to reduce the relative importance attached to the development of tourism and the downturn in arrivals in 1983, and income in 1984, prompted the government to reassess its strategies. Whilst depressed world economic conditions imposed a cyclical effect, it was also recognised that structural changes, associated with modernisation within Singapore, were influencing its traditional attractiveness as an Oriental tourist destination.

Singapore reacted quickly and positively by elevating the role of the STPB and also set up in 1984 a Tourism Task Force to advise on future development, which resulted in a Tourism Product Development Plan (1986–90) designed to revitalise existing attractions and develop new areas of interest. In line with the Tourism Development Plan the government committed S$1 billion to infrastructural development, and improved tax concessions and investment privileges available to private investors.

Since 1986 tourist arrivals and income have resumed their upward trend and in 1988 tourism accounted for 5.4 per cent of GDP, contributed 11 per cent to foreign exchange earnings and employed directly and indirectly 100,000 persons or 8 per cent of the total labour force (STPB Annual Report, 1988–89).

Although the hotel sector in Thailand has played a significant role in attracting tourists and was granted investment privileges by the Board of Investment in the 1960s, the tourist industry was not given any special emphasis until the Fourth Five-Year Development Plan (1977–81). The Fifth Plan (1982–86) and Sixth Plan (1987–91) increasingly attached importance to tourism as a foreign exchange earner and provider of employment opportunities.

Recent policy stems from the Tourism Act of 1979 which established the Tourism Authority of Thailand (TAT) in its present structure with responsibility for formulating policy and promotional marketing. In the 1980s visitors to Thailand increased rapidly and the successful promotion of Visit Thailand Year (1987) contributed to Thailand displacing Singapore in 1988 as the leading ASEAN tourist destination both in terms of arrivals and revenue.

In Malaysia the Tourist Development Corporation (TDC), established in 1972, played a relatively passive role in promoting international tourism in the early years of its formation, and it was not until the mid-1980s and the poor performance of traditional exports that international tourism was accorded high priority.

In 1987 the establishment of the Ministry of Culture and Tourism and the elevation of the industry to cabinet status marked the beginning of an aggressive campaign to promote tourism, especially through overseas marketing with Fascinating Malaysia in 1988 and Visit Malaysia Year in 1990. Vastly increased budget allowances to the TDC and additional tax concessions granted in the 1990 National Budget have served to maintain the stimulus to develop the tourist industry, not only in promotional matters but also to develop and raise skills and professionalism within the industry. The above measures have resulted in a dramatic increase in tourist arrivals to 7.4 million in 1990 (of which 70 per cent originate from Singapore) which firmly established Malaysia as the leading ASEAN country in terms of tourist arrivals. However, in terms of receipts, despite an almost three-fold increase from US$545 million in 1985 to US$1.52 billion in 1990, Malaysia remains at the bottom of the income table, mainly due to the predominance of the short-stay visitor from Singapore.

In the Philippines, while the government established a commitment to developing a tourist industry in the early 1970s in recognition of its potential benefits to the economy, this earlier initiative was largely suppressed by the negative publicity associated with political unrest and instability. As a consequence, whilst other ASEAN countries experienced rapid growth in tourist arrivals with their number of visitors increasing two-fold or three-fold in the decade of the 1980s, the Philippines in contrast experienced a general decline for most part of this period and it was not until 1988 that arrivals recovered to the 1 million total achieved in 1980. Renewed efforts to promote tourism have yet to overcome the major problem of negative publicity and arrivals remain around the 1 million mark. Nevertheless tourism is an important industry within the economy and accounted for 8 per cent of export earnings in 1987 and 2.4 per cent of employment (ESCAP Tourism Review No. 4, 1988).

The major commitment to developing the tourist industry in Indonesia can be traced to the early 1980s when the collapse in the price of oil, which had previously underpinned economic growth, forced the government vigorously to promote the non-oil sector, including the tourist industry. Deregulation, the move to dismantle the highly bureaucratic framework of licensing and regulation prevalent in Indonesia, greatly benefited the tourism sector, as did the relaxation of visa requirements in 1983. Although visitor arrivals and tourist income rose rapidly in the 1980s the Indonesian government tended to lack the degree of commitment shown by neighbouring ASEAN countries in their promotional campaigns. For instance, it was not until 1989 that the Tourist Promotion Board was established, which in terms of political stature and government financial backing lacks the status of its counterparts in Singapore, Thailand and Malaysia. Instead it relies more heavily on support from the private sector. However, tourism's contribution to the economy is now considerable. In 1990 it became the third largest foreign exchange earner in the non-oil and gas sector after timber and textiles, with the expectation that it will become the leading export in this sector by 1993. It is estimated that 1.6 million people are employed, either directly or indirectly, as a result of tourism with a projected target of 2.5 million by the end of the current Five-Year Plan (Repelita V) in 1993 (EIU International Tourism Report No. 3, 1991).

## CONCLUSION

In the 1980s, and especially in the latter part of the decade, ASEAN governments strongly committed themselves to the development of their international tourist industries in the firm belief that to do so would bring substantial economic benefits to their respective countries. Foreign exchange earnings and the creation of employment opportunities were identified as the major reasons for tourism development, with other factors such as its ability to promote regional development also taken into consideration. Moreover, tourism as one of the world's fastest growing industries, if indeed not the most dynamic, could bring relatively rapid returns to investment.

Without question, the ASEAN governments (with the exception of Brunei) are committed to tourist development. Although there is some variation in strategies, governments have accorded high priority to tourism development including special investment and tax concessions and substantially increased financial backing to revitalised or recently established tourist promotion boards and programmes. This strong conviction is not shared by all members of ASEAN society, and tourism has been questioned from extreme and moderate points of view. The former argues that tourism should be banned altogether, whereas the latter suggests that the economic benefits from tourism should be weighed carefully against the environmental and social, as well as economic, costs of tourism development.

The few studies reviewed in this chapter suggest, perhaps with the exception of Singapore, that little serious research has been carried out to assess the economic impact of tourism on ASEAN countries. Apart from methodological considerations the few studies conducted have suffered from limitations of data.

Input–output analyses, like many other techniques, give a deceptive air of accuracy which, due to computational practices, portray results to several decimal places; in reality, due to choice of methodology and data limitations, these analyses may be far from accurate. Moreover, input–output analysis does not allow judgements to be made in relation to externalities such as pollution and environment. Nevertheless, acknowledging that considerable margins of error may exist, we may find partial or approximate answers from the above studies to some of the questions regarding the economic impact of tourism.

With regard to foreign exchange earnings, their net effect appears to be of significant benefit to ASEAN economies. Although estimates of foreign exchange leakages show a great deal of variation from 14 per cent in the Philippines to 59 per cent in Singapore, most estimates, even allowing for indirect or induced effects, fall below 40 per cent. The estimate of 59 per cent for Singapore contrasts with the findings of two recent studies (Khan *et al.* 38 per cent, Toh and Low 27 per cent). Furthermore, it is likely that Singapore as a small island economy with virtually no natural resources will have a higher propensity to import than other ASEAN countries.

In terms of income generation and employment creation the various studies show not only important direct effects but also powerful linkages to other sectors and therefore strong indirect effects.

Of significance are the studies of Malaysia and Singapore where comparisons with other export industries suggest that the tourist industry has a markedly greater economic impact and considerably less foreign exchange leakages than the modern electrical and textile industries.

The above studies clearly support the view that development of the international tourist industry offers ASEAN countries a way to increase substantially net foreign exchange earnings, generate income and employment and therefore stimulate economic growth.

Criticisms regarding the negative effects of tourism, including the inflationary effects of tourist expenditure on local prices and displacement of labour in other industries, are more difficult to assess since little or no research on these topics appears to have been conducted in ASEAN. Since ASEAN countries, apart from Singapore, generally have problems creating employment opportunities for their rapidly expanding labour forces it seems unlikely that labour demand from the tourism sector will have any significant effects on other industries.

The general conclusion that international tourism can be of significant economic benefit should not imply that ASEAN governments should allow tourism to develop in an entirely uncontrolled manner. Although an individual industry may have a unique situation, which warrants criticism and regulations specific to that particular industry, many of the criticisms voiced by anti-tourism groups apply to industrial development in general (e.g. allegations of exploitation by foreign multinational corporations, environmental pollution, social upheaval, lack of training and low wages, and so on). This of course does not make these criticisms less valid. On the other hand it is difficult to justify the singling out of the tourism industry for such criticism to the exclusion of other industries. This may suggest that the latter are more beneficial – an inference which is clearly open to question.

The rapid increase in tourist arrivals and income experienced in recent years appears likely to continue now that ASEAN governments have identified and committed themselves to the development of the tourist industry as a leading foreign exchange earner and provider of employment. The positive response to the recent more enlightened tourist development promotion has encouraged governments to support the development of the industry on a much greater scale than hitherto.

To increase receipts, tourist promotion boards essentially can consider three aspects: first, to promote measures to increase visitor arrivals; second, to encourage the visitor to stay for a longer period of time; and third, to persuade the tourist to increase daily expenditure. In the case of the first aspect, more aggressive overseas promotion, which is relatively easy to implement, has already significantly increased visitor arrivals and should continue to do so. However, increasing the length of stay and daily expenditure requires improvement in the quantity and quality of tourist services, and whilst this is recognised by the various tourist promotion plans, it will take longer to achieve.

The heightened awareness of tourism's potential economic benefits is encouraging greater efforts to identify those groups of tourists with higher spending patterns. Data collection and market surveys provide information on expenditure patterns, which can be classified according to various factors such as age groups, purpose of visit, length of stay, accommodation and nationality, etc. Through market segmentation promotional measures can be directed at specific groups. For instance, ASEAN countries are showing a keen interest in the MICE (Meetings, Incentives, Conventions and Exhibitions) market which is generally associated with higher per capita expenditure, but also demands high-quality services, often on a very large scale.

Emphasis is placed on building up the tourism infrastructure including hotels, leisure and recreational facilities as well as the need for manpower training and skill development. In a broader sense infrastructural problems, especially in regard to transportation, need to be addressed, particularly where tourists are encouraged to visit more remote areas in the interest of regional development.

National airlines are also identified as key factors in ASEAN tourism development, and airlines such as Thai International, Singapore Airlines (SIA), Malaysian Airline System (MAS), Philippine Airlines and Garuda, which in many cases have spearheaded overseas promotion, will continue to play a vital role. The on-going process to increase fleet capacity and expand the number of overseas destinations and bilateral agreements with foreign airlines in relation to landing rights is also seen as important.

Although members of a regional association, the individual countries of ASEAN have been involved in few areas of close cooperation and tend to formulate their policies independently. The easy land access and proximity of Singapore and Malaysia encourages cooperation between these two countries, and the development of industry and tourism as part of a growth triangle concept (Johore, Singapore and Riau Islands) in Batam Island, only 20 kilometres from Singapore, is also encouraging cooperation with Indonesia. More recently , however, through its Sub-Committee on Tourism (SCOT), the ASEAN countries have shown signs of closer cooperation with the designation of 1992 as Visit ASEAN Year. One of the main aims is to encourage overseas visitors to remain longer in ASEAN through the promotion of multidestination holidays, and, during 1992, visitors to one ASEAN country will be able, through the use of special promotional airfares, to travel to a second or third ASEAN country at no extra cost.[1]

During the 1990s the ASEAN countries expect the strong growth in tourist arrivals initiated in the 1980s to continue. These expectations appear realistic, especially since, as relative late-comers to the international tourist industry, they have much untapped potential to offer. Whilst political problems in the Philippines may continue to project a negative image as far as international tourism is concerned, prospects elsewhere in ASEAN appear favourable. The likelihood of more settled political conditions and the opening up of trade with Indo-China may also benefit ASEAN and in particular Thailand where Bangkok sees itself as a potential gateway or stopover point for the region.

Although the main focus of this chapter has been the international tourist, the impact of the domestic tourist should not be overlooked. Steadily increasing per capita incomes in ASEAN should stimulate the growth of domestic tourism which, though not important as a foreign exchange earner, will nevertheless impart significant economic benefits in terms of income and employment generation by creating demand for accommodation, shopping, transport and recreational services in a similar way to international tourism.

Finally, the increasing importance of the tourist industry in ASEAN is likely to encourage further research which may lead to a better understanding of its role within the economy. Likewise its rapid growth will raise the debate regarding its possible adverse effects, to which, it is hoped, ASEAN governments will react with a similar commitment to that now shown in their desire to promote the tourist industry.

## NOTE

1 Not implemented due to objections from IATA (International Air Transport Association).

# 12 Tourism and rural handicrafts in Thailand[1]

*Michael J. G. Parnwell*

## INTRODUCTION

Tourists to Thailand spent in the region of US$1,000 million on 'shopping' in 1989, or about one-third of total tourist expenditure. A significant proportion of this expenditure was on handicraft souvenirs, a factor which was helped considerably by the very successful promotion of Thailand Arts and Crafts Year, TACY (in fact a rather long 'year', from August 1988 until December 1989). The promotion campaign was aimed principally at boosting the country's exports of handicraft products, but it sought also to increase tourist spending – part of the broader strategy to turn Thailand into a 'shopping paradise' (*The Nation*, 14.8.88), in the process bolstering the country's earnings from international tourism.

The domestic component of TACY centred essentially upon a three-pronged assault on the tourist dollar: a general advertising campaign aimed at increasing tourists' awareness of the arts and crafts of Thailand, their cultural significance and the skills of the craftspeople involved; the establishment of national, regional and provincial showrooms, through which the handicraft products of particular areas could be promoted; and the organisation of exhibitions, demonstrations and 'side shows' whereby tourists could obtain a brief glimpse, albeit in rather artificial surroundings, of the various production techniques involved.

The Thai government has been concerned primarily with the perceived macroeconomic benefits to be obtained from boosting tourist spending and export earnings. None the less, the handicrafts sector also represents a means whereby some of the economic spoils of tourism development can be diffused to peripheral and rural parts of Thailand. Notwithstanding the fact that many Thai handicraft products for the international and tourist markets are manufactured in urban areas, particularly Bangkok, the growth in demand for Thai handicraft products is generally good news as far as the spread of economic benefits and activity is concerned. The more general tendency is towards the concentration of earnings from industrial development and tourism in the hands of national and multinational firms (Rodenberg, 1980), and the agglomeration of the tourism industry in a spatially restricted number of centres (see the chapters by Richter, Sinclair and Walton in this volume).

As with many aspects of tourism in South-East Asia, the economic and distributional benefits of handicrafts promotion are counter-balanced by a variety of costs, not least to Thailand's rich and diverse material culture. The modernisation and transformation of the traditional handicrafts sector – essential if producers are to satisfy the rapidly growing demand for their products – will by necessity involve changes in production methods, and may also lead to a decline in quality and craftsmanship. In catering to the tastes of foreign visitors, traditional designs may also be modified leading, *in extremis*, to the emergence of so-called 'airport art'.

Although, of course, Thailand's handicrafts industry need not inevitably follow an ultimately self-destructive path trading-off short-term economic gain against the longer-term degradation of its material culture, we are in essence faced with a dilemma which pitches the 'pragmatists' against the 'purists'. The former might argue that, given the high incidence of rural poverty in Thailand and the relatively depressed state of the economy away from the main centres of economic activity, the potential 'trickle-down effect' of handicrafts promotion provides a persuasive case in favour of the industry's modernisation and development. The latter, meanwhile, bemoan the effects that tourism is having on Thailand's traditional handicraft products, and argue the need to conserve this vital aspect of the country's cultural heritage.

This chapter assesses some of the economic and spatial arguments in favour of the promotion of rural handicraft industries in support of tourism, and finds that the pragmatists have a quite convincing case, especially in the country's peripheral and economically depressed regions. It also finds that many of the purists' fears are unfounded.

## TOURISM AND UNEVEN DEVELOPMENT

Tourism represents a potentially powerful means by which economic activity might be spread to peripheral, economically underdeveloped areas. In general, the more discerning tourists might be expected to shy away from the congested, polluted, frenetic metropolitan centres,

*Table 12.1* Regional economic disparities in Thailand, 1987

| | Per capita GRP (Baht) | % of national average | Share of GRP (%) Manufacturing | Agriculture |
|---|---|---|---|---|
| Bangkok and vicinity | 71,566 | 310.9 | 35.94 | 3.07 |
| Central Region | 18,742 | 81.4 | 17.91 | 22.02 |
| Western Region | 19,795 | 85.9 | 11.78 | 30.81 |
| Eastern Region | 31,094 | 135.1 | 19.62 | 21.96 |
| Southern Region | 17,506 | 76.0 | 5.04 | 33.69 |
| Northern Region | 13,185 | 57.3 | 7.34 | 33.96 |
| North-eastern Region | 8,343 | 36.2 | 8.37 | 33.17 |
| Whole Kingdom | 23,021 | 100.0 | 22.72 | 17.29 |

*Source:* Government of Thailand, NESDB, 1989, Gross Regional and Provincial Product, 1981–87; Bangkok: Office of the Prime Minister, NESDB.

which have provided the main foci for industry-centred economic growth in South-East Asia over the last few decades, preferring instead the more peaceful, pleasant and picturesque surroundings offered by up-country locations. Whilst the capital city may provide the point of entry for most international tourists, and may offer a variety of attractions on their sightseeing checklists, most will eventually wend their way to coastal resorts, mountainous interiors, ancient monuments and/or national parks. These are the features which underpin the 'differentness' and 'distinctiveness' of the region to Western tourists, and which partly explain the phenomenal growth of tourist arrivals from Europe, the United States and Australasia over the last decade or so.

Because many of the 'natural resources' (both physical and human) upon which tourism in South-East Asia has been built[2] are found some distance from, but usually within quite easy reach of, the main urban and economic centres, tourism might thus enable people in peripheral areas to claim for themselves a reasonable share of the spoils of economic development which are thought to be associated with the boom in international tourism. This is certainly the case in Thailand. The country evidences one of the most unbalanced and concentrated patterns of economic development in the Developing World. More than two-thirds of the country's urban population is located in the sprawling metropolis of Bangkok. Some four-fifths of total manufacturing value-added in Thailand is accounted for by the capital city and a small number of 'satellite' urban centres. The city provides the main focus for commercial and service sector activity, international trade, finance and political decision-making. The fertile alluvial plains of the adjoining Central Region determine that the region also dominates the country's rice economy and many other forms of non-industrial activity. Table 12.1 shows that per capita Gross Regional Product in Bangkok[3] is more than three times the national average, in stark contrast to the country's three principal peripheral regions (the south, the north and the north-east) which are all substantially below the national average.

The north-east is the poorest of the poor in this regard (see Parnwell, 1988). Here, adverse environmental conditions, locational disadvantages, relatively underdeveloped infrastructure and commu- nications, and decades of benign neglect by central government have combined to create what is often seen as a 'problem region' in a number of important respects (Keyes, 1989). Agriculture yields incomes and security only grudgingly, the rural non-agricultural economy is insufficiently developed to offer alternative local sources of income, industrial development in the north-east is minimal, and the region's human resources are being severely depleted by migration to the Bangkok-Central Region (Fuller *et al.*, 1983).

The pattern of tourism activity in Thailand to a certain extent represents the reverse-image of this unbalanced pattern of economic development, although it is clear from Figure 12.1 that the north-east also rarely figures on the tourists' itinerary. In general, however, the main centres of tourism are quite far removed from the Bangkok- Central Region. Although Pattaya forms part of the rapidly growing Eastern Seaboard Development Region (which the government has supported heavily as a way of decentralising industrial activity and alleviating some of Bangkok's very pressing problems), and Ayut- thaya, Kanchanaburi and Hua Hin are only an hour or so by tour bus from the capital city, the main centres of tourism are found in northern and southern Thailand.

The focus of tourism on peripheral areas may thus be desirable from the perspective of creating a slightly more balanced pattern of economic activity, but it does not necessarily follow that such areas will benefit substantially from such a situation. If we interpret spatially Britton's schema of expenditure patterns associated with tourism (Figure 12.2), we might conclude that, figuratively speaking, peri- pheral rural areas enjoy only a few of the crumbs which fall from the

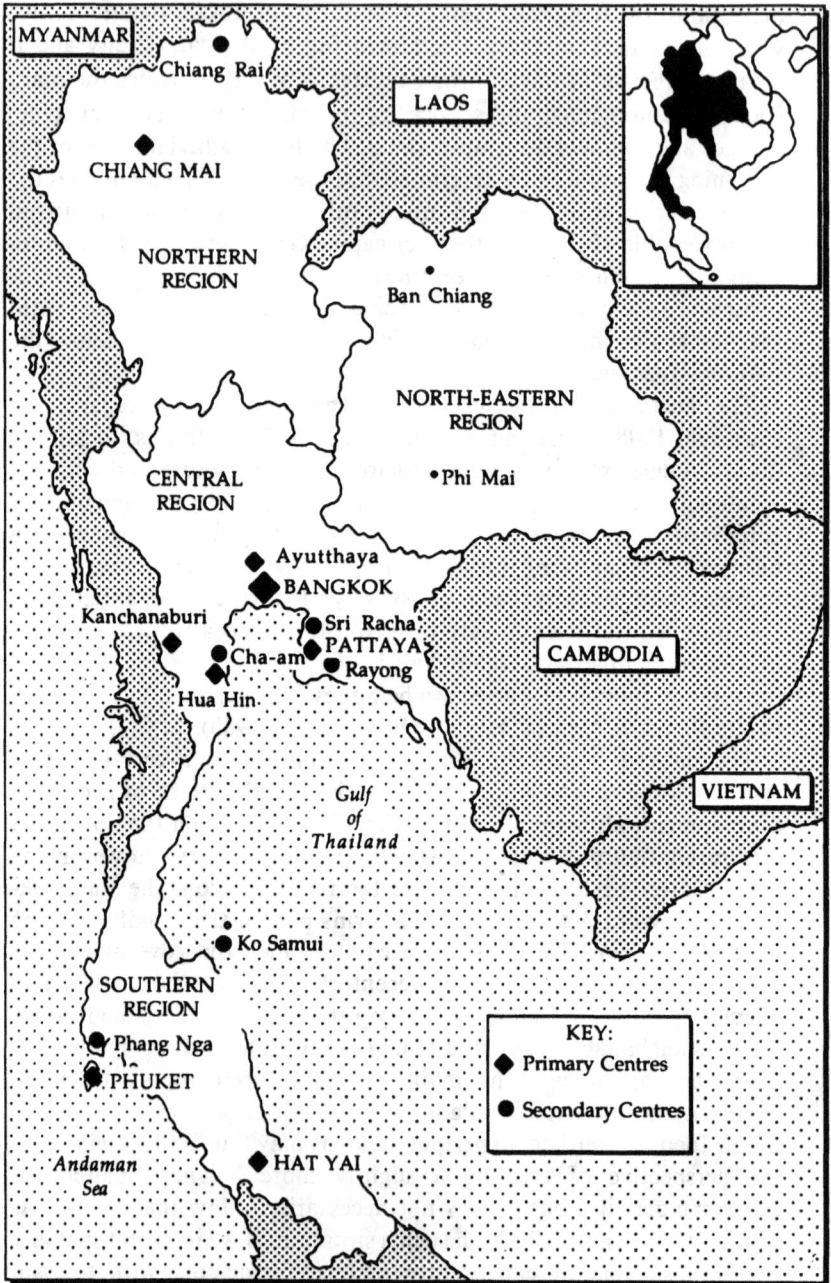

*Figure 12.1* Thailand: primary and secondary centres of tourism

high table of international tourism. This may be, first, because such areas do not possess to a sufficient degree the capital, expertise, entrepreneurship, experience, vision, power and influence which are necessary to claim a stake in the infrastructure of tourism (accommodation, transportation, excursions, retailing), which thus falls mainly into the hands of 'outsiders' (i.e. national and international businesspeople). Second, it may be because rural areas in peripheral regions possess few of the means which might potentially be employed to persuade tourists to part with their money. Tourists may pass quickly through these areas on nationwide tours (organised by national or international tour operators), on the way catching a glimpse of the 'real' Thailand, but the bulk of their shopping and spending is likely to take place in urban as opposed to rural areas. Thus, whilst tourism may indeed be quite heavily focused on peripheral regions, in the main it is urban entrepreneurs who appear to derive the greatest economic benefit. The phenomenon of 'hill tribe tourism' in northern Thailand may be exceptional in this regard, although one might still debate the utility (economic and otherwise) of such a form of tourism for the people concerned (Cohen, n.d.).

The situation in north-east Thailand is even more precarious. Because it lacks the kinds of resources which have attracted large numbers of tourists to other regions (sea and sand, mountains and 'hill tribes', fauna and flora), the economic benefits of Thailand's tourism boom have largely passed the north-east by. The region does, of course, have an interesting history and rich cultural traditions, but to a large extent these are not manifest in the kinds of features which make places such as Ayutthaya, Chiang Mai and Kanchanaburi such major centres of tourism. The Khmer architecture on view at Phi Mai, the archaeological finds at Ban Chiang, rock paintings in Ubon Ratchathani, the elephant round-up in Surin and the chance to peer across the Mekong River from Nong Khai at the last vestiges of communism are perhaps the main features of the north-east which attract albeit relatively small numbers of tourists to the region. Efforts are currently being made by the Thai government, in conjunction with the European Commission, to further develop and exploit the region's tourism potential, but in the main the prospects for mass tourism in the region remain extremely limited.

## TOURISM AND THAI HANDICRAFTS

Set against this back-drop of uneven development in Thailand and, in spite of its potential, the rather disappointing level of achievement of

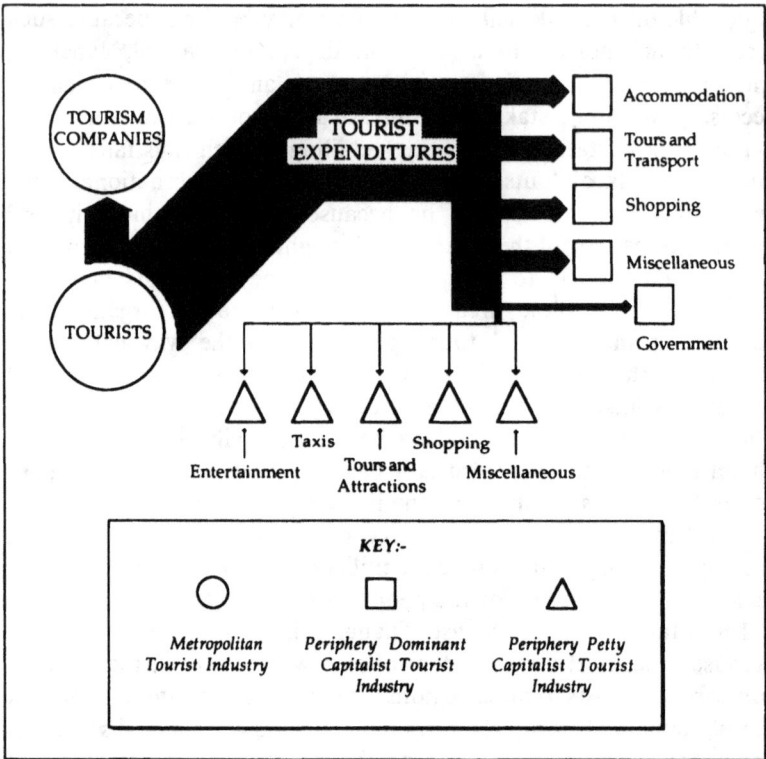

*Figure 12.2* Distribution of tourist industry expenditure
*Source*: Lea, 1988, 14.

tourism in contributing to the development of peripheral rural areas, it is interesting to note the recent development of the Thai handicrafts industry in relation to the growth of tourism. The promotion of Thai handicrafts represents a potentially important means of bolstering the tourism industry, inasmuch that the country's material and aesthetic culture, most manifest in its traditional handicraft products, forms a crucial element of the cultural package which is used in selling the country to the foreign tourist. At the same time, the sale of Thai handicrafts may help to increase substantially the revenue which Thailand derives from international tourism. Furthermore, in the context of the foregoing discussion, a growing demand for traditional handicraft products represents a potentially significant means whereby rural areas in peripheral regions may be able to claim for themselves a share of the tourist dollar.

The promotion of handicrafts has thus been used by the Thai

*Table 12.2* Thailand: selected craft exports, by product (various years)

| Product | Value (million Baht) | | | |
|---|---|---|---|---|
| | 1970 | 1974 | 1978 | 1982 |
| Precious stones | 115.0 | 760.0 | 1,669.1 | 4,645.0 |
| Leather products | 0.4 | 56.7 | 379.5 | 1,059.8 |
| Wood and carved wood products | 25.8 | 256.1 | 548.0 | 743.0 |
| Jewellery and ornaments | 7.2 | 41.9 | 258.6 | 466.4 |
| Wooden and carved furniture | 0.2 | 36.6 | 96.9 | 336.8 |
| Rattan furniture | 0.1 | 23.9 | 75.7 | 346.8 |
| Silk | 35.8 | 40.1· | 47.4 | 175.5 |
| Bronzeware | 15.0 | 37.3 | 77.9 | 115.3 |
| Silver and nickelware | 10.4 | 40.1 | 139.5 | 212.2 |
| Wicker | 0.8 | 32.6 | 44.5 | 115.1 |
| Handwoven cotton textiles | 0.9 | 23.7 | 47.9 | 92.4 |
| Artificial flowers and fruit | 0.3 | 5.5 | 30.2 | 94.1 |
| Paintings and sculptures | 0.5 | 52.4 | 11.9 | 17.5 |
| Metal castings and statuettes | – | – | 24.9 | 65.2 |
| Pearl, ivory, horn and bone products | 0.1 | 10.8 | 39.1 | 11.7 |
| Ceramic products | 1.0 | 0.7 | 9.8 | 36.7 |
| Thai dolls | 0.3 | 2.3 | 5.2 | 29.9 |
| Lacquerware | n/a | n/a | 6.5 | 9.4 |
| Umbrellas | – | 0.1 | 3.2 | 4.8 |
| Other craft products | – | 0.3 | 3.8 | 9.5 |
| Total: | 213.8 | 1,421.1 | 3,549.6 | 8,587.1 |

*Source:* Pye, 1988

government as an important means of boosting earnings from tourism and, at the same time, underpinning the development of the country's export economy.[4] Since the early 1970s there has occurred a substantial increase in handicraft exports from Thailand. Table 12.2 shows that there was a more than forty-fold increase in exports of Thailand's main handicraft products between 1970 and 1982. Certain handicraft products have experienced a particularly dramatic growth in exports, especially leather products, precious stones, jewellery, wooden products and furniture. By 1987 Thai handicraft exports had exceeded a value of 26,600 million Baht[5] – a 300 per cent increase over 1982 – and were projected to surpass 30,000 million Baht in 1988 (*The Nation*, 13.8.88).

Table 12.3 shows that, although the performance of Thailand and other South-East Asian countries in boosting handicraft exports during the 1980s has been impressive, a number of East Asian countries have not only enjoyed a faster rate of growth in handicrafts exports but they also claim a considerably larger share of the world

*Table 12.3* Exports of 71 main handicraft products from selected East and South-East Asian countries to the major market economies

|  | Value ($US m.) 1980 | 1984 | % change 1980–84 |
|---|---|---|---|
| Thailand | 406.5 | 479.3 | 17.9 |
| Philippines | 281.8 | 323.8 | 13.8 |
| Singapore | 199.4 | 346.5 | 73.8 |
| Malaysia | 87.9 | 113.0 | 28.6 |
| Indonesia | 31.1 | 42.1 | 35.4 |
| China | 1,108.8 | 1,589.3 | 43.3 |
| Hong Kong | 1,975.1 | 2,531.9 | 28.2 |
| Taiwan | 1,620.8 | 3,039.9 | 87.6 |
| South Korea | 786.6 | 1,258.6 | 60.0 |

*Source:* Kathuria *et al.*, 1988, 5

market than is the case with the South-East Asian countries. This at least suggests that there may still be considerable scope for a further expansion in the market for Thai handicrafts in the years ahead (see also, in the context of Malaysia, Nolten and Tempelman, 1986).

In addition to promoting handicrafts production in Thailand in support of the country's export trade, the government is also seeking to increase tourist spending in the country as a way of bolstering foreign exchange earnings, increasing employment and raising taxation revenues from this booming industry. In 1987, total spending by tourists on 'shopping' (souvenirs, handicrafts, and so on) amounted to more than 13,000 million Baht, or approximately 26 per cent of total tourist spending in the country. The aim was to increase this proportion to 35 per cent by 1990. It was in support of this objective that the government devised the 'Thailand Arts and Crafts Year' promotion, following the very successful 'Visit Thailand Year' campaign in 1987. The Secretary to the organising committee of TACY (also Deputy Governor of the Tourism Authority of Thailand), Khun Saree Wangpaichitr, indicated the intention to 'make Thailand a shopping paradise for visitors' (*The Nation*, 14.8.88). The 'Shopping' guide produced by the Tourism Authority of Thailand follows up this objective:

Fine handicrafts are traditional to the country, and many of the most popular items are created in small cottage industries, employing skills handed down for generations. Others are produced in factories boasting the latest in advanced technology and quality control. Both are distinguished by the superb

craftsmanship that makes a 'Made in Thailand' purchase something special to treasure for years to come.

                    (Tourism Authority of Thailand, 1989, 1)

In 1988 the Thai government set aside more than 100 million Baht for
various promotional and developmental activities in support of this
handicrafts promotion campaign (*The Nation*, 14.8.88), just under
two-thirds of which was to be invested in support of training
programmes, seminars and exhibitions, one-third was to be spent on
the promotion of Thai handicrafts overseas, and a small amount was
to be allocated to the domestic component of the campaign. Various
crafts exhibitions were organised, with high-spending tourists very
much in mind, first in Bangkok (organised by the Department of
Industrial Promotion) where the products of some 66 provinces were
represented, and later in selected provincial centres up-country. One of
the former Prime Minister Chatichai Choonhavan's first tasks in office
was to open the national handicraft exhibition which heralded the
start of Thailand Arts and Crafts Year (ibid.).

In addition to directly promoting Thai handicrafts, the Tourism
Authority of Thailand in 1989 developed the slogan *wattanathammachart* or 'culture and nature' as a cornerstone of its tourism promotion
strategy into the 1990s.[6] The aim of this strategy is to attempt to
diffuse tourism more effectively to the provinces thus, in theory,
ensuring that the benefits of the tourism boom are spread more widely.
Aspects of material culture, such as traditional handicrafts, are clearly
likely to represent an important component of this strategy, especially
in areas such as the north-east where, as we have seen, there are few
other major tourist attractions or centres.

Thus it is clear that traditional handicraft products have been
singled out to play an important future role not only in boosting
earnings from the tourism industry but also in drawing provinces in
the peripheral regions more centrally into the limelight through
contributing what they, arguably, produce best to the country's
portfolio of tourist resources.

In view of the projected role of handicraft industries in support of
tourism in Thailand, a number of important questions need to be
addressed:

First, in what ways may the promotion of handicrafts production in
support of tourism assist in the development of peripheral rural areas
and, thus, help in ameliorating the pattern and consequences of
uneven development?

Second, to what extent are traditional handicraft industries, especially in peripheral areas, in a position to respond to the stimulus provided by a rapidly growing market for their products?

Third, assuming that handicrafts producers *are* able to adapt their manufacturing techniques to enable them to capitalise on this increasing 'external' demand, what will be the possible effects of these changes on the products (and producers) themselves? In other words, will the almost inevitable shift to mass production methods and commercially more marketable designs result in a decline in workmanship and a denigration of the cultural significance of traditional arts and crafts, as many analysts have suggested?

The following discussion will attempt to cast some light on each of these key questions, drawing primarily on information derived from field-work in the north-eastern region of Thailand between 1987 and 1990.

## HANDICRAFTS AND RURAL DEVELOPMENT

I have discussed in some detail elsewhere (Parnwell and Khamanarong, 1990) the potential role to be played by rural industries in the process of rural and regional development in Thailand. Put very simply, the modernisation and development of small-scale industries in peripheral rural areas, such as in the north-east, might help to achieve a number of the development objectives of national policy-makers which 'conventional' planning approaches, such as urban-industrial decentralisation and rural job creation, have been singularly unsuccessful in accomplishing. In particular, 'rural industrialisation' holds out the prospect of diversifying the rural economy, helping both to reduce the reliance of villagers on agricultural production and at the same time creating opportunities for employment and income-generation *in situ* (Romijn, 1987, 211, 224). Furthermore, given that the insufficiency of income in their local areas is one reason why large numbers of people regularly migrate to urban centres, especially Bangkok, the promotion of industrial production in the countryside might also help to stem the haemorrhage of the region's human resources towards the capital primate city (see also Singhanetra-Renard, 1987, 273).

Rural industrialisation might therefore also help not only to achieve a more balanced pattern of industrial activity in Thailand – one of the government's underlying development objectives – but it would also serve to slow, admittedly only slightly, the pace of urban growth and the rate of urban concentration. A further potential benefit of rural industrialisation would be to increase the female labour participation rate in rural areas, given that women are often the main component in the cottage industry workforce (Islam, 1987, 4: Romijn, 1987, 229). Whilst not wishing to suggest rural industrialisation as a developmental panacea, it is clear that, by focusing on building rural and regional development 'from below' (Stöhr and Taylor, 1981) through investing in the modernisation of existing production structures, rather than relying on the 'filtering down' of the benefits of rapid urban industry-centred economic growth towards the periphery, a number of potential advantages may accrue to the country's hitherto underdeveloped areas.

Whilst such a principle might be laudable from the perspective of social and distributive justice (Mabogunje, 1989), there are clearly a number of significant barriers which must first be confronted if the potential of rural industrialisation as a tool of spatial and economic development policy is to be realised. Some of these constraints, and potential means of overcoming them, will be examined later in this chapter. Meanwhile, we first assess the current 'state of the art' of handicrafts production in north-east Thailand.

Figure 12.3 shows quite clearly that there already exists a quite substantial foundation upon which such a rural industrialisation strategy in the north-east might be built. The region features a wide variety of forms of rural industrial production some of which, as with pottery production in Ban Chiang, Udon Thani province,[7] and 'diamond' cutting in many north-eastern provinces,[8] have already shown considerable innovation in responding to the potential demand for their products from tourists and the wider international market. Although the map makes no reference to the number of such industries, or to their present level of development and sophistication, field-work in the region has identified a number of industries which have either been substantially transformed over the last decade or so, in response both to external and internal stimuli, or which might be considered to offer some potential for future modernisation, particularly in response to tourism and export demand.

On the other hand, many of the symbols on the map represent traditional rural cottage industries which have changed little in their structure and production methods over perhaps a century or more and which, because of the nature of the goods produced and the techniques employed, have few prospects for development and change in the longer term. The World Bank's assessment is equally gloomy: 'We can expect an almost total disappearance of (rural craft) activities in the near future' (World Bank, 1983, 82). Perhaps the World Bank reckoned without tourism and handicraft exports:

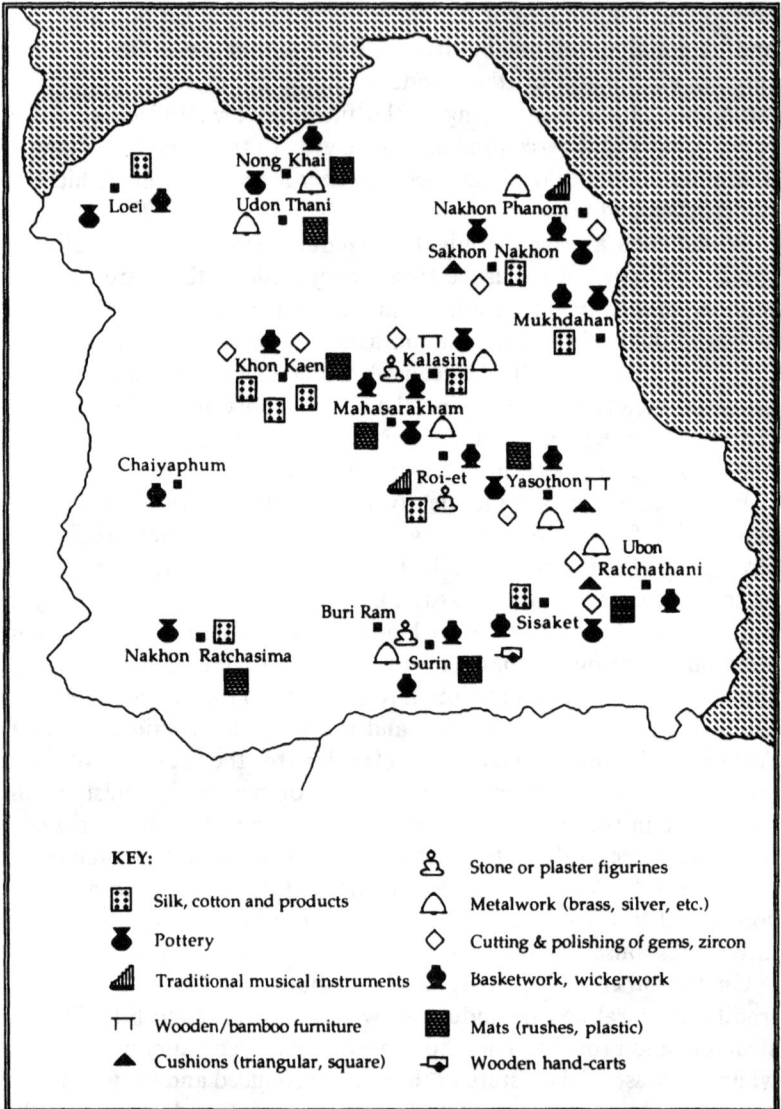

*Figure 12.3* North-east Thailand: main locations and forms of handicraft production

Exports are the key to the future. Domestic demand for utilitarian goods is weak in most Asian countries and sales to tourists are still negligible. The tourist market, though, will increase and should be emphasised as these goods are the same as those made for export.

(*IDRC Reports*, 1988, 6)

These two statements are perhaps not as contradictory as they may at first appear. Elwood Pye has suggested that there are two distinct types of craft industries in Thailand: on the one hand, there are a number of 'large factories and workshops in major metropolitan centres such as Bangkok and Chiang Mai'[9] from which 'the vast majority of the country's exports come', and on the other 'a large number of small, part-time artisans who are primarily farmers, but who draw on craft income to supplement agricultural earnings' (Pye, 1988, 68–69). As one might expect, it has been primarily the urban-centred, large-scale enterprises which have capitalised to the greatest extent on the growing demand for handicraft products. The inertia and backwardness which dog the rural handicrafts sector have left them ill-prepared to respond to the challenges presented by these changing market conditions.

How then might rural handicraft industries claim for themselves a larger and, some would suggest, their rightful share of the spoils of tourism and export-led demand for Thai craft products? The following section will discuss how this might be achieved, and will outline the prerequisite changes which must first be introduced.

## CAPACITY TO CHANGE

In a recent article (Parnwell and Khamanarong, 1990) I have outlined the many areas where change is necessary if traditional rural cottage industries are to be 'brought into the modern world' in order to achieve some of these objectives. In essence, a larger volume of more marketable and better quality goods must be produced more cheaply, more reliably and more efficiently. To achieve this, the supply of raw materials and finance capital must be improved, production skills enhanced, entrepreneurship developed, designs changed, new technology introduced and marketing systems extended (see also Islam, 1987). These are also precisely the kinds of changes which will be necessary if peripheral rural areas are to be able to share in the growing demand for souvenirs and handicrafts associated with tourism and international trade.

It is clearly unrealistic to expect all of these changes to take place spontaneously and independently of external involvement and support. Whilst the countryside may be considered to have a certain comparative advantage over the major metropolitan areas in terms of, for example, land and labour costs, there are also a great many constraints which impinge on rural areas relative to towns and cities. Some of the more important of these are outlined below.

First, most rural areas are quite far removed from the main market centres, particularly, as in the case of handicrafts, where that market is principally urban or international in nature. Second, the generally small size and scale of rural handicraft industries does little to underpin their efficiency and competitiveness *vis à vis* their larger and generally more sophisticated urban counterpart industries. Third, Elwood Pye has suggested that the predominant role of rural craft industries is as a means of supplementing agricultural earnings, and as such there may be a number of attitudinal and perceptual barriers to change which must be confronted in any effort to promote greater efficiency and market-orientation in these industries (Pye, 1988; see also Romijn, 1987, 226). Fourth, linked to this, because of the cyclical shift of labour between agriculture and cottage industry there may, at certain times of the year, be significant shortages in the availability of labour for handicrafts production:

> Craft entrepreneurs often find it extremely difficult to meet production deadlines as a result of labour shortages during periods of peak agricultural activity. In weaving . . . 81% of workers left their jobs for farming at some time during the year.
> (Pye, 1988, 74)

Fifth, the part-time and traditional nature of many forms of rural handicrafts production may determine that few people possess the kinds of production skills, managerial expertise and entrepreneurship which may be essential prerequisites for the modernisation and development of the industry. Finally, there may also be quite severe local capital formation constraints which may similarly restrict the capacity for technological change in rural industrial production.

Thus, before rural areas can expect to capitalise on the growing demand for traditional craft products, a number of quite fundamental changes must be instigated. In essence, there are six key areas where changes must be concentrated:

1 first, training and education, in order to up-grade production skills,

develop entrepreneurship and, perhaps also, overcome attitudinal barriers to change;

2 second, design and market orientation, in order to ensure that rural handicraft products are not only more directly targeted at the booming tourism and export market but also that they are of a style, quality and price which will guarantee that they will capitalise on this external demand;

3 third, input delivery systems will have to be improved in order to ensure that producers can keep abreast of a potentially rapid increase in demand for their products;

4 fourth, there may be a need to introduce entirely different production techniques in order to increase levels of productivity;

5 fifth, there must be adequate provision of finance capital in order to support such changes as may be deemed necessary in the process of handicrafts production; and finally,

6 there is perhaps a strong case for strengthening linkages between rural and urban areas in support of rural industrialisation, such as through sub-contracting and putting-out arrangements, as a way of combining the comparative advantages of both villages and towns in the field of industrial production.

Rather than dealing with these elements separately, as has happened on several occasions with disastrous results,[10] there is a need for a coordinated and integrated approach wherein all constraints are tackled simultaneously.

Since the early 1980s, the Thai government has afforded a relatively high priority to improvements in the rural handicrafts sector. The Fifth National Plan (1982–86) placed particular emphasis on economic restructuring, centred on export-oriented industrialisation and the diversification of the rural economy (Pye, 1988, 72). The underlying objective of the latter strategy was to ameliorate the growing problem of seasonal unemployment in rural areas. Because of their capacity to absorb labour during slack periods in the agricultural calendar, rural handicraft and agro-processing industries have provided the cornerstone of this policy.

The Sixth National Plan (1987–91) places even stronger emphasis on rural industrialisation, seeking to encourage the development of small-scale industries through the promotion of entrepreneurship, the strengthening of management, improving market information and easing financial constraints (Government of Thailand, 1987, 232).

Support for handicraft industries is very much facilitated by prevailing attitudes towards the rural industrial sector:

The overall environment for promotion is more favourable in countries that view artisans as a natural resource. Thailand is the best example of this. Here, artisans do not suffer from a low social standing and the industry is not viewed as a residual. No doubt, the promotional work of the Royal Family on behalf of the artisans is partly responsible for this.

(Pye, 1988, 30)

Thai government agencies have also redoubled their efforts in an attempt to strengthen the rural industrial sector. In contrast to neighbouring countries, Thailand does not have a particularly difficult task in coordinating the work of a large number of agencies which have overlapping responsibility for handicraft industries: Thailand has fewer than half the number of such agencies found in Malaysia, for example (Nolten and Tempelman, 1986). The main agency for supporting craft industries is the Department of Industrial Promotion (especially the Handicrafts Promotion Division, which was responsible for coordinating Thailand Arts and Crafts Year). Some 40 per cent of the DIP's disbursements are targeted at the cottage and craft industry sector (Pye, 1988, 73). Other agencies with partial responsibility for supporting small-scale industries include the Board of Investment, the Small Industries Finance Office and the Industrial Finance Corporation of Thailand (see Parnwell and Khamanarong, 1990).

The following short case studies of rural industries in north-east Thailand help to illustrate both the difficulties and the potential which exist for the transformation of handicrafts production in connection with tourism.

## Brassware manufacture in *Ban* Pa Ao, Ubon Ratchathani Province

The first case study, of brassware manufacture in *Ban* (village) Pa Ao, provides an interesting example of how an essentially backward rural industry employing quite rudimentary production techniques has managed to capitalise directly on the growing tourism industry. The brassware products of this village industry are, even to an uncultured eye, very basic. Items such as ornamental buffalo bells and betel containers are produced using the 'lost wax method'. Thin strands of beeswax are wound around clay moulds, rudimentary patterns are applied by hand using simple wooden and plastic wheels, and then molten bronze is added to the moulds. The pattern is imprinted on the bronze, before the heat discharges the wax. The bronze, brought into the village in blocks from the nearby town of Ubon Ratchathani, is smelted in a small furnace using charcoal and hand-operated bellows.

Although the eleven or so households which are involved in the brassware industry in *Ban* Pa Ao all contain highly skilled craftsmen and craftswomen, the techniques used are very basic, and are unlikely to have changed significantly over a considerable period of time. The finished products are generally quite shoddy, and are certainly of inferior quality when compared with bronzeware produced in larger urban factories. The products are prepared in a fairly haphazard, unstandardised manner; it is extremely difficult to maintain a constantly high temperature in the furnace; and there is little or no polishing or finishing of products prior to retail. A high proportion of the finished articles are damaged and unsaleable. Nonetheless, the villagers have no difficulty in selling all the reasonable quality goods that they produce: large orders are constantly coming in from afar, and a retailing outlet in Ubon Ratchathani reports a brisk trade in the products of *Ban* Pa Ao.

In connection with the earlier discussion, which suggested that the only way that rural handicraft industries would be able to capitalise on the growing external market would be by radically transforming their production techniques, how is it that *Ban* Pa Ao has managed to thrive using centuries old technologies? The answer would appear to be that it has survived *because* of the techniques used. The industry has carved a niche for itself in the regional tourist market based on the rustic charm of its products and the traditional nature of the production process. Enterprising local entrepreneurs have actively promoted *Ban* Pa Ao on this basis, and now fairly large numbers of foreign tourists stop by on their tour of the north-east to marvel or giggle at the production process – buying a few momentos before they leave. However, one cannot help but ask whether foreign visitors are being given a very accurate or representative impression of handicrafts production in Thailand through their short glimpse of the brassware industry in *Ban* Pa Ao.

The industry provides an important source of income for the 40 or so villagers who are directly involved in the industry, although in the main the manufacture of brassware represents a useful sideline which occupies a number of older villagers when they are not working in the fields. However, by effectively fossilising the industry on behalf of the tourist, changes are also being prevented which might possibly allow the industry to change with the times and develop into a stronger nucleus for a more diversified local economy. Perhaps not: any such changes would probably undermine the basis of the industry's marketability, its rustic and rudimentary charm, and would expose not only the industry but also its products to competition from much higher-quality brassware produced elsewhere.

### Cushion-making in *Tambon* Paa Tiw, Yasothon Province

The cushion-making industry in *Tambon* (commune) Paa Tiw provides a strikingly different case study to that of *Ban* Pa Ao. This collection of six contiguous villages is famous for producing the *morn sam liang* (triangular cushions) and *morn sii liang* (square cushions) which are found in handicraft shops throughout Thailand, and which are now exported to Europe, the United States, Japan, the Middle East and elsewhere (see also Parnwell and Khamanarong, 1990). It is a booming industry, but also one which has changed substantially over the last decade or so in response to changing market conditions and demand.

The industry has switched very effectively from being a relatively small-scale undertaking producing traditionally styled cushions largely for the local (i.e. north-eastern) market but also for the broader national market, into one which now serves an international market both directly through handicraft exports and indirectly through tourist purchases of Paa Tiw cushions as souvenirs. Whilst the style of the product remains essentially the same (although the square cushions are a more recent innovation), their design and manufacture have undergone significant changes in recent years. Villagers now produce cushions in a wide range of sizes to suit the tastes of Saudi Arabian clients, for example, who prefer thin mattresses to be attached to the cushions, and tourists, who prefer scaled-down versions of the traditional cushions which are more easily carried as hand luggage on the flight home. Brighter colours, fast dyes, new materials and more elaborate patterns are also incorporated in the modified designs, again to suit the tastes of the main body of consumers.

Such changes in design are very readily adapted on account of the way that the industry itself has been restructured. Instead of the previous situation wherein individual households were engaged in all parts of the production process (weaving, dyeing, sewing, stuffing, and so on), the industry now evidences a complex division of labour which sees different households specialising in separate parts of the production process. Through such production specialisation productivity is increased, product quality is enhanced and changes in design are more readily incorporated.

Such a transformation of the industry is attributable almost entirely to the role of six key entrepreneurs who not only organise the industry very effectively but who also liaise with the business community in Bangkok through whom most of their products are channelled for sale in the capital city and for export. The entrepreneurs have been principally responsible for introducing new designs, providing training and skills up-grading, purchasing sewing machines, supplying raw materials,[11] organising distribution and marketing, and arranging finance. The considerable material wealth of these entrepreneurs suggests where the majority of financial benefits from the industry go, but there is little doubt that, without their involvement and entrepreneurial flair, the industry would not have been able to respond so readily and effectively to changing market conditions, and the villagers as a whole would not have derived such substantial financial rewards from their one-time traditional cottage industry.

Although villagers in *Tambon* Paa Tiw still consider themselves to be farmers first and foremost, for most the cushion industry provides their main source of livelihood. The production process is also flexible enough to allow a certain seasonal movement of labour between farming and cushion-making. Significantly, however, the level of out-migration from *Tambon* Paa Tiw, particularly of females (hardly any men are involved in cushion-making) has been kept at a very low level as a result of the recent transformation of this handicraft industry.

## TO CHANGE OR NOT TO CHANGE?

We return finally to the dilemma of the 'purists' versus the 'pragmatists'. The two short case studies above have suggested that producers in peripheral areas have been able to obtain a reasonable source of livelihood from their involvement in the handicrafts industry, and in this way have derived some benefit from the tourism boom and the opening-up of international markets for Thai handicraft products. As such their living standards are better, and their economic options more varied, than might otherwise have been the case.

At the same time, however, the literature is replete with statements which bemoan the decline in craftsmanship and the denigration of aesthetic and material culture which tourism has apparently wrought in the traditional rural handicraft sector. Evelyne Hong conveys the flavour of the purists' objections in the context of Malaysian handicrafts:

arts and crafts have become commercialised under the impact of tourism. Today one can find dozens of batik factories . . . which produce batik to satisfy the tastes of the souvenir-hunting tourists. Batik, which was once traditionally produced on natural fibre, is now commercially produced in synthetic materials . . . Malaysian pewter ware made from refined local tin is pandered in a wide range from the utilitarian to the decorative – beer mugs, ash trays, candle holders, goblets, salvers, coffee or tea sets and time pieces.

(Hong, 1985, 61)

Nolten and Tempelman warn that such changes call into question the notion of 'handicrafts as heritage' (Nolten and Tempelman, 1986, 45), whilst Ichaporia claims that the facsimiles of 'folk' art and crafts which are produced for the external audience may, in the long-term, 'acquire their own traditions and a place for themselves in the producers' culture' (Ichaporia, 1982, 12).

There are a number of reasons why change is necessary if producers are to capitalise on the opportunities provided by the development of an external market for their products. Leaving aside the demand for fine arts and crafts (both authentic and replicas) emanating from museums and private collectors, the tourist market can not, or will not, in general bear the full economic cost of the time and skill which goes into the production of many traditional handicraft products. For example, the textiles which Meo and Yao 'hill tribeswomen' in Northern Thailand produce for their own use, and particularly for their New Year celebrations, may involve several months of intricate weaving and needlework (see Cohen, 1983c). Only one, or at most a handful of pieces will be made by a woman each year. A high social and cultural value is placed on the technical virtuosity that a woman is able to demonstrate in her work. To produce garments to the same high standard for the voracious tourist market would demand a price which few tourists would be willing to pay. Accordingly, production techniques and standards are modified to allow more items to be produced, and at a lower cost to the consumer.

Similar adaptations may occur in response to the nature of consumer demand. The typical tourist may be interested, not so much in the functionality or cultural significance of traditional handicrafts, as in their aesthetic appeal and their ability to remind him or her of superficial aspects of their experience abroad. As such, there is also pressure for the products to comply to visitors' popular stereotypes of the host society, which may deviate quite significantly from reality (Graburn, 1982). Thus, tourists may be looking for something quite different from the handicrafts they purchase than is the case for the culture groups from which they originate. In this way it is almost inevitable that, in catering for an external market, changes in design, style, materials and so on will occur. The extent to which the new styles and designs differ from the old may depend, *inter alia*, upon whether the adaptation occurs spontaneously from within the society or takes place at the behest of outside agents (Cohen, 1983c).

Critics of this process of change thus focus quite logically upon the perceived link between, on the one hand, the growth in mass tourism and the associated increase in demand for handicraft products, and, on the other, the declining quality, standard and cultural relevance of traditional handicrafts. The association may, however, be spurious, for at least two reasons. First, there may occur a separation between the items which are produced for the external market and those which continue to be produced for the maker's own use. Even though the same orthogenetic tradition may be recognisable in both, the former may bear little resemblance to the latter in terms of their quality, design and functionality. Furthermore, '(o)nly a small proportion of the souvenir arts and crafts usually associated with the peoples of the Third and Fourth Worlds stem directly from traditional arts' (Graburn, 1982, 9). Second, much so-called 'tourist art' or 'airport art' may in fact be produced not by the traditional artisans but by others who are seeking to capitalise on a market niche. This may include people who have no formal skills or training in handicrafts production, and people who are outside the culture group from which the handicrafts may have originated (ibid., 8).

It also does not necessarily follow, even in societies which do become involved in producing handicrafts for the tourist market, that this will lead to a deterioration in the quality of their traditional arts and crafts, and the denigration of their cultural position and significance. Cohen claims that 'commercialization of folk art is not identical with their destruction' (Cohen, 1983c, 21). Furthermore, in the admittedly atypical case of resettled and refugee Meo and Yao in Thailand, 'commercialization keeps the folk arts alive; indeed, in its absence, they would wither away' (ibid.). The tourism market created an opportunity for producers to innovate and, where commercial activities remained under their control, provided an outlet for nascent entrepreneurship. Graburn concludes that, in many cases, the only real significance of souvenir arts to the producing culture is the fact that they can be sold (Graburn, 1982, 8). The effect of their inculcation into the market economy may be several times more profound than that resulting from changes to their arts and crafts.

The argument that tourism undermines traditional arts and crafts is therefore far from being conclusive. As we have seen, the effects of reorientating handicraft products towards a wider market may, on occasions, be negative or at best neutral, but in some instances may be responsible for breathing new life into moribund industries (*Cultural Survival Quarterly*, 1982, 5). They may provide the necessary means for supporting artisans' skills and techniques which, in rapidly changing societies, might otherwise find no outlet for cultural expression. The promotion of traditional handicrafts in support of tourism may rekindle people's awareness of their role and importance, and also their vulnerability in the face of modernisation and rapid social change.

An equally convincing argument, especially for the peoples of peripheral, economically depressed areas, is provided by the economic benefits that may accrue from their claiming a share of the spoils from the rapid development of the tourism industry. I leave the last word to the owner of a small workshop in Bor Sang, a tourism-oriented handicrafts centre near Chiang Mai in Northern Thailand: 'if we don't make umbrellas, we won't have enough money to live' (King, 1977, 27).

## NOTES

1 I wish to express my thanks to Dr Koson Srisaeng of the Ecumenical Coalition on Third World Tourism in Bangkok for comments on an earlier draft of this chapter, and to Associate Professor Suranart Khamanarong of the Department of Social Sciences, Khon Kaen University, with whom I have been working on rural industrialisation in North-East Thailand. The field research upon which this chapter is based received generous financial support from the British Academy Committee for South-East Asian Studies. Permission to conduct research in Thailand was kindly granted by the National Research Council of Thailand.

2 Certainly the sun, sea, sand, society and sightseeing aspects; less so sex and shopping (cf. Crick, 1989).

3 Because of differences in sources used, the regional divisions used in Table 12.1 are slightly different from those used in Figure 12.1. The western, eastern and central region used in the former coincide with the Central Region used in the latter.

4 Because tourism is generally seen as part of a country's 'invisible' export trade, there is a great deal of overlap between handicraft sales to tourists *in situ* and sales of handicrafts through international trade. The latter involves transporting the products to the consumer; the former, in effect, involves the consumer travelling to, and purchasing the products in, the country of manufacture.

5 £1 sterling equals approximately 45 Baht.

6 The Thai word for 'culture' is *wattanatham*, and that for 'nature' *thama-*

*chart*. Strictly speaking, the phrase should be *wattanatham-thamachart*. The literal meaning of *wattanathammachart* is something like 'the protection of nature', which is a little ironic given the considerable impact that tourism has had on the natural environment (see Parnwell, Chapter 15 in this volume).

7 A small number of rural household industries in and around Ban Chiang specialise in the manufacture of reproduction pots which reflect quite closely the designs, shape and texture of the 4,000-year-old pots uncovered in the famous archaeological site which now serves as an important centre of tourism (domestic as well as international) in the area.

8 The cutting and polishing of gems and zirconium 'diamonds' in central north-eastern provinces has experienced a phenomenal boom over the last six to seven years. Hundreds of workshops have sprung up in villages throughout the region, in which stones are prepared for eventual setting in the large cosmetic jewellery factories in Bangkok, prior to export. I have suggested elsewhere (Parnwell and Khamanarong, 1990) that the growth of this unusual rural industry represents the utilisation of the region's comparative advantage over the Bangkok-Central Region.

9 Major handicraft centres in Chiang Mai, such as Sankamphaeng and Bor Sang, might be considered 'intermediate' between the purely rural and the predominantly urban in that, although they bear many of the organisational hallmarks of urban industries, production is in many cases still structured around relatively small workshops.

10 The pottery industry in *Ban* Mor, Mahasarakham province, provides an illustration of the folly in dealing with elements of the production process in isolation. In view of the very primitive production methods which were being employed, a well-meaning NGO provided the village with a mechanical potter's wheel. This helped substantially to increase productivity but, because product design and marketing had been largely ignored, the villagers were unable to sell all the pots they produced. The resultant glut in production and fall in prices meant that villagers were no longer able to afford the diesel fuel needed to power the potter's wheel. They reverted to their former methods, and the gift from the NGO lay rusting in a corner of the village.

11 Because of the rapid rate of expansion that the cushion industry in *Tambon* Paa Tiw has undergone in recent years, severe shortages of kapok (a fibre not unlike cotton wool which is used to stuff the cushions) were experienced. Two solutions were forthcoming: kapok was recycled from old cushions and mattresses purchased from Bangkok and elsewhere; and another locally-abundant material, straw, was also used for stuffing the cushions.

# 13 Early tourism in Malaya[1]

*A. J. Stockwell*

Much of the growth in the 'heritage industry' during the 1980s and 1990s is to be attributed to the tourist industry. With respect to Malaysia and Singapore, paperback reprints of early travel writings which are readily accessible in airport shops and published collections of postcards and photographs have pandered to nostalgia, while a romantic past – if not the historic past – has been recreated round a number of icons of the raj, such as the Raffles Hotel or the Selangor Club, which have been saved from the scourge of developers. Many Western visitors to Singapore, one suspects, are prone to equate the Raffles Hotel with the island's history and pay pilgrimage to what has become a garish shrine to Conrad, Kipling and Maugham. As myth fosters tourism, so tourism encourages myth. But this chapter is less concerned with the images of the past projected in contemporary tourist literature than with establishing the historical context in which tourism began to develop during the period of imperial expansion and colonial consolidation.

## DEFINITIONS: EXPLORERS, TRAVELLERS AND TOURISTS

> *I am a traveller – thou art a tourist – he, she, or they are trippers.* The distinctions implied in this statement of the view of nearly every Englishman or American abroad are among the most subtle in the English language – so subtle, indeed, that I am quite unable to grasp them.
>
> (Gorer, 1936, 232)

The purpose of exploration is geographical discovery. The methods of the explorer are semi-military: he may hire guides, impress porters and make demands on local peoples for supplies and transport, but, expecting few amenities *en route*, he mounts a self-contained expedition across uncharted seas and into unmapped lands. European exploration blazed the trail for European expansion; explorers were agents of Western commercial, cultural and political penetration of South-East Asia. At the turn of the century Europeans generally accepted that the age of exploration had ended with the establishment of colonial rule. Concluding his history of exploration in South-East Asia, Hugh Clifford wrote:

> Our task is now completed: the tale is told, and Chryse the Golden stands revealed to us, robbed of its magic and mystery, just a common fragment of the earth upon which we also tread. It has still a few, a very few, secrets left for discovery by the adventuresome – the actual sources of the Salwin and the Irawadi among the number; but for the rest it has been traversed again and again by alien explorers, and a man must go far afield indeed if to-day he would break new ground. The geographer has done his work, and has done the most of it in less than a century of time; and it remains for the scientist and the ethnologist – above all the ethnologist – to complete the task.
>
> (Clifford, 1904, 345–6)

Unlike explorers, travellers move within known geographical limits and often follow established routes; the places they visit may be alien, exotic and dangerous but they do not lie beyond the frontiers of the 'known world'. Within these territorial confines, however, the traveller sets out to encounter and investigate unfamiliar peoples and places. Unlike migrants, merchants and tourists, who travel hoping to arrive and are generally impatient with delays and obstacles in their way, the traveller would accept that to travel hopefully is better than to arrive since reaching journey's end is less important than enjoying or learning from the journey itself. Some travellers make it their business to examine a country and its flora, fauna and people according to the scientific criteria of geology, botany, zoology, entomology, ethnology, anthropology and so on. Others employ the arts of painting (North, 1980) or writing (Bruce Lockhart, 1936; Maugham, 1922; Maugham, 1963) to record their observations of an unfamiliar environment and, regarding travel as an aspect of self-discovery and education, in these ways hold a mirror up to nature to reflect the human condition and their own place in it. Unlike the explorer, the traveller does not mount a self-contained expedition but extemporises, making use of what is to hand in the way of transport and accommodation. But unlike the tourist, the traveller neither relies upon nor expects to find a broad range of amenities.

Tourists travel for pleasure, visiting places of cultural interest, enjoying natural scenery, participating in recreational activities. The tourist differs from both the explorer and the traveller in being a short-stay and semi-detached visitor. Tourists take interest in the journey itself but, unlike travellers, do not readily reconcile themselves to the fate of not reaching their destination. If the traveller seeks the unfamiliar, the tourist finds comfort in the familiar. Whereas the traveller shuns the company of his own countrymen – Laurence Sterne observed in *The Sentimental Journey* (1768) that 'an Englishman does not travel to see Englishmen' – the tourist, as G. K. Chesterton observed in 'The Resurrection of Father Brown', is 'rather disposed to dismiss people from the scene when once he had convicted them of being native to it'. While the explorer is self-sufficient and the traveller adaptable to circumstances, the tourist is dependent upon the travel industry. Tourism requires a smoothly functioning support system including reliable transport, accommodation, information, financial services and leisure facilities.

The categories explorer, traveller and tourist are useful but not watertight. Two, conceivably all three, of the activities may be blended in a single journey. When a tourist establishes his individuality by going his own way or publicising his own observations, he becomes, or at least sees himself as, a traveller. Each term is value laden, judgemental and subjective; they are labels which travellers stick on fellow-travellers, they are prisms through which they view each other. 'Explorer' has connotations of the epic and heroic, 'traveller' of thoughtful individualism, while the image of the twentieth-century tourist has been tarnished by all the attributes of the crowd in its brashness and insensitivity to its surroundings.

## TOURISM AND EUROPEAN EXPANSION TO SOUTH-EAST ASIA: TRANSPORT DEVELOPMENTS AND THE TRAVEL INDUSTRY

If exploration was a factor in European expansion then tourism was one of its results. Just as exploration paved the way for formal imperialism, so empire – and the security, amenities and gadgetry associated with it – in turn enabled the development of tourism. The growing orderliness of Malaya, which was an important aspect of the country's appeal to tourists, is illustrated by J. H. M. Robson's changing advice to motorists: before the First World War he stated that 'a revolver is not necessary, but there is no harm in carrying one', while in the early 1920s he pointed out that 'a revolver is not necessary, but if carried a police permit is necessary' (Robson, 1911, 212; 1923, 215).

Not only did the emergence of tourism reflect the spread of European political control in the region; it was also indicative of the phenomenal growth in the travel industry in the late nineteenth and early twentieth centuries. Shipping, railways, roads, even hotels and resorts and the other paraphernalia upon which a tourist industry would thrive were originally developed in South-East Asia for purposes other than attracting holiday traffic. Until the jet age of popular packages, tourism outside Europe remained the icing on the cake of the travel industry. The lucrative travel services provided by J. M. Cook, the son of the founder of Thomas Cook and Co., for example, included the transportation of Wolseley's ill-fated expedition to relieve Gordon at Khartoum in 1884 and of Kitchener's troops advancing upon Omdurman in 1896–98. In transporting 18,000 British and Egyptian troops, 130,000 tons of stores, and 800 whalers to Wadi Halfa in 1884, Cook employed 5,000 men, 28 ships (on the Tyne to Alexandria leg), 6,000 railway trucks and then 27 steamers and 650 sailing boats on the Nile (Brandon, 1991, 34ff, 190–91). Similarly, long-haul passenger-shipping flourished in those cases where a company managed to negotiate a mail contract with government.

In addition to major contributions from advances in navigation and technology, the early predominance of Britain's mercantile marine was greatly assisted by subsidies through royal mail contracts. In the 1830s the British government adopted the policy of developing ocean steam navigation by way of mail contracts. This support was essential because the primitive state of early steam navigation made operating costs high and subsidies at this juncture enabled British shipyards and shipping companies to establish a lead which was not surpassed for a century. By the 1840s three major contracts had been concluded by the British government: with Cunard on the North Atlantic, with the RMS (Royal Mail Service) for the West Indies and South America, and with P & O in the Mediterranean. In 1845 P & O's contract was extended to India and China (Harcourt, 1988). In the 1860s there were further changes: perfection of the compound engine led to the decline in costs of building ships and in operating costs while the opening of the Suez canal encouraged expansion of steamshipping on the Far East run (see Table 13.1).

The fierce competition which ensued strengthened demands from companies for government protection. The new maritime nationalism was seen, for example, in Napoleon III's huge subsidy to Messageries Imperiales in 1860 to challenge the P & O monopoly in the China silk

*Table 13.1* Shipping through Suez

| Year | Tons |
|------|-----:|
| 1870 | 436,000 |
| 1875 | 2,000,000 |
| 1895 | 8,400,000 |
| 1913 | 20,000,000 |

*Source*: Broeze *et al.*, 1986, 4.

trade and in Bismarck's mail agreement with the North German Lloyd Company which made full use of Singapore from the 1880s. P & O's new mail contract, however, for a long time sustained the company's position in Eastern waters. The mutual advantages derived from the mail contracts were clear: companies gained subsidies and support while they also contributed to the integration and defence of the empire. On the other hand, P & O's favoured position was criticised by Members of Parliament, by rival shipping owners like Alfred Holt and by commercial communities in India and the colonies which not only protested against high P & O charges and its near monopoly but were also obliged to contribute to the government subsidy (Harcourt, 1988). Although P & O by no means snuffed out competition – Blue Funnel Line (under Holt), for example, responded successfully to establish a huge organisation at Singapore and emerge as an unquestioned leader in Britain's carrying trade with the East – by the First World War it had taken over Blue Anchor and British India Lines in a disparate grouping symptomatic of the tendency to agglomerate in pre-1914 British shipping generally (Cooper, 1989).

Meanwhile, local shipping firms grew up centred on Singapore, notably the Straits Steamship Company (Tregonning, 1967; Hyde, 1964; 1973). Coastal shipping, which provided links between the Straits ports and the Malay States, enjoyed subventions from the colonial authorities just as long-distance lines did from the metropolitan government. Coasters plying from port to port brought mail and visitors; the latter were usually government officials, officers from the Straits garrison, traders and missionaries, but occasionally an outsider, like Isabella Bird, would step ashore. The latter's account of her travels in Malaya in 1879 vividly illustrates the challenges of transport in the early days of the Residential system and are worth recounting at some length here.

Having broken her return journey from the Far East to Britain at Singapore, Isabella Bird decided to make a foray into the peninsula. At this time none of the European steamers called on the peninsula and she sailed from Singapore to Malacca on board the *Rainbow* which she described as 'a very small vessel, her captain half Portuguese and half Malay, her crew Chinese, and her cabin passengers . . . all Chinese merchants'. Since she was the only European passenger and the only woman aboard, the Welsh engineer was solicitous for her comfort. Concluding that 'it was obviously impossible for (her) to sleep in a very dirty and very small hole, tenanted by cockroaches disproportionately large, and with a temperature of eighty-eight degrees, he took a mattress and pillows upon the bridge, told me his history, and that of his coloured wife and sixteen children under seventeen, of his pay of £35 a month, lent me a box of matches, and vanished into the lower regions with the consoling words "If you want anything in the night, just call 'Engineer' down the engine sky-light." ' Miss Bird was reassured by this attention: 'It does one's heart good to meet with such a countryman.' Passing 'a very comfortable night lying on the deck in the brisk breeze on the waveless sea', she was roused at dawn by crew wanting to wash the deck, so '(she) lifted (her) mattress on a bench and fell asleep again' and did not wake finally until the dropping of the anchor announced that the *Rainbow* had reached Malacca six hours ahead of schedule (Bird, 1883, 121–23).

The *Rainbow* subsequently took her to Klang whence, after staying with the Douglas family at the Residency, she embarked for Penang (via Bernam and the Dindings) on the steam-launch *Abdulsamat*, 'a very small vessel' which 'tumble(d) about a good deal', was over-crowded and awfully hot. 'Perfect though the *Abdulsamat* (was), there (was) very little rest to be got', and after the first night aboard her cabin-companion, Mrs Daly, who was 'comely' and had 'a very nice complexion', 'looked haggard, yellow, and much shaken' (ibid., 244). By the time she reached Penang she was glad of a brief rest at the Hotel de l'Europe before Mr Justice Wood took her to his home. After two days in Georgetown she was rowed across to Province Wellesley and was later picked up by the *Kinta*, a steam-launch of the Perak Government but 'not nearly so fine as the *Abdulsamat*' (ibid., 276). In the company of William Maxwell, Captain Walker, Mr and Mrs Innes and two young sons of the exiled Abdullah (formerly Sultan of Perak), Isabella landed at Teluk Kartang (later renamed Port Weld) three weeks after leaving Singapore and proceeded by land to Taiping.

Expansion of shipping east of Suez from the late nineteenth century led to the development of port facilities. In 1906 the five most important ports in the British empire (measured in terms of in-coming tonnage) were London, Hong Kong, Liverpool, Singapore and Colombo. Notable developments occurred in the ports of Madras,

Colombo, Batavia (where Tanjong Priok, 10 kilometres from Batavia, succeeded in rescuing Batavia from the Singapore grip), the island of Sabang (off Sumatra) which was a compulsory mail stop, and Belawan which became the outlet for Deli tobacco. In Singapore the Tanjong Pagar Company started to construct the wharf which was extended and completed by the Straits government between 1905 and 1917, after it had taken over the company, and named the King's and Empire docks (Broeze *et al.*, 1986, 4).

After the First World War, and particularly during the 1930s, cruise ships brought tourists to South-East Asian waters. Recalling his time as immigration officer in the Straits, Purcell wrote:

> Round-the-world luxury cruises were a feature of the inter-war period. I lunched on board the ill-fated *Empress of Britain* more than once; also on the *Lurline*, a steamship of the American Matson Line on her maiden voyage; I inspected the *Anandorra Star*. These luxury ships were replete with ingenious devices to attract the wealthy tourist. Some had flower gardens on their upper decks, others had air-conditioning in its earlier forms (one liner had a dining-room cooled by hundreds of tons of ice – entering it, one was frozen stiff where one stood; leaving it, one was struck down by the boiling heat of the Penang wharf). The menus on these ships were a mile long, and they offered every dish that could titillate the jaded palate from *tamales*, *sukiaki*, and caviare to American pumpkin pie; the gymnasiums on board were fitted with stationary bicycles, rowing-machines, oscillators, vibrators, and electric horses, and every gadget that could delight the contortionist or enable the nonagenerian to massage his unwilling liver into fitful functioning; the Italian Line ornamented its saloons with rococo frescoes and bas-reliefs of petrified macaroni, while the first-class cabins on the American Line had restrained decorations of the highest 'snob appeal' (e.g. interiors of the White House or Buckingham Palace and engravings of dukes in full Garter robes). After all this luxury, the coolies on the wharves in sweaty singlets afforded a notable anti-climax.
>
> (Purcell, 1965, 236–37)

Having been commandeered as troop ships, ocean liners returned to South-East Asian waters after the Second World War and enjoyed a brief fillip from the boom in emigration to Australia. From the 1960s, however, long-haul passenger shipping to the Far East became burdened with operating costs (especially the expenditure on crew and, after 1973, fuel) and could not compete with air transport. Imperial Airways, founded in 1924 and absorbed by BOAC in 1940 (Quin-Harkin, 1954), had sent its first commercial flights into Singapore in 1933, but it was the jet age, and particularly the advent of the jumbo, which popularised South-East Asian tourism. Ocean liners were sent to Taiwan for scrap or converted for container traffic or into cruise ships for the Aegean, Caribbean or South Pacific (Miller, 1986).

## TOURISM AND BRITISH MALAYA: AMENITIES AND ATTITUDES

As extra-European tourism began to develop in the twentieth century, South-East Asia attracted less attention than Egypt, India and the Far East. Nonetheless, first or last landfalls in the region were usually made in the Straits Settlements, and Singapore in particular capitalised on its position as 'Clapham Junction of the East'. Lacking historical sites or the magnetism of Bali, Penang and Singapore were regarded by those with the money and leisure to travel for pleasure as convenient rather than compelling stopping-off points offering opportunities to break the monotony of an ocean voyage (Peninsula & Oriental Steam Navigation Company, 1908, 226–30). Alternatively the traveller from Europe could disembark at Georgetown, take the train south or spend nearly a fortnight motoring through the peninsula before picking up a ship in Singapore, while those approaching from Australia, China and Japan could follow the same itinerary but in reverse order (Robson, 1911, 1923). Few tourists strayed beyond the Straits Settlements and west-coast states though non-residents could obtain licences for big game hunting in Pahang, Kelantan and Trengganu, and a proposal to create a National Game Park in Malaya, which was put forward in April 1927, was welcomed as 'a great addition to the country's attractions and a valuable asset' (Braddell, 1934, 127; Hubback, 1923).

It appears, therefore, that early in the development of Malaysian tourism the pattern, with which we are now familiar, of short-term stop-overs was being set. For example, in his tour of 1925–26 Horace Bleackley visited Malaya between French Indo-China (including, of course, Angkor) and the Dutch East Indies (taking in Borobodur) (Bleackley, 1928). Ten years later R. H. Bruce Lockhart completed his return to Malaya before proceeding as far as Macassar (Bruce Lockhart, 1936). In the mid 1950s Harold Nicolson, *en route* for Java, disembarked in Singapore and received hospitality from the British Commissioner-General, Robert Scott (Nicolson, 1957).

Before the period of popular tourism probably the majority of Europeans holidaying in South-East Asia at any time would have been resident members of the various colonial communities on weekend breaks or local leave rather than visitors coming in from outside. In the 1920s, for example, local leave for Malayan Civil Servants amounted to 14 days which could be spent in Fraser's Hill and later in the Cameron Highlands or further afield at Brastagi (northern Sumatra), Thailand, Ceylon or Hong Kong (Butcher, 1979, 157–66).

Despite the accessibility and amenities of the Straits Settlements and the west-coast states, the growth areas of South-East Asian tourism in the 1930s were elsewhere, particularly Java and Bali. Nor, it seemed, did the British promote tourism as vigorously as did the Dutch. 'Unlike the Dutch, who have made a religion of tourist propaganda,' observed Robert Bruce Lockhart, 'the British in Malaya do little to attract the passing stranger' (Bruce Lockhart, 1936, 10). As regards publicity, J. F. McNair, for example, attempted to portray life in Perak in the best possible light following the war of 1875–76. He larded description of the state with hints to 'settlers, travellers, or sportsmen', including the recommendation of 'modern tinned meats' as a supplement to standard provisions: he insisted that barbecuing sausages in the jungle 'outrivals the efforts of the most famous Pall Mall *chef*' (McNair, 1878, 418–20). The first recognisable guidebooks were for the Straits Settlements not the Malay States. In 1887 T. J. Keaughran's *Picturesque and Busy Singapore* was reprinted from the *Straits Times* and in 1890 B. E. D'Aranjo produced the *Stranger's Guide to Singapore*. Both books were superseded in 1892 by the Reverend G. M. Reith's *Handbook to Singapore* which Walter Makepeace revised fifteen years later (Reith, 1907).

With respect to the peninsula, just as tourism was dependent upon an infrastructure originally created for other purposes, so much of the early promotional material was a by-product of publicity campaigns primarily designed to attract young men with money to come out as planters. One of the first projects of the Malay States Information Agency was the publication of *The Illustrated Guide to the Federated Malay States* in 1910. The *Guide* was edited by C. W. Harrison (of the Malayan Civil Service) and was illustrated with watercolours by Mrs Barnard (wife of H. C. Barnard, a railway engineer) and photographs by C. J. Kleingrothe (who took most of the celebrated group shots of this period). It went through several impressions and 15,400 copies were printed between 1910 and 1923 (Harrison, 1911; 1923). Similarly the FMS Railway was issuing a brochure from at least 1920. From time to time, particularly on grand imperial occasions such as the

British Empire Exhibition of 1924, the London *Times*, Manchester *Guardian* and other British newspapers would carry comprehensive supplements surveying the potential of British Malaya and providing information on travel facilities. Individual residents also published accounts of life in the region and hints to travellers while travellers themselves clambered onto the lecture circuit with their lantern slides or published their globe-trotting jottings. This literature was uneven in its quality and authenticity. Least reliable, one suspects, were the travellers' tales of the exotic put about in British high society and amongst North American plutocrats who by the 1930s, after 'Hollywood or Mr. Roosevelt had "discovered" Bali', were 'in the process of going Bali-mad' (Bruce Lockhart, 1936, 11).

Early travellers in colonial Malaya moved through a network of personal contacts and introductions, staying, as did Isabella Bird, at Government House or the Residency and, if they tarried, being offered temporary membership of the club. In this way, as Kipling wrote of India, they were able to 'travel anywhere and everywhere without paying hotel bills' (Sandison, 1967, 103). As government rest houses and private hotels were built in response to the requirements of colonial society at work and at play, they came to be patronised by visitors as well as residents, though in the period before the Second World War the hotel never completely supplanted private hospitality offered to friends and acquaintances coming in from Britain.

The first, and for many years, the leading hotel in Singapore was the Hotel de l'Europe, established in 1845 as the London Hotel in a house built by Coleman for Edward Boustead on the Esplanade. In 1865 it was renamed Hotel de l'Europe and in 1905 it moved into a new building. Because of financial problems, its site was acquired by the government for the Supreme Court in 1934 though the Hotel de l'Europe survived to the present day as the Cockpit (Turnbull, 1977, 47; National Archives Collection, n.d., 46) The Adelphi Hotel was originally established in 1863 in Raffles Place. It later moved to High Street and finally to the junction of Coleman Street and North Bridge Road where a new building was opened in 1906 but torn down in the 1970s (ibid., 32, 49). The Raffles Hotel opened in 1887 and was refurbished in 1899. Of the other Singapore hotels mention should be made of the Goodwood, which grew out of the German Teutonia Club, and the Seaview which was established in the mid 1930s.

The Eastern & Oriental was the premier hotel in Penang. By 1910 Kuala Lumpur had two hotels, the FMS and the Empire, and on 1 July 1911 the Station Hotel was opened, a second Station Hotel being subsequently built at Ipoh.

Hotels in the Straits Settlements had an uneven reputation. 'There is only one thing which in 1902 the inhabitants of either place (Penang and Singapore) would confess to be inferior in quality – the hotels', wrote Clifford. 'As the globe-trotters of those now distant days usually spent their time in these hostelries, that fact was held to account for the unflattering opinions which passing travellers were wont to form of these, the world's most notoriously fascinating cities' (Clifford, 1928, 24). Purcell commented similarly that Singapore's 'first-rate order, sanitation, solidity, and discipline (was) spoilt by a second-rate decor and nowhere decent to eat' (Purcell, 1965, 239).

As against these jaundiced views, however, economiums abounded not least, though not only, in publicity material. The new premises of the Hotel de l'Europe were advertised in 1905 as being 'magnificently furnished with elegant simplicity and modern in construction, offering every advantage and necessity conducive to comfort and health' (National Archives Collection, n.d., 46). Under the management of Henry L. Schutz (late of the Taj Mahal Place, Bombay, and Galle Face Hotel, Colombo) it boasted 'the finest Dining Room in the East' (Reith, 1907, 5), though an early twentieth-century visitor put it on a par with the Raffles: 'It is generally agreed that there is no choice between the Raffles and the Europe, both are good first class, comfortable hotels and the best you can find in the Orient. . . . The food is quite good enough' (National Archives Collection, n.d., 49). The manager of the Hotel de l'Europe in the 1920s was Arthur Odell who was lauded by one tourist as 'a genius', 'a master of his craft' and 'a splendid asset to the colony' who 'will occupy a niche in the temple of fame beside three other paramount benefactors of Malaya – (?Ernest) Birch and Swettenham and Raffles' (Bleackley, 1928, 12). Under the management of the Sarkies brothers the Adelphi also acquired a fine reputation; its dining-room had seating capacity of 300 and an advertisement for the hotel in 1905 proclaimed: 'The interior presents a palatial, imposing bright appearance with magnificent marble effects and sumptuous apartments' (National Archives Collection, n.d., 49). In the mid 1890s the Sarkies also ran two Penang hotels, the Eastern & Oriental and the Sea View. Up-country Kuala Lumpur was slower and less sophisticated in its provision of hotels; the facilities of the Station Hotel, Kuala Lumpur, were distinctly more modest than those of, say, Singapore's Hotel de l'Europe. When it opened in 1911 the Station Hotel advertised: 'Moderate and fixed Tariff. Inclusive Terms from $4 (14s.) per day. Electric Light and Electric Fans. High-class Restaurant adjoining. No gratuities' (Harrison, 1911, frontispiece).

Western tourists to Malaya, whether they came from Britain, continental Europe or the United States, were associated with British colonialism by their contacts and by the colour of their skin. Although 'trains, government rest houses, cinemas, hotels, and churches were not segregated in the same way that similar institutions were in the Southern states of the United States' (Butcher, 1979, 97), travellers saw themselves, and were treated by others, as guests of the British not the indigenous community. The visitor was promised 'a universal and ready disposition to oblige you merely because you are an *orang puteh*, and because, happily for your present comfort and pleasure, the white people whom these Asiatics have known have treated them with comfort and kindliness' (Harrison, 1923, 4). Honorary members of colonial society during their sojourn, tourists were expected to marvel at the products of the Public Works Department rather than the customs of the non-European communities, and they were directed to inspect the flora and fauna of the countryside within the confines of botanical gardens or game parks. 'The attraction', as Paul Kratoska has put it, 'was not Asia but European activities in Asia' (Reith, 1907, vi). Thus the *P. & O. Handbook* drew attention to the 'many buildings' in Singapore 'of elegant and substantial appearance – Government House, the Victoria Memorial Hall, Cathedral, Banks, Esplanade, etc.', but was, on the other hand, dismissive of non-Europeans, merely referring to the 'large native quarter' as 'not very inviting, though its mixed population shows every variety of Eastern race' (Peninsula & Oriental Steamship Navigation Company, 1908, 229). Non-Europeans did sometimes intrude, nonetheless; for example, while Bleackley hailed Singapore's 'beautiful' *padang* and Cathedral as 'a vision of home', he lamented that the approach to Government House, instead of being 'the most splendid in Singapore', was 'disfigured by squalid Chinese dwellings' (Bleackley, 1928, 118–19).

Some unease was expressed in the inter-war years, however, about the deleterious effects of Western affluence, of which tourism was one. Some feared that the luxury of colonial life might sap the vigour of the regime and undermine its prestige; or that it would corrupt non-European subject peoples and damage their natural way of life; or, again, that it would upset the delicacy of race relations upon which depended Britain's continuing presence. The sensitivity which Europeans in rural and isolated postings supposedly displayed in their dealings with non-Europeans was regularly contrasted with the coarser attitudes born of an urban existence lapped by creature-comforts. For this reason Harrison thought it prudent to warn the outsider to tread warily: 'The white man has a good name amongst the

other races here, and one hopes that travellers of the white race will be
sensible enough not to resent being asked to remember that fact in
their passing' (Harrison, 1923, 4). For this reason he also felt it
apposite to print on the frontispiece of his *Guide* the following lines
from *The Merchant of Venice*:

> Mislike me not for my complexion,
> The shadow'd livery of the burnish'd sun,
> To whom I am a neighbour and near bred.

## CONCLUSION

This chapter has attempted to single out a number of avenues for the
historical examination of tourism in Malaya. One of these is the
identification of the characteristics of tourism as distinct from, say,
exploration in the history of European travel in the area. A second
issue, and one which is clearly related to the chronology of tourism in
South-East Asia, concerns the prerequisites or enabling factors for the
development of tourism in Malaya and more widely in the region. It
has been argued here that tourism was, to begin with, both a result and
a reflection of colonialism. It was, moreover, a product rather than a
cause of the phenomenal growth in the travel industry during the late
nineteenth and early twentieth centuries. Shipping, railways and
roads, even hotels, resorts and all the amenities upon which a tourist
industry thrives were originally developed for purposes other than
tourism. Third, we have discerned at the outset some of the features of
what subsequently became the pattern of tourism in modern Malaysia
and Singapore. Notable amongst these was the early popularity with
visitors from outside of the short-stay stop-over in the Straits Settlements and the more accessible parts of the west coast states. Finally, it
is clear that at an early stage in its development the question which has
bulked so large in the contemporary debate over tourism, namely its
impact upon non-European cultures and societies, was already arousing some concern with those who had acquired a lifelong interest in the
country and its people.

## NOTES

1  I wish to thank Mr J. M. Gullick for the information and guidance he gave
   me during the preparation of this chapter.

# 14 Early travellers in Borneo

*Graham Saunders*

Travellers to Borneo today arrive with certain expectations. There are certain sights they expect to see, certain experiences they expect to enjoy, certain activities they expect to undertake. They carry with them an idea or image of Borneo, an image which tourist brochures have conveyed and tourist authorities have cultivated. What that image is is the culmination of a process that began when the first European traveller to Borneo's shores recorded his impressions of what he had seen. Those who followed added their impressions to the store upon which the modern tourist draws and to which he may contribute. Travelling is interactive. A traveller cannot be a passive observer: he or she helps create the experience which he or she may record and pass on to others who follow, in turn affecting their image of Borneo and their reaction to their actual experience of it. Moreover each traveller leaves a mark upon the society he passes through so that society is never quite the same again. A memory remains which influences subsequent behaviour, and the self-image of a society that has been visited will be subtly altered. Where travellers are infrequent, change will not be readily detectable and any influence or effect may fade. Where mass tourism develops its impact may be profound.

The images now associated with Borneo are very largely those created by the impact of European travellers. Travellers there were from places as far apart as China and Arabia, pre-dating the first European contacts, and some left accounts which refer to Borneo, but to which part or parts precisely scholars disagree. No doubt their reports created an image of Borneo among merchants and officials in their homelands, but the images now associated with Borneo are the product of European contact, which has been much more pervasive, particularly once Borneo came under European governance.

People who travelled to and within Borneo did so for a variety of reasons. The earlier contacts were largely exploratory, diplomatic and commercial, motives which remained through the nineteenth century and until the present day. These contacts added to European knowledge of Borneo and helped create an image of Borneo in the European mind, but those who contributed most in this regard were travellers who journeyed for their own interest and enjoyment and wrote about it afterwards. In these people we see the embryonic tourist and their published accounts were aimed at and appealed to a wider audience than the reports of diplomats, merchants, government officials and scientific collectors. In the following pages, these travellers will feature prominently and we will notice how attitudes we associate with the modern tourist gradually emerged and how the tourist image of Borneo gradually evolved.

There is not space to mention every traveller who visited Borneo and any selection may be disputed. Human beings are complex. The most indefatigable collector of specimens may travel also to see the sights, and a naval officer, missionary or government official may well delight in the scenes and peoples he meets in the course of his duties. Moreover, any selection from published sources is an inadequate presentation of the total European experience of Borneo. A large number of travellers left no record that has been preserved. Humble folk, in particular, and the nineteenth-century equivalent of the modern backpacker, travelling on the cheap, working his passage, were unlikely to have their experiences published.

What we are looking for is evidence of that urge to travel to strange places which inspires the modern tourist. We need to consider not only the physical aspects of travelling, but also the intellectual or mental approach to travelling. To a large extent, being a tourist is a matter of attitude. A tourist is not an explorer, for example, entering the unknown. Tourists generally follow. Almost indispensable to the tourist is the guide. Tourism as a common activity occurred only with the improvements in transportation which by the end of the nineteenth century were making travel safer and more comfortable. Mass tourism had to wait for the development of cheap, reliable transport and the provision of accommodation and services for large numbers of people. Early travellers lacked these amenities, but they could still display attitudes common to present-day tourists. A tourist travels for pleasure in order to see new places and to meet people from societies different from his own. A tourist looks for the exotic, but does not wish to stray too far from the familiar, or from home comforts. A tourist collects mementoes of his or her travels, be they artefacts, sketches and drawings or, in modern times, photographs and videos. A tourist will not, except in the most superficial way, enter into the society which he or she visits. We are all of us tourists at some time when we travel, however much we may wish to eschew the name when applied to ourselves.

Travellers, be they tourists or not, inevitably make some impact, however slight, upon the society they visit. If no other traveller appears that impact will fade, but when other visitants arrive they add to the accumulated experience and subtle changes occur. Later travellers are influenced by the reports of their predecessors and arrive with preconceptions not held by those who went before. Moreover, every traveller carries his own cultural impedimenta which affect the manner of his travel and his interpretations of what is seen and experienced. On the other side, the reactions and attitudes of those inhabitants who have had experience of travellers are also affected by that experience. A complex cultural exchange begins and a new relationship develops along with new perceptions of each other and of one's own identity, society and culture. In the next several paragraphs we shall see this interaction at work. In particular, we shall observe the emergence of a European image of Borneo which has been taken over by the tourist industry of the present day. In addition, many of these travellers' accounts are interesting in their own right, often entertaining and offering rare insights into Bornean societies of the time.

The first European to leave an account of Borneo in any detail was Antonio Pigafetta, the chronicler of Magellan's voyage, who visited Brunei in 1521. In the circumstances, he was hardly a tourist, but he illustrates the importance of travellers to historians, because his is the best description we have of the Sultanate of Brunei at the height of its power. It has been quoted many times and has contributed greatly to modern Brunei's perception of its past and of its present role (Nicholl, 1975, 8–13). The later Spanish visitors in 1578 attacked and burnt the place and their accounts are largely official depositions (ibid., 35–54). Nevertheless, the Spanish (and Portuguese) accounts of Brunei in the sixteenth century are important historical documents, while the events themselves shaped both European perceptions of the Brunei Sultanate and Brunei perceptions of Europeans as a threat; although, as the Spanish, in the Brunei version of events, were repulsed heroically, the attack of 1578 is strongly and proudly imbedded in the national consciousness.

The first Englishman to leave an account of part of Borneo was Daniel Beeckman, who called at Banjarmasin in 1714 on a commercial venture. His comments on life in Banjarmasin and other places he visited are often perceptive and lively, but his portrayal of the orangutan is of a creature of fable, the progenitor of those mainly mythical,

*Figure 14.1* The Orang-ootan
*Source*: Beeckman, 1718, 37.

Wild Men of Borneo to which tourist literature still alludes (Beeckman, 1718, 37). From the north-west coast we have a lively description of Brunei in 1776 by Thomas Forrest, who called there after concluding his main purpose, his voyage to New Guinea. He had no business to conduct with Brunei and his description of Brunei's Kampong Ayer or water village and its floating market set the pattern for the many that followed, including his comparison with Venice (for its 'water lanes', not its architecture). Brunei was still a considerable place and Forrest's account reflected this (Forrest, 1969, 378-85).

> In those divisions of the town (of Brunei), made by the water lanes, is neither firm land nor island; the houses standing on posts, as has been said, in shallow water; and the public market is kept sometimes in one part, sometimes in another part of the river. Imagine, a fleet of London wherries, loaded with fish, fowl, greens, &c floating up with the tide, from London Bridge towards Westminster; then down again, with many buyers floating up and down with them; this will give some idea of a Borneo market. Those boats do not always drive with the tide, but sometimes hold by the stairs of houses, or by stakes, driven purposely into the river, and sometimes by one another: yet, in the course of a forenoon, they visit most part of the town, where the water lanes are broad. The boat people (mostly women) are provided with large bamboo hats, the shade of which covers great part of the body, as they draw themselves up under it, and sit, as it were, upon their heels.
>
> (Forrest, 1969, 380).

In the nineteenth century, the number of travellers visiting Borneo considerably increased, especially after the arrival of James Brooke and his acquisition of Sarawak. When Brooke first arrived in 1839, he had no fixed purpose in mind. His excursions under the guidance of the Brunei nobles who governed the place were genuinely the travels of a man who was out to see the sights. Only later, disappointed by his reception in the Celebes (Sulawesi), did he return to the Sarawak river with other purposes in mind. Brooke's journals, published in part by Captains Keppel and Mundy of the Royal Navy, and his letters, published later by his friend John Templer, tell us much about the condition of the country and its people, but even more about the ambitions, objectives and prejudices of James Brooke. The traveller of 1839 is transformed into the ruler, with severe damage to objectivity (Keppel, 1847; Mundy, 1848; Templer, 1853).

Amongst those who were drawn to Borneo by Brooke's activities were at least two with a genuine interest in what they saw and the ability to convey their impressions in picture as well as words. One was the young Frank Marryat, then a midshipman on HMS *Samarang*, a keen observer whose vivid writing has the enthusiasm of youth and is fleshed out by numerous illustrations (Marryat, 1848). Indeed, the illustrations which appeared in this and other contemporary publications created visual impressions perhaps more important than words in developing an image of Borneo in European, particularly British, minds. Not all accounts and illustrations were published. Naval Surgeon Edward Cree, attached to the British naval force combating piracy on the Borneo coast, was an accomplished water-colourist whose official duties left him time for casual exploration and painting in between periods of intense activity treating casualties in various skirmishes. His work was not published until very recently, but no doubt his paintings and, possibly, his journal had a small private circulation. His paintings give us our most impressive visual impression on Brunei in the mid-1840s, while his smaller illustrations are the equivalent of the modern traveller's snapshots (Levien, 1981, 153–69).

Neither Marryat nor Cree travelled just for the sake of travelling, nor did they choose Borneo as a destination. Their itineraries were chosen for them and they made the best they could with what they encountered. Hugh Low and Spenser St John would not qualify as tourists, but they were intrepid travellers and made exploratory journeys of great importance. Low's book on Sarawak publicised that country and the role of James Brooke (Low, 1848). It was the product of two years' residence there rather than the impressions of a traveller. Low then moved on to Labuan, where his duties in the Colonial Service were not so arduous as to prevent him becoming the first European to climb Mount Kinabalu in north Borneo in 1851, nor accompanying St John, since 1856 British Consul-General in Brunei, on a second climb in 1858. St John's account and its illustrations and Low's botanical and zoological discoveries, particularly of spectacular specimens of pitcher plants (*nepenthesis*), placed Mount Kinabalu firmly among the images of Borneo (St John, 1862, I, 230–355). Tourists today tread in Low's steps as the names Low's Peak, Low's Gulley and various animals and plants bearing his name testify. Kinabalu had a special place in the native Sabahan consciousness before Low and St John appeared on the scene, but they gave the mountain new dimensions which were added to by travellers like Guillemard and Whitehead to name but two (Guillemard, 1886, I, 109–12; Whitehead, 1893). Kinabalu became a sight that all travellers to northern Borneo had to see and came to symbolise the country itself.

> We never had a finer view of Kina Balu than this evening. A white cloud in the form of a turban, its edges richly fringed with gold, encompassed most of the highest peaks, while the brightness of the setting sun rendered every other portion of the mountain distinctly visible, except those dark valleys cut deep in its sides, where the Dahombang and the Pinokok have their rise; and even here a succession of cascades reflected back the sun's rays from the shadowy gloom.
>
> We were standing opposite its western face, and having no high buttress between us and the mountain, we could observe the great precipice, which is here nearly perpendicular from the sloping summit down to an elevation of about 5,000 feet. As we stood there admiring the extreme beauty of the scene, a double rainbow began to appear, and apparently arching over the mountain, formed, as it were, a bright framework to the picture. We stayed there until the sun setting beyond the distant hills threw the valley into shade, but left its brightness on the craggy peaks above. Gradually the wind rose and drove the clouds over the heavens, and the form of the mountain and the brilliant rainbows vanished.
>
> (St John, 1862, 318–19)

The adventurer and trader Robert Burns cannot be classified as a tourist, although he travelled with interests other than commercial and became, as Tom Harrisson has called him, the 'first Ethnologist and Explorer of Interior Sarawak'. His study of the Kayans was the product of a keen and alert mind fascinated by and sympathetic to Kayan society, but his rivalry with James Brooke over mineral rights in Brunei territory caused him to receive a bad press from Brooke's supporters, while he was undoubtedly of hasty temper and immoderate habits. His decapitation by Sulu or Illanun pirates in Marudu Bay in 1851 did not bring posthumous recognition and sympathy. The general feeling at the time appears to have been that he had it coming to him (Harrisson, 1951).

A formidable and genuine traveller who arrived in Sarawak in that year was Madame Ida Pfeiffer, on her 'Second Voyage Around the World'. Using her own funds and a grant from the Austrian government, she obtained free passages from generous Dutch officials in the East Indies and from her own German countrymen in Java. She was on her way to Adelaide, South Australia, in 1851 when she decided to visit Sarawak, attracted by the reputation of Rajah James Brooke. The Rajah was not in Sarawak when she arrived, but she was met by his nephew, Captain Brooke Brooke, who installed her in the Rajah's bungalow and with two other Europeans escorted her on a tour of the gold mining area at Bau. She soon exhausted what Sarawak could offer, writing, 'When I had nothing more to see in Sarawak I wished to continue my journey'. And so she did, brushing aside Captain Brooke's objections to her travelling to Pontianak in Dutch Borneo via the Skrang river, where Brooke's authority had only very recently been established. In the end he sent her in a government gun-boat to the mouth of the river and in a *prahu* to the fort, braving high seas which deterred a missionary who was supposed to accompany her to Skrang. As the first white woman in the area, she became a major attraction in her own right, visiting a longhouse, discussing head-hunting and ignoring warnings that she should proceed no further. In the end, Alan Lee, the young Brooke officer at the fort, gave way and provided her with eight Malay boatmen and his own Chinese cook. With these, and a servant provided by Captain Brooke, she ascended the Batang Lupar, collecting insects, 'to the merriment of the Dayaks', irritated by the slackness of her companions and the slow progress made and relying on the Brooke flag to see her through – which it did. Her own behaviour disarmed suspicion among the Dayaks. On entering a longhouse she would shake hands with the men and women and then sit down and take children on to her lap. Probably her own confidence and fearlessness disarmed hostility as much as the Brooke flag, for these same people were shortly to rise against the Rajah and to kill the young officer Lee (Pfeiffer, 1855).

Ida Pfeiffer was perhaps a phenomenon rather than a tourist, one of that remarkable breed of nineteenth-century women travellers who defied the conventions of their day. In Frederick Boyle, however, we have a man who was a tourist at heart. Travelling with his brother, Arthur, he arrived in Sarawak in 1863 on the Rajah's steamer, the *Rainbow*. The brothers stayed at the Rajah's guest bungalow, toured the Borneo Company's mines, collected artefacts, travelled in the Sarawak gun-boat *Jolly Bachelor* to Kanowit, Mukah and the Saribas, and enjoyed themselves immensely. Boyle's narrative is informative, colourful and light-hearted. His description of the dinner held to farewell the Rajah, returning to England in September 1863, when the Resident's pet bear drank the punch, the rockets for the fire-works display would not work and the sailors of HMS *Rifleman* providing the music practically danced the jigs and hornpipes they played, is reminiscent of the lively caricatures produced by Charles

Dickens. That Boyle was the quintessential tourist is demonstrated by his concluding comments to his readers, whom he advises to travel by the French shipping line east of Suez and to avoid the P. & O.; like his modern counterpart comparing airlines (Boyle, 1865).

> Though this expedition (ascending the Upper Rejang to its source, then traversing a tract of jungle, to reach a large lake of the interior from which descends the river of Pontianak) was prohibited by such unfortunate circumstances (the hostility of the Kayans), we had hitherto made an active use of our time. We had visited every fort and station of the Sarawak territory, and had probably seen more of the outward aspect of the country than any European connected with it. We had visited both the Land and Sea Dyaks in their own homes, and had made acquaintance with some of their most celebrated chiefs. If, by ill-fortune, the main object of our voyage had failed, at least our travels had introduced us to most of the points of interest in a kingdom whose history in connection with Rajah Brooke has been the most romantic story of modern times. And, therefore, since we regarded ourselves as mere wanderers, neither scientific nor anthropological, we decided that, our curiosity being already satisfied by the experiences of four months, nothing more remained for us to do in this country but to take our passage by the *Rainbow* and return to England.
>
> (ibid., 263)

By the mid-1870s Sarawak was a more settled country under the firm and autocratic rule of Rajah Charles Brooke, who had succeeded his uncle, Rajah James, in 1868. Moreover, he had married and Ranee Margaret presided over Sarawak society. Amenities were slowly improving, although travellers of any substance still relied on private hospitality. In 1876, the celebrated traveller and artist Marianne North, whose paintings of exotic plants fill a pavilion at Kew Gardens, visited Sarawak. She stayed at the Astana and was a welcome guest for Ranee Margaret. She spent some time on Mattang, the prominent mountain near Kuching, painting and, escorted by the Borneo Company manager and the Rajah's treasurer, went up the Sarawak river and on jungle walks. However, much as she enjoyed her visit, Marianne North travelled with a purpose, which was to paint (North, 1980, 95–102).

Other travellers visited Borneo with purposes other than pleasure. The island was becoming opened up to European influence and was becoming more widely known. The Dutch extended their influence more completely over their large area of the island, while in the 1880s the British North Borneo Company laid claim to what is now Sabah and Rajah Charles extended his territory at the expense of Brunei, an increasingly run-down and ramshackle state rescued from oblivion by the appointment of a British Resident in 1906. With entry points to the hinterland under European control and that hinterland rendered more accessible to traders and government officials, Borneo and its exotic flora and fauna attracted a succession of naturalists, beginning with Hugh Low himself in 1845 and with the more eminent Alfred Wallace in 1854. Wallace was in Sarawak for fifteen months. One of his particular studies was of the orang-utan, of which he killed seventeen in the interests of science (he mentions naturalists in Dutch Borneo who conducted similar research). The orang-utan was becoming part of the image of Borneo although still linked in the popular mind with the idea of 'Wild Men'. Wallace's descriptions of 'remarkable beetles', a 'flying frog', and the strange plants to be found in Borneo's luxurious forests, contributed to an image of tropical Borneo to which later naturalists added (Wallace, 1922, 26–72). One of these was Carl Bock, a Norwegian, who was commissioned by the Governor-General of the Netherlands East Indies in 1879 to travel through and report on the interior of south-east Borneo. Bock's report was published in English in 1881 as *The Head-Hunters of Borneo*, a lively, somewhat sensational account of his travels which included a report of cannibalism among the Tring Dayaks and his prolonged efforts to locate a tribe of men with tails, of whom he had heard. The book was illustrated with 30 colour plates depicting native artefacts, housing and dress. That native dress was clearly scanty no doubt contributed to the book's success. A second edition was published in 1882 and it appeared also in German and Norwegian. It contributed greatly to the popular image of Borneo as a place inhabited by wild head-hunters and dusky bare-breasted women (Bock, 1881).

> I made enquiries in the village, and found a strong general belief in the existence of people with tails in a country only a few day's journey from Long Puti. Such definite statements were made to me on the subject that I could hardly resist the temptation to penetrate myself into the stronghold of my ancestral representatives. Tjiropon, an old and faithful servant of the Sultan, assured me, in the presence of his Highness and of several Pangerans, that he had himself some years ago seen the people in Passir. He called them 'Orang-boentoet' - literally, tail-people. The chief of the tribe, he said, presented a very remarkable appearance,

having white hair and white eyes – a description which exactly agreed with one I had received some time previously from a young Boegis, when travelling by steamer to Samarinda from Paré Paré in Celebes. As to the all-important item of the tail, Tjiropon declared with a grave face that the caudal appendage of these people was from two to four inches long; and that in their homes they had little holes cut or dug in the floor on purpose to receive the tail, so that they might sit down in comfort. This ludicrous anti-climax to the narrative of the trusty Tjiropon almost induced me to discredit the whole story. At any rate, I thought, the Orang boentoet must be in a very high state of development – rather, perhaps, in the last stages of retrogression – if the extremely sensitive prehensile tail of the spider-monkey has so lost its elasticity in these people as to incommodate its wearer to such a degree.

The Sultan, however, was highly impressed with the truth of Tjiropon's story. He had often heard that there were among his neighbours, if not among his own subjects, a tribe with tails; but he had hitherto discredited the rumours. 'Now', he said, 'I do believe there are such people, because Tjiropon has told us. I have known him for twenty years, and he dare not tell a lie in my face, in presence of us all'.

(Bock, 1988, 144–45)

Most travellers with a scientific purpose did not have such a popular impact. Of those who followed Bock into Dutch Borneo, the most notable are probably A. W. Nieuwenhuis (Nieuwenhuis, 1900) and Bock's compatriot Carl Lumholtz (Lumholtz, 1920). On the British side of the island, the American William T. Hornaday had a more light-hearted passage in 1878 (Hornaday, 1885) while the Italian Odoardo Beccari, who travelled in Sarawak between June 1865 and January 1868, published only in scientific journals. It was not until 1902 that his account of his travels appeared in book form in Italian and not until 1904 did it appear in English, by which time the tourist image of Borneo had been largely completed by more popular writers with less serious purposes (Beccari, 1904).

One of these was Annie Brassey, travelling with her husband on their yacht and arriving at Kuching in April 1887. Annie Brassey was a genuine tourist although, obviously, not of the packaged variety. She and her party had been hesitant about going up the river to Kuching when they heard that the Rajah was away, 'but it seemed a pity to be so near and to miss the opportunity of seeing Kuching'. They were amused by the quaintness of some of the direction-boards along the river which indicated the course to follow; signs such as 'Hug this close on the outside'. They admired the scenery inland from the town, visited the public buildings and the market, above which was housed the museum where they examined the artefacts with great attention. They were escorted by Mr Maxwell, in charge during the Rajah's absence, and the Brasseys were given lunch at his bungalow. Caught in a sudden rainstorm which compelled them to shelter in the government offices by the river, Annie Brassey rather envied the rest of the party which had been lunching at the fort 'where they had much enjoyed the view from the heights'. By this date, photography had made its appearance, and the Rajah's officers, like modern tour guides, were not above providing 'two Dyak soldiers in full war-costume, in readiness to be sketched or photographed'. Thus ended the Brasseys' tour of Kuching and by evening they were again at sea. At Labuan, a couple of days later, Annie Brassey exhibited the same attributes of a tourist, buying from a group of Dayaks from the Baram 'jackets made of cotton, grown, dyed, and woven by the Dyaks, horn and tortoiseshell combs, kreises (*sic*), parongs (*sic*), knives, pipes, tobacco pouches, travelling-bags of plaited matting and sumpitans or blowpipes from which poisoned arrows are discharged'. They visited all the shops in the town and went for a drive in the country. While waiting for a boat to take them back to their yacht in the evening they amused themselves with a Chinese open-air theatre, a wax-work exhibition and a puppet-show. The word 'amused' is hers. In Brunei, which they next visited, the attraction was an audience with the Sultan, 'an ugly, smiling, feeble old man', who greeted them affably. The Brasseys went on to visit north Borneo, stopping at Kudat and Sandakan and making an expedition to the birds'-nests caves at Madai. Her husband could not go on this expedition, but Annie and her companions were escorted by officers and police of the North Borneo Company. This was, then, a somewhat privileged form of tourism and until the mid-twentieth century and the improvement of communication with and within Borneo this was to remain the case, travellers tending to depend on the hospitality and assistance of government, the commercial companies and the Christian Missions whose personnel usually welcomed the diversion such travellers occasioned (Brassey, 1889).

Perhaps the Sultan of Brunei also welcomed the diversion offered by his visitors, but one wonders what he made of Walter J. Clutterbuck, FRGS, who clattered across from Labuan in a rickety Chinese launch with a young Englishman as his guide, and supplies that consisted largely of alcohol: eight dozen bottles of beer, a bottle of whiskey and two dozen soda water. Clutterbuck was a traveller somewhat down market from the Brasseys, less protected and less aloof from the local population. He and his companions were as much objects of curiosity as the Bruneians were to him and they were constantly surrounded by crowds of children fascinated by their every action.

> The Chinamen live on a small island in the middle of this river-paved town (Brunei), and the street outside our dining-room was full of little Chinese children, who with a quantity of Malay men examined our performance through the door and window bars with the most eager interest . . .
>
> At first we thought it a bore having every mouthful of food that we ate criticised in a whispered under-tone by such an admiring audience. But it is wonderful how one can become acclimatised to the scorching gaze of the multitude in this worn-out world. Anyway, *they* seemed to enjoy it and think us extraordinary.
>
> It seemed, looking out at these naked savages, as though we had suddenly got back to the early morning of history. We were now in a country where almost every adjunct of civilization was unknown – a country where marmalade, beer, and potatoes had never been introduced – and, after all, our being eyed from the street was merely savage curiosity. . . . We stayed at Brunei two or three days, cruising about in a family boat, as, like the rest of the inhabitants, we had to annex a boat to pace the street in. We wandered through the city taking photographs of nearly all we saw. I say of *nearly all*, as the females always ran away as soon as our eye was fixed on them. . . . We were looked at everywhere as quite strange beings, so that in wending our way amid the watery streets of the town we felt most incongruous mortals.
>
> (Clutterbuck, 1891, 217, 221–22).

The tourist syndrome takes hold in the twentieth century. Ella Christie has been called Sarawak's first tourist and, reading her diary entries, it is easy to see why. She was in the country for only a few days in May 1904, when the Rajah was absent, and was accommodated in the Astana by Mr Deshon, the Resident. On 7th May she tried shopping in the bazaar and went for a rickshaw ride in the countryside. On the 8th she was taken by the sister of the Anglican Archdeacon to see what she calls a Dayak princess. On the 9th she excitedly writes that the Commandant of the Sarawak Rangers, Sir Percy Cunynghame, provided 'a show of Dyaks for me to Kodak. All in war-paint, really savages. I do hope they will come out. I did Sir Percy beside them in one, as a contrast . . . I have got some very good Borneo savage relics and hats' (Christie, 1961).

By this time a tourist image of Borneo had clearly emerged, so that in 1922, for instance, Elizabeth Mershon could entitle her book, *With the Wild Men of Borneo*. In the same year, that royal tourist, Edward Prince of Wales, was greeted in Singapore by Dayak warriors brought over from Sarawak who performed war dances in full regalia. The pictorial record of his voyage shows Dayak women, modestly covered, lined up for his arrival and a Dayak woman holding, in the words of the caption, 'the skull of a fallen enemy tribesman'. Another photograph is captioned 'Wild Men of Borneo at Singapore'. The prince did not call at Sarawak, but he visited Labuan and Jesselton, now Kota Kinabalu. At Jesselton, we are told, he spent three hours with wild tribesmen, watched pony racing, presumably by Bajaus, and saw a demonstration with the blowpipe, presumably by Muruts. He then made his visit to Brunei and to the Sultan (Phillips, 1922). A 57-page, well-illustrated and no doubt widely read article in *The National Geographic Magazine* in 1919 contained only four photographs of Chinese (in one of which appeared a Malay fisherwoman) and one of the Malay section of Kuching. All the rest were of Dayaks and jungle (Smith, 1919).

It is clear that by the 1920s the images of Borneo in the public mind were those of the tourist brochures of today, certainly for the British-controlled part of the island. Once those images were established, then travellers to Borneo were going to expect to see them be they orang-utans, Dayak head-hunters, longhouses, Brunei's Kampong Ayer, Mount Kinabalu, Bajau horsemen or whatever. For the tourist, these are the images which define Borneo and set it apart from other places. These are what makes Borneo unique. They are what the tour guides, tour operators, travel agents and local residents guarantee they see. They are the subject matter of travel guides, coffee-table books and government tourist authority briefings. To see encapsulated the tourist image of Sarawak, for example, visit the Sarawak resort of Damai Beach, near Kuching, and attend the stage presentation there. It is a slick, professional and spectacular piece of entertainment, aimed at the packaged tourist. As a cultural presentation it is highly effective and the audience loves it.

There are some who see all this as falsifying the true picture of Borneo. At one level, of course, it does. At another, however, it reflects a reality. The images grew out of the experiences, observations and imaginations of travellers who saw and reported – and interpreted. These travellers carried with them their own intellectual and cultural baggage along with their physical luggage; and concepts like the Noble Savage, the Romantic view of nature, Darwinian theory and the scientist's impulse to collect and classify, combined with a human fascination with the unusual and the exotic. From Daniel Beeckman and Pigafetta on travellers to Borneo did not only observe. They interpreted what they saw and accommodated what they observed to their own prejudices, to their own cultural values, to their own intellectual world. In doing so they created, developed and passed on an image of Borneo which has taken on a life of its own – as the existence of a tourist industry testifies. Moreover, it is an image which has affected the attitudes and self-perceptions of the people of Borneo themselves. It has been no one-sided exchange. Borneans have responded to European contact in ways which have helped develop the European image of Borneo: but they have also themselves been affected and influenced by that image so that their behaviour has been changed by it. We can see this most clearly in the tourist industry itself, where Borneans exploit the tourist image of Borneo in order to fulfil the expectations of modern travellers. This is not as cynical as the word 'exploit' perhaps implies, for many Borneans have come to accept that image at least in part as reflecting a reality which at one time existed, even if they regard it as being kept artificially alive now. Moreover, the image has acquired a new dimension as an expression of a Bornean identity. Kalimantan, within Indonesia, and Sabah and Sarawak, within Malaysia, have political reasons for perpetuating an image of Borneo which emphasises its uniqueness.

Early European travellers to Borneo thus had a profound if unintended impact upon Bornean society and upon later events. In the present context, what is fascinating in these travellers' accounts of their journeys through Borneo is seeing how an image of Borneo gradually emerged and how the traveller was transformed eventually into the tourist.

# 15 Environmental issues and tourism in Thailand[1]

*Michael J. G. Parnwell*

> Tourism is potentially the least damaging of the profit-making initiatives, because it is in its own interests to preserve the environment.
>
> (Hamilton, 1990)

Tourism is a form of resource exploitation. Where, as in many developing countries, the natural environment constitutes the principal resource upon which tourism has been built, it is clearly in the industry's best interests to minimise the extent to which the environment is degraded by tourism activity and associated infrastructural development. Without adequate safeguards, the sustainability of the industry in the longer term may be threatened.

With so many tropical countries now vying for a slice of a steadily growing tourism cake, each offering a fairly similar range of attractions and 'unspoilt' environments, the established tourist destinations can ill-afford to neglect their tourism resource-base. International tourism has become what economists might call a 'buyers' market', particularly since the Gulf War, with environmental quality representing a key commodity: 'Increasingly, tourists are demanding that their environments be high-quality and pollution-free as well as inherently interesting, and some tourists will change travel patterns if environmental quality expectations are not met' (Inskeep, 1987, 119). The potential long-term economic effects of uncontrolled tourism development, especially in countries which have come to rely heavily on the 'tourists' dollar', might therefore serve to focus the minds of planners and policy-makers on the need to prevent or ameliorate the negative effects of tourism on the natural (and, for that matter, human) environment.

Edward Inskeep takes the argument a stage further: in addition to pursuing a greater harmony between tourism and the natural environment, careful management of the industry might even help to engender environmental consciousness in the public and private sectors, and may promote conservation-mindedness amongst hosts and guests alike (ibid., 131). The growth of special interest tourism, such as 'eco-tourism' (safaris, bird-watching tours, wildlife photography, landscape painting, even organised hunting trips – see Janet Cochrane's chapter in this volume), has in many instances helped to generate a greater awareness of the aesthetic value of natural ecosystems amongst both the promoters and consumers of tourism resources.

Set against this backdrop, it is very disappointing to find that in important international tourist destinations, the various news media regularly feature 'horror stories' about the ways in which the environment is being severely damaged as a result of the tourism boom. Striking headlines such as 'Tourism Boom, Environment Doomed' (*Utusan Konsumer*, mid-June 1991), 'Samui Environment Under Threat' (*Bangkok Post*, 8.9.89), 'Golf Course Mania in Malaysia' (*Utusan Konsumer*, October 1991) and 'Tourism Boom Threatens Paradise Islands' (ibid., 6.12.88) appear with increasing regularity in the newspapers of some of South-East Asia's main tourism centres. Whilst we might attribute this partly to media hype, newspapers presenting a somewhat distorted image of the effects of tourism in playing to a growing interest in environmentalism amongst their readership, a trip to any of the region's main tourism 'honeypots' will reveal that there is more than a grain of truth in these stories. Tourism is responsible for fundamentally transforming, and in some cases severely damaging, the natural resources upon which the industry has been built over the last two decades or so. Even areas which are ostensibly being 'protected' because of their natural beauty or ecological vulnerability, such as the Pulau Redang marine park off the coast of Terengganu in Malaysia, and the marine parks of Phang Nga province off Thailand's southern Andaman coastline, are currently being developed for their tourism potential.

The aim of this chapter is to highlight some of the issues which underlie the negative effects of tourism on the natural environment in Thailand, and to examine the likely longer-term impact of the *laissez faire* policies which appear to predominate in many areas of tourism resource 'management'. In other words, is Thailand's tourism boom environmentally sustainable? We start with a brief description of some of the ways in which tourism is affecting the natural environment in Thailand.

## TOURISM AND ENVIRONMENT IN THAILAND

An important feature of the tourism industry in Thailand is its close association with ecosystems which have proven to be of only marginal value for other forms of economic activity. These include the upland regions of northern Thailand, which evince significant pockets of poverty and deprivation, and the coastal areas of southern Thailand which hitherto mainly have featured small fishing communities, coconut plantations and, on a larger scale, tin-mining. Coincidentally, such environments contain many of the features which attract international tourists to the country: long sandy beaches fringed by swaying palm trees, picturesque cool mountain ranges, interesting peoples with their rich cultural traditions, and so on. Whilst the development of tourism in such locations may be seen as desirable from the point of view of spreading economic development to peripheral and marginal locations, it is also responsible for exerting sometimes excessive pressure on what are in general very fragile and vulnerable ecological zones (see also Wong Poh-Poh, 1990).[2]

The present tendency for the infrastructure of tourism to be concentrated in a relatively small number of key tourism centres may restrict the spatial extent of environmental degradation, but this is traded off against the very intensive exploitation of natural environmental resources which occurs in these key locations. Where such development is carefully planned and controlled (e.g. restrictions of the expansion and style of buildings, measures to protect vulnerable locations), and with sufficient infrastructural investment (e.g. sewerage and refuse disposal systems), the environmental impact of tourism development may be minimised. Where, however, for reasons which will be discussed shortly, such safeguards are not forthcoming, not only will environmental degradation almost inevitably result, but this may also have the effect of pushing dissatisfied tourists (via equally disgruntled travel agencies) into new and hitherto unspoilt locations which, a few years later on, will undergo a similar destructive process of change.

The following short case study of the tiny island of Ko Samui, in the Gulf of Thailand near Surat Thani, provides an illustration of some of the environmental pressures which have been associated with the relatively unplanned and uncontrolled growth of tourism.

### Ko Samui: paradise lost?

An island of only some 250 square kilometres, Ko Samui will play host to a projected 1.1 million visitors annually by the end of the century. Yet little more than a decade ago Ko Samui was well off the beaten track for all but the most intrepid back-packing tourists who were willing to hitch a ride on a local fishing boat in order to enjoy the dramatic and unspoilt beauty of the island.[3] By 1987 this trickle of visitors had turned into a torrent, with around 250,000[4] people annually (*The Nation*, 20.12.90) enjoying the crystal clear azure waters and pure sandy beaches, the island's extensive coral reef systems with their rich marine life, the friendly locals and relaxed atmosphere.[5] There is little doubt, then, that the natural environment represents one of the island's principal resources as far as tourism is concerned.[6]

The phenomenal growth in tourism to the island has been facilitated by the introduction of a regular ferry service, frequent flights to a newly constructed airstrip, considerable extension and improvement of the road system, and the construction of more than 220 hotels and bungalows which line the beaches (*Bangkok Post*, 4.9.89). It has also been accompanied by the bars, restaurants, shops, entertainments, vehicle rental facilities, prostitution, and so on which are a familiar feature of many coastal resorts in Thailand today. Recognising the attractiveness of the island's natural environment, Ko Samui has been very vigorously promoted as a major tourism destination by both private sector firms and the Tourism Authority of Thailand. Big business has capitalised on the island's tourism potential. An important point in connection with the later discussion is that very little of this business is locally based. National and international firms have flocked to the island. As a result of the promotion programme, the clientele has started to change, with more affluent tourists joining the shoestring travellers who were principally responsible for 'discovering' the island's tourism potential. With this change in clientele has come further pressure for the construction of more up-market accommodation and recreational facilities.

Unfortunately, the very fragile coastal, marine and small island environment upon which tourism has been built has come under increasing pressure as a result of the largely uncontrolled, and hardly anticipated, tourism boom. The phenomenal amount of construction work which has taken place over the last decade or so has, in the main, proceeded unbridled by planning controls. Such building restrictions that exist have been largely ignored, often quite wilfully. As a result, the coastal landscape, so important an element of the aesthetic environment, has in places been changed quite dramatically. Clearly it would be impossible for the development of the island's tourism industry, with all its potential benefits for the local population, to have been accomplished without some quite fundamental changes. However, there is little doubt that the natural environment, upon which the industry has developed, has undergone irreversible changes as a result of the tourism boom. We must also question the extent to which the local people have benefited from the growth in tourism.

In addition to the above changes, others of a more sinister nature have taken place. The coral reefs and their associated marine life have come under considerable pressure from a number of sources. The scores of pleasure boats which take tourists to the coral have added pollution to the more direct impact of dropping anchor on the reefs (*The Nation*, 9.5.89). Scuba-diving and souvenir-hunting, both inside and outside formally organised parties, has caused considerable damage to the reefs.[8] So too has the massive volume of untreated effluent which is discharged into the sea from the island. The authorities have been unable to cope with anything more than a fraction of the island's rapidly increasing tourist population in respect of sewerage treatment and refuse disposal facilities. Although a survey conducted by the Technical and Training Division of the Tourism Authority of Thailand found no significant evidence of marine pollution resulting from the discharge of waste water into the sea, a newspaper report revealed that Ko Samui has the capacity to cope with only 25 per cent of the total amount of garbage created each day (ibid., 20.12.89). The remainder is either burned, buried or dumped at sea, with obvious consequences. The authorities are also finding it difficult to cope with the rapidly increasing demand for water on the island.

Rather late in the day, the Tourism Authority of Thailand, in conjunction with the National Environment Board, has sought to introduce a conservation plan for Ko Samui in which 63 development projects costing some 345 million Baht would commence in 1992, focusing on the improvement of public utilities (water supply, sewerage treatment, refuse disposal) and the preservation of the environment (ibid., 21.6.90). This figure compares with the more than 500 million Baht that tourists exchanged in cash and traveller's cheques at the island's bank in 1988 (ibid., 24.6.90), and the 3 million Baht which was received yearly in the early 1980s for the island's principal export to the mainland – coconuts (Cohen, 1982b, 194). The island people themselves have come together to form the Nature and Environment Conservation Group of Samui, which campaigns against pollution and destruction of natural resources such as the island's forest reserves (*Bangkok Post*, 8.9.89).

The structure plan for southern Thailand, which was produced by the Japan International Cooperation Agency (JICA) in 1989, in conjunction with the TAT, also pays particular attention to the need for the growth of tourism to be accompanied by quite stern and far-reaching conservation measures. The report pointed to the need for better coordination amongst government agencies which have overlapping responsibility for tourism and the environment (JICA, 1989, 7), adding that 'the government has an extremely important role to play in terms of legislative, monitoring, supervising and directing actions' (ibid., 19). The report also called for the designation of 'Marine and Shoreline Conservation Areas' on Phuket, Ko Samui and Ko Pha-ngan.[9]

Until such recommendations and planning objectives can be effectively implemented, the relatively uncontrolled growth of tourism on Ko Samui and elsewhere in the southern region will continue to exert considerable, perhaps irreversible, pressure on the natural environment – the principal resource upon which the industry has been built. There are already signs that the more discerning tourists are rejecting Ko Samui in favour of other hitherto 'undiscovered' islands which, a few years from now, will almost certainly go the same way as Ko Samui unless the government acts quickly and decisively. The case of Ko Samui is far from being unique or atypical in the broader Thai context.

An important question which underlies the negative effects of tourism on the natural environment, in Ko Samui and elsewhere, is 'how can this have been allowed to happen?' The following section aims to consider some of the factors which may help not only to answer this question but also to inform policy-making decisions aimed at ameliorating the negative effects of tourism on the natural environment.

## SEEKING AN EXPLANATION: SOME UNANSWERED QUESTIONS

Before proceeding to look at some of the issues which underlie the environmental effects of tourism, we ought at this stage to introduce two notes of caution. First, it is very difficult, and indeed not altogether desirable, to isolate the environmental effects of tourism from those of other processes of development and change. In multifunctional centres such as Bangkok tourism represents just one of a number of activities which are exerting pressure on the urban environment. In areas where tourism is perhaps the dominant activity, as in many coastal resorts, one can more safely point to the ways in which tourism is affecting the local area. Nonetheless, tourism represents just one of a number of forms of resource exploitation and economic activity which may be taking place simultaneously and contiguously. It may therefore be very difficult to draw up an action agenda for tackling the environmental effects of tourism in isolation from other forms of economic activity.

Second, it is very misleading to talk, as is often the case, of tourism and tourists as a homogeneous entity. Tourism in Thailand takes a wide variety of forms, drawing people from very diverse economic and social backgrounds, both from abroad and nearer to home. Motives for travel vary greatly, as do visitors' levels of knowledge about, interest in and concern for the socio-cultural and environmental features of the destination area. The term 'tourism' is often taken to be synonymous with 'holiday-making', whereas most accepted definitions include such phenomena as business travel, educational visits and family reunions (Murphy, 1985). Just as the characteristics of tourism vary considerably, so we might expect the effects of tourism, environmental and otherwise, to be equally variable.

In seeking to explain the negative environmental impact of tourism, and the relative prioritisation of environmental exploitation versus environmental conservation, there are a number of issues which need to be addressed.

## A question of management and planning

'It is not tourism, *per se*, that is destructive, but mismanaged and unmanaged tourism' (Hamilton, 1990). It is perhaps customary to blame the planners for the problems which result from the process of development. Certainly, they are far from being blameless: planning to off-set the environmental consequences of tourism should, in theory, be much more straightforward in newly developing centres of tourism, as in many parts of South-East Asia, than in those that have been longer established, where the environmental effects of tourism may first have become apparent.

Not only should it be possible to make a 'fresh start', with a more or less clean sheet of paper for the planner and a green-field site for the developer, both should also be able to approach their task armed with the considerable accumulated wisdom and land management techniques which have been developed by the recreation and leisure industries world-wide over a considerable period of time. Techniques of Environment Impact Assessment are very advanced and sophisticated, and there are a whole range of standards and criteria which can be employed in determining the potential carrying capacity of a proposed tourism centre. Armed with such standards and techniques, tourism *could* be made to exist symbiotically with nature.

There are also myriad techniques available for increasing the carrying capacity of tourism centres, such as through the development of purpose-built tourist resort complexes, investment in and careful design of tourism infrastructure, the construction of nature trails through areas of fragile flora and fauna, and so on. Thus, it is not necessarily the sheer volume of tourists which is causing environmental degradation, but the failure of planners and managers to anticipate and cater adequately for the large numbers of visitors who travel to newly developing tourist destinations (see Hitchcock, on Komodo Island in Chapter 16 of this volume). A number of factors may help to explain this situation

1  There may have been insufficient international communication and technology transfer in the fields of land and recreation management. Added to this may be the fact that land management techniques which have been developed for temperate regions are not necessarily applicable to tropical locations.
2  Thai planners may not adequately be trained in the skills and techniques of recreation management.
3  Planners and practitioners may lack the authority which is needed to enable them to enforce effectively environmental legislation, be it in connection with tourism or other forms of economic activity. Sriracha Charoenpanij shows how the Thai legal system may in some cases undermine planners' attempts to regulate economic expansion (Charoenpanij, 1988). Environmental standards may be set at unrealistically high levels, making compliance unlikely, or they may be too lax to stand much chance of preventing ecological damage. Penalties may be laughably low, principally because maximum fines are sometimes formally stipulated in environmental acts which are infrequently up-dated (e.g. the Public Health Act, 1941) giving wrongdoers little disincentive against breaking environmental laws (Charoenpanij, 1988, 471).
4  There is also frequently a lack of coordination, and a great deal of overlapping responsibility, between the various government departments and agencies under whose aegis environmental matters fall. Measures to control pollution in the eastern coastal resort of Pattaya, for example, have involved the National Environment Board, the Public Health Department, the Police Department, the Royal Irrigation Department, the Land Department, the Civil

Engineering Department, as well as the Pattaya City administration (Tourism Authority of Thailand, 1990). Only with the Improvement and Conservation of National Environmental Quality Act, promulgated as recently as 1975, has any meaningful provision been made for dealing with the problem of overlapping responsibility (Charoenpanij, 1988, 463–64).

5  The government may be insufficiently aware of the likely long-term effects of rapid tourism development on the natural environment. This is doubtful. Considerable pressure has been put on the government, via the media and through other channels, to act decisively to ameliorate the harmful effects of tourism on the natural environment. The government, through the Tourism Authority of Thailand, has responded positively, arranging a number of seminars and fora where practitioners, academics and local communities have had an opportunity to air grievances and contribute to the process of policy decision-making (*The Nation*, 17.7.90). The environment does appear to have been placed much further up the planning agenda as a result.

6  Finally, even though Thailand may, in international terms, constitute a relative newcomer to the tourism 'big league', it is of course naive to suggest that planners and developers are able to make a fresh start in the development of tourism centres. In the main they have been heavily preoccupied with reacting to problems as they have presented themselves, rather than anticipating and seeking to accommodate future tourism demand. They lack the resources, personnel and authority to do much more than chip away at the edges of the environmental nuisance resulting from tourism. Whilst the Thai government may have the authority to manipulate and control the actions of the larger organisations involved in the tourist industry, it has much less influence over the more informal, small-scale, fly-by-night enterprises which are a characteristic feature of most tourism centres, and which often represent the vanguard of the tourism industry in more remote and hitherto underdeveloped tourist locations. Also, whilst the custom-built tourist resort may represent the most effective means for restricting the environmental effect of tourism, not all tourists are happy to be crowded into such 'sterile' centres, quite far removed from the 'real' Thailand.

## A question of ownership

The ownership of the infrastructure of tourism (hotels, recreation facilities, etc.) may be of crucial importance in determining the extent to which environmental degradation occurs or is tolerated. It is seldom the perpetrators of environmental damage who suffer the direct consequences. The tourists, of course, may remain in one location for only a handful of days, and may decide not to return if they are not satisfied with the quality of the environment in that location. Alex Hamilton's notion (*Environment Guardian*, 10.8.90) – that it is in the industry's best interests to protect the environment – applies only where the owners and operators of the industry have a long-term commitment to remaining involved in tourism in a particular location Where there has been considerable local involvement in the development of the industry, we might expect people to demonstrate a clearer commitment to maintaining the quality of the natural environment than in instances where a large number of 'outsiders' have capitalised on the growth of the industry. Local inhabitants are not as free as outsiders to pack up and leave if environmental degradation reaches such a stage that it begins to have a negative impact on the industry. In the case of Ko Samui, as Kamnuan Somwongse, chairman of the Tourism Business Association, reports:

> most tourism business owners are outsiders who emigrated to the island after tourism boomed. Some local residents even pessimistically commented that business owners do not realize the importance of environment conservation because they just came to make profit. When the island is totally destroyed and cannot give benefits to them anymore, they will leave.
>
> (*The Nation*, 9.5.89)

Because of constraints on capital formation, expertise, entrepreneurship, awareness and influence amongst local populations in the more peripheral loci of tourism in Thailand (and in some other parts of South-East Asia[10]), we often find that the development of the industry has largely become the prerogative of outside capitalists and entrepreneurs (both domestic and foreign). Although, on the Ko Samui beach studied by Cohen in 1979, levels of local participation in the early development of the industry were quite high (Cohen, 1982b, 216–17), the more recent rapid expansion of the industry on the island has involved 'outsiders' to a much greater degree (similarly on the island of Phuket: Cohen, 1982b). Only some 20 per cent of Ko Samui islanders enjoy the benefits of employment in the tourism industry (*The Nation*, 20.12.89).

Although it is far from certain that the powerful, local entrepreneurial families who control part of the tourism industry on Ko Samui are any more conservation-minded than the outsiders, there is evidence from elsewhere in South-East Asia (the Philippines, for example) that, where local people have become more centrally involved in the development of tourism in their home areas (such as through 'tourism co-operatives'), many of the environmental and other side-effects of tourism have been considerably reduced (ibid., 9.5.89).

## A question of responsibility and attitude

In seeking to understand why the natural environment is being allowed to become degraded by tourism, we might briefly dwell on the attitudes of the people who are most centrally involved in the industry. It has been suggested that many members of the tourism business community on Ko Samui, for instance, see it as the government's responsibility, not theirs, to deal with environmental damage. Fly-tipping of refuse, because of the shortage and expense of formal systems of disposal, is rationalised by the government's failure to provide adequate facilities, and by the fact that tourism businesses pay taxes to the local authorities to enable them to deal with such problems:

> Some (businesspeople) don't think it's their duty to preserve the environment because they have a wrong idea that they pay taxes to the government. So it should be the government who should deal with all problems.
>
> (Kamnuan Somwongse, *The Nation*, 9.5.89)

Although there is little evidence to support such a theory, it may also be the case that the tourists themselves rationalise any harmful effects that their presence may have on the environment in terms of the considerable sums of money that they bring into the local economy.

## A question of awareness and concern

Because 'environmentalism' is still very much in its infancy in Thailand, the power of the environmental lobby is generally weak relative to the larger, better organised, longer established and arguably more influential business lobby. The situation, however, is changing very rapidly. The national (and international) outcry in the mid-1980s surrounding the proposed construction by the Electricity Generating Authority of Thailand (EGAT) of a dam across the Nam Choan river in Kanchanaburi province (which would have flooded some unique, and legally protected, wildlife reserves) is considered by many to have represented a watershed in terms of formal protests on environmental matters in Thailand. Active campaigning by groups from all levels of Thai society was successful ultimately in bringing about the cancellation of the project in March 1988. Since that time many more very vocal protests have been staged concerning such phenomena as illegal tree-felling in southern Thailand and illegal salt-mining in north-east Thailand. In both instances the principal protestors were people who had directly been affected, respectively, by devastating floods and the salinisation of water courses and fields. In the context of tourism, a number of local environmental organisations have also been established to raise the public's awareness of the environmental consequences of rapid and largely uncontrolled tourism development, including the Nature and Environment Conservation Group of (Ko) Samui and the Phuket Environmental Protection Club (*The Nation,* 23.3.91).

## A question of priority

Given the nature of many of Thailand's contemporary development problems (quite widespread poverty in peripheral rural areas, a lack of alternative sources of income in rural and coastal regions, limited diversification of local economies, and so on), one might understand the tendency to give the promotion of economic growth a higher priority than the imposition of environmental safeguards which, in some eyes, may be expected to restrict the pace of development. This is a rather short-sighted view, given first the possible longer-term consequences of neglecting the environment (particularly so in the case of tourism, where the natural environment is of such importance to the industry), and second given the rather questionable assumption that the fostering of economic growth through the promotion of tourism will help directly to alleviate problems such as rural poverty.

## A question of power

Finally, the thorny issue of corruption, patronage and vested interest must at least be mentioned as a possible contributor to the negative environmental effects of tourism development. Kamnuan Somwongse, chairman of the Tourism Business Association, has suggested a certain degree of 'eco-blindness' amongst various echelons of the business community on Ko Samui when it comes to making profits from tourism (*The Nation*, 9.5.89). Such a phenomenon, however unfortunate, pales into insignificance when one considers the extent to which powerful business interests may go to exploit loopholes in legislative provisions for environmental conservation, and shortcomings in law enforcement, to underpin their own vested interests. Set against a back-drop of both the self-indulgence of the greedy, and the self-preservation of the needy, the weakness of the conservation cause becomes all the more apparent.

## TOURISM AND THE ENVIRONMENT: TOWARDS A SUSTAINABLE FUTURE?

It may be quite some time before tourism destroys tourism in Thailand. Almost regardless of the ways in which the environment is exploited and manipulated to suit the needs of the tourism industry, people may be expected to continue to flock to Thailand in large numbers. This is partly because of the changing character of the tourism industry. With the continued growth of cheap excursion air fares and package holidays, mass tourism has displaced élite or specialist tourism as the predominant form of international tourism in Thailand. With increasing numbers of people seeking something 'different' from their annual holiday, and with more people possessing the financial means to enjoy Thailand's 'differentness', the country's position as one of South-East Asia's pre-eminent tourism destinations would appear reasonably assured in the short term (*ceteris paribus* – i.e. provided the country remains politically 'stable' and socially 'open').

A further factor in favour of a continued tourism boom is the power of the advertising and promotional media to attract new customers and, increasingly, to gloss over some of the harmful effects that their growing presence is having. In the context of the earlier discussion, the term 'paradise' is used liberally in the promotional literature for coastal locations like Ko Samui, particularly that which is produced by domestic and foreign tourism agencies. For the escapist, 'mass tourist' in particular, the concept of 'paradise' (definition: a state of bliss) is very much a relative one: a relaxed holiday by a palm-fringed sandy shore dampened by an azure sea may appear paradisaic compared with the places from which they are seeking to escape and, indeed, in comparison with the Costa del Sol and other centres of mass tourism which they previously may have experienced.

This is not to advocate a *laissez-faire* attitude towards tourism development, but to emphasise that the expansion of the tourism industry in Thailand and several other South-East Asian countries is quite likely to be sustained, at least in the short term, even though the natural environment is becoming despoiled as a consequence. There are many hitherto undeveloped areas to which the tourism industry might potentially spread, and as the more discerning tourists 'vote with their feet' against environmental despoilation so others will doubtless take their place.

However, the concept of 'sustainable development', or in the present context 'sustainable tourism', is concerned with more than this simple numbers game - keeping the customers rolling in and reasonably contented, if only because the yardsticks by which they judge environmental quality are already quite tarnished. It increasingly draws in questions of political economy, the distribution of wealth and opportunity, and the avariciousness of *laissez-faire* capitalism (see Redclift, 1987). It also takes a more long-term view of the impact of development on the environment: 'Sustainable development is development that meets the needs of the present without compromising the ability of future generations to meet their own needs' (World Commission on Environment and Development, 1987, 43). Environmentally sustainable forms of development must involve a high degree of 'saving' for the future, even if this means compromising economic efficiency and levels of profit in the short term (Brookfield, 1988). Moreover, 'the saving is required at all levels from the individual, through the state, to the international community' (ibid., 133).

In the longer term, tourism (ably assisted, it should be said, by other media of economic, social and cultural change) will destroy tourism in Thailand, unless certain safeguards are instituted. These safeguards must consist, first, of scientific, technological and managerial measures to protect the environment, such as proper investment in infrastructure, restricted access to fragile ecosystems, and forward planning in the design and construction of tourism centres.

However, these environmental safeguards may be quite useless until other, more fundamental issues are addressed. Thailand's capacity to support sustainable tourism is limited by structural and sectoral weaknesses in the country's development to which the rapid exploitation of tourism resources is seen as a partial solution. The 'pressure of production' (ibid., 134), and the rationalisation of its environmental consequences, becomes all the more intense in the face of peristent poverty in peripheral rural areas.

For sustainable development to become a reality it is necessary for the livelihoods of the poor to be given priority, but how can this priority be pursued at the local level while the effects of international development systematically 'marginalizes' them?

(Redclift, 1987, 36)

Thus, Thailand's capacity to confront structural and distributional problems in an environmentally benign manner would appear to be further restricted by the country's relatively weak and dependent position in the international economy. Tourism is a case in point: not only is there growing international pressure from the demand side of the industry, which the government finds hard to withstand, but the heavy involvement of transnational corporations in the country's tourism industry also leaves at least one of the government's hands tied behind its back. Tourism might thus be seen as an almost irresistible force coming up against, in Thailand, a relatively compliant and acquiescent object.

A similar line of argument can be developed in connection with the domestic scene. Tourism cannot be isolated from the broader economic, social and political environment within which 'decisions against nature' are being made: 'consideration of natural environmental factors cannot be separated from socio-economic and aesthetic considerations in the actual practice of envrionmental planning' (Inskeep, 1987, 121). Thai development strategies place heavy emphasis on facilitating economic growth, which in reality appears to receive a much higher priority than the pursuit of social and distributive justice. Set against this backdrop, policy prescriptions in relation to tourism and the environment, however laudable, are subject to severe constraints in practice.

With sufficient political resolve Thailand should be capable of, and indeed is already introducing, technological and managerial measures which may underpin a greater harmony between economic growth and the environment, and which may thus support the sustainability of the tourism industry in the short term. However, it is much harder to envisage Thailand breaking away from, or modifying its position in, the world economy, not least in the context of such an internationalised industry as tourism. And yet, as Redclift notes, 'sustainable development options . . . can only be achieved through political changes at the local, national and international level' (Redclift, 1987, 36).

Given the foregoing, it is even more difficult to see how tourism might be used as a *positive* force in conserving nature and the environment (Inskeep, 1987). Edward Inskeep has suggested that greater emphasis should be placed on 'special interest tourism' (wildlife safaris, bird-watching holidays, and so on) as a way of attracting the kinds of tourists who are themselves concerned for the conservation of natural habitats. Alternatively, selective tourism marketing techniques can be applied 'in order to attract environmentally conscious tourists who will show respect for tourism environments and be conservation-minded in their use of them' (ibid., 1987, 122).

Additionally, greater attention should be paid to educating guests and hosts alike, through such media as promotional brochures and training courses, in the modes of conduct which might be considered appropriate to the environmental and cultural codes of the tourist destination area. There may thus be a strong case for promoting 'alternative' forms of tourism, such as 'eco-tourism', as a way of engendering a greater harmony between people and nature through tourism (although note the criticism of 'alternative tourism' in the introductory chapter of this volume). Unfortunately, such principles would appear to be at variance with the economic arguments in favour of mass tourism. On the other hand, 'rather than contrasting alternative with "mass" tourism, policy-makers concerned with tourism development should strive to make the conventional more sustainable' (de Kadt, 1990, i).

'Sustainable development' is not anti-development, but advocates a form of development which is more in tune with the needs of environmental conservation than has generally been the case hitherto. In Thailand, where the environment represents such an important 'natural resource' for tourism, a blatant disregard for the environmental consequences of rapid tourism development in pursuit of short-term economic rewards is undoubtedly short-sighted. This chapter hopefully has shown that, in seeking to underpin the sustainability of Thailand's tourism industry in the longer term, there are a number of quite fundamental political, structural, distributional and attitudinal issues which must first be addressed. In addressing these issues, planners might be guided by the notion that 'poverty is the greatest pollution' (Brookfield, 1988, 126).

## NOTES

1 I would like to express my thanks to the Ecumenical Coalition on Third World Tourism in Bangkok for providing many of the newspaper cuttings and other sources from which the following case studies are developed. Thanks also to Pauline Kh'ng for her assistance in unearthing some references on the environmental impact of tourism.
2 Of course, tourism also contributes quite significantly to environmental problems in the country's main economic centres and cities (e.g. Bangkok-

Central Region and Chiang Mai), such as air and noise pollution, traffic congestion, increased energy demand and the associated burning of fossil fuels, sewerage and refuse disposal difficulties, and so on.

3  According to Cohen, the first beach 'resort' (consisting of a row of cabins, later replaced by bamboo huts) was opened in 1976 (Cohen, 1982b, 195–96). By the early 1980s there were 25 such resorts.

4  According to one report, some 480,000 tourists arrived on Ko Samui in 1988 (*Bangkok Post*, 4.9.89).

5  A point which is often overlooked, but which may be of significance in connection with the impact of tourism, is that the majority of tourists to Ko Samui are in fact Thai, not foreign.

6  Fishing and the tending of coconut groves were the island's main economic activities before the advent of tourism, and continue today where they have not been displaced or rendered unprofitable by tourism.

7  The reefs are important in protecting the beaches from erosion, especially during the typhoon season. They also support a great diversity of marine life which is itself important for the local economy and the tourism industry itself.

8  It should also be pointed out that the phenomenon of illegal dynamite-fishing around the coral reefs by locals does little to help with the conservation of this very vulnerable ecosystem.

9  The JICA report also outlined plans for a substantial expansion of the tourism industry in southern Thailand over the next decade or so. It remains to be seen whether the two broad objectives – exploitation and conservation – can both be achieved.

10  Capital and human resource constraints appear to be less of a problem in hindering local involvement in the tourism industry in Indonesia.

# 16 Dragon tourism in Komodo, eastern Indonesia[1]

*Michael Hitchcock*

## INTRODUCTION

During the second half of the twentieth century it became increasingly apparent to many scientists and park managers in Europe and the USA that in order to survive wildlife reserves must bring in revenue (Joffe, 1969). It was argued that the monies raised would not only help cover the overheads of these establishments, but would also help stave off demands for other kinds of commercial exploitation, which might be more environmentally detrimental. A wide variety of means of generating income have been tried – ranging from hunting to small-scale farming – and these have usually been tightly regulated by the various park authorities. Tourism, however, has emerged as one of the most popular sources of finance, not least because it is widely regarded by conservationists as being one of the more eco-friendly industries, especially when set against such interests as logging and mining.

The above concerns are of particular relevance to the Republic of Indonesia which maintains more wildlife reserves than any other South-East Asian nation. As a developing nation Indonesia has limited funds to devote to its conservation effort, although it is responsible for internationally renowned parks, such as Ujung Kulon in Java and Komodo in eastern Indonesia, as well as a large number of less well-known reserves. Throughout the 1980s Indonesia expanded its tourism industry and aimed at a target of 1 million visitors per year by the end of 1987 (Bagus, 1987, 169). The republic has also sought to increase its share, which stood at 8.7 per cent in 1987, of the lucrative ASEAN tourist market (ibid.). Indonesia has been strongly involved in the coordinated ASEAN approach to tourism and 1991 was designated Visit Indonesia Year. Ecological tourism has played an important part in these developments, not least because Indonesia's natural environment is especially attractive to some of the country's high-spending visitors, particularly the Japanese (cf. Moeran, 1983).

This chapter deals with the development of tourism in the 1980s in the Komodo National Park. It traces the implementation of a management plan that was prepared for the Indonesian government by the UNDP and the FAO. Attention is paid to the impact these developments have had upon a small-scale society within the park and examines some of the problems these people have experienced in coping with tourism. In particular it deals with the question of how the priorities of wildlife conservation and national development can be set against the needs of distinctive ethnic minorities.

The Komodo National Park is located between the islands of Sumbawa and Flores in the eastern Indonesian province of Nusa Tenggara Timur (NTT). The park forms part of the regency at Manggarai and comprises the islands of Komodo, Padar and Rinca. With many rare plant and animal species, the reserve has a unique ecosystem and is of great scientific interest. Komodo is best known as the home of the giant lizard, *Varanus komodoensis*, which is popularly referred to as the 'Komodo dragon'. The lizard is the world's largest land-dwelling reptile, though it is a good swimmer and is sometimes sighted outside the national park. It has powerful jaws, a long tail and can grow to around 3 metres in length. In recognition of Komodo's international significance the Indonesian authorities made the reserve into a national park in 1978, though the lizards themselves have been protected by various kinds of legislation since the early twentieth century.

The scientific community first became aware of the existence of the giant lizard through the work of P. A. Ouwens, the curator of the Zoological Museum in Bogor. Ouwens learned of the whereabouts of the 'dragon' from J. K. H. van Steyn van Hensbroek, an officer serving in the army at the Netherlands East Indies. A description based on collected specimens was published by Ouwens in 1912 in the *Bulletin du Jardin Botanique de Buitenzorg*, and on realising that the lizard's habitat was restricted to the Komodo region, the Netherlands Indies Society for the Protection of Nature tried to introduce conservation measures. The society, which was founded in 1912, approached the Sultan of Bima, the ruler of Komodo and the surrounding area. As a result of this application the Sultan issued a decree prohibiting the hunting and capture of the giant lizard, though the legislation could be enforced only within the Sultanate. In 1926 another decree was issued by the authorities in Manggarai in western Flores; but this did not become effective until Manggarai and Komodo were removed from Bimanese jurisdiction in 1930 by the colonial government. The Resident of Timor, who had taken responsibility for Komodo and

Flores, later ratified the second decree and it became applicable throughout the Netherlands East Indies (Blower *et al.*, 1977, 6).

Some idea of the effectiveness of the early examples of conservation law in a remote part of Indonesia can be deduced from the accounts of travellers and scientists who visited the reserve. Douglas Burden, for example, who was collecting on behalf of the American Museum of Natural History before the regulations were strengthened, describes the acquisition of fourteen lizards, two of which were alive (Burden, 1927, 216). In contrast, Lady Broughton, who sailed to Komodo several years later on Lord Moyne's yacht the *Rosaura*, was permitted by the authorities to take only three out of the seven 'dragons' that she and her party had trapped. Lady Broughton, however, was able to confirm the hypothesis that the giant lizards were deaf by the simple expedient of discharging a shotgun near some of these animals (Broughton, 1936, 321). After independence the Indonesian government continued to enforce the legislation with, it would appear, equal vigour. David Attenborough, for instance, who like the *Rosaura* group was collecting on behalf of London Zoo, was obliged to release the specimen that he had caught (Attenborough, 1959, 160).

Although scientists learned of the existence of *Varanus komodoensis* only in the early twentieth century, the giant lizards were well known to local populations. The Komodo islanders call these animals *ora*, whereas their neighbours in eastern Sumbawa refer to them as *mbou*, though the term 'Komodo' is used in Bima town, especially when talking to tourists. Given their dramatic appearance, it is not surprising that there is a certain amount of local folklore regarding these creatures. The inhabitants of Komodo, for example, have long lived in close proximity to the lizard and there are various myths surrounding their relationship with them. According to I Gusti Ngurah Bagus, an anthropologist, it is said that the dragons are the islanders' siblings and that, if one of these animals is injured, then its relatives, who have taken the form of human beings, will also become ill (Bagus, 1987, 175). The Bimanese claim that the giant lizards used to live in Sumbawa until they were driven out by a local folk hero known as La Hami.[2] Dragon imagery also features in the legend of the foundation of the Bimanese state, in which a prince marries a Naga princess. The latter creature, however, belongs to the wider Asian tradition and need not necessarily be linked to Komodo. Nevertheless, it has been suggested that some of the dragon mythology of the Far East was inspired by travellers' accounts of the giant lizard (Broughton, 1936, 321). Without the relevant documentary evidence one can only speculate that the *ora*, with its long tail and flickering tongue, was transformed into a fire-breathing dragon by story-tellers.

## ENVIRONMENT AND PEOPLE

The rugged islands of Komodo, Padar and Rinca are separated by channels with strong tidal currents. As a result of the continual interchange of water between the Flores Sea and the Savu Sea, the seas around the national park have a high degree of oxygenation and are among the richest in the world (Blower *et al.*, 1977, 16). There is abundant plankton and the islands lie close to migratory routes for whales, blue and sperm whales being among those seen in the vicinity. In addition to numerous varieties of sharks, ten species of dolphin have been recorded, and though the dugong is said to be found in these waters it is probably rare (ibid.).

Komodo has a dry maritime environment and is covered in monsoon forests and open savannah. The climate is influenced to a lesser degree by the wet north-west monsoon than, for instance, Java and to a much greater extent by the dry south-east winds. Rainfall, therefore, tends to be concentrated between November and April, and there is a pronounced dry season from May to October. Although there are no meteorological data available for the reserve, Bagus has provided estimates based on data obtained in Sapé (50 kilometres west of Komodo) and Labuhanbajo (40 kilometres east of Komodo). It is reasonable to assume that the average is around 800–1,000 millimetres per annum (Bagus, 1987, 173).

The national park is situated to the east of the Wallace Line and belongs to a transitional zone lying between Australia and Asia. Wildlife associated with both continental regions is, therefore, found in the reserve. Wild pigs, feral buffalo and Timor deer (*Cervus timorensis*) forage in the interior, while crab-eating macaques live at the edge of the woodland (Blower *et al.*, 1977, 17). Jungle fowl and sulphur-crested cockatoos can be seen in the forests, as well as the monopod, which buries its eggs in huge mounds of leaves and twigs. In addition to the 'dragons', there are many kinds of reptiles, including green pit vipers that live in the rafters of local houses (Burden, 1927, 255). Wildlife is equally abundant along the coastline, where there are sea eagles, estuarine crocodiles and giant turtles.

In spite of the diversity of the wildlife, the park is sparsely populated in human terms, largely because of the scarcity of water. During the dry season streambeds near the coasts often dry up, though some water can be obtained by digging. There are also small rivers and springs in the interior of Komodo, though these are mainly restricted to the upper slopes of Arab mountain and Satalibo mountain (Blower *et al.*, 1977, 12). Local villages, therefore, are located close to the few reasonably reliable sources of fresh water, and the two main settlements are Kampung Komodo and Kampung Rinca. The villages hug the shoreline and comprise wooden framed houses with bamboo screens and thatched or corrugated iron roofs.

Very little is known about the early history of the Komodo islanders, though some grave sites and artefacts have been found. Bagus has suggested that the present inhabitants of the national park do not have a very extensive history in the area, and that Komodo may have been used only on an occasional basis in the past when water supplies were more abundant than they are today (Bagus, 1987, 175). Until 1930, when the Dutch colonial authorities placed Komodo under the jurisdiction of their representative in Timor, the islanders were technically subjects of the Sultan of Bima. Komodo lies strategically between Bima and its former territories in Manggarai in Flores, though it does not appear to have been closely integrated into the Sultanate. Komodo's population was probably always quite small and Bimanese rule amounted to little more than periodic demands for tribute. The Sultanate also does not appear to have been able to defend Komodo from marauders and there is a report of a raid in the mid-nineteenth century (Zollinger, 1856, 243). So remote was Komodo, in the eyes of the Bimanese court, that it was regarded as a place of exile, though it is not clear how many people were banished to the island. In spite of its isolation from the capital, Komodo was drawn into Bimanese trading networks and Bimanese is one of the languages spoken by the inhabitants of the national park. Like the Bimanese the Komodo islanders profess Islam, though the latter live in the Christian-dominated province of NTT.

In addition to the paucity of historical sources regarding Komodo, there was until the last decade a lack of detailed ethno-linguistic data. This situation changed radically with the publication of Jilis Verheijen's *Komodo: Het Eiland, Het Volk en de Taal* in 1982 since it revealed the existence of a hitherto unrecorded ethnic group, the Ata Modo. Verheijen's study has shown that, although the language of the Ata Modo contains many Bimanese loanwords, it is a separate language within the Bima-Sumba group. It also contains many Manggarai words and lexical affinities between Komodo and the eastern half of Sumba have been noted by Gregory Forth (1983, 57). Not only is the Komodo language distinctive, but so is their social organisation. Interestingly, Verheijen has suggested that marriage in

Komodo is permitted with all four types of cousin, there being only a weak preference for the daughter of the prospective groom's mother's brother. There is also some evidence that clans are known on the island and that special powers are inherited down the female line. In many respects the islanders have much in common with the neighbouring Manggarai and the terms used in classifying kinsmen are similar (ibid.).

The Komodo islanders' traditional way of life is well adapted to local conditions, which can be quite variable depending on the rainfall. Their mixed economy includes some cultivation and animal husbandry, hunting and fishing, and the collection of woodland products. One of the islanders' most important staples is sago, which is obtained from the starchy core of the *gebang* palm. Canoes are used to bring home sections of the palm, which grow in various locations throughout the national park (Verheijen, 1982, 10). A sugar palm, *Arenga pinnata*, is also used as a source of starch in times of scarcity, as well as a tree belonging to the genus *Cycas*. Bananas, maize, cassava and sweet potato are grown near Kampung Komodo and, though rice is esteemed, it has to be imported from neighbouring Bima and is consequently quite expensive.[3] Other garden produce includes pumpkins, watermelons and papaya. Small domestic fowl forage around the houses, while goats are kept on small off-shore islands to protect them from the giant lizards (Blower *et al.*, 1977, 24).

Hunting has long been a mainstay of the local economy and Blower *et al.* have suggested that the extensive areas of fire climax grassland on the island were 'probably due to deliberate burning for hunting purposes' (ibid., 25). The main quarry is deer, a source of both food and hides, and during the inter war years hides were exported, sometimes at a rate of around two hundred per year (ibid., 1978, 25, citing Hoogerwerf, 1954). The 'Komodo dragon' has never been extensively hunted for commercial reasons, perhaps because its skin, unlike that of the common monitor lizard, has little financial value. It is also possible that the giant lizard was never hunted by the islanders for cultural reasons and Bagus has suggested that the Ata Modo believe that they have a kinship link with the animal (1987, 175). There is some evidence, however, that the Chinese valued the fat in the 'dragon's' tail on account of its medicinal value. According to colonial sources, a group of Chinese illegally killed about a 100 giant lizards in 1926, 65 of which were later confiscated by the authorities (Blower *et al.*, 1977, 25).

A variety of woodland products are also exported by the islanders. Tamarind, for example, is picked during the dry season and is either shipped by canoe or is taken overland to Kampung Komodo, from where it is sent to Sumbawa and other destinations. Edible nests of swiftlets, which fetch high prices in urban centres, are found in caves within the reserve.

Virtually the whole male population of Komodo is involved in fishing and the collection of marine products. They use cast nets, scoop nets and handlines, and set up traps in shallow water. They fish from outrigger canoes and fishing platforms, *bagan*, and use pressure lamps at night to attract their prey. Dolphins are, in theory, protected, though they are sometimes harpooned; turtles are captured and exported to Bali (ibid., 24). Squid are caught in Liang Bay and shellfish are gathered along the coast. Shrimps may be pounded in long wooden mortars to make *terasi*, the Indonesian seafood paste. Both sun-dried and salted fish are exported from Komodo, though the catch does not fetch a good price in Bima market if it is too heavily salted. Sea grass (*Zostera* sp) is harvested for sale to Japan for pharmaceutical purposes; but because the plants are pulled up by their roots the park authorities have tried to curtail this activity (ibid., 34). Marine products such as bêche-de-mer and agar-agar, a gelatin made from seaweed, are obtained around Komodo.

The Komodo islanders themselves do not necessarily profit greatly from fishing since many are indebted to local skippers. Bagus, for example, mentions a recent study which shows how these credit arrangements, known as *ijon*, hamper local development (Bagus, 1987, 174–75). Furthermore, not all the fishermen in the national park are Komodo islanders, since seafarers from other Indonesian regions make use of these waters. Bagus has, for example, published a breakdown of ethnic groups within the reserve which shows that the indigenous inhabitants comprise a mere 18.4 per cent of the population. They are outnumbered by maritime groups such as the Bajo (33.3 per cent) and Bugis (27.6 per cent), though it remains uncertain whether or not these groups are made up of temporary residents (Bagus, 1987, 175). It is also not clear how these statistics were compiled and the figures are expressed only in terms of percentages. Certain marine activities always seem to have been beyond the scope of the local people, presumably because they lack both resources and good trading networks. Blower *et al.*, for example, mentioned a Chinese company in the 1970s which was engaged in shipping mother-of-pearl and shells to Ujung Pandang and thence to Korea (Blower *et al.*, 1977, 24). From time to time there are reports from Komodo of pearl divers operating from ships owned by Chinese Indonesians or even Japanese, but these are difficult to verify.

## THE DEVELOPMENT OF TOURISM

A national park was established in Komodo to protect its environment for scientific purposes. To assist in the implementation of this initiative, a management plan was drawn up by a multinational team of experts under the auspices of the United Nations. The authors of the plan organised field research in the reserve and were involved in lengthy negotiations with the Indonesian authorities. The scientists realised that the agricultural potential of the reserve was limited and that it would make an unsuitable destination for settlers from more densely populated islands under Indonesia's transmigration scheme (Blower *et al.*, 1977, 30). The team appreciated that in order to survive the national park must bring in revenue, not least because it was located in one of the country's most underdeveloped regions. It was proposed, therefore, that tourism should be introduced to protect the reserve from the kinds of commercial exploitation that might be environmentally destructive and to help develop the local economy.

In addition to providing a detailed account of the equipment and personnel that would be needed to maintain the park, the management plan made a series of proposals concerning visitor services. It was suggested that although tourists should not be too restricted, they should be encouraged to make use of signposted nature trails near to Liang Bay, thereby reducing their impact on the environment. When travelling further afield it was envisaged that the tourists would be accompanied by guides. The scientists proposed building hides so that visitors would be able to see the giant lizards within their natural habitat. They were particularly anxious to curtail the use of goats as bait to attract the lizards, a practice they described as 'aesthetically unattractive' and 'artificial' (ibid., 44). The scientists were concerned that the lizards might lose their natural fear of human beings and become dangerous. Emphasis was placed on the need to employ some English-speaking guides and plans for a visitor centre within the park were included. Many of the recommendations were ecologically sensitive, such as the need to build a 'tourist village' with local materials and the imposition of a ceiling of 40 visitors at any one time, rising to 80 as the facilities improved. But they also proposed building an airstrip within the park so that it could be connected to Bali, a major tourist centre, by a regular air service (ibid.).

Although the authors of the management plant were primarily scientists interested in the zoology and botany of Komodo, they also made various proposals that would have an impact on the lives of the islanders. They recommended that cultivation should be restricted to the village enclaves outlined in the plan and that designated conservation areas should be established. It was anticipated that the islanders would be able to continue fishing, but that some of their other traditional activities, such as hunting and tree felling, would be regulated. The scientists hoped that the islanders would eventually become engaged in the work of the park and would find employment as guides, boatmen, labourers and hotel workers. Some islanders, it was suggested, could become involved in making handicrafts for sale to tourists (ibid., 37). Bagus later reiterated the idea that tourism could be used to improve the economic prosperity of the Komodo islanders, though he did not go into detail (Bagus, 1987, 175).

In the management plan concern was expressed about the size of the human population within the park. While the authors of the report argued that Kampung Komodo and Kampung Rinca should be allowed to remain in the reserve, they did recommend relocating three other settlements. The villages in question were on the island of Rinca and the scientists believed that they were recently established communities, though it is not clear how they reached that conclusion (Blower, *et al.*, 1977, 37). The ethnic affiliation of the inhabitants of the villages also remains uncertain and it is unclear whether or not they were ever consulted about these proposals. The scientists did, however, suggest that, in the event of resettlement, the villagers should be awarded compensation, possibly in the form of land on the coastline of neighbouring Flores. The introduction of a registration scheme to prevent further immigration was proposed and the scientists argued that the only new buildings that should be permitted within the reserve should be those that replaced existing houses (ibid.).

Komodo was well known to the outside world long before it achieved the status of a national park, though it is not clear precisely when it became a major tourist destination. *National Geographic*, for instance, included features on Komodo in the 1920s (Burden, 1927) and 1930s (Broughton, 1936), and in the 1950s the reserve was brought to a wide readership through the work of Ton Schilling (1957) and David Attenborough (1959). Komodo appeared for a third time in *National Geographic* in an account of a journey through eastern Indonesia in an amphibious vehicle (Schreider and Schreider, 1962). By the 1970s Komodo was being mentioned in popular guidebooks, though the tourist facilities within the reserve were still very basic. A *losman* (traditional Indonesian guesthouse) is, for example, referred to in the *Indonesia Handbook* (Dalton, 1978, 242); however, at the time of my visit in 1981 this amounted to no more than a small brick building divided into two rooms.

Although few of the tourist developments envisaged by the authors of the Komodo management plan had taken place by the end of the 1970s, the situation began to change rapidly during the next decade. Eastern Indonesia, hitherto one of the country's most inaccessible regions, became more closely integrated into the national mainstream. By 1980, for example, a telephone system had been installed in neighbouring Bima, which provided a long-distance service of somewhat variable quality through a series of microwave relays (Just, 1986, 37). In the following year the overland route to Komodo was improved by the completion of the highway across Sumbawa linking the harbours of Sapé and Alas. The Indonesian Directorate General of Tourism also began to investigate the possibility of upgrading the existing, though infrequent, ferry service between Bali and Komodo through the introduction of special cruise ships. Initially, however, it was thought that the sea route would be unattractive to visitors on package holidays of limited duration and the authorities concentrated on improving the air services. The airstrip proposed by the national park planners was not built, though a piece of land was cleared so that helicopters could land on Komodo. Most airborne visitors, however, continued to make use of local ferries after landing in either western Flores or eastern Sumbawa. Because of the time factor little enthusiasm was shown by the tourist authorities in the overland route, though this was later promoted as being suitable for young travellers with limited means and a sense of adventure. Eventually the potential of cruise ships was recognised by the authorities and by the mid 1980s all three principal routes were in constant use by visitors to Komodo. A new ferry service, which greatly reduced the travelling time between Sapé harbour and Komodo was also introduced and the national park authorities acquired a launch to take visitors to Padar and Rinca.

Much of the park's infrastructure was upgraded in the 1980s. Two small hostels – each divided into nine compartments – were built, along with a cafeteria and information centre (Jonathan Agranoff, personal communication). In accordance with the management plant these new developments were located as far away as possible from Kampung Komodo to avoid disrupting the local population. This socially-sensitive decision, however, proved to be quite expensive since the island's water supplies were limited and many metres of new pipes had to be installed in order to bring water to the tourist enclave. The number of visitors also rose steadily towards the end of the 1980s and began to exceed the quota recommended by the planners, placing a strain on the already overstretched resources.

## TOURISM AND THE KOMODO ISLANDERS

Generally speaking, the strategies proposed by the authors of the management plan have been adhered to and the Komodo National Park is undoubtedly a success. The establishment of the reserve not only helped to conserve a unique ecosystem, but it also provided an important boost, through tourism, for both the national and provincial economies. Locally run hotels, shops, restaurants and transport companies have all benefited from their proximity to an internationally renowned wildlife reserve. Although the local authorities do not publish any statistics regarding the people employed either directly or indirectly through tourism, the numbers are probably quite substantial. Partly as a result of the introduction of tourism local communications have been improved and this has also helped to develop the regional economy. But with regard to the small-scale populations of eastern Indonesia, particularly the Komodo islanders, the growth of tourism has been a mixed blessing. Overlooked by the authorities and lacking the appropriate skills and education, the islanders have been unable to participate in the new developments.

Although the Komodo islanders have had to accept the restrictions imposed on them by the park's managers and share their water with the new hostels, they have not benefited from tourism in the ways envisaged by the authors of the management plan. In common with demographic trends throughout Indonesia the population of Komodo grew rapidly in the 1980s; but the number of jobs generated by the reserve could not keep pace with the rising number of people coming on to the job market. Ideally this should have been taken into account by the planners; they were, however, primarily concerned with environmental conservation rather than the needs of the local population. Admittedly the planners had hoped to stave off some of these problems by resettling several villages outside the reserve, but the Indonesian authorities have yet to act on these recommendations. Although it remains unclear whether or not the local government intends to implement these proposals, it is possible that they are unwilling to take any action that offers no immediate economic advantage. When viewed from the perspective of the province as a whole the recommendations may not appear to be especially attractive since they simply involve relocating poor populations between equally economically depressed regions.

In accordance with the management plan some **Komodo islanders did secure employment within the national park, though they were largely restricted to unskilled posts. The local people were unable to** apply for the better-paid administrative and scientific posts which became available because very few of them were educated beyond the elementary level.[4] Islanders who wish to progress to high school and beyond have to study in neighbouring Bima, which few of them can afford. Trained personnel, therefore, have been brought in from elsewhere in Indonesia to run the park.

The jobs issue became critical not only because of the rising population, but also because the islanders were drawn into the monetary economy without the appropriate skills. This seems to have occurred for a number of reasons, some of which can be linked to the development of tourism. First, the islanders were prevented by the authorities from bringing more land under cultivation and this led to a growing dependence on imported food, which had to be paid for in cash. Second, prices rose in Komodo as the local economy became geared to the needs of foreign visitors. Third, the islanders did not become involved in making handicrafts for tourists, as was proposed by the planners, because they lacked a strong craft tradition, having obtained the goods they needed in the past through trade with the Bimanese.[5] The generalist skills of the Komodo islanders are well suited to local conditions and, unlike neighbouring Bima, there are hardly any specialist artisans. Fourth, the **inhabitants of Komodo had insufficient capital to invest in the small businesses associated with tourism, such as the ferry service from Sapé harbour, which was introduced by a Balinese entrepreneur (Jonathan Agranoff, personal communication).** These factors may partially explain the indebtedness of the islanders noted by Bagus (1987, 174–75).

Aside from the limited employment opportunities provided by the national park, the islanders have gained little in economic terms through tourism. Curiously, one of the major sources of income remains the sale of goats for use as bait, though this is one of the practices which the planners had hoped to discourage. This is cause for concern since it remains unknown what effect the use of bait is having on the behaviour of the giant lizards in their natural habitat. Furthermore, there is evidence that some visitors, in common with the authors of the management plan, find this practice artificial and ecologically suspect; in the long term this may reduce Komodo's attractiveness as a tourist destination. Given the low standard of living it seems unlikely that the park authorities will be able to curtail this activity, unless alternative means of making a living can be found.

Clearly both the provincial authorities and the managers of the national park are presented with a series of intractable problems when trying to counterbalance the needs of the local economy, environmental conservation and the cultural rights of the Komodo islanders. Closing down the tourism industry is not a realistic option given the number of jobs, both locally and nationally, that depend on the reserve. Resettlement of the Komodo islanders might also prove to be problematic, not least because of the limited availability of suitable land within the province. Another consideration is the fact that the Ata Modo in particular are well adapted to the conditions on Komodo and it would probably be difficult for them to adjust readily to life elsewhere. In the circumstances it might be more realistic to involve the islanders more fully in debates about their future and the future of the national park. Perhaps a percentage of the revenues derived from tourism could be devoted to training the islanders so that they can participate more readily in the industry. Administrative, linguistic and craft skills are priorities. In view of their close relationship with the environment the islanders themselves could conceivably be able to suggest ways of diversifying the local economy that are not ecologically harmful. A starting point would be to build on skills that already exist. Revitalising the fishing industry might turn out to be a workable option providing steps were taken to help resolve the idebtedness of the islanders. Whatever the outcome, adherence to the tenets of both national and provincial administrations is not an option. Neither is overreliance on a management plan, despite its merit, which is now over a decade old.

## NOTES

1 I am especially grateful to Prof. Dr I Gusti Ngurah Bagus, Jonathan Agranoff, Anton Fernhout and Janet Cochrane for their help in preparing this chapter. Thanks are also due to the Canadian International Development Association. The research was funded by the Economic and Social Research Council and the British Academy, and permits were granted by Lembaga Ilma Pengetahuan Indonesia.

2 The legend of La Hami is known in the Dompu regency of Sumbawa Island. In the story the child of a rajah is swapped by a minister and then is left in the forest. Local people bring up the prince who becomes an accomplished hunter. The rajah later encounters the young man in the forest and asks who he is. La Hami kills a giant serpent which is terrorising the district of Sanggar. The young man gives the serpent's head to the lord of Sanggar who then takes it to the rajah, falsely claiming that he did the deed. Later on La Hami appears and is identified as the rightful slayer of the serpent and is offered the hand of a princess in marriage. La Hami continues to work as a hunter and eventually drives out all the giant lizards from eastern Sumbawa.

3 According to Jonathan Agranoff the grains of rice are often cracked and damaged by the time they reach Komodo.

4 According to Jonathan Agranoff schooling is available in Komodo only as far as Grade 3 SMP.
5 According to Janet Cochrane some Komodo islanders have begun carving wooden models of the giant lizard for sale to tourists.

# 17 Tourism and conservation in Indonesia and Malaysia

*Janet Cochrane*

In industrialised countries, the establishment and continued existence of national parks and other conservation areas is justified in terms of their role in protecting natural ecosystems which would otherwise be altered by the pressures of industrial or agricultural development. It is also generally considered that protected areas add to the spiritual quality of life in an industrialised country, and one way in which they do this is by providing a recreational facility for the population of such countries.

In developing countries, the aim of protecting natural ecosystems is rarely sufficient to ensure that large areas of land will never be used for production. National parks have to be justified in terms of the economic benefits they will provide. The main benefits are usually cited as increasing the government's foreign exchange earnings through attracting foreign visitors or extending their length of stay, and the provision of local employment opportunities in rural areas through the diversification of tourism away from urban or beach resorts. If these economic benefits are great enough, it is expected that the political motivation to legislate for and enforce protection of the national parks will increase, while at the same time the need of the population surrounding the national park to rely on it for fuelwood and food will diminish. Another hope sometimes expressed is that the parks will both foster an awareness of conservation issues amongst the domestic population and serve their increasing desire to enjoy their leisure time in natural surroundings (National Conservation Plan for Indonesia, 1982).

It is arguable that these contentions are partially true in the case of some African countries with spectacular animals and easy access to major tourism markets, such as Kenya, where tourism is the largest earner of foreign exchange (MacKinnon and MacKinnon, 1986), or South Africa, where the income generated by gate receipts and overnight visitors to Kruger National Park far exceeds the cost of maintaining the park. In the past, local people and wildlife were often deemed incompatible, with the result that villagers were moved off their ancestral lands to make way for national parks, only to see the land apparently going to waste and used only by rich foreigners; naturally, a great deal of resentment was created in these circumstances. In recent years, however, governments and development agencies have learnt from such mistakes and are implementing protected areas policies in a different way. The approach has changed particularly since the World Congress on National Parks and Protected Areas held in Bali in 1982. An example of how this is being applied is in Madagascar, where Western tourists' willingness to pay to see the country's unique lemurs and other wildlife is being used as the focus for an integrated programme of employment creation, conservation and education which involves local people at all stages of decision-making and implementation (Bradt, 1991).

In South-East Asia, however, there are few examples up to the present of significant benefits accruing to conservation, foreign exchange reserves, or the local economy through wildlife tourism. There are, certainly, exceptions, notably Kinabalu Park, in east Malaysia, which as the state's principal tourist attraction has won the attention and investment to become an important source of employment and income in the area, while tourism-related enterprises centred on Bunaken Island, in north Sulawesi, Indonesia, have resulted in a substantial reduction in dynamiting and pollution of the coral reefs (Mason, 1990). Little research has been done into the reasons why conservation has been assisted by tourism in these areas while other national parks in South-East Asia have so far failed to fulfil their tourism potential.

National parks generally have a very low profile in South-East Asia. One reason for this is the different way in which Westerners and South-East Asians perceive wilderness areas. The world's first national parks were set up in the United States and Australia in the 1860s, followed by others in Europe and New Zealand, which particularly after the Second World War provided recreational facilities for increasing numbers of people. Parks like Yosemite in the US and the Peak District in England have entered people's consciousness as places where they can roam freely in natural surroundings (even though both places have been victims of their own success and are now having to implement visitor control schemes [Colthurst, 1991]) and have been fundamental to the creation of the current high level of conservation awareness in the West. In developing countries the colonial powers created game reserves which in many cases were converted to conservation areas in the years before or after independence, such as in

Indonesia and Malaysia, where the parks have been established only within the last 30 years and the concept of wanting to roam alone amidst nature has not yet developed, perhaps because there has not been time, but perhaps also for cultural reasons.

In the first place, the vernacular terms invented to describe the parks mitigate against the concept of wilderness: *Taman Nasional* is the Indonesian translation of national park and *Taman Negara* the Malaysian term. However, *taman* is normally translated as 'garden', and is certainly untainted by the associations of wildness automatically understood when Westerners think of a national park. For most people *taman* conjures up a highly controlled and artificial environment, as in a *Taman Hiburan Rakyat*, a People's Entertainment Park, or a *Taman Wisata*, a carefully manicured park created round a tourist attraction. While *taman* has a safe, cosy ring to it, *hutan*, or forest, does not. For most Indonesians and Malaysians the forest is a dark, wet place full of dangerous animals, with no value other than its potential as a source of food and timber.[1] Most people grow up in urban or agricultural areas, and feel that if the forest cannot be avoided entirely then it should be tamed and prettified, not left to its own uncontrolled devices. For people who work within the parks system, this innate belief is bound to cause a conflict with what they are supposed to be doing in their jobs: in Indonesia and Malaysia Western consultants have advised on the biological aspects of the parks and on the management structure, but in Indonesia in particular the later stages of management and development have been carried out by local civil servants who, as already discussed, lack the same basic consciousness as Westerners of what national parks are all about.

Another conflict with Western philosophy and practice concerning protected areas arises from the leisure behaviour of South-East Asians. Rather than seeking solitude or tranquillity, Indonesians and Malaysians tend to seek a holiday experience with a large group of their friends or colleagues (Wind and Heckman, 1988). The consequence of this is that when people become aware of national parks close to major urban centres, such as Gunung Gede-Pangrango National Park, 70 kilometres south of Jakarta, they tend to go there in very large numbers on Sundays and public holidays. Within or beside the national parks subject to such heavy use, facilities more usually found in pleasure parks have sprung up – souvenir stalls, sports halls, cafes and restaurants. This type of heavy utilisation is not necessarily inconsistent with the conservation aims of the national parks, as it is intermittent and tends to be limited either naturally or by planning measures to 'honeypot' zones, and studies have shown that although many animals leave the most crowded areas while visitors are present they return and behave normally during the rest of the week (Compost, personal communication, 1985). However, while these peaks in demand from domestic tourists are straightforward to predict, the popularity of a national park with domestic visitors imposes constraints on travel companies organising tours for Western visitors, who generally seek a more exclusive and private wilderness experience, and thus for the planning authorities a conflict between the desire to earn foreign exchange and the provision of domestic recreation facilities arises.

Awareness of the conservation functions of national parks and other protected areas, such as protection forests which safeguard watersheds of important rivers, is certainly increasing due to better education in the schools and more attention to the subject in the Indonesian and Malaysian media. Attempts are also being made to educate visitors to the national parks with exhibitions and visitor centres, some of which have excellent and expensively produced displays. However, many of the visitors to these are Western tourists.[2] On the other hand, the facilities which would give Western tourists the multifacetted learning experience which many of them demand generally do not exist, especially in Indonesian parks: there are very few properly marked trails with accompanying interpretive leaflets and natural history information such as species name labels on the trees (Cochrane, 1988), and knowledgeable, well-trained guides and rangers are present only in Malaysia.

Any comparison between the state of conservation awareness in South-East Asia and in industrialised countries should take into account the fact that in Europe, America and Australia the urge to wander off alone into the wilderness has arisen among large sections of the population only within the last fifty years, and still only affects a small proportion of visitors to national parks. As Pigram says, 'for much of history, wilderness held a negative connotation, either as waste land or some vast, hostile and dangerous place to be avoided if at all possible, or else to be tamed, controlled and exploited' (Pigram, 1983, 174). In the nineteenth century when people first started leaving cities on day-trips to the seaside they did so in big groups, and the present-day phenomenon of people who visit national parks but stay within ten minutes' walk of their cars is well known (Colthurst, 1991). Some Western conservationists working in South-East Asia see their role partly as one of stewardship, to look after the rainforests and other wild areas of their adopted countries until the local population is in a psychological and economic position to do so itself (Heckman, personal communication, 1988). Their confidence is probably well judged: with the increasing urbanisation and affluence of Indonesia and Malaysia a desire for 'getting back to nature' is beginning to show. In Malaysia there is an increasing number of excellent bird-watchers and other amateur naturalists, and in both countries young people are joining organisations such as the Malay Nature Society, the Consumers' Association of Penang, and the Indonesian Environmental Forum, all of which actively campaign for environmental protection.

'There is a basic and permanent conflict between the preservationists, for whom the preservation of the natural inheritance is an absolute priority, and the utilitarians who want people to benefit from the activities the resources could provide' (Baud-Bovy and Lawson, 1977, 186). Many national parks in Indonesia were apparently established by people who belonged to the 'preservationists' camp, as until fairly recently no more than lip-service was paid to the concept of encouraging tourism in the parks. It was somehow believed that it was enough to create the basic structure of a park by defining its territory on a map and in the bureaucracy, and visitors would then automatically appear; no effort was put into marketing the parks or into providing suitable accommodation or other facilities (Cochrane, 1988). More recently, the 'utilitarians' have won more influence in how funding is allocated to developing the parks. An example of this is the shift in emphasis of the World Wide Fund for Nature programme in Indonesia, which now takes wildlife tourism seriously as a way of helping to ensure that the national parks can 'earn their keep' and thereby win support from the political and administrative powers (Betts, personal communication, 1991).

The question of which philosophical approach to the existence of national parks is currently in vogue with Western development agencies and the government departments they influence has left the legacy of another obstacle to the smooth running of the protected areas system, in that many of the people in more senior positions were trained overseas under a different philosophy to that which now prevails. Once back in their home environment it is often difficult for them to have access to the journals and conferences in which new approaches are aired.

It might be assumed that, because local nationals rather than Western consultants are in charge of the national parks, conflicts between the parks authorities and the surrounding population might be negated, but unfortunately this is rarely the case. The more senior and skilled posts in the parks hierarchy generally have to be filled by officials who are not from that area of the country because sufficiently qualified people are not available locally – particularly since national parks tend by definition to be in the more remote and under-developed parts of the country. The parks authorities, however, do generally try to employ people from nearby villages as wardens, and this can certainly lead to greater acceptance of the park. For instance, it is reported from Kinabalu Park that infringement of park boundaries is less from villages where a substantial number of staff are recruited (Wong, personal communication, 1991).

Another problem as far as tourism is concerned is that the senior staff are generally forestry graduates. Naturally, they have no experience of or training in tourism. Unlike in the West, where being a ranger is a much sought-after form of employment, the job of park warden in Indonesia and Malaysia is considered rather menial and of low status. In Indonesia, the only qualification needed is a primary school certificate, which guarantees only a basic level of literacy. The salaries are very low and in Indonesia often paid irregularly, and it is difficult for the wardens to enforce anti-poaching and anti-wood-cutting regulations amongst their fellow villagers. The wardens are generally well disposed towards visitors but have no training in tourism, and therefore have no idea what the tourists want to see or how to show it to them. Yet it is precisely these people who could be most useful as guides because they often have much more practical knowledge of which animals are present and how they behave than the more senior staff because they are from the local area and spend much more time in the forest. It should be said, however, that the situation is changing in that better-qualified park staff who are graduates in biology or other natural sciences are being appointed in the more popular parks to liaise with tourists, and they are likely to be able to provide a more satisfactory experience for foreign visitors.

A more satisfactory situation already prevails in Malaysia, where the wardens generally have a better understanding of what the tourists are likely to want from their visit, and several of the tour companies employ specialist guides who are good bird-watchers or botanists in their own right. It is also, of course, highly significant for wildlife tourism, as in so many other fields, that communication between parks staff and visitors is not such a problem in Malaysia as in Indonesia because English is so much more widely spoken.

The national parks and nature reserves in Indonesia and Malaysia have been carefully selected to preserve a representative sample of the ecosystems in both areas (MacKinnon and MacKinnon, 1986). Standards of facilities and enforcement of regulations are generally higher in Malaysia, but in neither country does wildlife tourism receive much attention from either the government or private enterprise, given that cultural tourism is well developed in both countries and that neither is as dependent on tourism for foreign exchange as some African countries. In Indonesia the number of international tourists visiting the national parks is too low to have any significant impact on foreign exchange. There are unfortunately no consistent visitor figures available for the parks, but it is quite apparent that the numbers are insignificant. The only exceptions to this are the orang-utan rehabilitation centre at Bohorok, in north Sumatra, where the orang-utan rehabilitants are relatively easy to see, and Komodo National Park, where the so-called 'dragons' are readily spotted. Certain other national parks (Ujung Kulon, Gunung Gede-Pangrango, Baluran, Bali Barat) also receive a regular stream of visitors, although this is principally because of their proximity to major tourist routes and the ease of incorporating them into standard itineraries; visits to them are generally of very short duration and at the wrong time of day (i.e. around midday when the animals are at their least active).

In Malaysia the number of visits to national parks is well documented and is much higher than in Indonesia – there were 16,803 foreign visitors to Mount Kinabalu Park in 1990 – but this is still insignificant as a proportion of foreign visitors overall to Malaysia, which reached 4.5 million in 1990.

The potential of South-East Asian wildlife as a tourist attraction is in any case limited because of the nature of the terrain and the animals themselves. It is difficult to penetrate and explore the rainforest because of the luxuriant growth of vegetation, and it is even more difficult to catch sight of a rainforest animal, other than invertebrates such as ants, mosquitoes and leeches. The holiday-going public is used to seeing large, spectacular mammals in television documentaries or on previous holidays to eastern or southern Africa, and is therefore unlikely to be enthusiastic about creatures which are mostly small, shy, nocturnal and living high up in the canopy of the forest. Indonesia has a greater diversity and complexity of wildlife than any other nation in the world (Whitten, 1987) because of its position astride two major biogeographical zones – the Asian and the Australian. This means that in the western half of the country Asian-related species of animal such as orang-utans, elephants, tigers and wild cattle are found, while in the eastern part of the archipelago live Australian-related fauna such as kangaroos and other marsupials and birds like cockatoos and honey-eaters. Yet most visitors to Indonesia (and indeed many Indonesians) are unaware of this great diversity and see nothing of it.

One consequence of this is that specialist guides and tour leaders are unable to show their clients many animals in the wild. This largely accounts for the popularity with tour groups and individual travellers of semi-tame animals such as the orang-utans at Bohorok and Sepilok, in Sabah, and the giant lizards of Komodo. There are well-established ways of making wildlife easier to see, for instance by building hides or walkways through the trees at canopy level or planning nature-trails with good interpretive labels, but this requires a higher level of investment and skills than is generally available in either Indonesia or Malaysia – although again, the situation is significantly better in Malaysia in this respect. Taman Negara in west Malaysia has some very good hides and salt-licks, and there is a popular canopy walkway in Kinabalu Park in Sabah.

Given that the conservation lobbies in Malaysia and Indonesia are still in an early stage of development, practical ways have to be found of generating sufficient political will to protect ecologically viable tracts of land. If wildlife tourism in Indonesia and Malaysia were seen to generate substantial revenues the industry would undoubtedly receive more attention from influential quarters than at present. Current regulations do not permit entry fees to be charged to parks in Indonesia, although a nominal sum is occasionally charged for the permit, and there is no standard fee for entry in Malaysia. If the parks were allowed to charge for entry and to be accountable locally for the money, rather than having to send it to the national headquarters of the conservation authority, they could use the revenue to develop facilities or give staff bonuses, which could generate a great deal more interest in encouraging tourists.[3] Indonesian environmentalists are also in favour of this, as they feel it would not only help conservation but also that it is important to stress 'value rather than volume' in their tourism industry (Reuter, 1991).

It could also be beneficial in some cases to involve private groups in upgrading visitor facilities where the park authorities are unable to do so. This has begun to happen in Indonesia, where in Ujung Kulon National Park a privately managed guest-house has recently been built. Allowing private entrepreneurs into the parks is generally considered inappropriate because it is feared that their principal aim will be to maximise the return from their investment in the short term, which could be incompatible with the long-term needs of the environment in which they operate. Nevertheless, if tourism utilisation of parks and reserves is properly zoned and controlled, so that a certain area is dedicated to intensive use while keeping most of the park's territory as wilderness, the aims of providing employment and earning income while at the same time guaranteeing conservation can be reconciled.

In Indonesia in December 1990 an Association for Wildlife and Nature Tourism was formed, which is in fact dedicated to promoting hunting tourism. This should not necessarily be viewed as a negative development, because of the current high level of illegal hunting in Indonesia; it was felt necessary to establish official game reserves to impose some control on hunting. Several influential people are involved in the association and in the consortia formed to manage the game reserves, and their involvement undoubtedly stems from the two-fold aim of commercial exploitation of the game and of providing recreation for themselves and their friends. (It is to be hoped that legitimised hunting activities are confined to the one species of animal which can currently be legally hunted, namely wild boar.) It would probably be too optimistic to predict that a pure, altruistic sense of the need for conservation will become strong enough in the near future to ensure that the national parks are properly funded. But if influential individuals such as those involved in hunting could be made aware that large sums of money can also be earned from 'soft' forms of wildlife tourism such as photography and trekking, and if proper controls on development are enforced, then the prospects for tourism aiding conservation in Indonesia and Malaysia would be much greater.

In Malaysia the national parks are reasonably well established and the country is sufficiently prosperous for the fact that wildlife tourism does not contribute greatly to foreign exchange reserves to be of limited importance. In Indonesia, wildlife tourism could contribute significantly to the overall tourism product by extending the average length of visitor stay and helping to spread tourists out into the more remote areas. However, a substantial amount of work needs to be carried out both on the infrastructure of visitor facilities in the parks and on developing markets in the principal tourism generating countries before there can be a real prospect of tourism making a significant contribution to conservation.

## NOTES

1 A brochure promoting the tourist attractions of Lampung province, in southern Sumatra, includes a few paragraphs on the Way Kambas nature reserve. It explains that 'deer, gibbons, wild elephants, tigers, etc.' live in the reserve, and that 'those animals are just going around freely in their environment, which illustrates to us that we are surrounded by the horrible jungle'.

2 The visitor's centre at the Bohorok orang-utan rehabilitation centre, in North Sumatra, has excellent facilities and a good exhibition, but the majority of local visitors on day excursions from the nearby major city of Medan do not enter the centre.

3 There is a 5 Malaysian dollar charge for going on the canopy walkway at Kinabalu, which is a realistic fee and is certainly no barrier for people who want a closer view of the rainforest.

# 18 Dialogue with the hosts

## An educational strategy towards sustainable tourism

*Kadir H. Din*

## INTRODUCTION

Current projections suggest that world tourist arrivals will reach 666 million in the year 2000, with nearly a third landing at Asian destinations (Hiemstra, 1991, 62). This estimate anticipates an annual growth of 4.5 per cent for the whole world between 1988 and 2000, with the highest growth (12.1 per cent per annum) expected to occur in Asia. Within the Asian region, Malaysia has already started to enjoy a rapid and sustained growth in tourist arrivals: the industry has expanded at an annual average of 17.3 per cent over the last decade, and by a phenomenal 50 per cent in each of the last two years (Tourism Development Corporation, 1991, 32). Tourism has emerged from the backwaters of the Malaysian economy to become its third largest foreign exchange earner, surpassing the contributions from traditional commodity items, namely palm oil, sawn logs, rubber and tin.

The above trend has given rise to considerable concern among observers world-wide, both within and outside the industry, regarding the socio-cultural, economic and environmental effects of the tourism 'boom'. Of late there has been a noticeable convergence in areas of concern among researchers, and foremost among these is the concern for an appropriate role for the tourist industry in the world economy. Economists, anthropologists and others appear to have fallen in line with philosophers in discussing the implications of the rapid growth in tourism beyond the singular emphasis on the numeric aspect of the industry. Thus, one reads more frequent exhortations of the notion of 'appropriate', 'responsible' or at least 'sustainable' tourism (see also Chapter 15 by Parnwell in this volume). One of the core issues underlying the above notions is the question of how and to what extent can tourism benefit the host community, meaning the original (particularly the native or indigenous) residents in destination areas.

## HOST COMMUNITY AS BENEFICIARIES

Although the category 'host community' has been widely mentioned in the literature since the 1960s, it was only through the more focused efforts of Peter Murphy at the University of Victoria, Canada, that the concept became a subject of popular scrutiny (Murphy, 1985, *passim*; see also D'Amore, 1983; Gunn, 1988). Whereas earlier studies tended to view the host community as a unitary receptacle, the above authors demonstrate that the host community is in fact a highly differentiated group, always with a small minority deriving actual pecuniary benefits from tourism. The benefit structure becomes conspicuously narrower when one proceeds to examine the situation in Third World destinations.

In two previous papers on the subject, I have suggested that the benefit structure may also follow ethnic affiliation (Kadir Din, 1986; 1988b), and part of the explanation lies in the lack of entrepreneurial capability of the local residents who may belong to a group that is less than adequately pre-adapted to the demands of a new type of economic activity. It follows that any meaningful local involvement in the new-found opportunities associated with tourism would have to be initiated 'top-down' through a proper assessment of the needs of the host community (Kadir Din, 1989b).

While the proposition for a 'top-down' incentive programme would readily appeal to common sense, the effective implementation of such a programme, which may range from fiscal incentives to manpower training, would require enormous development efforts which should commence by making local residents fully aware of the new force of change that is affecting their community. The purpose of this chapter is to draw attention to the relevance of an education strategy towards host community involvement in tourism. The following section provides a general overview of the Malaysian approach to tourism planning, which illustrates the lack of emphasis on community education in contemporary tourism planning. Following this, a more detailed account of the recent developments in the island destination of Langkawi is presented; the choice of Langkawi is prompted by the writer's long familiarity with the island, and its status as an emergent tourist principal destination in Malaysia.

## THE HOST FACTOR IN MALAYSIAN TOURISM PLANNING

Since the late 1950s, the attitude of the Malaysian authorities to tourism development has centred primarily on two major concerns: to project a positive image of the country abroad, and to promote growth as a means of earning foreign exchange. As a result of this, there has been little attempt to include the host factor in tourism planning. The sentiment of the host community was always presumed to be positive; this assumption was well borne out by positive remarks by tourists in the media, and the high tourist ratings obtained on the friendliness of locals as indicated by results of the occasional surveys of departing tourists. As in the sectoral plans covering other economic activities, tourism planning helped to perpetuate a myth that tourism has always been a harmless activity which operates with few socio-cultural consequences.

The 1970s saw occasional criticisms by observers, mostly of the protest genre, directed against what appeared to be negative issues surrounding the impact of tourism on society. These issues included environmental deterioration, moral decadence, and certain kinds of unacceptable behaviour by the stereotypical tourist. By the late 1970s some consideration was given towards addressing these concerns (for example, see Anonymous, 1976, 7, 46), and by the early 1980s concern over the abrasive consequences of tourism projects on the local residents became recognised and was subsequently embedded in planning laws as found in the provision of the Town and Country Planning Act (1976) and the Environmental Quality Act (Amendment 1985). Whereas the former calls for the submission of Structure Plans which, where applicable, address the impact of tourism on local residents, the latter makes mandatory the submission of Environmental Impact Assessment reports on tourism impacts (including the socio-cultural impact of tourism), prior to the approval of projects of certain scales and at certain locations.

The above explicit injunctions on the host factor in tourism development is a far cry from the earlier 'presumed acceptability' of tourism among residents in destination areas. The position prior to this was well reflected in a statement made by the Kedah Chief Minister that 'we do not have to consult with the local people; we know what is good for them' (*Dewan Masyarakat*, 1984). The need to increase resident awareness of tourism as a new force of change was considered a non-issue so that, so long as there was potential for development in an area, tourism projects were presumed to be beneficial to the host community.

## HOST PARTICIPATION IN MALAYSIAN DESTINATIONS: THE EXAMPLE OF LANGKAWI

Since the Dutch decided to treat Langkawi as a destination for the recuperation of their soldiers serving the region in 1642, Langkawi has undergone three discernible stages in its development as a tourism centre. The inception stage began in 1948 when the first hotel on the island (Fairwinds Hotel) was built. A number of rest-houses was built in the 1950s and 1960s. During the subsequent stage (1970s), Langkawi grew to become a popular destination among domestic tourists until the island was proposed for a US$1 billion resort development in the early 1980s. By the late 1980s, Langkawi was poised to become the largest single resort destination in the region, following the government's decision to turn the island into a free port.

Throughout the above three stages, tourism development proceeded without any consideration being given to its acceptability to the local population. In the early 1980s there were frequent complaints concerning outside intrusion; a number of protests surfaced, including two against the government's decision to acquire land for the extension of the existing airstrip, and the exploitation of Telaga Tujuh mountain stream as a source of water supply. These two complaints later extended to complaints on environmental pollution, moral decadence, and inflation (especially land prices – see Bird, 1989). It was only in the late 1980s that efforts were made to implement the provisions of the Environmental Quality Act and the Town and Country Planning Act, mentioned earlier.

### The Langkawi Structure Plan, 1990–2005

The Survey Report for the Langkawi Structure Plan was completed and displayed to the public for one month after 25 February 1990. Subsequently, pursuant to the Town and Country Planning Act, the Structure Plan was launched by the Prime Minister and exhibited in Kuah on 5 January 1991. As three years have now passed since the island was conferred the status of a free port, it will be useful to examine planning considerations affecting tourism – in particular, considerations of host involvement in the planning process itself. Although the public had the opportunity, on two occasions, to express their views and make representations on matters with which they disagreed, as provided in the Town and Country Planning Act (1976, Section 9/2 and 3), it is usually during the second review after publicity of the draft plan that members of the public become more effective in airing their protests.

The effectiveness of the review process depends to a large extent on two main factors: how literate and vocal are the community, and how objective is the conduct of the review process. It is often claimed that the public are usually apathetic, partly because of their own ignorance of the subject, and partly because of their lack of familiarity with the procedures involved (Jafari, 1991, personal communication). It seems more likely, however, that the method of canvassing residents' opinions does not involve creative efforts seriously to obtain information on their reactions to the proposals contained in the plan. The standard procedure in the review process is to begin with the appointment of a Public Reactions Sub-Committee which then arranges for a meeting with the representatives of the resident community. The minutes of the meeting are then used as a source for making necessary alterations to the draft plan before it is submitted for approval and assent by the State Executive Council, following which the Structure Plan comes into effect.

The public exhibition for the Structure Plan for Langkawi was announced in the newspapers over a period of three days in early January 1991. Further publicity was given through announcements on the radio and two television channels, plus a display of 100 posters and ten large cloth posters at strategic locations in Kedah. The event gained extended publicity since it was announced by the Prime Minister, who for some time had taken a special interest in the development of the island. A total of 1,000 copies of the report was printed in English and Malay. Out of this only 93 copies of the English version were sold, as compared to the sale of 189 Malay version copies, representing some 5 per cent of the attendees (4,577 people, mostly Malays). Altogether, 39 protest letters were received by the Sub-Committee. Although 32 of the complainants indicated their willingness to participate in the meeting, only 14 showed up in three separate sessions. The total number of disagreements received was significantly more than the total received during similar public exhibitions held for Alor Setar (31 letters) and Kangar (23 letters) two to three years previously.

It is significant to note that membership of the Sub-Committee clearly represented the government (state politicians and administrators), with four of the members bearing conferred titles. Questions can be raised as to whether the members realistically can be taken as an independent body to oversee a public review process. The complainants, however, represented a wide range of interest groups, six of which have pro-government connections. The only group which is known for its vocal criticism of government projects is the Consumers Association of Penang (CAP), which does not have a home base in Langkawi, and which therefore may not represent the true sentiment of the local population. The majority of protests, mostly less sophisticated in presentation, came from individual farmers, fishermen and chalet operators, who can claim to have their stake in the future of Langkawi.

From the protest letters, it is evident that tourism-related issues predominate. These include:

1 Land reclamation for tourism-related projects.
2 Acquisition of land from local residents for development.
3 The development of golf ranges.
4 Soil erosion problems at the hill sites for tourism.
5 Quota for *Bumiputera*[1] involvement in the new projects.
6 Relocation of fishing communities.
7 Increases in ferry fares.
8 Problems relating to improper conduct of tourists.
9 Erosion of spiritual values as commercialism creeps in.

As one might expect, the Sub-Committee's comments on many of the complaints raised concerning tourism was a simple 'outside the scope of the study', meaning that such complaints will not be heeded to. In particular, nearly every complaint on moral issues relating to tourism development was declared to be outside the purview of the Sub-Committee.

## THE ENVIRONMENTAL QUALITY ACT
## (AMENDMENT, 1985)

Pursuant to Section 34A of the Environmental Quality Act (Amendment, 1985), the Department of the Environment published the *Handbook of Environmental Impact Assessment Guidelines* which contains specifications for tourism-related projects. These include 'any area with tourism potential'. Activities which fall under the aegis of the Environmental Impact Assessment legislation include:

1 construction of coastal resort facilities with more than 80 rooms;

2 hill station resort or hotel development covering an area of 50 hectares of more;

3 development of tourist or recreational facilities in national parks;

4 development of tourist or recreational facilities on islands in surrounding waters which are gazetted as national marine parks.

One of the three components contained in the Environmental Impact Assessment checklist for studies covers the human aspects, which include aesthetic, cultural, socio-economic, health and safety aspects. At the time of writing (February 1991), I am not aware of any serious attempt to observe these provisions (first published in 1987), in all the new tourism projects on Langkawi. It should be emphasised at this point that the problems relating to environmental deterioration on the island of Langkawi also arose from the rapid growth of chalets which were not built with proper sewage disposal and beach protection measures. Although individually these premises may fall outside the scope of the relevant Acts (being less than 50 hectares, or having fewer than 80 rooms), when the combined effect of dozens of operators is taken into account, the gross effect can be a tyranny of the small, and clearly leaves room for concern.

## OVERCOMING THE FREE-RIDER SITUATION

The above account of the failure in the implementation of the provisions of the two relevant Acts towards achieving sustainable goals in tourism development suggests that full cooperation is needed from local residents, who can act as complainants and who can provide the basis for effective control programmes. A prerequisite for such cooperation calls for a sensitive and informed public because, without their cooperation (through protests and participation), it may be difficult to enforce the regulations contained in the relevant control Acts. To achieve the desired effect, it is therefore important that the local residents be made aware of the implications of changes brought about by the rapid growth of tourism, so that they will be in a position to assist in addressing the risks associated with such rapid changes.

It is proposed that instead of relying solely on spontaneous involvement by locals, planners can act more effectively by first introducing measures which would serve to educate the public so that they can become more involved in shaping the future course of their community (see for example Hall, 1988). Although such an approach assumes a 'top-down' posture in terms of source of initiative, the end result may produce a blend of both 'top-down' and 'bottom-up' approaches in participatory planning. Granted this proposition, what would be the best approach towards encouraging more locals to participate in the decision-making process?

Bennett (n.d., 124) suggests that we ought to create 'agents of change' who can educate the public about the 'sources' of change – in this case tourism. To be effective, such agents should comprise local 'knowledgeables who are politically independent, or at least are impartial to political considerations'. Once such agents are identified, Murphy recommends that workshops should be held to familiarise locals with the nature and implications of tourism development (Murphy, 1988, 135–38). To avoid ineffective conduct of meetings such as these, it is necessary that parallel workshops in the form of focus groups be organised to provide opportunities for improving awareness among different interested parties in the host community. Through such workshops, it is possible to canvass the views, preferences and grievances of all the different groups in the locality. A delphi technique can then be introduced to determine the needs and priorities of the host society. To achieve this, a bigger forum should be organised which can amalgamate both the contending and common viewpoints among the different 'focus groups' in society, so that debates can be held to determine the needs and priorities of the larger group – i.e. the entire community.

A key consideration to the above goal is that the viewpoints synthesised in the end would represent the collective sentiment of the local population, and not just 'top-down' pronouncements as evident in the current practice, especially when such pronouncements come from outsiders who may not fully be able to empathise with the predicament of the locals. This approach, however, does not reject the policies decided at the centre. It merely attempts to translate them through a dialogue with the receiving communities so that they can understand the perspective of the policy-maker and vice versa, and will be in a better position to provide the support in the implementation of the relevant policy. Whenever there are disagreements, they can be sorted out at the combined forum before a particular ruling is adopted for enforcement.

## IDENTIFYING THE NEEDS OF THE HOSTS AND THE GUESTS

An optimal tourism planning decision is one that takes into consideration the needs of both the tourists and the resident population. It is only through careful articulation of these needs that the future of the industry can be sustained, and local resentment can be averted. Whereas the needs of the locals can be identified through the above-mentioned workshops and fora, the needs of the tourist are easier to determine: regular questionnaire surveys or focus group workshops on their preferences and complaints are sufficient to solicit their points of view.

As for the residents, tourism represents an economic opportunity which should not be by-passed simply because residents are not ready to participate in the opportunities that arise. In a study among longhouse dwellers in Limbang, Sarawak, and on the local residents in Penang, Langkawi, Tioman and Taman Negara, I found that local residents are more knowledgeable than they are commonly presumed to be. They were enthusiastic in desiring to participate directly in tourism businesses, although they may have little prior experience in the conduct of a business.

In most new destinations, the religious leaders appear to be the least receptive among the locals since tourism has for long been associated with certain immoral behaviour, both among the locals as well as the tourists. Rather than by-passing them or ignoring them, prudence suggests that they should be allowed to express their views, and should be given some consideration before the planners proceed with the tourism projects.

## CONCLUSION

A sustainable mode of tourism development is one which considers both the ecological and the social carrying capacity of the destination area. I have argued that, because tourism involves an encounter situation, between the values of outsiders and insiders, it is important to pay attention to the needs of the host community who are the rightful custodians of the area. Their needs, in the final analysis, cannot be superseded by outside interests, nor can they be determined by outsiders. They must come from locals and be in touch with local sentiments. Local 'knowledgeables' and other members of the local community must be given a greater say. The main weakness of the current 'top-down' strategy is that it fails to solicit the 'objective' views of the locals, who in any case will inevitably have to accommodate all the impacts arising from tourism development. Local sentiments are also dynamic in nature but are critical in a successful hospitality industry. This calls for a trial and error approach at the beginning, but in the long run as more locals become aware of the consequences, the host community will be in a better position to address whatever problems may arise in their midst. If the planner is seriously intent on realising the good of sustainable tourism, it is imperative that the concept, and the spirit of law behind it, be made intelligible, so that these values ultimately become a part of the local ethos.

## NOTE

1 Literally 'sons of the soil'; term applied to the Malays and other indigenous peoples of Malaysia.

# References

Acciaioli, G., 1985, 'Culture as Art: From Practice to Spectacle in Indonesia', *Canberra Anthropology*, 8/1 and 2, pp. 148-74.

Adams, Kathleen M., 1984, 'Come to Tana Toraja, "Land of the Heavenly Kings": Travel Agents as Brokers in Ethnicity', *Annals of Tourism Research*, 11, 3, pp. 469-85.

—— 1990, 'Cultural Commoditization in Tana Toraja, Indonesia', *Cultural Survival Quarterly*, 14, 1, pp. 31-33; 77.

—— 1991, 'Touristic Pilgrimages, Identity, and Nation-Building in Indonesia', paper delivered at annual meetings of Association of Asian Studies, New Orleans.

Agung, I. A. A. G., 1989, *Bali Pada Abad XIX. Perjuangan Rakyat dan Raja-Raja Menentang Kolonialisme Belanda 1808-1908*, Yogyakarta: Gadjah Mada University Press.

D'Amore, L. J., 1983, 'Guidelines to Planning in Harmony with the Host Community', in Peter Murphy, ed., *Tourism in Canada: Selected Issues and Options*, Western Geographical Series, 21, pp. 135-57.

Anderson, B. O'G., 1983, *Imagined Communities: Reflections on the Origins and Spread of Nationalism*, London: Verso Editions.

Anderson, Dennis and Mark W. Leiserson, 1980, 'Rural Nonfarm Employment in Developing Countries', *Economic Development and Cultural Change*, 28, pp. 227-48.

Anonymous, 1976, *A Report of the Advisory Panel on Tourism Development in Malaysia*, Kuala Lumpur: Tourism Development Corporation.

Appadurai, Arjun, 1990, 'Disjuncture and Difference in the Global Cultural Economy', *Theory, Culture and Society*, 7, pp. 295-310.

Apter, David, 1971, *The Political Kingdom in Uganda*, Princeton: Princeton University Press.

—— 1987, *Rethinking Development: Modernization, Dependency, and Postmodern Politics*, Newbury Park: Sage.

Archer, B. H., 1977, *Tourism Multipliers: The State of the Art*, Occasional Papers in Economics, No. 11, Bangor: University of Wales Press.

—— 1989, 'Tourism and Island Economies: Impact Analyses', in C. P. Cooper, ed., *Progress in Tourism, Recreation and Hospitality Management*, Volume One, London: Belhaven, pp. 125-34.

Ariel, Heryanto, 1988, 'The Development of "Development" ', *Indonesia*, 46, pp. 1-24.

Arndell, R., 1990, 'Tourism as a Development Concept in the South Pacific', *The Courier*, 122, pp. 83–86.

Ashford, Douglas, 1978, 'The Structural Analysis of Policy or Institutions Really Do Matter', in Douglas Ashford, *Comparing Public Policies: New Concepts and Methods*, Beverly Hills: Sage.

*Asia Travel Trade*, 1990, various issues.

*Asia Yearbook*, 1989, Hong Kong, Far Eastern Economic Review Publishing Company.

Association of Indonesian Travel Agencies, n.d., *Lampung Tourism*, Lampung, Sumatra: Association of Indonesian Travel Agencies.

Attanayake, A., H. M. S. Samaranayake and N. Ratnapala, 1983, 'Sri Lanka', in Elwood A. Pye and Txong-biau Lin, eds, *Tourism in Asia: The Economic Impact*, Singapore: Singapore University Press, pp. 241–351.

Attenborough, David, 1959, *Zoo Quest for a Dragon*, 2nd edition, London: Companion Book Club.

Ayal, E. B., 1963, 'Value Systems and Economic Development in Japan and Thailand', *Journal of Social Issues*, 19, 1, pp. 35–51.

Aznam, S., 1990, 'Wish You Were Here', *Far Eastern Economic Review* (22 March), pp. 31–33.

Babb, L. A., 1973, 'Heat and Control in Chhattisgarhi Ritual', *Eastern Anthropologist*, 26.

Bachrach, Peter and Morton S. Baratz, 1963, 'Decisions and Non-Decisions: An Analytical Framework', *American Political Science Review* (September), pp. 632–42.

Bacon, F., 1597, 'Of Travel', *Bacon's Essays*, London: Normal Tutorial Services (reprinted 1904).

Bagus, I Gusti Ngurah, ed., 1986, *Sumbangan Nilai Budaya Bali dalam Pembangunan Kebudayaan Nasional (The Value of the Contribution of Balinese Culture in the Development of National Culture)*, Jakarta: Departemen Pendidikan dan Kebudayaan.

—— 1987, 'Komodo National Park: Its Role in Tourism Development in Indonesia', *Man and Culture in Oceania*, 3 (special issue), pp. 169–76.

Bakdi Soemanto, 1989, 'Jagat Pariwisata Kita di Yogyakarta' (Our Tourist World in Yogyakarta), *Citra Yogya*, 2, pp. 5–14.

*Bangkok Bank Monthly Review*, 1991, 'The Impact of the Visit Malaysia Year on Thai Tourism', *Bangkok Bank Monthly Review*, 32 (May), pp. 182–84.

*Bangkok Post*, 1990, 'Hotels: Oversupply of Rooms Ahead', *Bangkok Post, Mid-Year Economic Review* (30 June), pp. 39–43.

—— 1991, 'Room Rates Under Pressure', *Bangkok Post, Mid-Year Economic Review* (30 June), pp. 48–49.

Banuazizi, Ali, 1987, 'Social-Psychological Approaches to Political Development', in M. Weiner and S. P. Huntington, eds, *Understanding Political Development*, Boston: Little, Brown.

Barang, M., 1988, 'Tourism in Thailand', *South* (December), 71, 73.

Barthes, R., 1983, *The Eiffel Tower*, New York: Hill and Wang.

Bateson, G., 1949, 'Bali: The Value System of a Steady State', in J. Belo, ed., *Traditional Balinese Culture*, New York: Columbia University Press (reprinted 1970), 384–401.

Bateson, G. and M. Mead, 1942, *Balinese Character: A Photographic Analysis*, New York: New York Academy of Sciences (reprinted 1962).

Batt, H. W., 1974, 'Obligation and Decision in Thai Administration: From Patrimonial to Rational Legal Bureaucracy', unpublished Ph.D. thesis, SUNY, Albany.

Baud-Bovy, M. and F. Lawson, 1977, *Tourism and Recreation Development*, The Architectural Press Ltd.

Baudrillard, J., 1988, *Selected Writings*, Cambridge: Basil Blackwell.

Baum, V., 1937, *A Tale from Bali*, Singapore: Oxford University Press (reprinted 1986).

Beccari, Odoardo, 1904, *Wanderings in the Great Forests of Borneo. Travels and Researches of a Naturalist in Sarawak*, London: Constable.

Beck, B., 1969, 'Colour and Heat in South Indian Ritual', *Man*, 4, 4, pp. 553–72.

Beeckman, Daniel, 1718, *A Voyage to and from the Island of Borneo*, London (reprinted 1973, Folkstone and London: Dawsons of Pall Mall).

Belo, J., ed., 1970, *Traditional Balinese Culture*, New York: Columbia University Press.

Ben-Amos, Dan, 1984, 'The Seven Strands of *Tradition*: Varieties in Its Meaning in American Folklore Studies', *Journal of Folklore Research*, 21, 2/3, pp. 97–131.

Bendesa, K. G. and M. Sukarsa, 1980, 'An Economic Survey of Bali', *Bulletin of Indonesian Economic Studies*, 16/2, pp. 31–53.

Bendix, Regina, 1989, 'Tourism and Cultural Displays: Inventing Tradition for Whom?', *Journal of American Folklore*, 102, 404, pp. 131–45.

Bennett, N., n.d., *Barriers and Bridges for Rural Development*, Bangkok: The Foundation for Social Sciences and Humanities.

Berger, P., B. Berger and H. Kellner, 1973–4, *The Homeless Mind*, Harmondsworth: Penguin.

Bird, Bella D. M., 1989, *Langkawi: from Mahsuri to Mahathir: Tourism for Whom?*, Kuala Lumpur: Institute for Social Analysis.

Bird, Isabella L., 1883, *The Golden Chersonese and the Way Thither*, Kuala Lumpur: Oxford University Press (reprinted 1967).

Blau, P., 1967, *Exchange and Power in Social Life*, New York: Wiley.

Bleackley, Horace, 1928, *A Tour of Southern Asia (Indo-China, Malaya, Java, Sumatra, and Ceylon, 1925–1926)*, London: John Lane the Bodley Head.

Blower, J. H., *et al.*, 1977, *Proposed National Park Komodo, Management Plan 1978/79–1982/83*, based on the work of Blower, J. H., A. P. M. van der Zon and Yaya Malyana, (mimeographed), Bogor: Nature Conservation and Wildlife Project of the Food and Agricultural Organisation of the United Nations, Directorate General of Forestry.

Bock, Carl, 1881, *The Head-Hunters of Borneo: A Narrative of Travel up the Mahakkam and down the Barito; Also, Journeyings in Sumatra*, London, Sampson and Low (reprinted with an Introduction by R. H. W. Reece, 1985, Singapore: Oxford University Press).

de Boer, F. E., 1989, 'Balinese Sendratari, a Modern Dramatic Dance Genre', *Asian Theatre Journal*, 6/2, pp. 179–93.

Boissevain, J., 1978, 'Tourism and Development in Malta', in V. L. Smith, ed., *Tourism and Economic Change: Studies in Third World Societies*, 6, pp. 37–56.

Boon, J. A., 1977, *The Anthropological Romance of Bali, 1597–1972:*

*Dynamic Perspectives in Marriage and Caste, Politics and Religion*, Cambridge: Cambridge University Press.

Booth, A., 1990, 'The Tourism Boom in Indonesia', *Bulletin of Indonesian Economic Studies*, 26, 3, pp. 45–73.

Bourdieu, P., 1977, *Outline of a Theory of Practice*, Cambridge: Cambridge University Press.

Boyle, Frederick, 1865, *Adventures Among the Dayaks of Borneo*, London: Hurst and Blackett.

Braddell, Roland, 1934, *The Lights of Singapore*, London: Methuen (reprinted 1941).

Bradt, H., 1991, *Guide to Madagascar*, 3rd edition, London: Bradt Publications.

Brandon, Piers, 1991, *Thomas Cook: 150 Years of Popular Tourism*, London: Secker and Warburg.

Brassey, Annie, 1889, *The Last Voyage*, London: Longmans, Green and Co.

Broeze, Frank, Peter Reeves and Kenneth McPherson, 1986, 'Imperial Ports and the Modern World Economy: The Case of the Indian Ocean', *Journal of Transport History*, 3rd series, 7, 2, pp. 1–20.

Brookfield, Harold, 1988, 'Sustainable Development and the Environment', *Journal of Development Studies*, 25, 1, pp. 126–35.

Broomfield, J., 1991, 'Demand for Tourism in Fiji', M.A. dissertation in Economics, University of Kent at Canterbury.

Broughton, Lady, 1936, 'A Modern Dragon Hunt on Komodo: An English Yachting Party Traps and Photographs the Huge and Carniverous Dragon Lizard of the Lesser Sundas', *National Geographic* (September), pp. 321–31.

Brown, Carolyn Henning, 1984, 'Tourism and Ethnic Competition in a Ritual Form: The Firewalkers of Fiji', *Oceania*, 54, pp. 223–44.

Bruce Lockhart, R. H., 1936, *Return to Malaya*, London: Putnam.

Buck, R. C., 1978, 'Boundary Maintenance Revisited: Tourist Experience in an Old Order Amish Community', *Rural Sociology*, 43, pp. 221–34.

—— 1982, 'On Tourism as an Anthropological Subject', *Current Anthropology*, 23, pp. 326–27.

Bugnicourt, Jacques, 1977a, 'Tourism with No Return!', *Development Forum*, 5, 5, pp. 1–2.

—— 1977b, 'The Other Face', *Development Forum*, 5, 6, p. 8.

Burden, W. Douglas, 1927, 'Stalking the Dragon Lizard on the Island of Komodo', *National Geographic* (August), pp. 216–30.

Burkart, A. J. and S. Medlik, 1974, *Tourism: Past, Present and Future*, London: William Heinemann.

Butcher, John G., 1979, *The British in Malaya, 1880–1941: The Social History of a European Community in Colonial South-East Asia*, Kuala Lumpur: Oxford University Press.

Carver, E., 1987, 'Tourism: Offers of Natural Delights', *Far Eastern Economic Review* (5 February), p. 56.

Catholic Bishops of Thailand, 1990, 'Pastoral Letter on Tourism', *Contours*, 4, 6 (June), p. 5.

Charoenpanij, Sriracha, 1988, 'The Thai Legal System: The Law as an Agent of Environmental Protection', in The Siam Society, *Culture and Environment in Thailand*, Bangkok: The Siam Society, pp 463–73.

Christie, Ella, 1961, 'The First Tourist: Astana Guest, Kuchin, 1904', *Sarawak Museum Journal*, Volume X, Nos. 17–18 (new series), July–December, pp. 43–49.

City Desk, 1987, 'Prison, AIDS and Condoms: The Controversy Continues', *The Nation*, (20 October) p. 4.

Clifford, Hugh, 1904, *Further India. Being the Story of Exploration from the Earliest Times in Burma, Malaya, Siam, and Indo-China*, London: Lawrence and Bullen (in the series *The Story of Exploration*, ed. J. S. Keltie, Secretary, Royal Geographical Society).

—— 1928, *A Free Lance of To-day*, London: Methuen.

Clifford, James, 1986, 'Introduction: Partial Truths', in J. Clifford and G. E. Marcus, eds, *Writing Culture: The Poetics and Politics of Ethnography*, Berkeley and Los Angeles: University of California Press.

—— 1988, *The Predicament of Culture: Twentieth-Century Ethnography, Literature, and Art*, Cambridge: Harvard University Press.

Clutterbuck, Walter J., 1891, *About Ceylon and Borneo, Being an Account of Two Visits to Ceylon, One to Borneo, and How We Fell Out on Our Homeward Journey*, London: Longmans, Green and Co.

Cochrane, J., 1988, 'The Potential for Wildlife Tourism in Indonesia', unpublished MA thesis, University of Surrey.

Cohen, Erik, 1972, 'Towards a Sociology of International Tourism', *Social Research*, 39, pp. 164–82.

—— 1979a, 'A Phenomonology of Tourist Types', *Sociology*, 13, pp. 179–201.

—— 1979b, 'Rethinking the Sociology of Tourism', *Annals of Tourism Research*, 6, 1, pp. 18–35.

—— 1982a, 'Jungle Guides in Northern Thailand – The Dynamics of a Marginal Occupational Role', *Sociological Review*, 30, pp. 236–66.

—— 1982b, 'Marginal Paradises: Bungalow Tourism on the Islands of Southern Thailand', *Annals of Tourism Research*, 9, 2, pp. 189–228.

—— 1982c, 'Thai Girls and Farang Men: The Edge of Ambiguity', *Annals of Tourism Research*, 9, pp. 403–28.

—— 1983a, 'Insiders and Outsiders: The Dynamics of Bungalow Tourism on the Islands of Southern Thailand', *Human Organization*, 42, 2, pp. 158–62.

—— 1983b, 'Hill Tribe Tourism', in John McKinnon and Wanat Bhruksasri, eds, *Highlanders of Thailand*, Kuala Lumpur: Oxford University Press, pp. 307–25.

—— 1983c, 'The Dynamics of Commercialized Arts: The Meo and Yeo of Northern Thailand', *Journal of the National Research Council of Thailand*, 15, 1, pp. 1–34.

—— n.d., 'Hill Tribe Tourism', report presented to the H. S. Truman Research Institute at the Hebrew University of Jerusalem.

—— 1984a, 'The Dropout Expatriates: A Study of Marginal *Farangs* in Bangkok', *Urban Anthropology*, 13, 1, pp. 91–114.

—— 1984b, 'Social Change in Thailand: A Reconceptualization', in E. Cohen, M. Lissak and U. Almagor, eds, *Comparative Social Dynamics*, Boulder, Co: Westview Press.

—— 1986, 'Lovelorn *Farangs*: The Correspondence Between Foreign Men and Thai Girls', *Anthropological Quarterly*, 59, 3, pp. 115–27.

—— 1987, 'Alternative Tourism – A Critique', *Journal of Recreation Research*, 12, 2, pp. 13–18.

—— 1988a, 'Authenticity and Commoditization in Tourism', *Annals of Tourism Research*, 15, 3, pp. 371–86.

—— 1988b, 'Traditions in the Qualitative Sociology of Tourism', *Annals of Tourism Research*, 15, pp. 29–46.

—— 1988c, 'Tourism and Aids in Thailand', *Annals of Tourism Research*, 15, 4, pp. 467–86.

—— 1989, ' "Primitive and Remote", Hill Tribe Trekking in Thailand', *Annals of Tourism Research*, 16, 1, pp. 30–61.

Collins, Daniel, 1990, 'Public Monuments in Malaysia and Indonesia: Cultural Expression and the Shape of Political Power', *Suvannabhumi*, 2, 1 (December).

Colthurst, D., 1991, 'The Failure of Success', *Geographical Magazine* (June).

*Contours*, various issues, *Contours: Concern for Tourism*, The Quarterly Newsletter of the Ecumenical Coalition on Third World Tourism, Bangkok: ECTWT.

—— 1989, 'Tourism in Burma', *Dawn* (October), No. 19, in *Contours*, 4, 4 (December), 1989, pp. 28–29.

—— 1990, 'Dangerous Greens', *Contours*, 4, 8 (December), pp. 22–23.

—— 1991, 'Big Tourism Drive Finds Indonesians Unprepared', *Contours*, 5 (March), 1, pp. 26–27.

Cooper, Malcolm, 1989, 'McGregor Gow and the Glen Line: The Rise and Fall of a British Shipping Firm in the Far East Trade, 1870–1911', *Journal of Transport History*, 3rd series, 10, pp. 166–79.

Cooper, Robert, 1984, *Resource Scarcity and the Hmong Response Patterns of Settlement and Economy*, Singapore: Singapore University Press.

Covarrubias, M., 1937, *Island of Bali*, Singapore: Oxford University Press (reprinted 1987).

Cribb, Robert, 1990, 'The Politics of Pollution Control in Indonesia', *Asian Survey*, XXX, 12 (December), pp. 1123–35.

Crick, Malcolm, 1985, 'Tracing the Anthropological Self: Quizzical Reflections on Field Work, Tourism, and the Ludic', *Social Analysis*, 17, pp. 71–92.

—— 1989, 'Representations of International Tourism in the Social Sciences: Sun, Sex, Sights, Savings, and Servility', *Annual Review of Anthropology*, 18, pp. 307–44.

Crowther, Geoff and Tony Wheeler, 1988, *Malaysia, Singapore and Brunei – A Travel Survival Kit*, Victoria: Lonely Planet Publications.

Crystal, Eric, 1989, 'Tourism in Toraja', in V. L. Smith, ed., *Hosts and Guests: The Anthropology of Tourism*, 2nd edition, Philadelphia: University of Pennsylvania Press.

*Cultural Survival Quarterly*, 1982, 'Ethnic Art: Works in Progress?', *Cultural Survival Quarterly*, 6, 4 (1982).

Dalton, Bill, 1978, *Indonesia Handbook*, 2nd edition, Vermont: Moon Publications.

Dann, G., 1988, 'Images of Cyprus Projected by Tour Operators', *Problems of Tourism*, 11, 3, Institute of Tourism, University of Warsaw.

—— forthcoming, 'The People of Tourist Brochures', forthcoming in T. Selwyn, ed., *Chasing Myths*.

Daroesman, Ruth, 1973, 'An Economic Survey of Bali', *Bulletin of Indonesian Economic Studies*, 9/3, pp. 1–34.

Davis, Gloria, 1979, 'What Is Modern Indonesian Culture? An Epilogue and

Example', in G. Davis, ed., *What Is Modern Indonesian Culture?*, Athens: Ohio University Center for International Studies.

Davis, Winston, 1987, 'Religion and Development: Weber and the East Asian Experience', in M. Weiner and S. P. Huntington, eds, *Understanding Political Development*, Boston: Little, Brown.

Deaton, A. S. and J. Muellbauer, 1980a, *Economics and Consumer Behaviour*, Cambridge: Cambridge University Press.

—— 1980b, 'An Almost Ideal Demand System', *American Economic Review*, 70, 3, pp. 312–26.

Demaine, Harvey, 1986, '*Kanpatthana:* Thai Views of Development', in M. Hobart and R. H. Taylor, eds, *Context, Meaning, and Power in Southeast Asia*, Ithaca: Cornell Southeast Asia Program.

Departemen Pendidikan dan Kebudayaan Kantor Wilayah Propinsi Daerah Istimewa Yogyakarta, 1984–5, *Proyek pengembangan kesenian D.I.Y.*, (*Project to develop the arts in the Special Region of Yogyakarta*), Yogyakarta: Departemen Pendidikan dan Kebudayaan Kantor Wilayah Propinsi Daerah Istimewa Yogyakarta.

—— 1987–88, *Laporan penyelenggaraan pergelaran teatre tradisional krumpyung dalam rangka pergelaran seni di Taman Budaya Yogyakarta* (*Report on the organisation of the performance of the traditional drama krumpyung for the performance at the Taman Budaya hall in Yogya*), Yogyakarta: Departemen Pendidikan dan Kebudayaan Kantor Wilayah Propinsi Daerah Istimewa Yogyakarta.

Department of Information, 1969, *The First Five-Year Development Plan* (1969/70–1973/74), Jakarta.

*Dewan Masyarakat*, 1984, Kuala Lumpur: Dewan Bahasa dan Pustaka.

Diamond, J., 1974, 'International Tourism and the Developing Countries: A Case Study in Failure', *Economia Internazionale*, 27, 3–4, pp. 601–15.

—— 1977, 'Tourism's Role in Economic Development: The Case Reexamined', *Economic Development and Cultural Change*, 25, 3, pp. 539–53.

—— 1979, *The Economic Impact of International Tourism on the Singapore Economy*, Harvard Institute for International Development Discussion Paper No. 77, Harvard University Press.

Dogan, Hasan Zafer, 1989, 'Forms of Adjustment: Sociocultural Impacts of Tourism', *Annals of Tourism Research*, 16, 2, pp. 216–36.

Duff-Cooper, A., 1986, 'A Balinese Form of Life in Western Lombok as a Totality', *JASO*, XVII, 3, pp. 207–30.

Dumont, L., 1970, *Homo Hierarchicus*, London: Weidenfeld and Nicolson.

Durkheim, Emile, 1976, *The Elementary Forms of the Religious Life*, (2nd edition) London: Allen and Unwin.

Eadington, William R. and Milton Redman, 1991, 'Economics and Tourism', *Annals of Tourism Research*, 18, 1, pp. 41–56.

Eco, U., 1986, *Faith in Fakes*, London: Secker and Warburg.

Economist Intelligence Unit, 1990, 'Malaysia', *EIU International Tourism Reports*, No. 3, pp. 67–94.

—— 1991, *International Tourism Report*, No. 3.

Edgell, David L., Sr., 1990, *Charting a Course of International Tourism in the 1990's: An Agenda for Managers and Executives*, Washington, DC: US Department of Commerce.

344    *References*

Edwards, Anthony, 1990, *Far East and Pacific Travel in the 1990s*, The Economist Intelligence Unit.

Eisenstadt, S. N. 1966, *Modernization: Protest and Change*, Englewood Cliffs: Prentice-Hall.

—— ed., 1968, *The Protestant Ethic and Modernization: A Comparative View*, New York: Basic Books.

—— and L. Roniger, 1980, 'Patron–Client Relations as a Model of Structuring Social Exchange', *Comparative Studies in Society and History*, 22, 1, pp. 42–77.

Elliott, James, 1983, 'Politics, Power and Tourism in Thailand', *Annals of Tourism Research*, 10, 3, pp. 377–93.

—— 1987, 'Government Management of Tourism – A Thai Case Study', *Tourism Management*, 8, 3, pp. 223–32.

English, E. P., 1986, *The Great Escape? An Examination of North–South Tourism*, Ottawa: North–South Institute.

Errington, Frederick and Deborah Gerwertz, 1989, 'Tourism and Anthropology in a Post-Modern World', *Oceania*, 60, 1, pp. 37–54.

Escobar, Arturo, 1988, 'Power and Visibility: Development and the Invention and Management of the Third World', *Cultural Anthropology*, 3, 4, pp. 428–43.

Evans, Peter B. and John Stephens, 1988a, 'Development and the World Economy', in N. J. Smelser, ed., *Handbook of Sociology*, Beverly Hills: Sage, pp. 739–73.

—— 1988b, 'Studying Development Since the Sixties', *Theory and Society*, 17, 5, pp. 713–45.

*Far Eastern Economic Review*, 1992, 'Facing up to AIDS: Thailand's Example', *Far Eastern Economic Review*, 155, 6, pp. 28–35.

Feiffer, Maxine, 1985, *Tourism in History*, New York: Stein and Day.

Fisher, James F., 1990, *Sherpas: Reflections on Change in Himalayan Nepal*, Berkeley and Los Angeles: University of California Press.

Fletcher, J. and H. Snee, 1989, 'Tourism in the South Pacific Island's', in C. P. Cooper, ed., *Progress in Tourism, Recreation and Hospitality Management*, Volume One, London: Belhaven, pp. 114–24.

te Flierhaar, H., 1941, 'De aanpassing van het inlandsch onderwijs op Bali aan de eigen sfeer' ('The Adaptation of Indigenous Education in the Private Sphere in Bali'), *Koloniaal Studien*, 25, pp. 1–24.

Forrest, Thomas, 1969, *A Voyage to New Guinea and the Moluccas, 1774–1776*, 2nd edition, Kuala Lumpur: Oxford University Press (originally published 1780, London).

Forster, John, 1964, 'The Sociological Consequences of Tourism', *International Journal of Comparative Sociology*, 5, 2, pp. 217–27.

Forth, Gregory, 1983, 'Review of *Komodo: het Eiland, het Volk en de Taal* ', *Indonesia Circle*, 32 (November), pp. 56–58.

Fox, Morris, 1976, 'The Social Impact of Tourism: A Challenge to Researchers and Planners', in Ben Finney and Karen Ann Watson, eds, *A New Kind of Sugar: Tourism in the Pacific*, Honolulu: East–West Center Press.

Francillon, G., 1979, *Bali: Tourism, Culture, Environment*, Paris: Unesco.

—— 1989, 'The Dilemma of Tourism in Bali', in W. Beller, P. d'Ayala and P. Hein, eds, *Sustainable Development and Environmental Management of Small Islands*, Paris: Unesco, MAB Series, pp. 267–72.

Frank, Andre Gunder, 1966, 'The Development of Underdevelopment', *Monthly Review*, 18, 4, pp. 17–31.

Fraser-Lu, Sylvia, 1988, *Handwoven Textiles of South-East Asia*, Singapore: Oxford University Press.

Fuller, Theodore D., Peerasit Kamnuansilpa, Paul Lightfoot and Sawaeng Rathanamongkolmas, 1983, *Migration and Development in Modern Thailand*, Bangkok: The Social Science Association of Thailand.

Furnham, Adrian and Stephen Bochner, 1990, *Culture Shock: Psychological Reactions to Unfamiliar Environments*, London: Routledge (reprint).

Gagnon, J. H., 1968, 'Prostitution', in *International Encyclopedia of the Social Sciences*, 12, pp. 592–98.

de Gallo, M. T. and H. Alzate, 1976, 'Brothel Prostituion in Columbia', *Archives of Sexual Behavior*, 5, 1, pp. 1–7.

Geertz, Clifford, 1963a, *Agricultural Involution: The Processes of Ecological Change in Indonesia*, Berkeley and Los Angeles: University of California Press.

—— 1963b, 'The Integrative Revolution: Primordial Sentiments and Civil Politics in the New States', in C. Geertz, ed., *Old Societies and New States*, New York: Free Press.

—— 1963c, *Peddlers and Princes: Social Development and Economic Change in Two Indonesian Towns*, Chicago: University of Chicago Press.

—— 1984, 'Culture and Social Change: The Indonesian Case', *Man* (n.s.), 19, pp. 511–32.

Gelston, Sally, 1989, 'The Golden Rule of Enforcement', *Asia Travel Trade* (December), p. 57.

Geriya, W., 1988, 'Peranan Kesenian dan Kebudayaan Bali dalam Diplomasi Kebudayaan' ('The role of Art and Culture in Bali in Diplomatic Culture'), in M. J. Atmaja, ed., *Puspanjali. Persembahan untuk Prof. Dr. Ida Bagus Mantra (Essays in Honour of Prof. Dr. Ida Bagus Mantra)*, Denpasar: Kayumas, pp. 149–59.

Gibbons, J. D. and M. Fish, 1989, 'Indonesia's International Tourism: A Shifting Industry in Bali', *International Journal of Hospitality Management*, 8/1, pp. 63–70.

Gittings, J. H., 1967, 'They Call It "R & R" ', *Presbyterian Life* (15 August) pp. 34–38.

Goffman, E., 1974, *Frame Analysis*, New York: Harper and Row.

Goldstein, Carl, 1990, 'Twist in the Trail', *Far Eastern Economic Review* (31 May) pp. 42–44.

Gorer, Geoffrey, 1936, *Bali and Angkor: A 1930s Pleasure Trip Looking at Life and Death*, Singapore, Oxford University Press (reprinted 1986).

Gottlieb, A., 1982, 'America's Vacations', *Annals of Tourism Research*, 9, 2, pp. 165–87.

Government of Thailand, NESDB (National Economic and Social Development Board), 1989, Gross Regional and Provincial Product, 1981–87, Bangkok: Office of the Prime Minister, NESDB.

Graburn, Nelson H. H., ed., 1976, *Ethnic and Tourist Arts: Cultural Expressions from the Fourth World*, Berkeley: University of California Press.

—— 1977, 'Tourism: The Sacred Journey', in Valene L. Smith, ed., *Hosts and Guests: The Anthropology of Tourism*, Philadelphia: University of Pennsylvania Press.

346 *References*

—— 1982, 'The Dynamics of Change in Tourist Arts', *Cultural Survival Quarterly*, 6, 2, pp. 7–11.

—— 1983, 'The Anthropology of Tourism', *Annals of Tourism Research*, 10, pp. 9–33.

—— 1984, 'The Evolution of Tourist Arts', *Annals of Tourism Research*, 11, 3, pp. 393–419.

Greenwood, Davyyd J., 1977, 'Culture by the Pound: An Anthropological Perspective on Tourism as Cultural Commoditization', in Valene L. Smith, ed., *Hosts and Guests: The Anthropology of Tourism*, Philadelphia: University of Pennsylvania Press, pp. 129–38.

—— 1989, 'Epilogue to "Culture by the Pound" ', in Valene L. Smith, ed., *Hosts and Guests: The Anthropology of Tourism*, 2nd edition, Philadelphia: University of Pennsylvania Press, pp. 171–86.

Grynbaum, Gail, 1971, 'Tourism and Underdevelopment', *NACLA Newsletter*, 5, 2, pp. 1–12.

Guillemard, F. H. H., 1886, *The Cruise of the Marchesa to Kamschatka and New Guinea with Notices of Formosa, Liu-Kiu, and Various Islands of the Malay Archipelago*, London: John Murray.

Guldin, Gregory Eliyu, 1989, 'The Anthropological Study Tour in China: A Call for Cultural Guides', *Human Organization*, 48, 2, pp. 126–34.

Gunadhi, H. and C. K. Boey, 1986, 'Demand Elasticities of Tourism in Singapore', *Tourism Management*, 7, 4, pp. 239–53.

Gunn, C., 1988, *Tourism Planning*, New York: Taylor and Francis.

Gusfield, Joseph R., 1967, 'Tradition and Modernity: Misplaced Polarities in the Study of Social Change', *American Journal of Sociology*, 72, 4, pp. 351–62.

Hail, J., 1980, 'Scant Options, Little Action', *Business Times Week*, 2, 2, pp. 11–16.

Hall, Anthony, 1988, 'Community Participation and Development Policy: A Sociological Perspective', in Anthony Hall and James Midgley, eds, *Development Policies: Sociological Perspectives*, Manchester: Manchester University Press, pp. 91–107.

Hamilton, Alex, 1990, *Environment Guardian* (10 August) p. 21.

Handler, Richard and Jocelyn Linnekin, 1984, 'Tradition, Genuine or Spurious', *Journal of American Folklore*, 97, 385, pp. 273–90.

Handley, P., 1989, 'Room to Expand', *Far Eastern Economic Review* (12 October), p. 65.

Hanks, L. M., 1962, 'Merit and Power in the Thai Social Order', *American Anthropologist*, 64, 2, pp. 1247–50.

—— 1975, 'The Thai Social Order as Entourage and Circle', in G. W. Skinner and A. T Kirsch, eds, *Change and Persistence in Thai Society: Essays in Honor of Lauriston Sharp*, pp. 197–218, Ithaca, New York: Cornell University Press.

—— and H. Phillips, 1961, 'A Young Thai from the Countryside', in B. Kaplan, ed., *Studying Personality Cross Culturally*, New York: Harper and Row, pp. 637–56.

Hanna, W. A., 1972, 'Bali in the Seventies. Part I: Cultural Tourism', *American Universities Field Staff Reports, Southeast Asia Series*, 20/2, pp. 1–7.

—— 1976, *Bali Profile: People, Events, Circumstances (1001/1976)*, New York: American Universities Field Staff.

Hannerz, Ulf, 1986, 'Theory in Anthropology: Small is Beautiful? The Problem of Complex Cultures', *Comparative Studies in Society and History*, 28, 2, pp. 362–67.

Hanson, Allan, 1989, 'The Making of the Maori: Cultural Invention and its Logic', *American Anthropologist*, 91, 4, pp. 890–902.

Hapgood, D. and M. Bennett, 1968, *Agents of Change: A Close Look at the Peace Corps*, Boston: Little, Brown.

Harcourt, Freda, 1988, 'British Oceanic Mail Contracts in the Age of Steam, 1838–1914', *Journal of Transport History*, 3rd series, 9, pp. 1–18.

Harrison, Cuthbert Woodville, ed., 1911, *An Illustrated Guide to the Federated Malay States* (second impression), London: The Malay States Information Agency.

—— ed., 1923, *An Illustrated Guide to the Federated Malay States* (fourth impression), London: The Malay States Information Agency.

Harrison, David, 1988, *The Sociology of Modernization and Development*, London: Unwin Hyman.

Harrisson, Tom, 1951, 'Robert Burns: The First Ethnologist and Explorer of Interior Sarawak', *Sarawak Museum Journal*, V, 3, (new series), November, pp. 463–94.

Harvey, D., 1989, *The Condition of Postmodernity*, Oxford: Basil Blackwell.

Hawkins, Donald, ed., 1990, *Tourism Policy Forum*, George Washington University, International Institute of Tourism Studies (November), p. 10.

Heyl, B. S., 1977, 'The Madam as Teacher: The Training of House Prostitutes', *Social Problems*, 24, pp. 545–55.

Hiemstra, S. J., 1991, 'World Tourism Outlook for 1990s', *World Travel and Tourism Review*, Volume 1.

Hirschman, Albert O., 1975, 'Policy-Making and Policy Analysis in Latin America: A Return Journey', *Policy Sciences*, 6, pp. 385–402.

Hoben, Allan and Robert Hefner, 1991, 'The Integrative Revolution Revisited', *World Development*, 19, 2, pp. 17–30.

Hobsbawm, Eric and Terence Ranger, eds, 1983, *The Invention of Tradition*, Cambridge: Cambridge University Press.

Hofmann, Norbert, 1979, *A Survey of Tourism in West Malaysia and Some Socio-Economic Implications*, Singapore: ISEAS, Research Notes and Discussion, Paper No. 13.

*Holiday Which?*, 1990, 'Malaysia' (January) pp. 44–51.

Hon, Denis, 1989, 'Culture Designed for Tourism: The Sarawak Context', *Sarawak Museum Journal*, special issue, No. 4, pt. I, pp. 285–92.

Hong, Evelyne, 1985, *See the Third World While it Lasts: The Social and Environmental Impact of Tourism, With Particular Reference to Malaysia*, Penang: Consumers Association of Penang.

Hornaday, William T., 1885, *Two Years in the Jungle: The Experiences of a Hunter and Naturalist in India, Ceylon, The Malay Peninsula and Borneo*, London: Kegan, Paul, Trench and Co.

Hoselitz, Bert F., 1952, 'Non-Economic Barriers to Economic Development', *Economic Development and Cultural Change*, 1, 1, pp. 8–21.

Houbert, J., 1978, 'Report on the Seychelles', *Race and Class*, 19, pp. 294–300.

Hubback, Theodore R., 1923, 'Big Game Shooting', in Cuthbert Woodville Harrison, ed., 1911, *An Illustrated Guide to the Federated Malay States*, London: The Malay States Information Agency, pp. 230–53.

Hubegger, Larry and James O'Reilly, 1990, 'Tiny Brunei Retains Old World Charm', *Kansas City Star*, (29 July), p. 62.

Hughes-Freeland, Felicia, 1990, '*Tayuban*: Culture on the Edge', *Indonesia Circle*, 52, pp. 36–44.

—— 1991, 'A Throne for the People: Observations on the Jumenengen of Sultan Hamengku Buwono X', *Indonesia*, 51, pp. 129–52.

—— forthcoming, 'Golek Menak and Tayuban: Patronage and Professionalism in two Spheres of Central Javanese Culture', in a collection of papers on performance in Java and Bali, editor Bernard Arps.

Hunt, J., 1990, 'Hotels in Asia', *Travel and Tourism Analyst*, No. 4, pp. 16–36.

Huntington, Samuel P., 1968, *Political Order in Changing Societies*, New Haven: Yale University Press.

Hussey, Antonia, 1989, 'Tourism in a Balinese Village', *Geographical Review*, 79, pp. 311–25.

Hyde, Francis E., 1964, 'British Shipping Companies in East and South-East Asia, 1860–1939', in C. D. Cowan, ed., *The Economic Development of South-East Asia*, London: Allen and Unwin.

—— 1973, *Far Eastern Trade 1800–1914*, London: Black.

IBRD/IDA, 1974, *Bali Tourism Project: Appraisal Report*, Washington: Tourism Projects Department.

Ichaporia, Niloufer, 1982, 'Imports and Exportmania', *Cultural Survival Quarterly*, 6, 4, pp. 12–14.

*IDRC Reports*, 1988, 'Artisans of Progress', 17, 2 (April), pp. 1–15, Ottawa: International Development Research Centre.

*In Focus*, 1991, 'Sustainable Tourism: Pros and Cons', *In Focus* (Magazine of Tourism Concern), No. 1 (Summer 1991).

*Independent on Sunday*, 1990 (5 August).

Inkeles, Alex, 1983, *Exploring Individual Modernity*, New York: Columbia University Press.

Inkeles, Alex and D. H. Smith, 1974, *Becoming Modern: Individual Change in Six Developing Countries*, Cambridge: Harvard University Press.

Insight Guides, 1989, *Malaysia*, Singapore: APA Publications.

Inskeep, Edward, 1987, 'Environmental Planning for Tourism', *Annals of Tourism Research*, 14, 1, pp. 118–35.

Ireland, M. J., 1989, 'Tourism in Cornwall: An Anthropological Case Study', unpublished Ph.D. thesis, University College of Swansea.

Islam, Rizwanul, ed., 1985, *Strategies for Alleviating Poverty in Rural Asia*, Bangkok: International Labour Organization, Asian Employment Programme.

—— ed., 1987, *Rural Industrialization and Employment in Asia*, New Delhi: International Labour Organization, Asian Employment Programme.

Jafari, J., 1986, 'Tourism for Whom? Old Questions Still Echoing', *Annals of Tourism Research*, 13, pp. 129–37.

—— 1987, 'Tourism Models: The Sociocultural Aspects', *Tourism Management*, 8, 2.

Jameson, F., 1985, 'Postmodernism and Consumer Society', in H. Foster, ed., *Postmodern Culture*, London: Pluto.

Japan International Cooperation Agency, 1989, *Study on Potential Tourism Area Development for the Southern Region of Thailand*, Tokyo: JICA.

Jayasuriya, S. and K. Nehen, 1989, 'Bali: Economic Growth and Tourism', in H. Hill, ed., *Unity and Diversity: Regional Economic Development in Indonesia since 1970*, Singapore: Oxford University Press, pp. 330–48.

Jenkins, Ron, 1980, 'The Holy Humor of Bali's Clowns', *Asia*, 3, 2, pp. 29–35.

Jensen, I., 1990, 'Thailand's War on AIDS', *The Nation*, (16 August) p. 38.

Joffe, Joyce, 1969, *Conservation*, London: Aldus Books.

Johnston, Barbara R., 1990, 'Introduction: Breaking Out of the Tourist Trap', *Cultural Survival Quarterly*, 14, 1, pp. 2–5.

Joiner, Charles A., 1990, 'The Vietnam Communist Party Strives to Remain the "Only Force" ', *Asian Survey*, 30, 11 (November), pp. 1053–65.

Jones, Michael, 1986, *A Sunny Place for Shady People*, Sydney: Allen and Unwin.

Junaenah Sulehan and Fatimah Kari, 1989, 'Culture Designed for Tourism', *Sarawak Museum Journal*, Special Issue No. 4, pt I, pp. 279–84.

Just, Peter, 1986, 'Don/Donggo Social Organisation: Ideology, Structure and Action in an Indonesian Society', unpublished Ph.D. dissertation, Philadelphia: University of Pennsylvania.

Kadir H. Din, 1982, 'Tourism in Malaysia: Competing Needs in a Plural Society', *Annals of Tourism Research*, 9, pp. 453–80.

—— 1986, 'Differential Ethnic Involvement in the Penang Tourist Industry: Some Policy Implications', *Akademika*, 29, pp. 3–20.

—— 1988a, 'Social and Cultural Impacts of Tourism', *Annals of Tourism Research*, 15, 4, pp. 563–66.

—— 1988b, 'The Concept of Local Involvement and its Application to Malaysian Island Resorts', paper presented at the First Conference on Anthropology of Tourism, Roehampton Institute, London, 22–23 April 1988.

—— 1989a, 'Islam and Tourism: Patterns, Issues and Options', *Annals of Tourism Research*, 16, 4, pp. 542–63.

—— 1989b, 'Towards an Integrated Approach to Tourism Development: Observations from Malaysia', in Tej Vir Singh, H. L. Theuns and Frank M. Go, eds, *Towards Alternative Tourism: The Case of Developing Countries*, Frankfurt: Peter Lang, pp. 181–204.

de Kadt, Emanuel, ed., 1979, *Tourism: Passport to Development?*, New York: Oxford University Press.

—— 1990, 'Making the Alternative Sustainable: Lessons from Development for Tourism', in CEMP (Centre for Environmental Management and Planning), *Environment, Tourism and Development: An Agenda for Action?* A workshop to consider strategies for sustainable tourism development, Valetta, Malta, 4–10 March 1990.

Kathuria, Sanjay, Virginia Miralao and Rebecca Joseph, 1988, *Artisan Industries in Asia: Four Case Studies*, Ottawa: IDRC, Technical Study 60e.

Kedit, Peter M., 1980, *A Survey on the Effects of Tourism on Iban Longhouse Communities in the Skrang District, Sarawak*, Kuching: Sarawak Museum Field Report No. 2 (February).

Keppel, Henry, 1847, *The Expedition to Borneo of H.M.S. Dido for the*

*Suppression of Piracy: With Extracts from the Journal of James Brooke, Esq. of Sarawak, (now Her Majesty's Commissioner and Consul-General to the Sultan and Independent Chiefs of Borneo), Third edition, with an Additional Chapter, Comprising Recent Intelligence, by Walter V. Kelly*, 2 vols, London: Chapman and Hall.

Keyes, Charles F., 1984, 'Mother or Mistress But Never a Monk: Culture of Gender and Rural Women in Buddhist Thailand', *American Ethnologist*, 11, 2, pp. 223–41.

—— 1989, *Thailand: Buddhist Kingdom as Modern Nation State*, Bangkok: Duang Kamol.

Khan, Habibullah, 1986, 'Marine Intensive Tourism in ASEAN Countries', *Southeast Asian Economic Review*, 7, pp. 175–204.

Khan, Habibullah, F. S. Chou and K. C. Wong, 1990, 'Tourism Multiplier Effects on Singapore', *Annals of Tourism Research*, 17, 3, pp. 408–18.

Khin Thitsa, 1980, *Providence and Prostitution: Image and Reality for Women in Buddhist Thailand*, London: Change, International Reports.

King, William L., 1977, 'Umbrellas Make Their Day', *Journal of the National Research Council of Thailand*, 9, 2, pp. 1–33.

Kirkpatrick, C. H., N. Lee and F. I. Nixson, 1984, *Industrial Structure and Policy in Less Developed Countries*, London: Allen and Unwin.

Kirsch, A. T., 1975, 'Economy, Polity and Religion in Thailand', in G. W. Skinner and A. T Kirsch, eds, *Change and Persistence in Thai Society: Essays in Honor of Lauriston Sharp*, Ithaca, New York: Cornell University Press, pp. 172–96.

Klieger, P. Christian, 1990, 'Close Encounters: "Intimate" Tourism in Tibet', *Cultural Survival Quarterly*, 14, 2, pp. 38–41.

Krause, G., 1920, *Bali 1912*, Wellington: January Books (reprinted 1988).

Krell, Maya, 1989, 'Tourism in Centrally-Planned Economies – State of Cambodia as a Case Study', *Contours*, 4, 4 (December), pp. 16–17.

Krongkaew, Medhi, 1988, 'The Development of Small- and Medium-Scale Industries in Thailand', *Asian Development Review*, 6, 2, pp. 70–95.

*Kuoni Worldwide*, 10 December 1989–9 December 1990.

Langholz-Leymore, V., 1975, *Hidden Myth: Structure and Symbolism in Advertising*, London: Heinemann.

Lanfant, Marie-Francoise, 1980, 'Introduction: Tourism in the Process of Internationalization', *International Social Science Journal*, 37, 1, pp. 14–43.

Lansing, J. S., 1974, *Evil in the Morning of the World: Phenomenological Approaches to a Balinese Community*, Ann Arbor: The University of Michigan Center for South and Southeast Asian Studies.

Lash, S., 1990, *Sociology of Postmodernism*, London: Routledge.

Lasswell, Harold, 1936, *Politics: Who Gets What, When, and How*, New York: McGraw Hill.

Lea, John, 1988, *Tourism and Development in the Third World*, London: Routledge (Routledge Introductions to Development Series).

Lee, G., 1987, 'Tourism as a Factor in Development Cooperation', *Tourism Management*, 8, 1, pp. 2–19.

Lerner, Daniel, 1958, *The Passing of Traditional Society: Modernizing the Middle East*, New York: Free Press.

Levi-Strauss, Claude, 1962, *Le Totemisme Ajourd'hui*, Paris: Presses Universitaires de France.
—— 1964, *Mythologiques: Le Cru et le Cuit*, Paris: Plon.
—— 1966, *Mythologiques: Du Miel Aux Cendres*, Paris: Plon.
—— 1978, *Myth and Meaning*, London: Routledge and Kegan Paul.
—— 1985, *Anthropologie Structurale*, Paris: Plon.
Levien, Michael, ed., 1981, *The Cree Journals: The Voyages of Edward H. Cree, Surgeon R. N., as Related in His Journals, 1837-1856*, Exeter: Webb and Bowes.
Levy, Marion J. Jr., 1966, *Modernization and the Structure of Societies*, Princeton: Princeton University Press.
—— 1972, *Modernization: Latecomers and Survivors*, New York: Basic Books.
—— 1986, 'Modernization Exhumed', *Journal of Developing Societies*, 2, pp. 1-11.
Lin, T-B. and Sung, Y-W., 1983, 'Hong Kong' in Elwood A. Pye and Txong-biau Lin, eds, *Tourism in Asia: The Economic Impact*, Singapore: Singapore University Press, pp. 1-99.
Lindsay, J., 1985, 'Klasik, Kitsch or Contemporary: A Study of the Javanese Performing Arts', unpublished Ph.D. thesis, University of Sydney.
Long Chu and Fong Woon Siew, 1988, 'Country Paper on Singapore: Measurement of the Economic Impact of Tourism by Input–Output Analysis', *ESCAP Tourism Review*, No. 5.
Loose, Stefan and Renate Ramb, 1990, *Malaysia, Singapore and Brunei: The Traveller's Guide*, 2nd edition, Huddersfield: Springfield Books.
Low, Hugh, 1848, *Sarawak, Its Inhabitants and Productions: Being Notes During a Residence in That Country with His Excellency Mr Brooke*, London: Richard Bentley (reprinted 1968, London: Cass).
Lumholtz, Carl, 1920, *Through Central Borneo*, 2 vols, New York: Charles Scribner's Sons.
Mabbett, Hugh, 1987, *In Praise of Kuta - From Slave Port to Fishing Village to the Most Popular Resort in Bali*, Wellington: January Books.
Mabogunje, Akin L., 1989, *The Development Process: A Spatial Perspective*, 2nd edition. London: Hutchinson.
MacCannell, Dean, 1976, *The Tourist: A New Theory of the Leisure Class*, New York: Shocken.
—— 1984, 'Reconstructed Ethnicity: Tourism and Cultural Identity in Third World Communities', *Annals of Tourism Research*, 11, 3, pp. 375-91.
McDonald, H. and M. Schuman, 1991, 'Host of Woes', *Far Eastern Economic Review* (15 August), pp. 35-36.
McDowell, B., 1982, 'Thailand: Luck of a Land in the Middle', *National Geographic*, 162, 4, pp. 500-35.
McKean, Philip, 1973, 'Cultural Involution: Tourists, Balinese, and the Process of Modernization in Anthropological Perspective', unpublished Ph.D. dissertation, Department of Anthropology, Brown University.
—— 1976, 'Tourism, Culture Change and Culture Conservation', in D. Banks, ed., *World Anthropology: Ethnic Identity in Modern Southeast Asia*, The Hague: Mouton.
—— 1977a, 'Towards a Theoretical Analysis of Tourism, Economic Dualism and Cultural Involution in Bali', in V. Smith, ed., *Hosts and Guests: The*

*Anthropology of Tourism*, Philadelphia: University of Pennsylvania Press, pp. 93-108.

—— 1977b, 'From Purity to Pollution? A Symbolic Form in Transition', in A. Becker and A. Yengoyan, eds, *The Imagination of Realilty: Symbol Systems in Southeast Asia*, Tucson: University of Arizona Press, pp. 293-302.

—— 1982, 'Tourists and Balinese', *Cultural Survival Quarterly*, 6, 3, pp. 32-33.

MacKinnon, J., and K. MacKinnon, 1986, *Review of the Protected Areas System in the Indo-Malayan Realm*, Gland: United Nations Environment Programme.

McNair, J. F., 1878 *Perak and the Malays*, Kuala Lumpur: Oxford University Press (reprinted 1972).

McTaggart, W. Donald, 1980, 'Tourism and Tradition in Bali', *World Development*, 8, pp. 457-66.

Malaysian Government, 1989, *Mid-Term Review of the Fifth Malaysia Plan, 1986-90*, Kuala Lumpur: Government Printers.

Malaysian Tourist Development Corporation, 1989a, *A Visitor's Guide to Perlis*, Indera Kayangan, Kuala Lumpur: TDC.

—— 1989b, *A Visitor's Guide to Perak*, Darul Ridzuan, Kuala Lumpur: TDC.

—— 1990a, *Visit Malaysia Year 1990*, Consumer Brochure, Kuala Lumpur: TDC.

—— 1990b, *Malaysia Travel Planner*, Kuala Lumpur: TDC.

—— 1990c, *Incentive Malaysia*, Kuala Lumpur: TDC.

—— 1991, *Annual Tourism Statistical Report, 1990*, Kuala Lumpur: TDC.

*Malaysia Tourism News*, 1991, 'Visit Malaysia Year 1990: How Successful Was It?', (March).

*Manila Chronicle*, 1990, 'We Must Care For Our Home', *Manila Chronicle* (29 January).

Marcus, George E. and M. M. J. Fischer, 1986, *Anthropology as Cultural Critique*, Chicago: University of Chicago Press.

Marryat, Frank S., 1848, *Borneo and the Indian Archipelago with Drawings of Costume and Scenery*, London: Longman, Brown, Green and Longmans.

Mason, Peter, 1990, *Tourism: Environment and Development Perspectives*, London: Worldwide Fund for Nature.

Maugham, William Somerset, 1922, *On a Chinese Screen*, London: Heineman.

—— ed., 1963, *The Complete Short Stories*, Volume IV, Harmondsworth: Penguin.

Maurer, J. L., 1979, *Tourism and Development in a Socio-Cultural Perspective: Indonesia as a Case Study*, Genève: Institut Universitaire d'Etudes du Développement.

—— and A. Zeigler, 1988, 'Tourism and Indonesian Cultural Minorities', in P. Rossel, ed., *Tourism: Manufacturing the Exotic*, Copenhagen, pp. 64-92.

Melamid, A., 1978, 'Uncertainty in the Seychelles', *Geographical Review*, 68, pp. 228-29.

Mershon, Elizabeth, 1922, *With the Wild Men of Borneo*, Mountain View, California: Pacific Press Publishing Association.

Meyer, John W., 1987, 'The World Polity and the Authority of the Nation-

State', in G. M. Thomas, *et al.*, *Institutional Structure: Constituting State, Society and the Individual*, Beverly Hills: Sage, pp. 41–70.

Meyer, John and W. R. Scott, eds, 1983, *Organizational Environments: Ritual and Rationality*, Beverly Hills: Sage.

Miller, William H., 1986, *The Last Blue Water Liners*, London: Conway Maritime Press.

Mills, S., 1990 'AIDS: Images of a Grim Future', *Bangkok Post*, (1 December), p. 24.

Milne, S. S., 1987, 'Differential Multipliers', *Annals of Tourism Research*, 14, 4, pp. 499–515.

Moeran, B., 1983, 'The Language of Japanese Tourism', *Annals of Tourism Research* 10, 1, pp. 96–101.

Moore, Wendy, 1989, *Illustrated Guide to Malaysia*, London: Collins.

Moore, Wilbert E., 1979, *World Modernization: The Limits of Convergence*, New York: Elsevier.

Morgan, Prys, 1983, 'From a Death to a View: The Hunt for the Welsh Past in the Romantic Period', in Eric Hobsbawm and Terence Ranger, eds, *The Invention of Tradition*, Cambridge: Cambridge University Press.

Mosel, J. N., 1966, 'Fatalism in Thai Bureaucratic Decision Making', *Anthropological Quarterly*, 39, pp. 190–99.

Mouzelis, Nicos P., 1988, 'Sociology of Development: Reflections on the Present Crisis', *Sociology*, 22, 1, pp. 23–44.

Mowlana, Hamid and L. J. Wilson, 1990, *The Passing of Modernity*, New York: Longman.

Mukhopadhyay, Swapna and Chee Peng Lim, eds, 1985a, *Development and Diversification of Rural Industries in Asia*, Kuala Lumpur: Asian and Pacific Development Centre.

—— eds, 1985b, *The Rural Non-Farm Sector in Asia*, Kuala Lumpur: Asian and Pacific Development Centre.

Mundy, Rodney, 1848, *Narrative of Events in Borneo and Celebes, Down to the Occupation of Labuan: From the Journals of James Brooke, Esq., Rajah of Sarawak, and Governor of Labuan, Together with a Narrative of the Operations of H.M.S. Iris*, 2 vols, London: John Murray.

Murphy, Peter E., 1985, *Tourism: A Community Approach*, London: Routledge.

—— 1988, 'Tourism as a Force for Peace: The Local Picture', in L. J. D'Amore and J. Jafari, eds, *Tourism – A Vital Force for Peace*, Montreal: First Global Conference, pp. 132–39.

Museum voor Volkenkunde, 1989, *Toekang Potret: 100 Years of Photography in the Dutch Indies, 1839–1939*, Museum voor Volkenkunde, Rotterdam; Amsterdam: Fragment Uitgeverij.

Musyawarah Kerja, 1968, *Musyawarah Kerja Pariwisata Daerah Bali* (Workshop on Tourism in the District of Bali), Denpasar.

Narongchai, Akrasanee, *et al.*, 1983, *Rural Off-Farm Employment in Thailand*, Bangkok: Kasetsart University, Center for Applied Economics Research.

Nash, Dennison, 1977, 'Tourism as a Form of Imperialism', in V. Smith, ed., *Hosts and Guests: The Anthropology of Tourism*, Philadelphia: University of Pennsylvania Press, pp. 33–47.

354    *References*

—— 1981, 'Tourism as an Anthropological Subject', *Current Anthropology*, 22, pp. 461–68.
—— 1984, 'The Ritualization of Tourism: Comment on Graburn's *The Anthropology of Tourism*', *Annals of Tourism Research*, 11, pp. 503–22.
Nash, Dennison and Valene L. Smith, 1991, 'Anthropology and Tourism', *Annals of Tourism Research*, 18, 1, pp. 12–25.
Nash, Manning, 1984, *Unfinished Agenda: The Dynamics of Modernization in Developing Nations*, Boulder: Westview.
*The Nation*, 1987, 'Famous Massage Parlours not Banning "Farangs" ', (2 October), p. 2.
National Archives Collection, n.d., *Singapore Historical Postcards*, Singapore: Times Editions.
National Economic and Development Authority, 1989, *Philippine Economic Development Report, 1988*, Manila: National Economic and Development Authority.
Nehen, K., *et al.*, 1990, *Sumbangan Sektor Pariwisata Terhadap Pembentukan Nilai Tambah Produksi Daerah Bali* (The Role of the Tourism Sector in Increasing the Value of Production in Bali), Denpasar: Universitas Udayana.
Neumann, A. L., 1978, 'Hospitality Girls in the Philippines', *ISIS International Bulletin*, 13, pp. 13–16.
*New Straits Times*, 1991a, '$500,000 in Grants Given to Arts and Cultural Associations' 18 January, p. 4.
—— 1991b, 'Studying Effect of Ban on Tourism' 3 February, p. 3.
Nicholl, Robert, ed., 1975, *European Sources for the History of the Sultanate of Brunei in the Sixteenth Century*, Bandar Seri Begawan: Muzium Brunei.
Nicolson, Harold George, 1957, *Journey to Java*, London: Constable.
Nieuwenhuis, A. W., 1900, *In Centraal Borneo*, 2 vols, Leiden: E. J. Brill.
—— 1904–7, *Quer durch Borneo: Ergebnisse Seiner Reisen in den Jahren 1896–97 und 1898-1900* (Pathways Through Borneo: Report on his Journeys in the Years 1896–97 and 1898–1900), Leiden: Brill.
Niles, Edward, 1991, 'Sustainable Tourism Development – A Myth or a Reality?', *In Focus* (Magazine of Tourism Concern), 1 (Summer 1991), pp. 3–4.
Nolten, Marleen and Gert-Jan Tempelman, 1986, 'Handicrafts as a Means of Rural Development: A Case Study from Pahang, Peninsular Malaysia', *Malaysian Journal of Tropical Geography*, 13 (June), pp. 37–45.
Noronha, R., 1973, *A Report on the Proposed Tourism Project. Bali*, Washington: IBRD.
—— 1979a, 'Paradise Reviewed: Tourism in Bali', in E. de Kadt, ed., *Tourism. Passport to Development?*, New York: Oxford University Press, pp. 177–204.
—— 1979b, *Social and Cultural Dimensions of Tourism: A Review of the Literature in English*, World Bank Working Paper.
North, Marianne, 1980, *A Vision of Eden: The Life and Work of Marianne North* (foreword by Anthony Huxley, biographical note by Brenda E. Moon, published in collaboration with the Royal Botanic Gardens, Kew), New York: Holt, Rinehart and Winston.
Nunez, T., 1978, 'Touristic Studies in Anthropological Perspective', in: V. L. Smith, ed., *Hosts and Guests: The Anthropology of Tourism*, Oxford: Basil Blackwell.
Official Tourist Bureau, 1914, *Illustrated Tourist Guide to East Java, Bali and*

Lombok, Weltevreden: Vereeniging Toeristenverkeer.

O'Grady, Alison, ed., 1990, *The Challenge of Tourism: Learning Resources for Study and Action*, Bangkok: Ecumenical Coalition on Third World Tourism.

O'Grady, Ron, 1981, *Third World Stopover: The Tourism Debate*, Geneva: World Council of Churches.

—— 1990, 'Acceptable Tourism?', *Contours*, 4, 8 (December), pp. 9–11.

O'Hagen, J. W. and M. J. Harrison, 1984, 'Market Shares of U.S. Tourist Expenditure in Europe: An Econometric Analysis', *Applied Economics*, 16, 6, pp. 919–31.

O'Rourke, D., 1987, *Cannibal Tours* (film), O'Rourke and Associates, Filmakers, Australia (Available from Direct Cinema Ltd, Los Angeles, USA).

Ortner, Sherry B., 1989, 'Cultural Politics: Religious Activism and Ideological Transformation Among 20th Century Sherpas', *Dialectical Anthropology*, 14, pp. 197–211.

Otaganonta, W., 1991, 'Facing up to the AIDS Problem', *Bangkok Post*, (15 November), pp. 27, 48.

Pacific Consultants, 1973, *The Nusa Dua Area Development Plan*, Tokyo.

Panpiemras, Kosit, ed., 1987, *Rural Industrialization in Thailand*, Bangkok: National Economic and Social Development Board.

Parajuli, Pramod, 1991, 'Power and Knowledge in Development Discourse: New Social Movements and the State in India', *International Social Science Journal*, 43, 1, pp. 173–90.

Parenti, Michael, 1977, *Democracy for the Few*, New York: St Martin's Press.

Parnwell, Michael J. G., 1988, 'Rural Poverty, Development and the Environment: The Case of North-East Thailand', *Journal of Biogeography*, 15, 1 (January), pp. 199–208.

—— 1990, *Rural Industrialisation in Thailand*, Hull Papers in Developing Area Studies, No. 1.

—— and Suranart Khamanarong, 1990, 'Rural Industrialisation and Development Planning in Thailand', *Southeast Asian Journal of Social Science*, 18, 2 (December), pp. 1–26.

Peacock, James L., 1986, 'The Creativity of Tradition in Indonesian Religion', *History of Religions*, 25, pp. 341–51.

Pearce, Douglas, 1987, *Tourism Today: A Geographical Analysis*, Harlow: Longman; New York: John Wiley and Sons.

—— A. Markyanda and E. B. Barbier, 1989, *Blueprint for a Green Economy*, London: Earthscan Publications.

Peck, J. G. and A. S. Lepie, 1978, 'Tourism and Development in Three North Carolina Coastal Towns', in V. L. Smith, ed., *Hosts and Guests: The Anthropology of Tourism*, Oxford: Basil Blackwell.

Pemerintah Daerah (Regional Government), 1987, *Laporan Seminar Pembinaan dan Pengembangan Pariwisata Menuju Tahun 2000 di Propinsi Bali* (Report on a Seminar on the Creation and Development of Tourism for the year 2000 in the Province of Bali), Denpasar: Pemerintah Daerah Tingkat I Bali.

Peninsula and Oriental Steam Navigation Company, 1908, *The P. & O. Pocket Book* (3rd issue), London: Adam and Charles Black.

Pfeiffer, Ida, 1855, *A Lady's Second Journey Round the World*, London: Longman, Brown, Green and Longmans.

Philippine National Development Authority, 1988, *Philippines Development*

*Report*, Manilla: National Economic Development Authority.

Phillips, H., 1965, *Thai Peasant Personality*, Berkeley and Los Angeles: University of California Press.

Phongpaichit, Pasuk, 1981, 'Bangkok Masseuses: Holding Up the Family Sky', *Southeast Asia Chronicle*, 78, pp. 15–23.

—— 1982, *From Peasant Girls to Bangkok Masseuses*, Geneva: International Labour Office.

Picard, Michel, 1979, *Sociétés et Tourisme: Réflexions pour la Recherche et l'Action*, Paris: Unesco.

—— 1987, 'Du "tourisme culturel" à la "culture touristique" ', *Problems of Tourism*, 10, 2, pp. 38–52.

—— 1990, ' "Cultural Tourism" in Bali: Cultural Performances as Tourist Attraction', *Indonesia*, 49, pp. 37–74.

—— forthcoming, 'Balinese Culture: Cultural Heritage and Tourist Capital', in J. B. Allcock, E. M. Bruner and M.-F. Lanfant, eds, *International Tourism: Identity and Change: Anthropological and Sociological Studies*, London: Sage.

Picturesque Dutch East Indies, 1925, 'The Official Tourist Bureau of Weltevreden (Java)', *Inter Ocean*, 6, 8, pp. 526–29.

Pieterse, Jan Nederveen, 1991, 'Dilemmas of Development Discourse: The Crisis of Developmentalism and the Comparative Method', *Development and Change*, 22, pp. 5–29.

Pigram, J. P., 1983, *Outdoor Recreation and Resources Management*, London: Croom Helm.

—— 1990, 'Sustainable Tourism: Policy Considerations', *The Journal of Tourism Studies*, 1, 2, pp. 2–29.

Piker, S., 1968, 'The Relationship of Belief Systems to Behavior in Rural Thai Society', *Asian Survey*, 8, 5, pp. 384–99.

Pi-Sunyer, Oriel, 1979, 'The Politics of Tourism in Catalonia', *Mediterranean Studies*, 1, 2, pp. 46–69.

Pleumarom, Anita, 1990, 'Alternative Tourism: A Viable Solution?', *Contours*, 4, 8 (December), pp. 12–15.

Poe, E. A., 1927, 'Narratives of A. Gordon Pym', in E. A. Poe, *Poems and Miscellanies*, Oxford: Oxford University Press.

Pollman, Tessel, 1990, 'Margaret Mead's Balinese: The Fitting Symbols of the American Dream', *Indonesia*, 49, pp. 1–35.

Portes, Alejandro, 1980, 'Convergencies Between Conflicting Theoretical Perspectives in National Development', in H. B. Blalock Jr., ed., *Sociological Theory and Research: A Critical Appraisal*, New York: Free Press.

Postguide, 1989, *Malaysia*, Hong Kong: CFW Publications.

Powell, H., 1930, *The Last Paradise*, Singapore: Oxford University Press (reprinted 1986).

Powers, Ron, 1986, *White Town Drowsing*, New York: Penguin.

Prajogo, M. J., 1985, *Pengantar Pariwisata Indonesia (The Introduction of Tourism in Indonesia)*, Jakarta: Direktorat Jenderal Pariwisata.

Proyek Sasana Budaya Jakarta, 1979, *Naskah Kerjasama Ditjen Kebudayaan dan Ditjen Pariwisata (Document of Cooperation Between the Directorate General of Culture and the Directorate General of Tourism)*, Jakarta: Direktorat Jenderal Kebudayaan.

Pudyodyana, B., 1971, 'Thai Selective Social Change', unpublished Ph.D. thesis,

Cornell University.

Purcell, Victor, 1965, *The Memoirs of a Malayan Official*, London: Cassell.

Pye, Elwood A., 1988, *Artisans in Economic Development: Evidence from Asia*, Ottawa: IDRC, Research Report 262e.

—— and Txong-biau Lin, eds, 1983, *Tourism in Asia: The Economic Impact*, Singapore: Singapore University Press.

*Quantas Jetabout Holidays, Malaysia*, 1991/92.

Quin-Harkin, A. J, 1954, 'Imperial Airways, 1924–40', *Journal of Transport History*, I, 4, pp. 197–215.

Rabibhadana, A., 1975, 'Clientship and Class Structure in the Early Bangkok Period', in G. W. Skinner and A. T. Kirsch, eds, *Change and Persistence in Thai Society: Essays in Honor of Lauriston Sharp*, Ithaca, New York: Cornell University Press, pp. 93–124.

Rasmussen, P. R. and L. L. Kuhn, 1976, 'The New Masseuse: Play for Pay', *Urban Life*, 5, 3, pp. 271–92.

Rattanawannathip, M., 1992a, 'Will Girls Play the Game?' *The Nation*, (17 January), pp. C1, C8.

—— 1992b, 'Sommatra Does it Her Way', *The Nation*, (17 February), A10.

Redclift, Michael, 1984, *Development and the Environmental Crisis: Red or Green Alternatives?*, London: Methuen.

—— 1987, *Sustainable Development: Exploring the Contradictions*, London: Methuen.

—— 1988, 'Sustainable Development and the Market: A Framework for Analysis', *Futures* (December), pp. 635–50.

Redfoot, Donald L., 1984, 'Touristic Authenticity, Touristic Angst, and Modern Reality', *Qualitative Sociology*, 7, 4, pp. 291–309.

Reith, G. M., 1907, *Handbook to Singapore*, Singapore: Oxford University Press (reprinted 1985, revised by Walter Makepeace, with an introduction by Paul Kratoska).

Reuter, 1991, *Report on the Pacific Area Travel Conference*, Bali (10 April).

Richter, Linda K., 1980, 'The Political Uses of Tourism: A Philippine Case Study', *Journal of Developing Areas*, 14 (January), pp. 234–57.

—— 1982, *Land Reform and Tourism Development: Policy-Making in the Philippines*, Cambridge, MA: Schenkmen.

—— 1984a, 'The Potential and Pitfalls of Tourism Planning in Third World Nations: Case of Pakistan', *Tourism Recreation Research*, 1, pp. 9–13.

—— 1984b, 'The Political and Legal Dimensions of Tourism', in Peter Holden, ed., *Alternative Tourism, With a Focus on Asia*, Bangkok: Ecumenical Coalition on Third World Tourism, ATCM18/1–21.

—— 1985, 'The Fragmented Politics of U.S. Tourism', *Tourism Management*, 6, 3 (September), pp. 62–173.

—— 1989a, *The Politics of Tourism in Asia*, Honolulu: University Press of Hawaii.

—— 1989b, 'Indonesian Tourism: The Good, the Bad and the Ugly', *Contours*, 4, 1 (March), pp. 29–30.

—— 1991, 'Political Issues in Tourism Policy: A Forecast', in Donald E. Hawkins and J. R. Brent Ritchie, *World Travel and Tourism Review*, Volume 1, CAB International, London, pp. 189–94.

—— and William L. Richter, 1985, 'Policy Choices in South Asian Tourism

Development', *Annals of Tourism Research*, 12, 2, pp. 201–17.
—— and William L. Waugh, Jr., 1986, 'Terrorism and Tourism as Logical Companions', *Tourism Management* (December), pp. 230–38.
Robinson, H., 1976, *A Geography of Tourism*, London: MacDonald and Evans.
Robison, Richard, 1981, 'Culture, Politics and Economy in the Political History of the New Order', *Indonesia*, 31, pp. 1–29.
Robson, J. H. M., 1911 and 1923, 'Hints for Motorists', in Cuthbert Woodville Harrison, ed., *An Illustrated Guide to the Federated Malay States*, London: The Malay States Information Agency.
Rodenburg, Eric E., 1980, 'The Effects of Scale in Economic Development: Tourism in Bali', *Annals of Tourism Research*, 7, 2, pp. 177–96.
Roekaerts, Mil and Kris Savat, 1989, 'Mass Tourism in South and Southeast Asia – A Challenge to Christians and the Churches', in Tej Vir Singh, H. Leo Theuns and Frank M. Go, eds., *Towards Appropriate Tourism: The Case of Developing Countries*, pp. 35–69.
Romijn, Hendrika A., 1987, 'Employment Generation through Cottage Industries in Rural Thailand: Potentials and Constraints', in Rizwanul Islam, ed., *Rural Industrialisation and Employment in Asia*, New Delhi: International Labour Organization, Asian Employment Programme (ARTEP), pp. 211–40.
Rosaldo, Renato, 1989, *Culture and Truth: The Remaking of Social Analysis*, Boston: Beacon Press.
Roszak, T., 1986, *The Cult of Information*, Cambridge: Lutterworth.
Rudolph, Lloyd and Suzanne Rudolph, 1967, *The Modernity of Tradition: Political Development in India*, Chicago: Chicago University Press.
Phillips, Sir Percival, 1922, *The Prince of Wales' Eastern Book*, London: Hodder and Stoughton.
St John, Spenser, 1862, *Life in the Forests of the Far East*, 2 vols, London: Smith, Elder and Co.
Sandison, Alan, 1967, *The Wheel of Empire: A Study of the Imperial Idea in Some Late Nineteenth- and Early Twentieth-Century Fiction*, London: Macmillan.
Sanger, Annette, 1988, 'Blessing or Blight? The Effects of Touristic Dance-Drama on Village Life in Singapau, Bali', in *The Impact of Tourism on Traditional Music*, Kingston: Jamaica Memory Bank.
Santos, J. S. D., E. M. Ortiz, E. Huang and F. Secretario, 1983, 'Philippines', in Elwood A. Pye and Txong-biau Lin, eds, *Tourism in Asia: The Economic Impact*, Singapore: Singapore University Press, pp. 173–240.
SCETO, 1971, *Bali Tourism Study: Report to the Government of Indonesia*, Paris: UNDP/IBRD.
Schilling, Ton, 1957, *Tigermen of Anai*, London: Allen and Unwin.
Schreider, Helen and Frank Schreider, 1962, 'East from Bali by Seagoing Jeep to Timos', *National Geographic* (August), pp. 236–79.
Schulte Nordholt, H., 1986, *Bali: Colonial Conceptions and Political Change, 1700–1940. From Shifting Hierarchies to 'Fixed Order'*, Rotterdam: Erasmus University.
Schwarz, A., 1989, 'Tourism in Indonesia', *South*, (May), pp. 63, 66.
Schymyck P. W., 1983, 'The Impact of Tourism on the Singapore Economy', *Economic Survey of Singapore, 1983*.

Scott, David Clark, 1986, 'Manila Peddling Used Palaces, Tourism', *The Christian Science Monitor* (20 June), p. 21.

Scott, James C., 1976, *The Moral Economy of the Peasant: Rebellion and Subsistence in Southeast Asia*, New Haven: Yale University Press.

Sellato, B., 1990, 'Indonesia Goes Ethnic: Provincial Culture, Image, and Identity: Current Trends in Kalimantan', paper presented to the Centres and Peripheries in Insular Southeast Asia Round-Table, Paris: CNRS/DEVI.

Selwyn, T., 1990, 'Tourist Brochures as Postmodern Myths', in T. Selwyn, ed., *Problems of Tourism*, Vol. 13, 2, Warsaw: University of Warsaw.

Seminar Pariwisata Budaya, 1971, *Hasil Keputusan Seminar Pariwisata Budaya Daerah Bali (Proceedings of a Seminar on Cultural Tourism in Bali)*, Denpasar.

Senftleben, W., 1988, 'The Acquired Immune Deficiency Syndrome – The Case of Thailand: A New Task for Medical Geographers', *Philippine Geographical Journal*, 32, 2/3, pp. 56–65.

Seow, G., 1981, 'Economic Significance of Tourism in Singapore', *Singapore Economic Review*, October.

Shand, R. T., ed., 1986, *Off-Farm Employment in the Development of Rural Asia*, paper presented at a conference in Chiang Mai, 23–26 August 1983, Canberra: Australian National University, National Centre for Development Studies.

Shils, Edward, 1981, *Tradition*, Chicago: University of Chicago Press.

*Silk Cut Travel, Faraway Holidays* (Winter 1989/90; Summer 1990).

Sinclair, M. T., 1991, 'The Economics of Tourism', in C. P. Cooper, ed., *Progress in Tourism, Recreation and Hospitality Management*, Volume Three, London: Belhaven, pp. 1–27.

Sinclair, M. T., P. Alizadeh and E. Atieno Adero Onunga, 1992, 'The Structure of International Tourism and Tourism Development in Kenya', in D. Harrison, ed., *Tourism and the Less Developed Countries*, London: Belhaven.

Sinclair, M. T. and M. J. Stabler, eds, 1991, *The Tourism Industry: An International Analysis*, CAB. International, Wallingford.

Sinclair, M. T. and A. Tsegaye, 1990, 'International Tourism and Export Instability', *The Journal of Development Studies*, 26, 3, pp. 487–504.

Singer, Milton, 1956, 'Cultural Values in India's Economic Development', *Annals of the American Academy*, CCCV, pp. 81–91.

—— 1972, *When A Great Tradition Modernizes*, New York: Praeger.

Singh, Tej Vir, 1989, *The Kulu Valley: Impact of Tourism Development in the Mountain Areas*, New Delhi: Himalayan Books.

Sinha, Sanjay, 1985, *Planning for Rural Industrialization: A Review of Developing Country Programmes*, Occasional Paper No. 8, London: Intermediate Technology Development Group.

Singhanetra-Renard, Anchalee, 1987, 'Non-Farm Employment and Female Labour Mobility in Northern Thailand', in J. H. Morrisen and J. Townsend, eds, *Geography of Gender in the Third World*, London: Routledge, pp. 258–73.

Skinner, G. W. and A. Thomas Kirsch, eds, 1975, *Change and Persistence in Thai Society: Essays in Honor of Lauriston Sharp*, Ithaca, New York: Cornell University Press.

Smith, Harrison W., 1919, 'Sarawak: The Land of the White Rajahs', *The National Geographic Magazine*, Washington, Vol. XXXV, No. 1, January.

Smith, M. E., 1982, 'The Process of Sociocultural Continuity', *Current Anthropology*, 23, pp. 127–42.

Smith, Valene L., ed., 1977, *Hosts and Guests: The Anthropology of Tourism*, Philadelphia: University of Pennsylvania Press.

—— ed., 1978, *Hosts and Guests: The Anthropology of Tourism*, Oxford: Basil Blackwell.

—— ed., 1989, *Hosts and Guests: The Anthropology of Tourism*, second edition, Philadelphia: University of Pennsylvania Press.

Soebadio, H., 1985, *Cultural Policy in Indonesia*, Paris: Unesco, Studies and Documents on Cultural Policies.

Soedarsono, R. M., 1989, *Seni Pertunjjukan Jawa Tradisional dan Parawisata di Daerah Istimewa Yogyakarta*, (*Javanese Traditional and Tourist Performing Arts in the Special Region of Yogyakarta*), Dep. P & K.

*South China Morning Post*, 1988 (3 September).

*South Magazine*, 1988, 'Tourism in Thailand: Special Report', *South Magazine* (December), pp. 71–78.

*The Star*, 1990 (2 July).

Stöhr, Walter B. and D. R. Fraser Taylor, 1981, *Development from Above or Below? The Dialectics of Regional Planning in Developing Countries*, Chichester: John Wiley.

Sub-Committee on Tourism (SCOT), 1990, *ASEAN Tourism Industry 1990*, Kuala Lumpur, ASEAN Tourism Information Centre.

Sudhyatmaka Sugriwa, G. B., ed., 1991, *Bali Arts Festival: Pesta Kesenian Bali*, Denpasar: Cita Budaya.

Suhaini Aznam, 1990, 'Wish You Were Here', *Far Eastern Economic Review* (22 March), pp. 31–33.

Sullivan, Margaret, 1985, *Can Survive La: Cottage Industries in High-Rise Singapore*, Singapore: Graham Brash.

Suthaporn, S., 1983, 'VD and Prostitution: An Inseparable Problem', *Bangkok Post*, (1 July), p. 12.

Sutton, Margaret, 1989, 'From Five Star Hotels to Intimate Homestays', *World Development* (November), pp. 13–15.

Swidler, Ann, 1986, 'Culture in Action: Symbols and Strategies', *American Sociological Review*, 51, pp. 273–86.

—— 1990, 'Strategic Actors and Cultural Commitments: Variations in Culture's Transcendence', unpublished paper.

Syriopoulos, T. C., 1990, 'Modelling Tourism Demand for Mediterranean Destinations', Ph.D thesis in Economics, University of Kent at Canterbury.

Taylor, P., 1991a, 'Thais Face a Rising Tide of Pollution', *Financial Times* (12 February).

—— 1991b, 'Tourism Slump over Gulf War Extends to Thailand', *Financial Times* (6 February).

Techawongtham, W., 1991a, 'AIDS: A Warning for the Tea House Girls', *Bangkok Post*, (9 May), pp. 25–26.

—— 1991b, 'A Plan for All-Out War against AIDS', *Bangkok Post*, (29 November), 29, 31.

Teh, Sheila, 1989, *Asia Travel Trade* (December), pp. 60–61.

Templer, John C., ed., 1853, *The Private Letters of Sir James Brooke, K.C.B.*,

*Rajah of Sarawak, Narrating the Events of His Life from 1838 to the Present Time*, 3 vols, London: Richard Bentley.

*Thailand Foreign Affairs Newsletter*, various issues.

Thomas Cook, *Faraway Holidays, Far East* (December 1989–December 1990).

—— *The Faraway Collection* (December 1990–December 1991).

*Thomson Worldwide* (1 November 1990–9 December 1991) 2nd edition.

Thongthew-Ratarasarn, S., 1979, *The Social-Cultural Setting Of Love Magic in Central Thailand*, Madison, Wisconsin: University of Wisconsin, Center for Southeast Asian Studies, Wisconsin Papers on Southeast Asia.

Thorne, Ross and Margaret Munro-Clark, 1989, 'Hallmark Events as an Excuse for Autocracy in Urban Planning: A Case History', in Geoffrey Syme, *et al.* eds., *The Planning and Evaluation of Hallmark Events*, Sydney: Avebury Press, pp. 154–71.

*Time*, 1989, 'Destination Asia' (23 October), pp. 36–40.

Timm, Mark, 1990, 'A Search for Sustainable Tourism (in Thailand)', *Development Forum* (March–April), p. 24.

Toh Mun Heng and L. Low, 1990, 'Economic Impact of Tourism in Singapore', *Annals of Tourism Research*, 17, 2, pp. 246–69.

Tongroj, Onchan, 1986, *Rural Non-Farm Enterprises and Economic Development in Thailand*, Bangkok: Kasetsart University, Center for Applied Economics Research, Research Report No. 29 (November).

Tourism Authority of Thailand, 1989, *Shopping in Thailand*, Bangkok: Tourism Authority of Thailand.

—— 1990, 'Pattaya Leads the Way in Battle on Pollution', *Exotic Thailand*, (June), Bangkok: Tourism Authority of Thailand.

Tregonning, Kennedy Gordon, 1967, *Home Port Singapore: A History of the Straits Steamship Company Ltd.*, Singapore: Oxford University Press.

Truong, Thanh-Dam, 1983, 'The Dynamics of Sex Tourism: The Case of Southeast Asia', *Development and Change*, 14, 4, pp. 533–53.

—— 1990, *Sex, Money and Morality: Prostitution and Tourism in South-East Asia*, London: Zed.

Tucker, K., G. Seow, and M. Sundberg, 1984, *ASEAN–Australia Trade in Tourist Services*, Kuala Lumpur and Canberra: ASEAN–Australia Joint Research Project.

Turnbull, C., 1982, 'Bali's New Gods', *Natural History*, 1, pp. 26–32.

Turnbull, C. M., 1977, *A History of Singapore, 1819–1975*, Singapore: Oxford University Press.

Turner, Louis, and John Ash, 1975, *The Golden Hordes: International Tourism and the Pleasure Periphery*, London: Constable.

—— 1976, *The Golden Hordes: International Tourism and the Pleasure Periphery*, New York: St Martins Press.

Turner, V., 1969, *The Ritual Process*, Harmondsworth: Penguin.

Turner, V. and E. Turner, 1978, *Image and Pilgrimage in Christian Culture*, New York: Columbia University Press.

Tyler, Stephen A., 1986, 'Post-Modern Ethnography: From Document of the Occult to Occult Document', in J. Clifford and G. E. Marcus, eds, *Writing Culture: The Poetics and Politics of Ethnography*, Berkeley and Los Angeles: University of California Press.

United Nations Centre for Transnational Corporations, 1982, *Transnational*

## 362   References

*Corporations in International Tourism*, Report for the UNCTC by J. H. Dunning and M. McQueen, New York: United Nations.

United Nations Development Programme/Food and Agriculture Organisation, 1982, *National Conservation Plan for Indonesia, Vol. I*, Field Report of UNDP/FAO, Bogor, Indonesia.

United Nations Economic and Social Commission for Asia and the Pacific, 1988, *ESCAP Tourism Review*, Nos 4 and 5, Bangkok: ESCAP.

—— 1990, *Strategy for Rural Poverty Alleviation: Agriculture-Industry Linkages*, Bangkok: United Nations, ESCAP.

Universitas Udayana and Gerard Francillon, 1975, 'Tourism in Bali – Its Economic and Socio-Cultural Impact: Three Points of View', *International Social Science Journal*, 27, 4, pp. 721-57.

Urry, John, 1988, 'Cultural Change and Contemporary Holiday-Making', *Theory, Culture and Society*, 5, pp. 35-55.

—— 1990, *The Tourist Gaze: Leisure and Travel in Contemporary Societies*, London: Sage.

Usher, A. D., 1988a, 'Behind the Numbers: Addicts with AIDS', *The Nation*, (7 September), p. 31.

—— 1988b, 'Addicts and AIDS: The New Government's Challenge', *The Nation*, (22 August), p. 31.

—— 1991, 'Law to be Used as a Cure for AIDS?', *The Nation*, (24 March), p. 83.

*Utusan Konsumer*, 1989, 'What Price Tourism' (November) p. 4.

—— 1991, various issues (Paper of the Consumers Association of Penang).

van den Berghe, Pierre L., 1980, 'Tourism as Ethnic Relations: A Case Study of Cuzco, Peru', *Ethnic and Racial Studies*, 3, 4, pp. 375-92.

van der Velden, L., 1982, *'Tussen Prostituee en Maitress: de Hospitality Girls van Ermite, Manila, Amsterdam'*, Univesrity van Amsterdam, Antrop – Sociol Centrum, Vakgroup Zuid -en Zuidoost Asie (mimeo).

Varley, R. C. G., 1978, *Tourism in Fiji: Some Economic and Social Problems*, Occasional Papers in Economics, No. 12, Bangor: University of Wales Press.

Varma, Baidya Nath, 1980, *The Sociology and Politics of Development: A Theoretical Study*, London: Routledge and Kegan Paul.

Verheijen, J. A. J. 1982, *Komodo: het Eiland, het Volk en de Taal*, Verhandelingen van het Koninklijk Instituut voor Taal- Land- en Volkenkunde, 96, The Hague: Martinus Nijhoff.

Vickers, A., 1989, *Bali: A Paradise Created*, Berkeley: Periplus.

Volkman, Toby Alice, 1982, 'Tana Toraja: A Decade of Tourism', *Cultural Survival Quarterly*, 6, 3, pp. 30-31.

—— 1984, 'Great Performances: Toraja Cultural Identity in the 1970s', *American Ethnologist*, 11, 1, pp. 152-69.

—— 1987, 'Mortuary Tourism in Tana Toraja', in R. S. Kipp and S. Rodgers, eds, *Indonesian Religions in Transition*, Tucson: University of Arizona Press.

—— 1990, 'Visions and Revisions: Toraja Culture and the Tourist Gaze', *American Ethnologist*, 17, 1, pp. 91-110.

Waldman, Marilyn Robinson, 1986, 'Tradition as a Modality of Change: Islamic Examples', *History of Religions*, 25, pp. 318-46.

Wallace, Alfred Russel, 1922, *The Malay Archipelago*, Singapore: Graham

Brash (reprinted 1983).

Waters, Somerset, 1986, *The Travel Industry World Yearbook, 1986*, New York: Child and Waters.

—— 1987, *The Travel Industry World Yearbook, 1987*, New York: Child and Waters.

—— 1989, *The Travel Industry World Yearbook, 1989*, New York: Child and Waters.

—— 1990, The Travel Industry World Yearbook, 1990, New York: Child and Waters.

Weiner, Myron, 1969, 'Review of L. and S. Rudolph, *The Modernity of Tradition*', *Economic Development and Cultural Change*, 17, 4, pp. 657–61.

Weiner, Myron and S. P. Huntington, eds, 1987, *Understanding Political Development*, Boston: Little, Brown.

White, K. J., 1985, 'An International Travel Demand Model: US Travel to Western Europe', *Annals of Tourism Research*, 12, 4, pp. 529–45.

Whitehead, John, 1893, *The Exploration of Mount Kinabalu, North Borneo*, London: Gurney and Jackson.

Whitten, A. J., 1987, *The Ecology of Sulawesi*, Yogyakarta: Gadjah Mada University Press.

Wigglesworth, Zeke, 1990, 'Burma, Romania Seek Visitors', *Wichita Eagle* (19 August), 8E.

Wijaya, M., C. O. Pemayun and G. P. Raka, 1981, *Bali's Art Centre, Werdi Budaya, and the Annual Festival of the Arts*, Denpasar: Bali Government Tourist Office.

Wikan, Unni, 1990, *Managing Turbulent Hearts: A Balinese Formula for Living*, Chicago: University of Chicago Press.

Wilford, John Noble, 1990, 'Anthropology Seen as Father of Maori Lore', *New York Times* (20 February), C1, p. 12.

Wilson, David, 1979, 'The Early Effects of Tourism in the Seychelles', in E. de Kadt, ed., *Tourism: Passport to Development?*, Oxford: Oxford University Press.

—— 1981, 'Comment', *Current Anthropology*, 22, 5, p. 477.

Wind, J., and D. Heckman, 1988, 'Nature Tourism Services to Attract Foreign Visitors', paper presented at a seminar held in Yogyakarta on Conservation and Nature Tourism.

Wong Poh Poh, 1986, 'Tourism Development and Resorts on the East Coast of Peninsular Malaysia', *Singapore Journal of Tropical Geography*, 7, pp. 152–62.

—— 1988, 'Beach Resort Sites on the East Coast of Peninsular Malaysia', *Singapore Journal of Tropical Geography*, 9, 1, pp. 72–85.

—— 1990, 'Coastal Resources Management: Tourism in Peninsular Malaysia', *ASEAN Economic Bulletin*, 7, 2, pp. 213–21.

Wong, Yoki, 1989, *Asia Travel Trade* (December), pp. 54–55.

Wood, Robert E., 1979, 'Tourism and Underdevelopment in Southeast Asia', *Journal of Contemporary Asia*, 9, 3, pp. 274–87.

—— 1980, 'International Tourism and Cultural Change in Southeast Asia', *Economic Development and Cultural Change*, 28, 3, pp. 561–81.

—— 1984, 'Ethnic Tourism, the State, and Cultural Change in Southeast Asia', *Annals of Tourism Research*, 11, 3, pp. 353–74.

World Bank, 1983, *Growth and Employment in Rural Thailand*, Washington: World Bank, Report No. 3906-TH.

World Commission on Environment and Development (Brundtland Report), 1987, *Our Common Future*, Oxford: Oxford University Press.

World Tourism Organization, 1988, *Economic Review of World Tourism: Tourism in the Context of Economic Crisis and the Dominance of the Service Economy*, Report for the WTO by V. Bote Gomez, Madrid: World Tourism Organization.

—— 1990, 'Tourism Activity in the 1980s and 1990s: Facts and Figures', *The Courier*, No. 122.

Worsley, Peter, 1984, *The Three Worlds: Culture and World Development*, Chicago: University of Chicago Press.

Yacoumis, J., 1990, 'Tourism in the South Pacific', *The Courier*, No. 122, pp. 81-83.

Yates, H. E., 1933, *Bali: Enchanted Isle. A Travel Book*, London: Allen and Unwin.

Yong, Frank, ed., 1991, 'Environmental Protection Through Ecotourism', *Alam Sekitar* (Magazine of the Environmental Protection Society Malaysia), 16, 1, pp. 1-6.

Young, S., 1989, 'The Alarde of Hondarrabia', unpublished B.A. dissertation, Belfast: The Queen's University.

de Zoete, B. and W. Spies, 1938, *Dance and Drama in Bali*, Singapore: Oxford University Press (reprinted 1987).

Zollinger, H., 1956, 'Bima and Sumbawa', *Journal of the Indian Archipelago and Eastern Asia*, 1, pp. 233-60.

Zulaika, J., 1981, *Terranova: The Ethos of Luck of Deep Sea Fishermen*, Philadelphia: ISHI.

# Index